GERMAN NOVELLAS
OF REALISM I

The German Library: Volume 37

Volkmar Sander, General Editor

GERMAN NOVELLAS
OF REALISM I

Edited by Jeffrey L. Sammons

CONTINUUM · NEW YORK

1989

The Continuum Publishing Company
370 Lexington Avenue, New York, NY 10017

The German Library
is published in cooperation with Deutsches Haus,
New York University.
This volume has been supported by a grant
from Robert Bosch GmbH.

Printed in the United States of America

Library of Congress Cataloging-in-Publication Data

German novellas of realism / edited by Jeffrey L. Sammons.
    p.   cm.—(The German library : v. 37–   )
    Contents: I. Preface to Many-colored stones /Adalbert Stifter.
Granite / Adalbert Stifter. Limestone / Adalbert Stifter. The Jew's
beech / Annette von Droste-Hülshoff. The black spider / Jeremias
Gotthelf. The poor musician / Franz Grillparzer. Mozart on the way
to Prague / Eduard Mörike.
    ISBN 0-8264-0317-4 (pbk.) ISBN 0-8264-0316-6 (hard)
    1. German Fiction—19th century—Translations into English.
2. Short stories, German—Translations into English.   3. English
fiction—Translations from German.   4. Short stories, English—
Translations from German.   I. Sammons, Jeffrey L.   II. Series.
PT1327.G385   1989   87-30505
833'.01'0912—dc19   CIP

Acknowledgments will be found on page 313,
which constitutes an extension of this page.

Contents

FRANZ GRILLPARZER

EDUARD MÖRIKE

Introduction

As regards "realism" in nineteenth-century Germany, literary history conveys two received opinions: first, that realism as it is known in Western countries was unable to thrive in Germany, where instead an alternative, more idealistic but also more parochial mode developed under the rubric of "poetic realism," and second, as a corollary to the first, that the realistic novel characteristic of Western countries, especially France and England, failed to emerge in German literature, which is distinguished by a particular predilection for the genre of the novella. Like all received opinions, these have a substantial basis in reality, and like all such opinions, they invite reconsideration and reassessment. It is well to remember that there can be no such thing as comprehensive literary history, for the range and mass of all existing literature is too great. Literary history selects and excludes in a process of canonization that purports to winnow out the "best" and often succeeds in doing so, but it is a process that can also be subject to sociological and ideological determinants. This is especially the case with the German canon, which was formed under particularly intense nationalistic and ideological pressures in the Wilhelminian period.

Realism did develop differently in Germany as compared with France and England, as the writers themselves were often aware; one of them, Otto Ludwig, articulated the idea of a "poetic realism" as a mode appropriate to his society. The reasons traditionally given for the difference are themselves sociological. Germany was a poor and relatively undereducated country through most of the nineteenth century. The market for serious literature was thin; by the standards of Scott or Dickens, Balzac or Dumas, no major German writer became prosperous from his literary work, and the great majority earned their living in other professions. Books were relatively expensive and editions were correspondingly small, in optimistic cases running to around 1,500 copies. A work that sold ten thousand copies was a spectacular best seller. For three-quarters of the century the nation had no capital city capable of drawing the literary life into an urban setting as Paris and London did. German society continued to be polarized between its Protestant and Catholic populations and splintered into small and, with the exception of Prussia and Austria, powerless states. Even after the foundation of the Reich in 1871 regional particularism remained strong. The development of urban civilization, industrial capitalism, and middle-class power, though certainly going forward, was somewhat stunted, especially in its political dimensions.

For the progressive middle class, to which the majority of writers belonged, the largely failed revolution of 1848 was a traumatic caesura. It capped with what seemed like an ultimate defeat a third of a century of disappointment, torpor, and oppression in the Metternichian age. This sense of defeat, with its concomitant requirements of lowered expectations and compromising accommodations, affected the tone of the so-called "poetic realism," which inclines to the elegiac, the melancholy, or the tragic. While the absence of a sense of humor among German writers is exaggerated in received opinion, it does appear that the gaiety sometimes found in Romanticism and in Goethe in some moods, and still detectable in subdued form in a writer with Romantic roots like Mörike, has dissipated; German wit, where it survived, tended to be satirical and sometimes bitter. In addition to these burdens German literature continued to function as a surrogate for the national unity that was so difficult to bring into being; thus, through its retained idealism it sought a national ethical definition in conscious contrast to the more robust, less inhibited, more cheerfully vulgar realism of the West, and thus retrospectively drew upon itself the charge of a parochial social and political evasiveness.

This charge is not wholly without foundation, but it measures German realism by a standard foreign to it. I hope that my way of putting the case shows that German writers did not hermetically seal themselves off from society and current history, were not indifferent to the world around them. Their particular mode of realism was a considered response to that world; its "poetic" character is an effort to assert and retain humanistic values in a discouraging environment. The elegiac tone, found in Stifter, Grillparzer, Mörike, and Meyer, is a form of resistance to a perceived deterioration of values, and the tragic tone, pervasive in Raabe and Storm and frequently encountered elsewhere, is a form of criticism of a society that frustrates and balks ordinary human aspirations. Furthermore, it is always wise to counter the abstractions of literary history by looking more closely at individual writers and texts. The selection in our two volumes will show, I hope, that German "realism" was not a cohesive mode governed by shared superintending principles. The writers can be very different from one another in outlook, style, and artistic strategy. The attentive reader may find much that fits rather awkwardly into the categories of received opinion, for example, the empathic probe of a noblewoman into the consciousness of a semi-criminalized underclass in Droste-Hülshoff's *The Jew's Beech,* or Storm's technological man in *The White Horse Rider,* which, though set in the middle of the eighteenth century, explores the modern antinomies of science and superstition, rationality and tradition, elitist arrogance and communal inertia in a manner that may remind the reader of Ibsen's *An Enemy of the People,* written in the previous decade. Even the most conservative, even reactionary, of our authors, Jeremias Gotthelf, is by any definition a writer of intense social consciousness. The somewhat disreputable comedy of Raabe's *Gedelöcke* or Meyer's *Plautus* may also not fit preconceived notions of German humor or its absence.

This brings us to the vexed question of the novella, upon which a vast amount of theoretical discourse has been and continues to be expended. No one will question that this genre occupies a prominent position in the canon of German literature. Minimally definable as a prose fiction of intermediate length located between the short story and the novel, it is characterized by more depth than breadth of focus, a silhouetted profile, often enhanced by the widely employed technique of narrative framing, a somewhat introverted perspective, and a tendency toward symbolism. Some though by no means all writers were concerned with the theoretical definition of the genre, which continued to generate variants well into our own century, Kafka and Thomas Mann being perhaps the most famous exemplars. But this is a matter in which it is especially important to be attentive to the limitations of conventional literary history, which can be misleading insofar as it implies that the "Western" form of the novel did not occur in nineteenth-century Germany. This is simply not true; ambitious, wide-ranging, social and political novels focusing on every aspect of contemporary life abounded. Many were widely read and some had international reputations. Their authors tended to be quite cosmopolitan and were willing to look outward to foreign models, especially to the great British Victorian novels. These authors and their books are largely forgotten today, for they were read out of the canon around the turn of the century. No doubt this canonical process can be defended on aesthetic grounds, for none of the German novelists matched the peak achievements of their French and British counterparts. But there seem also to have been ideological motives for consigning these authors and works to oblivion—many general literary historians and comparatists are unaware that they even existed—and for establishing the novella as a distinctly German genre. German establishment intellectuals had always been suspicious of the novel, fearing popular meretriciousness in the form of time-wasting, delusory romances, an undermining of idealism in the forms of licentiousness and the exposure of the seamy, unbeautiful realities of modern society, and "un-German" infections from unwholesome foreign sources, especially France. These are not good reasons, however, for pretending that novelists and novels did not exist in Germany.

Furthermore, during the nineteenth century, the novella begins to converge toward the novel, simply by becoming longer. While Heinrich von Kleist at the beginning of the century wrote some novellas that fill but a few pages of print, in later times we encounter "novellas" running to two hundred pages and more. As they grow longer, in many cases they grow stronger, perhaps a sign that German writers were becoming more confident with experience. I draw attention to this point because the exigencies of space in this edition may serve to perpetuate rather than clarify conventional misconceptions about the actual state of fiction in nineteenth-century Germany. Some examples: Otto Ludwig (1813–65) made a major contribution to the theory of the novella, but his best-remembered fictional work is a socio-psychological near-novel, *Zwischen Himmel und Erde* (1856, "Between Heaven and Earth") that is too long to be included here. Conrad Ferdinand Meyer completed eleven novellas; the longest of them, *Jürg Jenatsch* (1876), is virtually a historical novel, and the longest of the remainder, *Der Heilige* (1879, "The Saint"), a subtly skeptical examination of the mysteries of Thomas à Becket's character through the eyes of an observant but plain-minded subordinate, is by general consent his best; it also is too long for inclusion here. Theodor Storm was a specialist in novellas if there ever was one, but the last and best of them, *Der Schimmelreiter* ("The White Horse Rider"), is also his longest; we have managed to fit it into *German Novellas of Realism* II. It is now increasingly recognized that Wilhelm Raabe, who wrote many novellas, some of genuine excellence, along with a number of short stories, nevertheless found his true vocation and his peak achievements in his late novels.

These remarks are not meant to detract from the genuine artistic achievement of the German novella, of which there are many fine examples. While it is myopic to suppose that the genre is distinctively German or that it uniquely expresses some mythical qualities of the German nation, it was a form in which major writers, for social and historical reasons, were able to create effectively and in some cases to achieve works of enduring international fame. Our selection generally follows this canon of endurance; it contains some of the most widely read and in many cases most frequently translated works of nineteenth-century German fiction. Where we have deviated somewhat from this main canonical line, the reasons are remarked upon in the introductions to the various authors. The writers in whom, by general consent, the realistic movement culminated in German letters, Gottfried Keller and Theodor Fontane, are absent here because they are more fully represented in individual volumes of The German Library.

At the head of our selection we have placed a major theoretical statement, Adalbert Stifter's preface to *Bunte Steine* (1853, "Many-colored Stones"). I trust that, in the light of what has been said so far, this will not be understood as a programmatic motto. It is not meant to suggest that the quietism, the hostility to passion, violence, and the unpleasant aspects of reality, the somewhat desperate idealism of the preface are characteristic of the time or even universally of what follows in our selection. Despite his very high standing today, Stifter was a more eccentric than representative writer in his time. Furthermore, it would seem logical that no one would write such a statement who was not contending within himself and in his world with threats of passion, moral and social anarchy, and elusive meaning. Thus it is not surprising that contemporary critics tend to read through the glaze of Stifter's intensely disciplined surface to the stresses and antinomies that it was devised to repress. With that observation we may turn from generalities to some brief remarks on the individual authors.

Adalbert Stifter was born in 1805 into modest circumstances in the village of Oberplan in southern Bohemia (now Horné Planà, Czechoslovakia). He was able to obtain an education and rise into middle-class status owing to mentors who recognized his intelligence and promising talents. After studying science at the University of Vienna, he supported himself for some years as a private tutor to noble families and then served as an education official in Linz from 1850 to 1865. Stifter was a neurotic personality who, like not a few of his fellow writers, had considerable difficulty in managing his personal life. Apart from literature and art (he was the most gifted painter among the German-language writers of the nineteenth century) his strongest aspirations were to public service, especially in pedagogy, and to marriage and parenthood—the family is one of the most important values in his fiction. In both these areas he encountered disappointment and failure, owing in large part to his naivety and unworldliness. His fiction, therefore, projects an idealized contrast to his experiences rather than a representation of them. His death in Linz in 1868 is now believed to have been a suicide. While some observers have taken this to be one more manifestation of the subliminal, contradictory dark forces in his consciousness, too much should not be made of it; he was suffering extreme pain from terminal liver cancer. In addition to a large number of novellas and novella cycles, Stifter completed two major novels, *Der Nachsommer* (1857, "Indian Summer"), which systematizes perhaps more than any other work the principles enunciated in the preface to *Many-colored Stones,* and a vast, highly stylized historical novel, *Witiko* (1865–67). In 1853 Stifter composed *Many-colored Stones* from, for the most part, previously published novellas, here rewritten and given the mineral titles that metaphorically bind them together. To this collection he prefixed his famous preface with its commitment to the "gentle law" of true reality, a concept with which Stifter is clearly, if somewhat reductively, attempting to place himself in the succession to Goethe. Of these novellas, *Bergkristall* ("Rock Crystal," originally *Der heilige Abend,* "Christmas Eve," 1845) is the most widely known and most frequently translated into English. Owing to prejudices of the editor it has been displaced here by two others, *Granit* ("Granite," originally *Der Pechbrenner,* "The Pitch-Burner", 1849), and *Kalkstein* ("Limestone," originally *Der arme Wohlthäter,* "The Poor Philanthropist," 1848). *Granite* sits on the boundary between fiction and autobiography; it is an idealized reminiscence of Stifter's boyhood milieu and his nurturing by his grandfather. As for *Limestone,* the reader of this volume should have no difficulty detecting a resemblance to Grillparzer's *The Poor Musician.* The resemblance is not fortuitous; Stifter greatly admired Grillparzer's novella and explicitly set out to write a counterpart to it. Stifter is famous for his nature descriptions, of which he was one of the greatest masters in German letters. Nature for him is an environment both real and metaphorical of ethical import. But the relationship between man and nature runs only one way. Nature itself is indifferent to human fates, often nurturing and lovely, but sometimes forbidding and alien, or bleak, as in *Limestone,* or even, despite the claims of the famous preface, violent and dangerous, as in the case of the plague described in *Granite,* which even dissolves the bonds between parents and children. This indifference of nature may be another of those underlying anxieties and antinomies that modern critics are wont to see in him.

Annette, Baroness von Droste-Hülshoff was born in 1797 in the family castle of Hülshoff near Münster, where she lived under the watchful eye of her family for the first twenty-nine years of her life. After her father's death she moved restlessly from place to place, living, however, always with family members and in the relative seclusion imposed upon her by her social position, against which her writing subtly strains. She had a number of hopeless love affairs, culminating in a long, equally doomed attachment to the critic Levin Schücking, eighteen years her junior, who was, however, a valuable intellectual companion. Always in delicate health, she died in 1848 in her brother-in-law's castle at Meersburg on Lake Constance. Droste was a gifted, deeply introspective poet; caught in a tension between her Catholic faith and her self-doubts, she became the outstanding religious poet of mid-nineteenth-century Germany. She attempted several works of fiction, but the only one she brought to completion was *Die Judenbuche* (1842, "The Jew's Beech"). In part this work is a product of her enduring fascination with the tales and superstitions of the Westphalian heaths and forests. But it is also interesting in regard to its insight into a social milieu very distant from the author's own. The baroness cannot be expected to have condoned poaching or the violence and moral chaos accompanying it, but she shows a remarkable sensitivity to the grimly impoverished conditions under which these people live and to their criminality as an expression of hostility to oppressive authority. She does not pretend, as another writer might have, that they would be less impoverished if they were to improve their moral condition. *The Jew's Beech* is also a kind of detective story, a genre that developed in Germany long before it did in England and the United States. But here the reader is the detective, and some of the most attentive detective-readers have found the case to be more opaque than it may appear to be on the surface, suggesting that the author invites us to reconsider the solution imposed upon us by the narrator with suspicious abruptness.

Albert Bitzius, who wrote under the name of one of his early fictional characters, Jeremias Gotthelf, was born in 1797 at Murten in the Canton of Berne; after his university studies and several appointments as curate he became pastor in the village of Lützelflüh in 1829, a position that he held until his death in 1854. His major achievement was doubtless his series of elaborate social novels of peasant life, some of which he wrote in both Bernese dialect and standard German versions, but his most famous work is an allegorical legend, *Die schwarze Spinne* (1842, "The Black Spider"). Of all the canonical German-language writers of the nineteenth century, Gotthelf was the most militantly conservative. Of a fundamentalist and, one must say, rather primitive Christian persuasion, he directly associated orthodox obedience in faith and morals with worldly prosperity, and deviation with moral anarchy and disaster in the conduct of life. He abhorred the liberal, humanistic strain in German culture to which most of the writers of his time in one way or another bore allegiance. The allegory of *The Black Spider* is certainly in some sense directed against revolution; even under the most oppressive, tyrannical circumstances, recourse to a solution outside the obedience of faith is recourse to the devil. By repeating his inner story in settings six hundred and four hundred years in the past and applying its lessons to the frame story set in the present, he projects an utterly immobile conception of society, oblivious to change and progress. But even those for whom his basic outlook is uncongenial must acknowledge the earthy power of his realism, especially in his major novels. He was sincerely concerned about not only the moral but also the social condition of the peasantry, on which he wrote vigorously and fearlessly. His narrative resources were impressive, as one can see in *The Black Spider,* which rises to a pitch of terror unparalleled in any other nineteenth-century German story of my acquaintance.

Franz Grillparzer was born in Vienna in 1791; he became a public official who served conscientiously in several posts but never obtained those he most wanted, as court or university librarian, and he retired from the civil service in 1856. He was a shy, insecure man, another of the self-sabotaging neurotics so frequently encountered among German-language writers in this period. He lurched from one abortive love affair to another; in 1821 he became engaged to a singer, Kathi Fröhlich, but never could make up his mind to marry her, even though he lived in the Fröhlich house in his later years. For fifty-one years they maintained an amazingly awkward relationship until his death in 1872. Grillparzer wrote in several genres from poetry to autobiography, but his major achievement was in the drama; he became the outstanding Austrian playwright of his time. He wrote tragedies on classical models as well as comedies and histories with which he, like other Austrian playwrights up to Hugo von Hofmannsthal, remained in close touch with the baroque theater of the seventeenth century. But the unfriendly reception given to his comedy, *Weh dem, der lügt* (1838, "Woe to Him Who Lies") determined him to withhold any further literary work from publication, a decision from which he deviated only rarely, so that a considerable body of the remainder of his life's work was posthumously published. One exception was *Der arme Spielmann* (1848, "The Poor Musician"). Grillparzer was quite musical, with a particular admiration for Mozart and for Beethoven, whom he knew personally and on whom he delivered a funeral eulogy. Yet *The Poor Musician* is one of the oddest of musical fictions, for it concerns a musician utterly incompetent except in his own imagined self, within which he pursues a high artistic commitment and ultimately exhibits a moral refinement that quite transcends the narrator's sincere but rather tepid sympathy. Many critics have taken the novella to be a wry and sorrowful self-reflection of the author, a rueful commentary on the gap between aspiration and achievement that he felt within himself, and such self-criticism may not have been altogether unjust, for Grillparzer's poetic imagination, historical insight, and psychological sensitivity were not always complemented by adequate stylistic resources.

Eduard Mörike was born in Ludwigsburg in 1804 and was trained as a clergyman, a vocation for which he was totally unfit, as he well knew, and which he tried to evade as far as was practicable. Eventually a sympathetic church consistory retired him on pension; later he was employed as a teacher in a young ladies' seminary, where the light duties suited him well. He was another of our shy, repressed neurotics; he was utterly without worldly ambition and seemed to dwell in a realm of his own imagination. His personal life was a shambles, punctuated by pathetic and sometimes faintly ludicrous episodes, including an unwise marriage that ended in separation after many unhappy years. He was inclined to remain rather aloof from social life, though he had a number of intimate friends; he died in Stuttgart in 1875. He was, however, a poet of major rank who has not unreasonably been compared with Wordsworth, although his full stature was not appreciated until our own century. Among German post-Romantic poets no one else can match the precision or his imagery or his symbolically charged epiphanies (examples in volume 39 of The German Library, *Poetry 1750–1900*). As a prose writer Mörike was more uneven. His one completed novel, *Maler Nolten* (1832; "Painter Nolten"), is interesting as a study of the interrelationship of psychopathological personalities but otherwise fails to satisfy. His novellas were mostly occasional pieces, some written for moralizing purposes. But in 1855 he achieved a work, *Mozarts Reise nach Prag* ("Mozart on the Way to Prague") that has become one of the best loved of German fictions. Although Mörike studied what could be learned about Mozart in his time, it is idle to ask whether the novella gives a true portrait of the composer. Rather it seems to project an idealized utopian self of the author, sharing Mörike's tender, childlike sensibility and unworldliness, but livelier and more urbane, and located, moreover, in a world in which art and society stood in a more substantial relationship to one another (although Mörike does not hesitate to point out that this lovingly and elegiacally portrayed world also contained the dissonances that were to lead to the cataclysm of the French Revolution). But even this sweet interlude in Mozart's otherwise rather plagued life comes to be overlaid with the tragic sense of Mörike's own age, perceivable, to be sure, only by Eugenia, the one character who shares to some degree Mozart's artistic sensitivity.

J. L. S.

GERMAN NOVELLAS
OF REALISM I

those of many other people. The flow of the air, the rippling of the water, the growth of the grain, the waves of the sea, the greening of the earth, the gleaming of the sky, the twinkling of the stars I consider great; the splendidly rising storm, the lightning that splits houses, the tempest that drives the surf, the fire-spewing mountain, the earthquake that buries whole countries, I consider not to be greater than the former phenomena; indeed, I consider them smaller because they are only effects of much higher laws. They appear at isolated places and are the results of one-sided causes. The force that makes the milk in the poor woman's pot surge up and overflow is the same one that drives up the lava in the fire-spewing mountain and makes it flow down the mountainsides. These phenomena are only more conspicuous and catch the eye of the ignorant and inattentive, while the mental processes of the true observer tend primarily to the whole and the general and can recognize magnificence only in them, for they alone sustain the world. The details pass away and in a short time their effects can hardly still be recognized. Let us elucidate what has been said with an example. If a man were to observe a magnetic needle, whose one end always points north, day after day at fixed times and were to write in a book the changes as the needle points north now more clearly, now less, certainly an ignorant person would look upon this activity as something small and frivolous; but how awesome does this small thing become and how inspiring this frivolity when we learn that these observations are really being made all over the world and from the tables compiled from them it emerges that many little changes in the magnetized needle often occur at all points of the earth at the same time and to the same degree, that the whole surface of the earth, as it were, feels a magnetic shiver at the same time. If we had a sensory organ for electricity and the magnetism emanating from it, such as we have eyes for the light, what a great world, what an abundance of immense phenomena would be open to us. But if we do not have this physical eye, we have the mental eye of science, and this teaches us that the electrical and magnetic force acts upon a huge scene, that it is spread over the whole earth and through the whole sky, that it flows around everything and manifests itself in gentle and incessant transmutation, by forming shapes and generating life. Lightning is just a small feature of this force, which itself is something great in nature. But because science only secures grain upon grain, only makes observation upon observation, only assembles the general out of the particular and because, after all, the quantity of phenomena and the field of the given are infinitely large, and God therefore has made the joy and bliss of research inexhaustible, we, too, in our workshops can only represent the particular, never the general, for that would be all Creation: so the history of what is great in nature subsists in a constant change of perspectives on this greatness. When humans were in their childhood, their mental eye still untouched by science, they were seized by what was nearby and conspicuous and swept away to fear and wonder; but when their faculties were opened, as they began to direct their attention to the connection of things, the particular phenomena sank ever more in importance and the law ascended ever higher; the marvels ceased, the miracles increased.

As it is in external nature, so it is in the internal nature of the human race. A whole life full of justice, simplicity, efficacy, mastering oneself, reasonableness, effectiveness in one's circle, admiration of the beautiful, combined with cheerful, tranquil effort, I consider great; mighty movements of temperament, frightful outbursts of anger, the lust for vengeance, the inflamed spirit that strives for activity, tears down, changes, destroys, and in its excitement often throws away its own life, I consider not greater, but smaller, for these things are as much products of individual and one-sided forces as storms, fire-spewing mountains, and earthquakes. We want to try to observe the gentle law that guides the human race. There are forces that aim for the survival of the individual. They take and use everything necessary to its survival and development. They secure the endurance of the one and thus of all. But if someone unreservedly seizes upon everything that his being needs, when he destroys the conditions of the existence of someone else, then something higher grows angry in us; we help the weak and the oppressed; we restore the state of affairs in which one person can survive beside the other and walk his human path; and when we have done that, we feel satisfied, we feel ourselves higher and more ardent than we feel as individuals, we feel ourselves as all humanity. Thus there are forces that work toward the survival of mankind as a whole that may not be checked by individual forces, indeed, that, on the contrary, must check the individual forces themselves. It is the law of these forces, the law that wants everyone to be respected, honored, and unthreatened beside the other, that he may walk his higher human path, may earn the love and admiration of his fellow men, that he may be protected as a precious object, as every person is a precious object for all other persons. This law obtains everywhere, wherever people live beside people and it manifests itself when people affect one another. It obtains in the love of husband and wife for one another, in the love of parents for their children, of children for their parents, in the love of brothers and sisters and of friends, in the sweet inclination of the sexes to one another, in the industriousness which sustains us, in the activity in which we work for our near and distant circle and for mankind, and finally in the order and form with which whole societies and states surround and conclude their existence. Therefore ancient and modern poets have often employed these subjects in order to submit their creations to the sympathy of immediate and distant generations. Therefore the true observer of mankind sees, wherever he sets his foot, only this law everywhere, because it is the only thing that is general, sustaining, and neverending. He sees it as well in the lowliest hut as in the highest palace, he sees it in the devotion of a poor woman and in the calm contempt for death of the hero of the fatherland or of mankind. There have been movements in the human race that have impressed a direction toward a goal upon the minds of men, when whole ages have enduringly acquired a different form. If the law of justice and morality is recognizable in these movements, if they are inaugurated and led by it, then we feel ourselves uplifted in all mankind, we feel ourselves humanly generalized, we feel the sublime that everywhere descends into the soul when immeasurably great forces in time or space are applied to a well-formed, reasonable whole. But when the law of justice and morality is not visible in these movements, when they struggle for one-sided and egotistical purposes, then the true observer of mankind will turn from them in disgust, as powerful and awesome as they may be, and regard them as something small, unworthy of a human being. So great is the power of this law of justice and morality that, wherever it has been attacked, it has at all times ultimately emerged from the fight victorious and glorious. Indeed, even when the individual or whole generations have perished for justice and morality, we do not feel that they have been defeated, we feel that they have triumphed; exultation and delight mixes with our compassion; because the whole stands higher than the part, because the good is greater than death, then we say that we sense the tragic quality and are lifted trembling into the pure ether of the moral law. When we see mankind in history approaching a great, eternal goal like a calm, silvery stream, then we sense the sublime, the especially epic quality. But as powerfully and capaciously as the tragic and the epic may affect us, excellent as they may be as levers in art, nevertheless it is mainly the ordinary, everyday, countlessly recurring actions of people in which this law most securely lies as a center of gravity, because these actions are the enduring, constitutive ones, as it were, the millions of rootlets of the tree of life. As in nature the general laws work silently and incessantly and the conspicuous is only an individual expression of these laws, so the moral law works silently, animating the soul, through the endless communion of men with men, and the miracles of the moment when deeds occur are only small tokens of this general force. Thus this law is the sustaining law of mankind as the law of nature is the sustaining law of the world.

As in the history of nature the attitudes toward greatness have continually changed, so it is in the moral history of mankind. In the beginning people were moved by what was nearest at hand; bodily strength and its victories in wrestling were praised, then came bravery and military courage, aimed at expressing and arousing violent feelings and passions against hostile hordes and alliances, then tribal authority and familial sovereignty were celebrated, in the meantime beauty and love, also, as well as friendship and sacrifice, but then people began to survey something greater: whole human groups and relations were ordered, the right of the whole united with that of the part, and generosity to the enemy and suppression of one's feelings and passions for the sake of justice were held sacred, as indeed moderation was regarded even by the ancients as the primary manly virtue, and finally a bond embracing all the peoples was imagined as something desirable, a bond that exchanges all the gifts of the one people with those of another, that furthers science, revealing its treasures for all people, and that in art and religion leads to what is as simple as it is high and heavenly.

As it is with the ascent of the human race, so it is with its descent. Declining peoples first lose their moderation. They go after the particular, they throw themselves shortsightedly upon what is limited and insignificant, they set the contingent above the general;

then they seek pleasure and the sensual, they seek satisfaction of their hatred and envy toward their neighbor, their art depicts what is one-sided, what is valid from only one standpoint, then the flighty, the inconsistent, the adventurous, finally the sensuous, the exciting, and ultimately immorality and vice; in religion the inner truth degenerates to a mere form or to opulent fanaticism, the distinction between good and evil is lost, the individual scorns the whole and pursues his pleasure and his destruction, and thus the nation becomes prey to its inner disarray or that of an external, more savage but more powerful enemy.——

Since in this preface I have gone so far in my views about the great and the small, so might I be allowed to say that I have endeavored to collect many exemplary cases in the history of the human race and that I have gathered particulars of these cases into creative efforts, but my views and experiences that have just been developing during the last few years have taught me to mistrust my powers; therefore these efforts may lie fallow until they have been better worked out or destroyed as insignificant.

May those, however, who have accompanied me through this preface that is in no way suitable for a young audience, not disdain to enjoy the product of modest powers and pass on with me to the harmless things that follow.

Autumn 1852

Translated by Jeffrey L. Sammons

Granite

Adalbert Stifter

In front of the house in which my father was born, close to the entrance, lies a large eight-cornered stone in the form of a very elongated cube. Its side surfaces are rough-hewn, but its top surface has become so fine and smooth from much sitting as though it had been covered with the most artful glaze. The stone is very old and no one can recall having heard of a time when it had been set there. The most ancient old men of our house had sat on the stone just as did those who had passed away in tender youth and who slumber beside all the others in the churchyard. Its age is also proved by the circumstance that the sandstone slabs upon which the stone rests have been completely worn out by having been trod upon and where they extend beyond the rain gutter they are marked with deep holes from the dripping water.

In my boyhood one of the youngest members of our household who sat upon the stone was myself. I liked to sit on the stone because, at least in those days, there was a wide view from it. Now the view has been somewhat obscured by buildings. I liked to sit there in the first days of spring, when the milder sunbeams generated the first warmth on the wall of the house. I looked out upon the tilled but not yet planted fields; I sometimes saw there a glass glisten and gleam as though with a white, fiery spark, or I saw a vulture fly by, or I looked into the distant, bluish wood, which with its sharp points stretched to the sky from which the storms and cloudbursts descend, a wood so high that I thought that if I could climb its highest tree, I would be able to touch the sky. At other times I looked at the road that passes near the house, now at a harvest wagon, now at a flock, now at a peddler passing by.

In summer Grandfather* also liked to sit on the stone in the

---

*Franz Friepes, Stifter's maternal grandfather, took on much of the role of a parent

evening and smoke his pipe, and sometimes, when I had already long been asleep or only heard disjointed sounds in my first slumber, young fellows and girls also sat partly on the stone, partly on the wooden benches next to it or on the pile of lumber and sang winsome songs into the dark night.

Among the things that I often saw from the stone was a man of a peculiar sort. He sometimes came driving up the Hossenreuth road† with a shiny black pushcart. On the pushcart he had a shiny black cask. His clothes had not been black from the beginning, but they had become very dark in time and were also shiny. When the sun shone on him he looked as though he had been greased with oil. On his head he had a broad hat, under which his long hair flowed down to his neck. He had a brown face and friendly eyes, and his hair already had the yellowish-white color that people of the lower classes who must work hard are wont to get. When he came close to the houses he usually cried out something that I did not understand. As a consequence of these cries our neighbors came out of their houses with utensils in their hands, which were usually black, wooden jugs, and came into our lane. While this happened the man had come all the way up and pushed his cart toward our lane. Here he stopped, turned the cock in the tap of his cask and poured for everyone who held his container under it a brown, viscous liquid, which I easily recognized as wagon grease and for which they gave him a number of kreuzers or groschen. When it was all over and the neighbors had left with their purchase, he straightened up his cask, scraped everything back into it that had spilled out of it, and went his way. I was present on these occasions just about every time; for even if I was not in the lane when the man came, I heard his cries as well as the neighbors did and was certainly on the scene sooner than all the others.

One day, when the spring sun was shining very amiably and made everyone cheerful and mischievous, I saw him again coming up the Hossenreuth road. He cried his usual chant when he had come near the houses, the neighbors came out, he gave them what they required, and they went away. After this had happened he cleaned up

---

after his father's early death. *Granite* consists of no doubt idealized versions of his grandfather's advice and stories.

†All the places named in the story are in southern Bohemia in the neighborhood of Stifter's birthplace of Oberplan.

his cask as always. In order to scrape into it what had accumulated around the cock or on the lower staves owing to the loosening of the tap, he had a long, narrow, flat spoon with a short handle. He dexterously scooped out every trace of liquid that had hid itself in a joint or corner and scraped it off on the sharp corners of the bunghole. While he was doing this I sat on the stone and watched him. By chance I had bare feet, as was often the case, and pants that had become too short with time. Suddenly he looked up at me from his work and said: "Would you like to have your feet greased?"

I had always regarded the man as a great curiosity, felt honored by his familiarity, and held up both my feet. He reached into the bunghole with his spoon, reached over, and put a slow streak on each of my feet. The liquid spread beautifully on my skin, had an extraordinarily clear, golden brown color, and wafted the pleasant aroma of resin up to me. According to its nature it flowed around the curve of my feet and down their sides. Meanwhile the man continued with his business, looked at me a couple of times with a smile, then put the spoon into a sheath next to the case, shut the bunghole on top, put on the shoulder straps of his pushcart, lifted it, and pushed it away. Since I was now alone and had a partly pleasant but nevertheless not quite reassured feeling, I wanted to show myself to Mother. Carefully holding up my pants, I went into the parlor. It was Saturday, and every Saturday the parlor had to be beautifully washed and scrubbed, which had been done this morning, as the wagon-grease man liked to come on Saturdays in order to remain on Sunday and go to church. The wood fibers of the floor, well leached and then dried, absorbed the wagon grease from my feet very greedily, so that after every one of my steps a pronounced footprint remained on the floor. As I came in Mother was sitting on the front window seat sewing. When she saw me coming and walking forward in this way, she jumped up. She remained hovering for a moment, either because she so admired me or because she was looking around for an instrument with which to receive me. Finally she cried: "What does this hopeless, obstinate son have on him today?"

And to keep me from going farther forward she hurried toward me, lifted me and carried me, ignoring my fright and her apron, out into the vestibule. There she set me down, and from under the loft steps, where we had to put all the switches and branches we brought home because they were not allowed anywhere else and where I myself had recently collected a large number of these things in recent days, she took whatever she could grab, and whipped my feet with it so long and so violently until the whole litter of switches, my pants, her apron, the stones of the floor, and everything around were full of pitch. Then she let me go and went back into the parlor.

Although from the beginning I had not been completely easy about the thing, nevertheless this awful turn of affairs and this discord with my dearest relative in the world left me all but annihilated. In the corner of the vestibule there was a big stone cube upon which the yarn for home weaving was beaten with a wooden maul. I staggered to this stone and sat on it. I could not even cry; my heart was crushed and my throat as though sewed up with thread. Inside I heard Mother discussing with the maid what to do, and I was afraid that, if the pitch prints did not go away, they would come out again and punish me further.

At this moment Grandfather came into the back door that leads to the well and the garden and walked toward me. He had always been the kind one and whenever any sort of misfortune fell upon us children, had never asked whose fault it was but always simply helped us. When he had come to the place where I was sitting he stopped and looked at me. When he had understood the condition I was in he asked what had happened and how I had got into this state. I wanted now to relieve my feelings, but I could still not say anything, for now, at the sight of his kind and well-meaning eyes all the tears that could not come out before poured out violently and ran down in streams, so that for weeping and sobbing I could only utter broken and mutilated sounds and could do nothing but raise my feet, on which the ugly red of the thrashing showed through the pitch.

But he smiled and said: "Just come over to me, come with me."

With these words he took me by the hand, pulled me gently down from the stone and led me, though in my emotional state I could hardly follow him, the length of the vestibule and into the yard. In the yard there is a broad walk paved with stones running around all the buildings. On this walk, under the eaves of the house, there are usually a few stools or things that serve for them, on which the maids can sit when combing the flax or doing similar jobs, in order to be protected from bad weather. He led me to such a stool and said: "Sit down there and wait a bit; I am coming right back."

With these words he went into the house, and after I had waited a while he came out again, carrying in his hands a big, green-glazed bowl, a pot of water, and soap and towels. He put these things down beside me on the stone pavement, pulled my pants off while I was sitting on the stool, threw them aside, poured warm water into the bowl, put my feet in it and washed them with soap and water until a big, white and brown flecked mountain of suds lay on the surface; the wagon grease, because it was still fresh, had completely gone away, and there was no more trace of pitch to be seen on my skin. Then he dried my feet with the towels and asked: "Is it all right now?"

I almost laughed under my tears; one stone after another had fallen from my heart while I was being washed, and if the tears had already been flowing more gently, now they only dropped one at a time from my eyes. He got me another pair of pants and put them on me. Then he took the end of the towel that had remained dry, wiped my tear-stained face with it and said: "Now go across the yard through the big entrance gate out to the lane, so that no one will see you and you won't be caught. Wait for me in the lane; I will bring you different clothes and change my own a little. I am going today to the village of Melm; you can come with me and you shall tell me how this misfortune occurred and how you got into the wagon grease. We will leave your things here; someone will pick them up."

With these words he pushed me toward the yard and went back into the house. I walked quietly across the yard and hurried out the entrance gate. In the lane I went very far from the large stone and the front door in order to be safe and placed myself so that I could look into the front door from afar. I saw that, in the place where I had been punished, two maids were busy kneeling on the floor and moving their hands back and forth. Probably they were trying to remove the traces of pitch remaining from my thrashing. Our house swallow flew screeching in and out of the door because today there had been a disturbance under its nest, first from my punishment and then from the maids at work. At the farthest boundary of our lane, very far from the front door, where the little hill on which our house stands already begins to decline toward the road going by, lay a few hewn tree trunks intended for a building or some similar purpose. I sat down on these and waited.

Finally Grandfather came out. He had his broad hat on his head, had on the long coat that he liked to wear on Sundays, and carried his stick in his hand. But in his other hand he had my blue-striped jacket, white stockings, black laced boots, and my gray felt hat. He helped me put all this on and said: "So, now let's go."

We walked along the narrow footpath through the green of our hill down to the road and continued on the road, first between the houses of the neighbors on which the spring sun lay and from which the people greeted us, and then out into the open country. There a broad field and beautiful green grass lay before us and bright, friendly sunshine spread over all the things of the world. We walked on a white path through the green field of grass. My pain and distress had almost disappeared; I knew that a good outcome could not fail because Grandfather was taking up the matter and protecting me; the open air and the sun exercised a calming influence, and I felt my jacket very pleasantly on my shoulders and the boots on my feet, and the air flowed gently through my hair.

When we had walked for a while on the meadow as we normally walked when he took me with him—that is, he shortened his great strides, but made great strides all the same and I sometimes had to trot after him—Grandfather said: "Now tell me once and for all how it happened that you got into so much wagon grease that not only your whole pair of pants are full of pitch, that your feet were full, that there is a pitch stain in the vestibule, switches fouled with pitch are lying around, and there are spots of wagon grease, too, in the whole house wherever you go. I already told your mother that you are coming with me; you need not worry any more; there will be no more punishment."

I now told him how I was sitting on the stone, how the wagon-grease man came, how he asked me if I wanted my feet greased, how I held them up to him and how he made a streak on each, how I went into the parlor in order to show myself to Mother, how she jumped up, how she took me, carried me into the vestibule, thrashed me with my own switch, and how afterwards I remained sitting on the stone.

"You are a silly little boy," said Grandfather, "and old Andreas is a wicked rascal; he has always played such tricks and now he will laugh to himself secretly and repeatedly for having had the idea. These details improve your case very much. But see, even old Andreas, as bad as we may think his case to be, is not as much to blame as we others think; for how should old Andreas know that wagon grease is such a terrible thing for people and that it can make such disorder in a house; because for him it is the only merchandise that he deals with, that nourishes him, that he loves, and that he always replenishes afresh when it runs out. And how should be know anything about washed floors, since he is on the road with his cask year in and year out, rain or shine, sleeps in a barn at night or on holidays and has hay or straw sticking to his clothes. But your mother is right, too; she had to think that you had thoughtlessly smeared your feet yourself with so much wagon grease and that you had gone into the parlor in order to dirty her beautiful floor. But give it time, she will come around, she will understand everything, and everything will be all right. When we get up to that height there, where we can see far around, I will tell you a story of pitchmen such as Andreas, one that happened long ago, before you were born and before I was born, and from which you will see what wondrous fates people can have in our dear Lord's world. And if you are strong enough and able to walk, I will let you come with me next week to Spitzenberg and into the Stag Mountains, and there you will see on the path in Spruce Glen the sort of still in which pitch is made and where old Andreas gets his supplies, and thus where the pitch came from with which your feet were greased today."

"Yes, Grandfather," I said, "I shall be quite strong."

"Well, that's good," he answered, "and you can go with me."

With these words we had arrived at a wall of loose stones, on the other side of which lay a green meadow with a white footpath. Grandfather climbed over the stone stile, pulling his stick and his coat behind him and helping me over it, since I was too small; and then we continued walking on the clean path. Approximately in the middle of the meadow he stopped and pointed to the ground, where a clear stream welled up from under a flat stone and ran on through the meadow.

"That is the Behring Spring," he said, "which has the best water in the neighborhood, except for the miracle-working water that is in the covered spring on Spring Mountain, near which stands the Shrine of the Good Water. Many people get their drinking water from this spring, many field workers come from far away to drink here, and many sick people have sent a flagon here from distant parts to have water brought to them. Be sure you remember the spring."

"Yes, Grandfather," I said.

After these words we walked on further. We walked on the footpath through the meadow, we walked up a path between fields and came to a glen that was covered with thick, short, almost gray grass and on which pine trees stood at fixed intervals from one another in every direction.

"Where we are walking now," said Grandfather, "is called Dry-beaks; it is a strange name that comes either from the dry, barren ground or from the scrawny weeds that sit by the thousands on the ground and whose flower has a white beak with a little yellow tongue in it. See, the mighty pines belong to the citizens of Oberplan according to their taxable property; they have their needles not in two rows but in sheaths like green bristle clusters, they have pliable, oily wood, they have yellow pitch, they make scant shadows, and when a weak breeze blows one can hear the needles rustling calmly and slowly."

As we went on I had an opportunity to observe the truth of what Grandfather had said. I saw a lot of the whitish-yellow little flowers on the ground, I saw the gray grass, I saw the pitch on many trunks like gold drops, I saw the innumerable needle clusters seeming to poke out of tiny, dark little boots on innumerable twigs, and I heard, although hardly a breeze was to be felt, the calm rustling in the needles.

We kept going on and the path became rather steep.

On a somewhat higher and more open place Grandfather stopped and said: "So, now we shall wait a little."

He turned around, and after we had caught our breath a little from the effort of climbing, he raised his stick and pointed to a great distant forest ridge in the direction from which we had come and asked: "Can you tell me what that is over there?"

"Yes, Grandfather," I answered, "it is the Alp where in the summer there is a herd of cattle that is driven down in the fall."

"And what is that, farther forward from the Alp?" he asked again.

"That is the Cottage Forest," I answered.

"And to the right of the Alp and the Cottage Forest?"

"That is the Philip George Mountain."

"And to the right of the Philip George Mountain?"

"That is the Lake Forest, where there are dark and deep lake waters."

"And still to the right of the Lake Forest?"

"That is the Boulder Stone and the Chair Forest."

"And farther right?"

"That is Tusset Forest."

"And farther you cannot see; but there is many a forest ridge with many a name, they go on many miles into the country. At one time the forests were much larger than they are now. When I was a boy they extended to Spitzenberg and the first buildings of the seminary; there were wolves in them, and in the night from under our beds we could hear the stags belling when it was their time. Do you see the column of smoke there, rising out of the Cottage Forest?"

"Yes, Grandfather, I see it."

"And farther behind another one out of the wood of the Alp?"

"Yes, Grandfather."

"And yet another from the dales of the Philip George Mountain?"

"I see it, Grandfather."

"And far back in the hollow of the Lake Forest, which you can hardly see, still another, so faint as though it were a little blue cloud?"

"I see it, too, Grandfather."

"You see, these columns of smoke all come from men who do their jobs in the forest. There are first of all the lumbermen who in places saw down the trees of the forest until nothing is left but stumps and underbrush. They light a fire to cook their food and also to burn up the brush and branches as necessary. Then there are the charcoal-burners who pile up a great stack, cover it with earth and brush, and from logs they burn the coals that you often see carried past our house in great sacks to distant places that have nothing to burn. Then there are the hay-gleaners who make hay in the little meadows and in the bare places of the forest or cut it from between stones with sickles. They, too, make a fire to cook on or so that their dray animals will lie down in the smoke in order to be less plagued by the flies. Then there are the collectors who look for fungi, medicinal herbs, berries, and other things, and also like to make fires to refresh themselves. Finally there are the pitch-burners who make kilns out of the forest earth or cover holes with clay and erect huts out of forest trees next to them in order to live in the huts and distill wagon grease in the kilns and holes, but also tar, turpentine, and other spirits. Where a quite thin thread of smoke rises it may be a hunter roasting his little piece of meat or resting. All these people have no permanent place in the forest, for they go here and there according to whether they have done their work or don't find what they need. Therefore the columns of smoke have no permanent place, and you see them here today and another time in another place."

"Yes, Grandfather."

"That is the life of the forests. But now let us look at what is outside them. Can you tell me what those white buildings are that we can see through the double pine?"

"Yes Grandfather, those are the Prang farms."

"And farther left from the Prang farms?"

"Those are the buildings of the Front and Rear Seminary."

"And still farther left?"

"That is Glöckelberg."

"And farther toward us on the water?"

"That is the Hammer Mill and Farmer David."

"And the many buildings quite close to us, among which the church rises, and behind which there is a mountain on which there is another little church?"

"But, Grandfather, that's our market town Oberplan, and the chapel on the mountain is the Chapel of the Good Water."

"And if the mountains weren't there and the heights that surround us, you would see many more buildings and villages: the Karl farms, Stuben, Schwarzbach, Langenbruck, Melm, Honneschlag, and on the opposite side Pichlern, Pernek, Salnau, and several others. You can see that there is much life in these villages, that in them many people labor day and night for their life's sustenance and enjoy the pleasure that is given to us here below. I have shown you these forests and the towns because in them the story took place that I promised on the way up to tell you. But let us go on, so that we shall soon reach our goal; I'll tell you the story as we walk."

Grandfather turned around; I did, too; he set the point of his stick into the meager grassy ground; we walked on, and he related: "In all these forests and in all these villages there was once a remarkable occurrence, and a great disaster came over them. My grandfather, your great-grandfather, who lived at that time, often told us about it. Once in the spring when the trees had hardly begun to leaf, when the blossoms had hardly fallen, a serious disease came over the region and broke out in the villages that you have seen and in all those you could not see because of the mountains in front of them, even in the forests you showed me. It had been in foreign lands long before and had taken off an incredible number of people there. Suddenly it came upon us. No one knows how it came: whether people brought it, whether it came with the mild spring air, or whether the winds and clouds carried it here; it is enough to say that it came and spread over all the places around us. The dead were carried away over the white blossoms that still lay on the path, and in the chamber into which the spring leaves looked lay a sick man, and the one nursing him would soon be sick himself. The pestilence was called the plague, and within five to six hours a man was healthy and dead, and even those who recovered from the illness were no longer quite healthy or quite ill and could not go about their business. Previously people had been telling on winter evenings how there was a sickness in other countries and people were dying of it as of a divine judgment; but no one had believed that it would come into our lands, because nothing foreign had ever come to us, until it came. It broke out first in the council houses, and everyone who caught it died immediately. The news spread in the neighborhood; people were frightened and ran at one another. Some waited to see whether it would spread, others fled and met the illness in the places to which they had repaired. After a few days they begin to bring the dead to the Oberplan churchyard to bury them, soon afterwards from villages near and far and from the market-town itself. The bells of the wagon trains could be heard almost all day long, and they could no longer ring the death knell for each corpse, but rang it in general for all of them. Soon they couldn't bury them any more in the churchyard, but made great pits in the open field, put the corpses in them and covered them with earth. From many a house no smoke rose, in many the cattle could be heard bellowing because no one had remembered to feed them, and many a cow ran around wild because there was no one to bring it from the pasture into the stall. Children didn't love their parents any more, nor parents their children, they merely threw the dead into the pit and went away. The red cherries ripened, but no one thought about them, and no one took them from the trees; the grain ripened, but it was not brought in with the usual order and cleanliness; indeed, much of it would not have been brought in at all if a sympathetic man had not helped a healthy little boy or old woman who had been left alone in a house bring it in. One Sunday, when the priest of Oberplan went up to the pulpit to give his sermon, there were seven persons with him in the church; the others were dead or ill or caring for the ill or stayed away out of confusion and obstinacy. When they saw this, they broke out in loud weeping; the priest could not give his sermon, but celebrated a low mass, and they went away. When the sickness had reached its peak, when people didn't know if they should seek help in heaven or on earth, it happened that a farmer from the Amish House of Melm went to Oberplan. A little bird sat on the Triple Pine singing:

> Eat gentian and pimpernel,
> Die not and rise up well.
> Eat gentian and pimpernel,
> Die not and rise up well.

The farmer fled; he ran to the priest at Oberplan and told him the words, and the priest told the people. They did what the bird had sung, and the sickness diminished more and more, and before the oats had gone to stubble and before the brown hazelnuts ripened on the bushes along the fences, it was no longer there. People ventured to come out again; smoke rose in the villages as they burned the beds and other things of the sick people, because the sickness had been very contagious; many houses were freshly whitewashed and scrubbed, and the church bells sounded peaceable tones again when they called either to prayer or to the holidays of the Church."

At that moment, as though called forth by these words, the great bell in the tower at Oberplan sounded clearly and purely with distinct deep tones, and the sounds came to us under the pines.

"See," said Grandfather, "it is already four o'clock and the bell is already ringing the close of work; you see, child, this tongue tells us almost with intelligible words how good and how happy and how peaceful everything is in this region again."

We had turned around at these words and looked back at the church. It rose with its dark tile roof and with its dark tower from which the tones came and the houses crowded around it like a gray flock of doves.

"Because it is the close of work," said Grandfather, "we must say a short prayer."

He took his hat from his head, crossed himself and prayed. I also took my cap off and prayed. When we had finished, crossed ourselves, and put on our headgear again, Grandfather said: "It is a lovely custom that this sign is given with the bell on Saturday afternoon to indicate that evening of the festival of Our Lord is beginning and that everything that is strictly worldly must rest, just as I on Saturday afternoon do not undertake any serious work but at most take a walk to neighboring villages. The custom comes from the pagans who used to be in the region, for whom every day was the same, and to whom, when they had been converted to Christianity, a sign had to be given to indicate that the Lord's day was drawing near. In the past this sign was very much heeded; for when the bell rang, people prayed and stopped their hard work at home or in the field. Your grandmother, when she was still a young girl, knelt every time when the bell sounded the close of work and said a short prayer. In those days, when I went to Glöckelberg on Saturday evenings, as I now go to other places—for your grandmother is from the nearer part of Glöckelberg—she often knelt at the sound of the village bell with her red bodice and snow-white skirts next to the hedge and the blossoms of the hedge were just as white and red as her clothes."

"Grandfather, she still always prays when the close of work is sounded, in the room next to the blue cupboard with the red flowers," I said.

"Yes, that she does," he replied, "but other people do not heed the sign, they keep working in the field and keep working in the house, just as the mallet of our neighbor, the weaver, continues to sound even on Saturday evenings until it is night and the stars appear in the sky."

"Yes, Grandfather."

"But you will not know that Oberplan has the most beautiful sound of bells in the whole region. The bells are tuned like the strings of a violin so that they sound well together. Therefore a new one could not be added if one were to break or get a crack, and the beauty of the sound would be over with. When your Uncle Simon was in the field against the enemy and was ill, he said, when I visited him, 'Father, if I could only hear the Oberplan bells once again!'— but he could not hear them any more and had to die."

In this moment the bell stopped ringing and there was nothing more in the fields but the friendly light of the sun.

"Come, let's go on," said Grandfather.

We walked further on the gray grass between the tree trunks, always from one trunk to another. There probably was a trodden path, but it was softer and nicer to walk on the grass. But the soles of my boots had already become so smooth from the short grass that I could hardly take another step and kept slipping in all directions while walking. When Grandfather noticed this state of affairs, he said: "You must not drag your feet so; on this grass you must set your foot down as though you meant it, otherwise you'll grind your soles smooth and no secure footing is possible. You see, everything must be learned, even walking. But come, give me your hand; I shall lead you so that you will proceed without difficulty."

He gave me his hand, I grasped it and went on now supported and secure.

After a while Grandfather pointed to a tree and said: "That is the Triple Pine."

A big trunk went high in the air and bore three slender trees that mixed their branches and twigs in the breezes. At its foot lay a lot of fallen needles.

"I don't know," said Grandfather, "whether the little bird sang the words or whether God put them in the man's heart: but the Triple Pine may not be cut down and no harm may come to its trunk and its branches."

I looked closely at the tree, then we went on and after a time we gradually came out of the Drybeaks. The trunks became thinner, they became scarcer, finally there were no more at all, and we were walking up a very stony path between fields that now reappeared. Here Grandfather showed me another tree and said: "See, that is the Power Beech; that is the most important tree around here; it grows out of the stoniest ground there is. See, that's why its wood is as firm as stone, that's why its trunk is so short; the branches are so close together and hold the leaves firmly so that the crown seems to form a sphere through which not a single eye of heaven can see. When it is about to become winter, people look at this tree and say: When the autumn winds roar through the dry foliage of the Power Beech and drive its leaves to the ground, then winter will come soon. And, in fact, the hills and fields cover themselves in a short time with the white blanket of snow. Take note of the tree and remember in later years, when I have long since been lying in the grave, that it was your grandfather who first showed it to you."

From this beech we walked up a little more and came to the crest of the ridge where we could look across to the places on the other side and saw the village of Melm in a mass of trees at our feet.

Grandfather stopped here, pointed with his stick to a distant forest, and said: "See, over there to the right, the dark forest is Rindlesberg, behind which lies the village of Rindles, which we cannot see. Farther left, it the evergreen forest were not there, you would see the great Alsch farm. At the time of the plague everyone had died in the Alsch farm except for a single maid, who had to take care of the cattle; two rows of cows who give the milk for the cheese that is made at the farm, then the steers and the calves. She had to feed all these for many weeks and wait, because the plague could not harm the animals and they remained cheerful and lively, until her masters learned of the events and sent her some help from the remaining people. In the great Hammer Mill that you showed me on the way up everyone had also died except for a single, crippled man who had to do all the work and satisfy the people who brought their grain to the mill after the plague and wanted their flour; that's where the saying comes from even today: 'I have more work than the cripple in the Hammer.' Of the clergy in Oberplan only the old priest remained to carry on the ministry; the two chaplains died along with the sexton and his son, who had already been ordained. Of the bathhouses that form the curved lane next to the short house row of the market three entirely died out."

After these words we went in the hollow passage and under a lovely play of colors of every sort caused by the sun in the green leaves of the shrubbery, down into the village of Melm.

Grandfather had something to do in the first house of the village, in the Power farm. Therefore we went into it through its great archway. The Power farmer stood in the yard in shirtsleeves with many deeply embossed metal buttons on his waistcoat. He greeted Grandfather when he saw him and took him into the parlor, but they left me sitting on a little wooden bench next to the door in the yard and sent me a slice of bread and butter, which I consumed. I rested, looking at the things that were there, such as the wagons that stood unloaded, pushed together under the roof of the shed, the plows and harrows that had been shoved together in a corner in order to make room, the farmhands and maids who went back and forth doing their Saturday work and preparing for the celebration of Sunday; and the things joined those with which my head was already filled, triple pines, the dead and dying, and singing birds.

After a while Grandfather came out again and said: "So, now I am finished and we shall start our way back."

I stood up from my bench; we went toward the archway; the farmer and his wife accompanied us that far, said goodbye at the archway, and wished us a safe journey home.

When we were alone again and were going along the hollow passage on our way back, Grandfather continued: "When it got to be late in the fall, when the whortleberries ripen and the fog already appears on the bogs, people turned again to that place in the earth in which the dead had been buried without consecration or ceremony. Many people went out and looked at the fresh pile of earth, others wanted to know the names of those buried there, and when religious service had been completely restored in Oberplan, the place was consecrated like a proper cemetery, a solemn worship service was held under the open sky, and all the prayers and blessings that had been left undone before were made up for. Then planking was put around the place and unslaked lime spread over it. From then on people retained the memory of the past in all sorts of things. You will know that many places around here still have names from the plague, for example Plague Meadow, Plague Path, Plague Slope; and if you were not so young, you would have seen the column that is no longer in existence but stood on the marketplace of Oberplan and on which you could read when the plague came and when it ceased, and on which there was a prayer of thanks to the crucified Christ who was displayed at the peak of the column."

"Grandmother told us about the Plague Column," said I.

"But afterwards other generations came," he continued, "who know nothing of the matter and scorn the past; the fences are gone, the places are covered with ordinary grass. People like to forget past suffering and consider their health a possession that God owes them and that they squander in flourishing times. They don't respect the places where the dead rest and they speak the name 'Plague' with a thoughtless tongue, as though it were any other name, like 'Hawthorn' or 'Yew.'"

Meanwhile we had come through the hollow passage to the crest of the ridge and now faced the forests that we had had to turn to see on our way up, and the sun was beginning to set over them in great glory.

"If the evening sun were not shining in our faces," said Grandfather, "and everything were not floating in fiery haze, I would be able to show you the place I am going to talk about now and that belongs to our story. It is many hours from here on foot; it is right across from us, where the sun is going down, and there is where the real forests begin. There are the firs and spruces, there are the alders and maples, the beeches and other trees like kings, and the common folk of the bushes and the thick tangle of the grasses and plants, the flowers, the berries and mosses under them. The springs come down from all the heights and gurgle and murmur and tell what they have always told; they flow over pebbles like light glass and combine into streams in order to go out into the far lands; the birds sing up above; the white clouds gleam; the rain pours down; and when it is night the moon shines on everything making it look like a dampened cloth made of silver threads. In this forest there is a very dark lake; behind it is a gray rock wall reflected in it; beside it stand dark trees that look into the water; and in front there are raspberry and blackberry hedges that form a barricade. On the rock wall lies a white jumble of fallen trees; rising out of the blackberries is many a white trunk that has been destroyed by lightning and looks at the lake; great gray stones lie around for a hundred years; and the birds and wild animals come to the lake to drink."

"That is the lake, Grandfather, that I named on the way up," I said; "Grandmother told us about its water and the strange fish that are in it, and when a white cloud comes over it there is a storm."

"And when a white cloud comes over it," Grandfather continued, "and otherwise the sky is clear, more and more join it; it becomes an army of clouds, and detaches itself from the forest, and draws out the storm that brings us heavy rain and frequently hail, too. On the edge of this forest, where there are fields today, but in those days there was still thick undergrowth, there was at the time of the plague a pitch-burner's hut. In it lived the man about whom I want to tell you. My grandfather still knew the hut, and he said that from time to time one could see smoke rising from the forest, just as today you saw the threads of smoke rising as we went up."

"Yes, Grandfather," I said.

"This pitch-burner," he continued, "wanted, during the plague, to escape the general visitation that God had inflicted on man. He wanted to go up into the highest forest where no one ever intrudes, where never a breath of men comes, where everything is different from down below, and where he hoped to stay healthy. But if someone were to get to him, he intended to kill him with his wooden poker rather than let him come nearer and bring the pestilence. When the sickness was long past, however, then he wanted to return and live on. Therefore, when the black-stained pushcarters, who obtained the wagon grease from him, brought the news that the plague had already appeared in the neighboring countries, he rose and went up into the high forest. But he went still farther than the lake, he went to where the forest is as it was at the time of creation, where no men have worked, where no tree falls unless it is struck by lightning or blown down by the wind; then it lies there, and new saplings and plants grow out of its body; the trunks stand tall, and between them are the unseen and untouched flowers and grasses and plants."

While Grandfather was saying this the sun had gone down. The fiery haze had suddenly disappeared; the sky, in which there was not a single cloud, had become a golden background such as one sees in old paintings; and the forest now stood out clear and dark blue from this background.

"See, child, now we can see the place I am talking about," said Grandfather; "look right at the forest, and you will see a deeper blue coloration; that is the basin in which the lake lies. I don't know if you can see it."

"I see it," I replied; "I also see the faint gray streaks that show where the rock wall of the lake is."

"Then you have sharper eyes than I," returned Grandfather; "now follow the wall with your eyes to the right and up to the edge, then you have those higher great forests. There is supposed to be a rock there that has an overhanging brim like a hat and can be seen like a little growth on the edge of the forest."

"Grandfather, I see the little growth."

"It is called the Hat Rock and is far above the lake in the high forest where hardly anyone has ever been. But on the lake there is supposed to have been a wooden dwelling. The Knight of Wittinghausen built it as a refuge for his two daughters in the Swedish War.* His castle was burned down then; the ruins still rise like a blue cube out of the Thomas Forest."

"I know the ruins, Grandfather."

"The house was behind the lake, where the wall protected it, and an old huntsman guarded the girls. Today there is not a trace of any of this left. From this lake the pitch-burner went up to the Hat Rock and looked for a suitable place. But he was not alone; his wife and children were with him, and his brothers, cousins, and servants; he had taken his cattle and his equipment. He had also taken all kinds of seeds and grain in order to be able to plant in the loosened earth, in order to gather provisions for future times. Now they built huts for men and animals, they built the ovens for distilling their product, and they spread the seed in the tilled fields. Among the people in the forest there was also a brother of the pitch-burner, who did not want to stay in the forest but wished to return to the hut. The pitch-burner told him that he should give a sign when the plague had broken out. He was to send up a column of smoke on the House Mountain at noon, let it continue without change for an hour, then extinguish the fire to make it stop. For the sake of certainty he was to do this three days in succession, so that the forest dwellers would recognize it as a sign that had been given to them. But when the plague had ceased, he was to send the news so that they could come down and not catch the disease. He was to send up a column of smoke at noon from the House Mountain, maintain it for an hour without change and then extinguish the fire. He was to do this four days in succession, but on each day an hour later; they would know from this particular procedure that all danger was past. But if he were to become ill, he should leave this commission as a testament to a friend or acquaintance, who should then pass it on to another friend or acquaintance, so that someone at last might send up the column of smoke and expect a reward from the pitch-burner. Do you know the House Mountain?"

"Yes, Grandfather," I replied; "it is the black, sharp-pointed forest that rises behind Pernek and on the peak of which there is a clump of rock."

---

*The phase of the Thirty Years' War extending from 1630 to 1635 and concluding with the Peace of Prague.

"Yes," said Grandfather, "that's it. Once there are supposed to have been three brothers, one on the Alp, one on the House Mountain, and one in the Thomas Forest. They are supposed to have given one another signs when danger threatened one of them, smoke by day, fire by night, so that it would be seen and the others might come with help. I don't know whether the brothers ever lived. But now the emigrants lived in the high forest, and when the plague had broken out in our region, a column of smoke rose from the House Mountain at noon, lasted an hour without change and then stopped. This occurred three days in succession, and the people in the forest knew what had happened.—But look how cool it has become and how the dew is already falling on the grass; come, I will button your jacket so that you won't be cold, and then I will continue to tell you the story."

During Grandfather's narration we had come into the Drybeaks; we had gone by the Triple Pine and come under the dark trunks on the almost colorless grass to the fields of Oberplan. Grandfather laid his stick on the ground, bent down to me, tightened my neckerchief, straightened my waistcoat, and buttoned up my jacket. Then he buttoned up his own coat, took his staff, and we went on.

"You see, my dear child," he continued, "none of it did any good, and it was only tempting God. When the bushes of the forest had got their blossoms, white and red, as nature wills, when the blossoms had turned to berries, when the things that the pitch-burner had planted in the forest earth had sprouted and grown, when the barley had got its golden beard, when the wheat had already become whitish, when the oat flakes hung on the little threads and the potato plants bore their green globes and bluish blossoms—all the pitch-burner's people, he himself and his wife, except for a single little boy, the pitch-burner's son, had died. The pitch-burner and his wife had been the last, and since the survivors had always buried the dead, but the pitch-burner and his wife had no one after them and the boy was too weak to bury them, they remained lying in the hut as corpses. The boy was now alone in the dreadful great forest. He let out the animals that were in the stalls because he could not feed them; he thought that they could find nourishment from the grass of the forest, and then he himself ran away from the hut, because he was terribly frightened of the dead man and the dead woman. He went to an open place in the forest, and there was now no one around, no one but death. When he knelt in the middle of flowers and undergrowth and prayed, or when he wept and wailed for his father and mother and the other people, and when he then stood up again, there was nothing around him but the flowers and undergrowth and the cattle, which grazed under the forest trees and made sounds with their bells. You see, that's how it was with the boy, who was perhaps just as big as you. But see, pitch-burners' children are not like those in the market towns or in the cities; they are already more instructed in the things of nature; they grow up in the forest; they know how to deal with fire; they are not afraid of storms and have few clothes, no shoes in the summer and, instead of a hat on their heads, their sooty hair. In the evening the boy took steel, stone, and tinder from his pocket and made himself a fire; the one in the pitch-burner's oven had long gone out. When he was hungry, he dug up potatoes with his hands from under the outgrown vines and roasted them in the heat of the fire. Springs and streams gave him water to drink. The next day he looked for a way out of the forest. He no longer knew how he had come up into the forest. He went up to the highest place on the mountain, climbed a tree and looked around, but he saw nothing but forest and more forest. He now thought that he would go to higher and higher places until he could finally look out and find the end of the forest. For food he took with him the kernels of the barley and the wheat, which he roasted together with their ears on a stone over the fire, burning the hairs and hulls, or he removed the small, delicate wheat kernels from their hulls, or he peeled carrots that grew in the cabbage patches. At night he wrapped himself in leaves and branches and covered himself with brush. The animals that he had let out had gone away, either because they had got lost in the forest or because they feared the death hut and fled it; he didn't hear their bells any more and they did not appear. One day when he was looking for the animals, he found on a hill, where there were blackberries and stones, a little girl lying in the middle of a blackberry patch. The boy's heart began to beat extraordinarily; he approached; the girl was alive, but had the sickness and lay there unconscious. He approached even closer; the girl had on white clothes and a black cape; she had tangled hair and lay awkwardly in the patch as though she had been thrown there. He called, but got no answer; he took the girl's hand, but her hand could not grasp anything and was lifeless. He ran into the valley, filled an old hat that he had taken out of the hut with water, brought it back to the girl and wet her lips. He did this several times. He did not know how to help the child and, if he had known, he had nothing to give her. Since he could not easily get through the tangled patch to the place where the girl was lying, he took a big stone, laid it on the creeping canes of the blackberries, and repeated this until he had covered the blackberries, until they were held down and the stones formed a pavement. He knelt on this pavement, moved the child, looked at her, straightened her hair, and, because he had no comb, he wiped off her wet locks with his hands, until they once again resembled beautiful, fine human hair. But because he could not lift the girl in order to carry her to a better place, he ran up the hill, tore out the dry grass there, tore off the stalks that grew high on the stones, collected the dry leaves that were left over from the previous autumn and that either hung in clumps or had been blown by the wind into crevices, and put all this in a pile. When it was enough he carried it to the girl and made her a softer bed. He put the things under her body where they were most needed. Then he cut twigs with his knife from the undergrowth, stuck them into the ground around the child, tied their tips together with grass and stalks and put light branches on top of them so as to make a roof. He laid twigs on the girl's body and covered them with broad-leafed plants, for example, coltsfoot, so that they made a blanket. He then got himself some food out of his dead father's fields. At night he made a fire out of wood and mold that he brought together. So he sat during the day next to the unconscious child, cared for her and protected her against animals and flies; at night he maintained a gleaming fire. See, the child did not die, but her sickness began to get better; her cheeks became lovelier and prettier again, her lips acquired a rosy color and were no longer so pale and yellowish, and her eyes opened and looked around. She also began to eat; she ate the strawberries that were still to be found; she ate raspberries that were already ripening; she ate the kernels of the hazelnuts that, to be sure, were not ripe but sweet and soft; she finally even ate the white meal of the roasted potatoes and the delicate kernels of the wheat, all of which the boy brought to her and handed to her; and when she slept he ran up the hill and climbed a rock in order to look all around; he also looked for the animals again because the milk would have been quite good just now. When the girl had grown stronger and was able to help, he took her to a place where over-hanging branches protected her, but, as he thought that a storm might come and the rain might pour through the branches, he sought out a cave that was dry, made a bed in it, and brought the girl there. There was a stone slab above the place and they could look nicely out into the forest. I told you that this sickness was very violent, that people within five to six hours were healthy and dead; but I tell you, too, that whoever survived the sickness was very soon healthy, except that he remained weak for a long time and had to be taken care of for a long time. Now the children remained in the cave, and the boy fed the girl and took care of everything she needed. Now the girl told him how she had got into the forest. Her father and mother and a number of people had left their faraway home as the sickness approached in order to seek higher ground where they would not be reached by the disease. They had got lost in the big forest, her father and mother had died, and the girl had been left behind alone. Where her father and mother had died, where the other people had gone, how she had got into the blackberries, she didn't know. Nor could she say where her home was. The boy told the girl how they had left their hut, how they had all gone into the forest, and how they had died and he alone had remained alive. You see, that's how the children sat in the cave when the day passed over the forest and illuminated the greenery, the birds sang, the trees shone, and the mountaintops gleamed; or they slumbered when it was night, when it was dark and still or when the cry of a wild animal sounded or the moon stood in the sky and poured its beams over the treetops. You can imagine how it was if you observe how beautiful it is here in the night, how the moon stands so stirringly in the clouds, even though we are so close to the houses, and how it shines down on our neighbor's black mountain ashes."

While Grandfather was telling his story we had gone down through the fields of Oberplan, we had crossed the meadow where the Behring Spring is, we had climbed over the stone wall, we had crossed the soft field of grass and were already nearing the houses of Oberplan. Meanwhile night had fully fallen, the half moon stood in the sky, lighting many clouds that had piled up, and its beams fell upon the mountain ashes standing in our neighbor's garden.

"After the girl had become very strong," Grandfather continued, "the children thought about getting out of the forest. They discussed

with each other how they might do that. The girl knew nothing at
all; but the boy said that all water runs downhill, that it runs on and
on without stopping, that the forest was very high and the dwellings
of people lay very low, that a bright running stream had gone by
their own hut, that they had climbed up from this hut into the forest,
that they had kept going up and up and had come across several
streams flowing downhill; therefore if they kept following a running
stream downwards, they would have to come out of the forest and
reach some people. The girl could see that, and joyfully they decided
to do it. They prepared themselves to leave. From the fields they
took potatoes, as many as they could carry, and many bunches of
grain tied together. The boy had made a sack out of his jacket, and
for strawberries and raspberries he made nice little pouches out of
birch bark. Then they departed. They looked first in the valley for
the stream from which they had drunk before and then followed it.
You see, the boy led the girl because she was weak and because he
was more experienced in the forest; he showed her the stones she
should step on, he showed her the thorns and sharp branches she
should avoid, he guided her in narrow places, and when they came
to big rocks or thickets and swamps, they went to the side and
cleverly kept to the direction of the stream. So on they went. When
they were tired, they sat down and rested; when they were rested up,
they went on. At noon he made a fire, and they roasted potatoes and
toasted their ears of grain. He looked for water in a spring or in a
cold creek that trickled over white sand out of the black forest earth
or from bushes and stones. When they came to places where there
were berries and nuts, they collected them. At night he made a fire,
made a bed for the girl, and bedded himself down as he had in the
first days in the forest. In this way they wandered on. They went past
many trees, past the fir with its bearded moss hanging down, past
the cleft spruce, past the long-armed maple, past the white-flecked
beech trunk with its light green leaves, they went past flowers,
plants, and stones, they went under the singing of the birds, they
went by hopping squirrels or a grazing deer. The stream went
around a hill, or it went in a straight line, or it wound around the
trunks of trees. It got bigger and bigger; innumerable side streams
came out of the valleys and went on with it; drops dropped into it
from the foliage of the trees and from the grass and joined it. It
gurgled over the pebbles and seemed to tell stories to the children.

Little by little the boy came to other trees that made him well aware that they were getting out; the pointy firs, the spruces with their rough trunks, the maples with their big branches, and the knobby beeches ceased; the trees were smaller, fresher, cleaner, and daintier.

At the edge of the water stood alder bushes; several willows stood there; the wild apple tree showed its fruit, and the wild cherry gave them its little, black, sweet cherries. Little by little came meadows; there came pastures; the trees grew less dense; there were only groups of them; and suddenly, when the stream was already running as a broad, calm river, they saw the fields and dwellings of people. The children rejoiced and went to a house. They had not come to the home of the boy; they didn't know where they had come, but they were received in a quite friendly way and taken care of by the people. In the meantime a column of smoke rose again from the House Mountain; it rose at noon, remained unchanged for an hour and then ceased. This happened four days in a row, on each day an hour later; but there was no one there to understand the sign."

When Grandfather had told the story this far, we had come to our house.

He said: "Since we are tired, and since it is so warm, let us sit a little on the stone; I will finish the story for you."

We sat on the stone, and Grandfather continued: "When people had learned who the boy was and where he belonged, he was taken with the girl to his uncle in the pitch-burner's hut. The uncle went up into the forest and with horror burned the forest hut in which the dead pitch-burner lay with his wife. The girl, too, was discovered by her relatives and picked up in the pitch-burner's hut. You see, in those days the plague broke out in other parts of the forest, too, and many people died of it; but other days came and health was restored to our regions. The boy now stayed with his uncle in the hut, and grew bigger and bigger; they pursued the business of distilling wagon grease, turpentine, and other things. When many years had gone by, when the boy was already almost a man, a buggy came driving up to the pitch-burner's hut. In the buggy sat a beautiful maiden, who was wearing a white dress and a black cape and wore a little sprig of blackberry at her breast. She had the cheeks, the eyes, and the fine hair of the forest girl. She had come to see the boy who had saved her and led her out of the forest. She and her old cousin, who accompanied her, asked the boy to come to the girl's manor house and live there. The boy, who liked the girl very much, went along. He learned all sorts of things there, became ever more skilled, and finally became the husband of the girl he had found in the forest at the time of the plague. You see, he got a manor house, he got fields, meadows, forests, inns, and servants, and, as he had been sensible and observant in his youth, so he increased and improved everything and was respected and loved by his subordinates, by his neighbors and friends, and by his wife. How different people's fates are. He often invited his uncle to come to him, to move in with him and live with him, but he stayed in his pitch-burner's hut and kept pursuing his pitch-burner's business, and as the forest became ever smaller, as the fields and meadows had spread to his hut, he went deeper into the woods and there kept on distilling wagon grease. His offspring, which he got after he had married, stayed with the same occupation, and from him is descended old Andreas, who is also only a wagon-grease carter and can't do anything but rove around the country with his black cask and smear wagon grease on the feet of foolish boys who don't know any better."

With these words Grandfather ended his story. But we continued to sit on the stone. The moon had been shining brighter and brighter, the clouds stretched themselves longer and longer, and I kept looking at our neighbor's black mountain ash.

Then Grandmother looked out the door and asked whether we did not want to come to eat. We went into my grandparents' parlor; from the wall Grandmother folded down a beautiful hanging table made of brown and white striped peachwood, covered it with white linen, gave us plates and utensils, and served chicken with rice. As we ate she said with an angry expression that Grandfather was even more foolish and thoughtless than her grandson, because he had taken a green-glazed bowl to wash wagon-greased feet, so that it was too disgusting to be used for anything else.

Grandfather smiled and said: "Then we will smash the bowl so that no one will take it by mistake, and buy a new one; after all, it is better than if the rascal had had to stay scared. You're looking after him, too."

With these words he pointed to the stove where my pitch-stained pants were being soaked in a little tub.

When we had eaten, Grandfather said I should go to bed, and he accompanied me into my bedchamber. As we went through the vestibule where I had had such a punishment, the young swallows twittered softly in their nest as though drunk with sleep; in the big parlor a little lamp was burning on the table, a lamp that burned every Saturday all night in honor of the Holy Virgin; in my parents' bedroom my father lay in bed with a light next to him, reading, as was his custom; Mother was not home because she was with a sick cousin. When we had greeted Father and he had answered in a friendly way, we went into the children's bedroom. My sister and my little brothers were already slumbering. Grandfather helped me undress and stayed with me until I had said my prayers and pulled up the covers. Then he went away. But I could not sleep; I kept thinking about the story that Grandfather had told me; I thought about one circumstance and another, and a number of things occurred to me that I must ask about. Finally, though, tiredness claimed its due and sleep descended onto my eyes. When I was still only half asleep, without being able to arouse myself to full consciousness I saw by the light that came from my parents' bedroom that Mother went in. She went to the font with the holy water, wet her fingers, came to me, sprinkled it on me, and made the sign of the Cross on my forehead, mouth, and breast; I saw that everything was forgiven and suddenly fell asleep with the joy of reconciliation—I can say, blissfully.

But my sleep was still not calm at first. I had many things with me, people dead, dying, ill with the plague, triple pines, the girl of the forest, the Power farmer, the neighbor's mountain ash, and old Andreas smeared my feet again. But the course of my sleep must have been good, for when they waked me the sun was shining through the windows; it was a lovely Sunday; everything was in a holiday spirit; after prayers we got a holiday breakfast, got our holiday clothes, and when I went out into the lane everything was pure, fresh, and clear; the things of the night were gone, and the neighbor's mountain ash was only half as big as it had been yesterday. We got our prayer books and went to church, where we saw Father and Grandfather in their places in the pew reserved for the leading citizens.

Since then many years have gone by; the stone still lies in front of my father's house, but now my sister's children play on it, and my old mother may often sit on it and look out toward the parts of the world where her sons are scattered.

Limestone

Adalbert Stifter

The story I here propose to tell is one which I once heard from a friend, one in which nothing out of the ordinary occurs, and yet one which I have never been able to forget. Nine out of ten readers will find fault with the man whom the story concerns, the tenth will not be able to get him out of his mind. The occasion of the story was a dispute that arose, as I was sitting with a number of our friends, about the ways in which it is possible for a man's mental qualities to be apportioned. Some declared that one can be endowed with a particular talent in an extraordinary degree, and nevertheless possess the others only to a slight extent. The so-called virtuosi were cited as examples of this. Others asserted that the qualities of the mind are always equally present, either all alike rich or all alike mediocre or all alike scanty, but that it is a matter of chance which gift is more especially developed, and that this gives an appearance of inequality. Raphael, if the impressions of his youth and the circumstances of his time had been different, might have become a great general instead of a great painter. Others again were of the opinion that since reason is man's metaphysical faculty and his highest faculty of all, it follows that where there is a rich endowment of reason, the other subordinate gifts must be present in abundance also. But the reverse (they said) is not the case; a man may particularly excel in one of the lower gifts, and not in any of the higher. And yet, of course, if there is any outstanding talent, whether high or low in itself, then the qualities subordinate to it must be outstanding as well. They argued that the lower gift is always the servant of the higher, and that it would be a contradiction to be endowed with the higher, commanding talent and lacking in the one which is lower and subservient. Finally there were others who said that men are as God made them, that we cannot tell how He has apportioned their qualities, and that it is idle to dispute the point, since we cannot be certain what relevant factors the future may reveal. It was then that my friend told his story.

As all of you know (he said) I have been working for many years now as a surveyor, I am employed by the State, and the Government has sent me on commissions of this kind to one place after another. In this way I have come to know different parts of the country and all sorts of people. On one occasion I was in the little town of Wengen, and it was evident that I should have to stay there for some time, since my business was becoming protracted and also extending in scope. It was then that I often visited the nearby village of Schauendorf, and made the acquaintance of the local priest, an excellent man who had introduced horticulture into the village, with the result that whereas it had formerly been surrounded by a tangle of thorny shrubs and gorse, it now looked like an orchard full of agreeable fruit trees. One day he invited me to a church festival, and I told him that I should come later on, as I had some necessary work to finish. When I had completed my tasks I set out for Schauendorf. I walked over the fields and through the fruit trees, and as I approached the priest's house I saw that the midday meal must have already begun. The garden, which was in front of the house as it often is in Catholic presbyteries, was empty; the windows overlooking it were open; I caught a glimpse of the kitchen and saw that the servants were hard at work around the fire; and from the dining room came the occasional clatter of plates and clink of cutlery. When I entered I found the guests sitting around the table and a place laid out and carefully kept for me. The priest led me to it and made me sit down. He said he would not introduce me to those present or tell me their names, since I knew some of them already anyway. Others I would soon get to know in the course of the meal, and he would tell me who the rest were when we had risen from table. So I sat down, and things turned out just as the priest had said they would. I made the acquaintance of many of those present, learned the names and circumstances of many others, and as the different courses were brought on and tongues were loosened by wine, many a new acquaintance seemed one of long standing. Only one guest remained unidentified. He sat there amiably smiling, attended carefully to everything that was said, always turning his face toward

whatever was the most animated center of conversation, as if he felt
that it was his duty to do so; his expression seemed to signify
agreement with everyone who spoke, and if livelier talk began to
come from another group, he would turn in their direction and
listen. But he himself did not speak a word. He was sitting rather far
down the table, his black-attired figure rising starkly above the white
linen tablecloth, and although he was not tall he never sat quite
upright, as if he felt that that would be unseemly. He was wearing the
costume of a poor country priest. His coat was very worn and
threadbare, it was shiny in some places and in others it had lost its
blackness and looked rusty and faded. It had strong bone buttons.
His black tunic was very long and its buttons were also made of
bone. The two tiny white bands that hung down over his black
neckcloth betokened his office and were the only white that he
displayed. Sometimes, as he sat there, a slight trace of his shirt cuffs
would become visible, and these he always carefully and surreptitiously pushed back into his sleeves. Perhaps their condition was
such that he must have been slightly ashamed of them. I noticed that
he helped himself to very little of any of the food, and always
courteously thanked the servant who was handing it around. At
dessert he scarcely tasted the fine wine, took only very small pieces
of confectionery, and put nothing aside on his plate, as the others of
course did in order to observe the custom of taking some small
souvenir back to their families.

It was by these oddities of behavior that the man attracted my
attention.

When the meal was over and the guests had risen, I was able to
view the remainder of his person. His breeches were of the same
material and in the same condition as his coat, they came down to
below his knee and were fastened there with buckles. Then followed
black stockings, which were, however, almost gray. On his feet he
wore broad shoes with large buckles. They were made of strong
leather and had thick soles. Such was the man's attire, and when the
rest of the company had divided into conversing groups he stood
almost alone, with his back nearly touching the wall between the
windows. His physical appearance was in keeping with his dress.
He had a long, gentle, almost timid face with very beautiful clear
blue eyes. His brown hair was gathered simply at the back, and there

were some white strands in it, which showed that he was already approaching his fiftieth year or that he must have had experience of anxiety and grief.

Before long he went to a corner and fetched his walking stick, a cane with a black knob made of bone like the buttons on his clothes, and approaching his host he began to take his leave. His host asked him whether he really must be going already, to which he replied that it was high time for him to set out, it would take him four hours to walk home and his feet were not as good as they had been in his younger days. The priest did not detain him. He took leave of the company, walked out of the house, and the next minute we saw him striding away through the cornfields; he climbed the hill that lay immediately to the west of the village, and there he seemed to vanish into the shining afternoon.

I asked who this man was and was told that he was the priest in a very poor parish, that he had been there for a very long time now, that he had no wish to move elsewhere, and that he seldom left his house except for some very urgent reason.

Many years had passed since that luncheon, and I had completely forgotten the man, when one day my professional duties took me into a fearful part of the country. I do not mean that it was full of wild scenery, ravines, chasms, cliffs, and waterfalls—I in fact find all these things attractive—merely that there was nothing there except innumerable hillocks or mounds; they were all of bare gray limestone, but the latter was not split into abrupt fragments as this kind of rock often is, on the contrary it had formed itself into broad roundish shapes, and each of these was surrounded at the foot by a long, narrow sand dune. Among these hills ran a little meandering river called the Zirder. The water of this river, which by reflection from the sky often looked dark blue amid the gray and yellow of the stone and the sand, combined with the narrow strips of green that often edged it, and with the other isolated patches of grass that lay here and there among the rock formations, to provide this landscape with the sole variety and refreshment it had to offer.

My lodging was an inn situated in a rather better part of the district and therefore some way away. The road near it, which passed over some rising ground, was called "the highway," as is usual in many parts of the country, and the inn was called after it. In order not to waste too much time walking to and from the inn, I always took cold food and wine with me to my place of work and did not have my main meal until the evening. Some of my assistants also lodged at the inn, the others accommodated themselves as best they could and built little wooden huts out on the rocky plateau.

This limestone region, which is called the Steinkar, is in fact not unduly remote but will be known to few people, since there is no occasion to travel to it.

One evening, when I was walking home alone from my work, having sent my assistants on ahead, I saw my poor priest. He was sitting on a mound of sand, with his big shoes almost buried in it, and sand on his coattails. I recognized him at once. He was dressed more or less as he had been on the occasion of our first meeting. His hair was much grayer now, as if it had hastened to assume this color; his longish face had become distinctly lined, and only his eyes were blue and clear as before. Leaning against him was the cane with the black bone knob.

I came to a halt, approached him, and greeted him.

He had not expected any greeting, and therefore hastily rose to his feet and thanked me. His face showed not the slightest sign of recognition; nor indeed was this to be expected, for at that luncheon he had certainly taken much less notice of me than I had of him. He simply stood before me and looked at me. So to begin a conversation I said: "Your Reverence will not remember me."

"I have not the honor," he answered.

"But I have had the honor," I said, reciprocating his courteous tone, "of eating at the same table as your Reverence."

"I have forgotten the occasion," he replied.

"You are surely the same man, sir," I said, "who once attended a church festival at Schauendorf, several years ago, and were the first to leave after lunch, because, as you said, it would take you four hours to walk back to your presbytery?"

"Yes, I am the same man," he answered. "I went eight years ago to the consecration festival at Schauendorf because it was my duty, I stayed to lunch because the priest invited me, and I was the first to leave after the meal because I had to walk four hours to get home. I have not been back to Schauendorf since then."

"Well, I was sitting at that table too," I said, "and today I recognized your Reverence immediately."

"That is surprising—after so many years," he said.

"My profession obliges me," I replied, "to associate with many people and to observe them, and accordingly I have developed such a talent for observation that I even recognize people whom I have seen years ago and only once. And so we have met again in this dreadful part of the country."

"It is as God made it," he answered. "There are not so many trees growing here as in Schauendorf, but there are many occasions when it is beautiful too, and sometimes it is more beautiful than anywhere else in the world."

I asked him whether he had settled in the district, and he answered that he had been parish priest in the Kar for twenty-seven years. I told him that I had been sent here to make a survey of the area, that I was mapping out the hills and valleys in order to reproduce them on paper on a smaller scale, and that I was living out at the Highway Inn. When I asked him whether he often came here, he replied: "I like to go out to give my feet some exercise, and then I sit on a rock to look at things."

During this conversation we had begun walking, he came with me and we talked of a number of other indifferent matters, the weather, the time of year, the local rock's characteristic tendency to absorb the sun's rays, and so forth.

If his clothes at the luncheon had been poor, they were if anything even poorer now. I could not remember having seen his hat on that occasion, but now I could not help glancing at it again and again, for there was not a single trace of nap left on it.

When we came to the place where his way diverged from mine and led down into the Kar to his house, we took leave of each other, expressing the hope that we should now meet quite frequently.

I continued on my way back to the inn and kept thinking about the priest. My mind ran constantly on his unusual poverty, which was such as I had never before encountered in a man whose rank was not that of a beggar, still less in any who are called upon to set others a shining example of cleanliness and neatness. The priest was, of course, almost overscrupulously clean, but it was this very cleanliness that made his poverty still more painfully obvious by revealing the utterly threadbare, thin, and dilapidated state of his clothing. I looked again at the hills with nothing but bare rock to cover them, I looked again at the valleys with nothing but long sand dunes in them, and then I went into my inn to eat my dinner of roast kid, a dish which they quite often served me there.

I asked no one about the priest, not wishing to hear him unkindly spoken of.

From now on I often met him. As I spent the whole day in the Steinkar and quite often wandered around it in the evening as well, getting my bearings and exploring different sections of the district, and as he too sometimes came out there, our paths could not fail to cross. And from time to time we fell into conversation. He seemed not displeased to meet me, and I too enjoyed our encounters. Later we often went on walks among the rocks together, or sat on one of them and looked at the others. He showed me many little animals and many plants that were indigenous to the area, he showed me its peculiarities, and drew my attention to distinguishing features in many of the mounds of rock which the closest of observers would have judged to be exactly alike in formation. I told him about my travels, showed him our instruments, and as we worked I would sometimes explain to him how they were used.

In due course I also occasionally went back with him to his house. From a place where the ground was a little less wild and rocky, we would walk by a gentler slope down to the Kar. At the edge of the stony plateau was a meadow with some trees in it, among them a fine tall linden tree, and behind this tree stood the presbytery. At that time it was a white building with one upper floor, and it stood out beautifully amid the kindlier green of the meadow and the trees and the gray of the rock. The roof was shingled, with shuttered dormer windows, and the main windows of the house also had heavy green shutters. Farther back, tucked away into a corner of the landscape, as if it were hiding among the rocks, stood the church with its red-painted wooden spire. In another part of the Kar was the school, with a scanty garden around it. The whole Kar consisted only of these three buildings. The remaining dwellings were scattered about the neighborhood. Perched here and there on a rockside and apparently clinging to it was a hut with its little garden of potatoes or goatweed. Some way out, toward the open country, there was also a more fertile area of arable land and meadows and clover fields, which belonged to the community.

From the windows of the presbytery one could see where the

Zirder flowed past along the edge of the meadow; a footbridge rose high above the water and curved down again to ground level, where the grass stood not much higher than the riverbed. Apart from the rocky plateau, this view of the arching footbridge over the lonely river was all that was visible from the house.

When the priest brought me home with him, he never took me upstairs, but always led me through a large entrance hall into a small sitting room. The entrance hall was quite empty, except for a very wide but shallow alcove in which there was a long wooden bench. On the bench, every time I visited the house, there was always a Bible lying, a large tome bound in strong leather. The little sitting room contained only an unpainted softwood table with a few chairs of the same material standing around it, a wooden bench by the wall, and two cupboards painted yellow. There was nothing else, only a small medieval pearwood crucifix, beautifully carved, hanging above the little stoup of holy water beside the door.

In the course of these visits I made a strange discovery. I had already noticed in Schauendorf how the poor priest kept surreptitiously pushing his shirt cuffs back into his sleeves, as if he felt ashamed of them. And he was now continually doing the same thing. I therefore made closer observations, and these, together with other glimpses which I caught of his attire, disclosed that so far from having reason to be ashamed of his cuffs, he wore the finest and most beautiful linen I have ever seen in my life. And this linen, moreover, was invariably in a faultlessly clean and gleaming white condition, such as the general state of his clothes would never have led one to expect. It followed that he must devote the most meticulous care and attention to this one item. Since he never alluded to the matter, it need hardly be said that I did not mention it either.

Such was our association as part of the summer went by.

One day when we were up among the rocks it was unusually sultry. The sun had not shone properly all day through the dull veil of cloud with which the whole sky was covered, but it had penetrated it far enough to be always palely visible; an unearthly light lay over everything in the rocky landscape, casting no shadow, and the few plants that grew there were drooping their leaves; for although the vaulted cloud layer was letting scarcely half the daylight through, the heat was nevertheless such that there might have been three tropical suns all blazing down from a clear sky. We had suffered great discomfort, so I let my assistants go shortly after two o'clock. I sat down under an overhanging rock which formed a kind of cave, where it was appreciably cooler than outside in the open air. There I ate my lunch, drank my chilled wine, and then read a book. In the late afternoon the cloud layer had not disintegrated as it very often does on such days, and it had not become denser, but stood exactly as it had done all day, evenly covering the sky. Consequently it was very late when I left the cave; for just as the overcast sky had not changed, so also the heat had scarcely lessened, and there was no likelihood of dew falling during the night. I was walking back very slowly through the hills when I saw the priest coming toward me through the sand dunes, looking up at the sky. We approached each other and exchanged greetings. He asked me where we had been working today, and I told him. I also told him how I had been sitting in the cave reading, and showed him my book. Then we walked on together through the sand.

Presently he said: "It will not be possible now for you to reach the Highway Inn."

"Why not?" I asked.

"Because the storm is going to break," he replied.

I looked at the sky. The cloud layer seemed to have thickened now, and there was a very strange livid coloring on all the bare rock surfaces we could see.

"I suppose we have had reason to expect a storm all day," I said, "but as to how soon the cloud will condense and cool and produce wind and electricity and precipitation, that I think is unpredictable."

"I daresay one cannot judge it exactly," he answered. "But I have lived in this district for twenty-seven years, I have learned a number of things by experience, and according to my observations the storm is going to break sooner than you might think, and it will be a very violent one. So I think that it would be best if you came with me to my house and spent the night there. My house is near enough for us to reach it easily in time, although the storm is already quite clearly there in the sky; you will be safe under my roof, and can go to your work tomorrow as soon as you please."

I replied that it was nevertheless not impossible that the cloud would produce nothing but steady rain. In that case I should be perfectly all right, because I had a little oilskin cape with me, which

I need only pull out of my pocket and put on, and the rain could then do me no harm. In fact, I said, even if I were not so protected, I had been so often soaked through in the course of my profession that in order to avoid such a misadventure I had no wish to be a burden and a cause of domestic disorder to anyone. But if there was really going to be a storm which might be accompanied by a heavy downpour, or hail, or even a cloudburst, then I would gratefully accept his offer and request shelter for the night. But I must stipulate that it should be nothing more than shelter, that he must not put himself about or give himself any domestic trouble beyond providing some spot for me under his roof; for such a spot would be all that I needed. In any case, I pointed out, our roads coincided for quite some way yet, so we could defer the problem, observe the sky as we went along, and finally decide in the light of events.

He consented, and said that if I did stay with him, I need have no apprehension that he would be in any way burdening himself; his home was a simple one, as I knew, and he would make no more than the minimum arrangements necessary to enable me to spend the night with him.

After arriving at this agreement, we proceeded on our way. We walked very slowly, partly on account of the heat, and partly because we had long ago fallen into the habit of doing so.

Suddenly there was a brief glimmer all around us, reddening the rocks.

It was the first flash of lightning, but it had been silent, and no thunder followed it.

We walked on. Presently there was more lightning, and as the evening had already darkened appreciably, and the light was diffused by the opaque cloud layer, the limestone turned rose-red before our eyes at every flash.

When we reached the point at which our ways parted, the priest stopped and looked at me. I conceded that the storm was breaking, and said that I would go home with him.

So we took the road leading to the Kar, and walked down the gentle rocky slope into the meadow.

On reaching the presbytery, we sat down for a little on the wooden bench in front of the house. The storm was now in full development and was standing from end to end of the sky like a dark rampart. Presently, against this unbroken darkness, across the foot of the storm wall, we saw long puffed-up streaks of drifting white vapor. So over there the storm had perhaps already begun, although where we were there was still not a leaf or a blade of grass stirring. Those drifting swollen clouds are often bad omens in stormy weather; they always presage violent gales and often hail and flooding. And the flashes of lightning were now being followed by clearly audible thunder.

Finally we went into the house.

The priest said that when there was a storm at night, it was his habit to place a lighted candle on his table and to sit quietly in front of it until the storm was over. During the day, he said, he sat at the table without a candle. He asked me whether I had any objection to his observing this custom on the present occasion too. I reminded him of his promise not to put himself out in the slightest degree on my account. So he accompanied me through the entrance hall into the familiar little room, and invited me to take off my things.

I usually carried with me on a leather strap over my shoulder a case containing drawing materials, drawings, and also some surveying instruments. Fastened next to the case was a satchel where I kept my cold food, my wine, my drinking glass, and my wine cooler. I took these things off and hung them over the back of a chair in a corner of the room. I stood my long measuring rod against one of the yellow cupboards.

Meanwhile the priest had left the room, and he now entered carrying a candle. It was a tallow candle in a brass candlestick. He placed the candlestick on the table and laid a pair of brass snuffers beside it. Then we both sat down at the table and remained seated, waiting for the storm.

It now seemed imminent. When the priest had brought the candle, the small remnant of daylight that was still coming in through the windows had vanished. The windows stood like black panels, and night had fallen completely. The lightning was more vivid, and in spite of the candle each flash lit up every corner of the room. The thunder became more solemn and menacing. Thus things continued for some time. Then at last came the first blast of the storm wind. The tree in front of the house trembled softly for a moment, as if stricken by a fleeting breeze, then it was still again. A little while later there was another tremor, more prolonged and profound. Shortly afterwards came a violent blast, all the leaves rustled, the branches seemed to be shuddering, to judge by the noise we heard from indoors; and now the roar continued unabated. The tree by the house, the hedges surrounding it, and all the bushes and trees of the neighborhood were caught up in one great rushing howl that merely waxed and waned by turns. Through it came the peals of thunder. They grew more and more frequent and penetrating. But the storm had still not reached us. There was still an interval between lightning and thunder, and the lightning, brilliant though it was, came in sheets and not in forked flashes.

At last the first raindrops struck the windows. They hammered singly against the glass, but soon there were more of them, and before long the rain was streaming down in torrents. It increased rapidly, with a hissing, rushing sound, until in the end it was as if whole continuous massive volumes of water were pouring down onto the house, as if the house were throbbing under the weight of it and one could feel the throbbing and groaning from inside. Even the rolling thunder was scarcely audible through the roar of the water; the roaring water became a second thunder. Finally the storm was immediately overhead. The lightning fell like lanyards of fire, the flashes were followed instantly by the hoarse thunderclaps which now triumphed over all the rest of the uproar, and the windowpanes shuddered and rattled under their deep reverberating echoes.

I was glad now that I had followed the priest's advice. I had seldom experienced such a storm. The priest was sitting quietly and simply by the table in his little room, with the light of the tallow candle shining on him.

At last there came a crash of thunder that seemed to try to lift the whole house up out of its foundations and hurl it down, and a second crash followed at once. Then there was a short pause, as often happens in the course of such phenomena; the rain broke off for a moment as if in alarm; even the wind stopped. But soon everything was as before; and yet the main onslaught had been broken, and everything continued more steadily. Little by little the storm abated. The gale fell to no more than a steady wind, the rain weakened, the lightning paled, and the thunder became a dull mutter that seemed to be retreating across-country.

At last, when the rain had died down to a mere continuous drizzle and the lightning to a flicker, the priest stood up and said: "It is over."

He lit a candle end and left the room. Presently he returned with a tray on which there were various things for supper. He put a jug of milk from the tray onto the table and poured out two glasses. Then he served some strawberries in a little green glazed dish, and put several pieces of black bread on a plate. He laid a place for each of us with a knife and a small spoon, then he took the tray out of the room again.

When he came back, he said: "This is our supper; I hope it will suffice for you."

He came to the table, folded his hands, and quietly said a blessing; I did the same, and then we sat down to our meal. We drank the milk from our glasses, cut slices of the black bread with our knives, and ate the strawberries with our spoons. When we had finished, he again said grace with folded hands, fetched the tray, and removed the remnants.

In my satchel I still had some of my lunch, and there was still wine in my bottle. So I said: "If you will allow me, sir, I shall take what was left over from my lunch today out of my knapsack, for otherwise the food would spoil."

"Please do exactly as you wish," he replied.

So I took my satchel and said: "This will also show your Reverence how such a wanderer as myself keeps table, and what sort of crockery and cutlery I have.

"I must tell you," I went on, "that for all the praise that is lavished on water and especially on mountain water, and despite the usefulness and excellence of this element in the great economy of nature, it is nevertheless—for a man working all day in the open country under the hot sun, or moving about amid arid rocks and sand, or climbing precipices—infinitely more refreshing and strengthening to drink water mixed with a little wine than to drink the purest and choicest water in the world. I soon learned this in the course of my work, and therefore always take a supply of wine on all my journeys. But only good wine gives good results. And so I had a consignment of good pure wine sent to the Highway Inn, and every day I carry a little of it with me to my rocky hills."

The poor priest watched me as I unpacked my paraphernalia. He looked at my little tin plates, of which several could be packed together into a conveniently small, thin disk. I put the plates on the table. Beside them I put knives and forks from my container. Then I cut slices of the fine white wheaten bread which I had sent to me twice a week, then slices of ham, cold roast meat, and cheese. I laid these things out on the plates. Thereupon I asked him for a bottleful of water; for that, I said, was the only thing I did not carry with me, knowing that nature would provide it wherever I went. When he had brought some water in a jug, I set out my drinking appliances. I took out the bottle which was still half full of wine, I put the two glasses—I always carry an extra one—on the table, and then I showed him my method of chilling wine. One stands the glass in a container of very porous material, the material is moistened with a very volatile liquid called ether which I always carry with me in a flask; this liquid then evaporates very rapidly and actively, and in so doing generates such a chill that the wine becomes cooler than if it had just been brought from the cellar or were even standing in ice. When I had freshened two glasses of wine in this manner, mixed them with water, and set one of them before him, I invited him to eat with me.

As if for courtesy's sake, he consumed a minute quantity of the food, sipped a little from his glass, and steadfastly declined to take any more.

I in turn now took only very little of the food I had set out, and proceeded to pack it all up again, feeling ashamed of the discourtesy into which in fact I had overhastily fallen.

I glanced quickly at the priest; but his expression showed not the slightest trace of ill-feeling.

When the table had been cleared, we sat on for a while by the tallow candle and talked. Then the priest set about preparing my bed. He brought in a large woolen blanket, folded it twice over, and laid it on the bench by the wall. From a similar blanket he made a pillow. Then he opened one of the yellow cupboards, took out an extraordinarily beautiful fine white sheet, unfolded it and spread it over my bed. By the faint light of the candle I could see that this was linen of exceptionally high quality, and could not help gazing at it; he noticed this and blushed.

He put a third blanket on the bed to cover my body.

"This is your bed, as good as I can make it," he said. "You need only say when you are ready to retire for the night."

"I leave that to your Reverence," I said. "Whatever may be your usual hour for going to bed, please be guided only by that. I am tied to no time; it is a consequence of my way of life that my sleep is sometimes short and sometimes long, and that I retire sometimes earlier and sometimes later."

"I too am tied to no time," he replied, "and I can arrange my hours of sleep according to my duties; but since the storm has made us later than usual tonight, and since I am sure you will get up very early tomorrow and probably go to your inn to fetch various things, I think it would be best for us to sleep and we should dispose ourselves to do so."

"I entirely agree with you, sir," I said.

After this conversation he left the room and I supposed that he had gone to his bedroom. I therefore undressed to the extent that I usually do, and lay down on my bed. I was just about to extinguish the candle which I had placed on a chair beside my bed, when the priest came in again. He had changed his clothes and was now wearing gray woolen stockings, gray woolen breeches, and a gray woolen jacket. He had no shoes on but was walking in his stocking feet. It was thus that he reappeared in the room.

"You have gone to bed already," he said. "I have come to wish you good night and then to lie down to sleep myself. Sleep well, then, so far as it is possible on that bed!"

"I shall sleep well," I replied, "and I bid you good night too."

Thereupon he went to the stoup that hung under the finely carved little crucifix, sprinkled himself with a few drops, and left the room.

By the light of my candle I saw him go into the large entrance hall and lie down on the wooden bench in the shallow alcove, placing the Bible under his head as a pillow.

On seeing this I leaped out of bed, went out into the hall in my night clothes, and said: "No, your Reverence, this will not do at all, it is not what we agreed—you must not sleep on this bare bench and give me the better bed. I am accustomed to sleeping on all sorts of beds, even in the open air under a tree; let me use this bench, and go yourself to the bed you were giving up for my sake!"

"No, my dear friend," he answered, "I have not given up any bed for your sake; normally no bed is ever made up in the place where yours is, and the place where I am lying now is where I sleep every night."

"You sleep every night on that hard wooden bench and with that book as a pillow?" I asked.

"Just as your profession has accustomed you to all kinds of beds, even to lying out in the open," he replied, "so I too have been accustomed by my profession to sleeping on this bench and to using this book as a pillow."

"Is that really possible?" I asked.

"Yes, it is so," he answered, "I am not telling you a lie. After all, I could have made up a bed for myself on this bench too, like the one I made on yours; but it is a very long time since I began sleeping in these clothes and here on this bench, just as you see me, and I am still doing it today." As I still hesitated skeptically, he said: "You can set your mind quite at ease, quite at ease."

There was nothing more I could say to this, especially in view of his quite convincing argument that he could after all have made up a bed for himself.

After a short time, during which I had gone on standing there, I said: "If this has long been your habit, reverend sir, then of course there is no more that I can say; but I think you will understand that I protested at first, because it is usual everywhere to sleep on a bed with bedclothes."

"Yes, it is usual," he said, "and we grow accustomed to it and think that that is how it must be. But it can also be otherwise. A man can get used to anything, and then the habit becomes very easy, very easy."

Thereupon, after wishing him a second good night, I left him and returned to my room and lay down again on my bed. And I did then remember that I had indeed never once seen a bed on any of my visits to the presbytery. I went on thinking about the matter for a long time, and could not help feeling soothed by the touch of the priest's exquisite linen sheet against my body. After a short while the priest did in fact give me proof that he was accustomed to his bed, for I heard by his gentle regular breathing that he was already fast asleep.

As I too was quiet now, and there was dead silence all through the house, and the wind had stopped, and the rain was now only just softly audible, and there was no more than an occasional faint last glimmer of lightning at the window, my eyes also grew drowsy, and after I had put out the candle I heard one or two more scattered drops falling on the windowpane, then they seemed to be followed by the gleam of a feeble flash, and then there was nothing more.

I slept very well, woke late, and it was already broad daylight when I opened my eyes. I had the impression that some slight sound had fully awakened me. When my eyes were wide open and I looked around, I saw the priest in the hall in his gray night attire, busy brushing the dust off my clothes. I quickly got up, went out, and interrupted him in his work, saying that he must not do it, that I could not accept such a service from him, it did not befit his position, the dust was of no consequence and if I wanted to be rid of it I could after all soon remove it with a brush myself.

"It does not befit my position as a priest, but it befits my position as your host," he said. "I have only one old servant who does not live in the house, she comes at certain times to give me the little help that I need, and today she is not here."

"No, no, that makes no difference," I answered. "I must remind you of your promise not to burden yourself in any way."

"It is no burden to me," he replied, "and it is already almost done."

So saying, he gave my coat a few more strokes with the brush, and then let me take both the brush and the clothes from him. He left the hall and went into another room which I had not yet seen. Meanwhile I got dressed. After a time he too came in fully dressed. He was wearing the old black clothes that he wore during the day and had worn on every previous day. We went to the window. The scene had changed completely. It was an absolutely beautiful morning, and the sun was rising radiantly through a measureless blue sky. How strange a thing such a storm is! So great an uproar is caused by the softest and most delicate elements in nature. The sky's subtle invisible vapors, harmlessly suspended in measureless space during the heat of the day or of many successive days, constantly accumulate until the air just above the earth has grown so hot and rarefied that the contents of its higher strata sink down through it; the vapors on a lower level are cooled in this way, or by some other breath of cold air, so that they at once condense into cloud masses, generating electricity, awakening the storm, bringing more cold and more cloud, until at last with the storm they rush across the earth and discharge their contents onto it in the form of ice drops or water drops. And when the discharge is complete and the air has been thoroughly mingled, it often reverts on the very next day to its former purity and clarity, and begins again to collect the vapors raised by the heat, so that gradually the whole process repeats itself and we have that alternation of rain and sunshine in which men and animals and plants thrive and rejoice.

The immense rainfall of the previous night had washed the limestone hills smooth, and they stood there white and gleaming under the blue of the sky and the rays of the sun. As they retreated one behind the other toward the horizon they displayed a delicate perspective of brilliant colors, a scale of broken grays and yellows and reds and rose tints, and between them lay the long shadows, blue as the sky and increasing in beauty as they stood farther away from us. The meadow in front of the presbytery was fresh and green, the linden tree had shed its older and weaker leaves in the gale and stood now as if newborn, and the other trees and bushes around the house lifted their wet gleaming branches and twigs toward the sun. Only near the footbridge had the storm left another and less pleasing spectacle. The Zirder had flooded, and part of the meadow, which as I have mentioned is scarcely higher than the riverbed, was lying under water. The end of the high arching bridge plunged straight down into this water. And yet this phenomenon too was beautiful, if one leaves out of account the damage that the flooding had probably caused by covering the meadow with sand. The wide watery surface glittered in the sunlight; to the green of the meadow and the gray of the rocks it added a third, harmonious, shimmering note, and the bridge rose up over the silver expanse like a dark fantastic line.

The priest pointed out to me several places a very long way away, which normally could not be seen but which today were distinctly visible, like clear pictures, in the purified air.

After we had spent a short time in contemplation of this morning view which had so compellingly attracted our gaze, the priest brought in some cold milk and black bread for our breakfast. We ate and drank it, and then I prepared to depart. I hung my case and my satchel with its leather strap over my shoulder, took my stick from the corner by the yellow cupboard, took the white hat which I wore on my expeditions, and thanked the priest heartily for giving me shelter during the heavy storm.

"I hope it was not too poor a lodging," he said.

"No, indeed, your Reverence," I replied, "you have been kindness itself, and I only regret having caused you trouble and inconvenience; in future I shall watch the weather and the sky very closely, and take care that I do not again let someone else be the sufferer by my foolhardiness."

I have given what I was able to give," he said.

"And I very much hope that I shall have an opportunity of doing you a service in return," I replied.

"Men live together, and there are many ways in which they can help each other," he said.

By this time we had reached the entrance hall.

"I must show you my third room too," he said; "I have one here in which I can get dressed and undressed without being seen, and where I keep various things."

So saying, he opened a door which I had not previously noticed, leading from the hall into a side room or rather a kind of vaulted recess. The furniture in here was again very meager. There was a large softwood wardrobe for storing clothes and other such things, including no doubt the woolen blankets that had been used for my bed; there were one or two chairs, and a tray with black bread and a jug of milk; those were the entire contents of the room. When we had left it he locked it up again, and we then took leave of each other, promising to meet again soon.

I walked out into the cool pure air and over the watersoaked meadow. I was, to be sure, still thinking how strange it was that while I had been in the presbytery we had never once gone upstairs, and that nevertheless, during the night and this morning, I had distinctly heard footsteps on the floor above us; but I put this thought from me and proceeded on my way.

I did not take my normal route, but walked in the direction of the Zirder. When one is surveying a country, when one has spent many years tracing the contours of different regions on paper, then one's interest in the characteristic features of a region is aroused and one becomes fond of it. I walked toward the Zirder because I wanted to see what the effects of its flooding had been and what changes it might have caused in the immediate neighborhood. As I was pausing by the water's edge and observing it, without being able to discern any effects other than its mere overflowing, I was suddenly confronted with a spectacle which I had not seen before, and found myself in company with which I had not yet been favored since my arrival in the Steinkar district. Apart from my workmen, whom I knew so well and who knew me so well that we were all as familiar to each other as instruments, I had met no one here except one or two residents at my inn, a number of people walking along the road, and the poor priest. It was now to be otherwise. As I watched, I saw a bright merry boy running over the bridge toward me from the opposite bank, which was on a higher level and had not been flooded. When he came to the end of the bridge which was immersed in the Zirder's floodwater, he stooped down and, so far as I could make out through my spyglass, untied his shoelaces and took off his shoes and stockings. But after removing them he did not step down into the water as I had supposed he would, but stayed where he was. He was followed at once by a second small boy who did the same. Then came one with bare feet who also stopped, then several others. Finally a whole swarm of children came running across the bridge; when they were just short of the end of it they crouched down, rather like a flock of birds swooping through the sky and all alighting together at the same point, and I could easily make out that they were all busy taking off their shoes and stockings.

When they had done this, one boy climbed carefully down off the bridge into the water. The others followed him. They made no attempt not to wet their breeches, but waded deep into the water with them on, and the little girls let their skirts float around their feet under water. To my astonishment I now also saw a taller, dark figure standing right out in the water: it was none other than my poor priest of the Kar. He was standing almost waist-deep. I had not seen him till now and had not noticed how he had got there, because I had been gazing beyond him toward the bridge all the time and did not turn my eyes to the foreground until now, as the children advanced in my direction. They all went up to the priest, and after pausing and talking to him for a little, they set out toward the bank where I was standing. They were not all equally careful in picking their way, and therefore strayed away from each other as they waded, approaching like black dots across the gleaming water, and reaching me one by one. As I saw that the floodwater was uniformly shallow and that there was no danger, I stayed where I was and let them come. The children arrived and stopped near me. They stared at me shyly and defiantly at first. But ever since I was a young man I have been fond of children, I have always dearly loved them as buds of the human flower, and my own marriage has been blessed with several; moreover, children are themselves the most sensitive of creatures when it comes to recognizing people who are well disposed toward them, and this quickly makes them confident and trusting. I was therefore soon surrounded by a circle of chattering, energetic children, eager to ask and answer questions. It could readily be guessed where they were going, as they all had their school satchels hanging over their shoulders by leather or linen straps. But since I too had my satchel and my case on a leather strap over my back, I daresay I must have been a comical sight, standing there rather like an overgrown schoolboy among the little ones. Some of them stooped down and set about putting their shoes and stockings on again, others went on holding them in their hands, looked up at me, and talked to me.

I asked them where they came from and was told that they were from the houses of the outlying Steinkar neighborhood, and were on their way to the Kar school.

When I asked them why they had all waited together on the bridge instead of just walking into the water one by one as they came, they said it was because their parents had told them that they must be very careful, and that if there was any water on the Zirder meadow beyond the bridge they were not to wade across it alone but to keep together.

"But supposing the water on the meadow were so deep that it would go over a grown-up person's head?"

"Then we would turn back," they answered.

"But supposing you had already crossed the bridge and were on the meadow, and then the water came with a rush, what would you do then?"

"We don't know."

I asked how long it took them to get here from the Steinkar houses, and was told that it took an hour. And the houses were indeed about that distance away. They were on the far side of the Zirder, built on a soil just as barren as that of the Kar, but the people living in them are actively engaged in business—in particular they burn lime from their rocks and export it over considerable distances.

I asked them whether their parents had also told them that they must keep their shoes and stockings dry; they said that they had, and I wondered at this inconsistency, standing there as they were with dry shoes and stockings in their hands and dreadfully wet trousers and skirts.

I asked them what they did in winter.

"We come over here then too," they said.

"But if there is snow water on the meadow?"

"Then we don't take our shoes off, but walk through it with them on."

"And if the bridge is icy?"

"Then we have to be careful."

"And if there is a very great deal of snow falling?"

"That doesn't matter."

"And if there's a tremendous lot of snow lying and no road through it?"

"Then we stay at home."

At this point the priest came up to me with the last of the children. It was high time too; for the children had already so lost all their shyness that a very tiny boy, who was carrying the basis and rudiment of all learning about with him on a little card, was about to recite his letters to me.

When the priest saw me surrounded by the children he greeted me very cordially and said it was very good of me to have come to the rescue as well.

I was startled by this suggestion, but at once said that I had in fact not come to the rescue, since I had not known that there would be children crossing the bridge, although of course if help had become needful I should certainly have offered it.

During this conversation, as I saw him standing there among the children, I noticed that he must have been much deeper in the water than they had; for he was wet to the waist, and with many of the children this would have been up to the neck. I was puzzled by the discrepancy and asked him about it. He said it could easily be explained. The farmer from the Wenn, who owned the flooded piece of meadow where he had just been standing in the water, had had some stones dug out of it and carted away the day before yesterday. The hole was still there. As he had seen today that the water was covering the meadow near the Zirder, it had occurred to him that the children's way probably passed quite close to this hole, and that one of them might accidentally fall into it. For this reason he had intended to stand beside the hole to prevent any such danger. But since the hole had steep sides, he had slipped into it himself, and once standing there in it he had just gone on doing so. One of the smaller children might even have got drowned in this hole, it had been dug so deep. He said that arrangements would have to be made for it to be filled up again; for the floodwater was muddy and it was impossible to judge the depth and unevenness of the ground under it.

The wet children crowded around the wet priest, they kissed his hand, they talked to him, he talked to them, or they just stood there gazing trustfully up at him.

But finally he said that they must now wring out their wet skirts, squeeze the water out of all their clothes or brush it off, and those who had shoes and stockings must put them on, and then they must start walking in order not to catch cold; they must keep in the sun to get dry all the sooner, and then they must go to school and be very good when they got there.

"Yes, we'll do that," they said.

And they followed his instructions immediately; they stooped or crouched down and wrung out their skirts or the bottoms of their trouser legs, or squeezed and brushed the water out of every fold and piece of cloth they were wearing, and I noticed that they did so with considerable skill. And the matter was, in fact, no very serious one; for their clothes were all made of a linen material, unbleached or with red or blue stripes, which would soon get dry and scarcely show that it had been wet; and as to the risk to their health, I thought, their vigorous young bodies would easily resist the damp. When they had finished squeezing out the water they proceeded to put on their shoes and stockings. And when they had finished this task too, the priest took his leave of me again, thanked me once more for coming here, and set out for the Kar with the children.

I called after the children, telling them to work hard at their lessons; they called back: "Yes, yes!" and off they went with the priest.

I watched the figure of the priest, surrounded by the children, walking across the wet meadow toward the Kar school; and then I too turned away and set out for my rocks. I decided that I would not return to the Highway Inn, but go straight to my place of work and look for my assistants, partly because I had no time to lose, and partly because in any case I still had with me the remains of my lunch of the previous day, which the priest has refused for supper. I also wanted to reassure my assistants, who would certainly have heard that I had not spent the night in the inn and might therefore be anxious on my account.

As I climbed up and up among the limestone hills, I thought of the children. How great a thing such inexperience and innocence is. On the authority of their parents they go to a place where they might meet their death; for the Zirder is extremely dangerous when it floods, and the children's ignorance can make the danger incalculable. But they do not know death. Their lips may speak its name, but they have no knowledge of its real nature, and their upsurging life cannot conceive of annihilation. Even if death were to come to them they would not know it, and they would be dead before they realized what was happening.

As I thus meditated, I heard the sound of the little bell from the steeple of the Kar church, drifting in among my rocky hills; it was just ringing for morning Mass, which the priest would be celebrating and which the children would be attending.

I went farther in among the rocks and found my assistants, who were glad to see me and who had brought food for me.

Owing to the length of my stay in the district, it was inevitable that I should hear a good deal about the priest from the people I met. I learned for example that it was really true (although in view of his own statement I in any case no longer doubted it) that for many years he had been sleeping in his entrance hall on the wooden bench, with the Bible under his head; that in summer he wore only his gray woolen clothes for this purpose, and used a blanket as well in winter. He had been wearing his clothes so long and preserving them so carefully that no one could remember when he had ever got himself new ones. He had let the upper floor of the presbytery to a lodger. A retired civil servant, they said, had come here to live on his pension in the district where he had been born. He had taken advantage of the fact that the priest was letting his rooms to settle here with his daughter and thus have the scenes of his childhood constantly before his eyes. This was yet another proof to me of how sweetly (as the poet remarks*) our native soil draws our affections and keeps itself in our remembrance: here was a man seeking out, for comfort and refreshment in his old age, a district from which anyone else would do his best to get away. I was also told that the priest ate nothing for breakfast and supper but a piece of black bread, and his lunch was provided for him by his servant Sabina, who cooked it at her house and brought it to the presbytery. It frequently consisted of hot milk or soup, or even of cold things in summer. When he was ill he did not send for any doctor or any medicine, but lay and refrained from eating until he got better. He used the money from the rent and from his stipend for charitable works, the recipients being persons whom he took pains to seek out. He had no relatives or friends. In all the years he had been here, no one had ever visited him. All his predecessors had only held the Kar parish for a short time and then gone elsewhere; but he had already been here for many years and it looked as if he would stay here for the rest of his life. He never paid visits in the neighborhood either, in fact he associated very little with his fellow men, and when he was not carrying out his duties or at the school, he would sit in his little room reading, or walk over the meadow to the Steinkar and wander around there in the sand or sit alone with his thoughts.

It had been rumored in the district that in view of his way of life he must have saved up money, and for this reason he had three times been robbed.

I was not in a position to distinguish true from false in these reports. Every time I met him, I saw his tranquil clear blue eyes, his simple ways, and his bitter, unfeigned poverty. As to what his past had been, I did not probe into this and had no wish to do so.

I had also heard a number of his sermons. They were simple and Christian, and although no doubt far from perfect in point of eloquence they were nevertheless clear and tranquil, and there was such goodness in them that they touched the heart.

My work in that district was taking longer and longer. The inhospitable territory with its clumps of rock was confronting us

---

*Stifter's reference is apparently to Ovid's lines *"Nescio qua natale solum dulcedine captos / ducit et immemores non sinit esse sui"* (Their native soil holds them captive by some sweet charm, and will not allow them to be forgetful of it) (translator's note).

with such obstacles that it was clearly going to take us twice the time we should have needed for an equal area in a region tamed and made fertile by man. In addition, the authorities now in effect set us a time limit by which we were to be finished, for they sent us instructions that on a certain date we were to be working in another part of the country. I was determined not to disgrace myself by being found behindhand. I therefore made a determined effort to hasten our progress. I left the Highway Inn, I had a wooden hut put up for me in the part of the Steinkar where we were working, I lived out in the hut, had my meals cooked there, and ate them sitting around the fire with my assistants. I got all my assistants to live on the site itself or nearby in temporary huts, and I also engaged a number of other men as casual laborers, so that we should now be able to press forward really fast and effectively.

And so we set to work hammering, measuring, driving in our stakes, stretching out our chains, setting up our plane tables, peering through our glasses, taking our bearings, measuring our angles, calculating, and so forth. We advanced across the rocky hills, and our marking-posts spread far and wide over the limestone landscape. As it was an honor to have this difficult terrain assigned to me for survey, I took pride in doing it really well and elaborately, and I often sat up in my hut working far into the night. I drew many sheets twice over, rejecting the less successful versions. The material was carefully arranged and filed.

As a result of all this work my association with the priest naturally fell rather into the background. But eventually, not having seen him in the Steinkar for some time, I became anxious. I was used to seeing his black figure among the rocks, visible from a long way off because he was the only dark point in the twilit gray of the limestone expanse, or in the pink tinge that it wore at sundown. I therefore inquired after him and was told that he was ill. I at once decided to visit him. I used my first free time for the purpose, or rather I made myself free on the first evening and went to his house.

I found him lying, not in his usual place in the hall, but on the wooden bench in the room where he had made a bed for me on the night of the storm. The woolen blankets I had had on that occasion had been laid under his body, and he had allowed this because he was ill. He had also been given a cover to spread over himself, and the pinewood table had been placed beside his bed so that he might put books and other things on it.

That was how I found him.

He was just lying there patiently, and no one had been able to persuade him, even now, to see a doctor or take any medicine, or even to accept the simplest of remedies which were brought into his room. He used the strange argument that it was tempting God to try to interfere, since it was God who sent the illness and God who would take it away again, or cause death to follow it if He had so ordained. And in any case he had no great faith in the efficacy of medicines or the skill of doctors.

When he saw me his face expressed great pleasure, and it was clear that he was glad that I had come. I said I hoped he would forgive me for not coming before, as I had not known that he was ill; I had had so much work to do that I had not been able to leave my hut in the Steinkar, but I had missed him, and had inquired after him, and now I was here.

"That is good of you, that is very good of you," he said.

I assured him that I would now visit him frequently.

When I had questioned him in greater detail about his condition, I realized that his illness was probably protracted rather than serious, and therefore left him with my anxiety somewhat allayed. Nevertheless, I ordered post horses some days later and drove into the town to consult a doctor whom I knew and to put before him all the symptoms which the priest had described to me in answer to my questions in the course of several visits. He was able to assure me that I had judged correctly, that the malady was not a dangerous one, that nature herself was in this case a better healer than man, and that although it would take some time there was no doubt that the priest would recover.

As I now came to see the priest quite often, I became so used to sitting for a little in the evening on the chair by his bed and chatting with him, that I gradually came to do so every evening. After my day's work I would walk from the Steinkar over the meadow to the presbytery, and would do my paperwork later by candlelight in my hut. This was made easier by the fact that I now lived quite close to the presbytery, which had by no means been the case when I had been staying at the inn. I was, however, not the only person to devote some care to the priest. Old Sabina, his servant, not only came across to his house oftener than her duty really demanded, but even spent most of the time she could spare from her own housekeeping, which was only for herself, in the presbytery doing the little services that the sick man needed. In addition to this old woman a young girl also came, the daughter of the lodger on the first floor of the presbytery. This girl, who was remarkably beautiful, would bring the priest some soup or something else, or ask how he was, or bring word from her father who sent to inquire whether he could be of assistance in any way. The priest would always lie quite motionless when the girl entered the room, he did not stir under his blanket and pulled it right up to his chin.

The schoolmaster called frequently too, and one or two of the priest's colleagues from nearby had also arrived to ask after his health.

Whether it was his illness that made him more amenable, or whether it was our daily association that brought us closer together, the priest and I got to know each other much better while he was ill. He talked more and was more communicative. I sat at the pinewood table by his bed, and arrived there punctually every day. As he could not go out and did not come to the Steinkar, I had to report to him the changes that were going on there. He asked me whether the blackberries on the Kulterloch were beginning to ripen already, whether the grass beside the upper Zirder, which always turned such a beautiful green in spring, was already yellowing and withering, whether the hips were ripening yet, how the weathering of the limestone was progressing, whether more pieces of it had crumbled off and fallen into the Zirder, whether the sand was accumulating, and so forth. I told him about these things and about others as well, I told him where we had been working, what progress we had made, and where we should be starting tomorrow. I took the opportunity of explaining a number of points about our work which were obscure to him. And I would sometimes read aloud to him, especially from newspapers, which a messenger brought to me in the Steinkar twice a week.

One day, when his illness had taken an agreeable turn for the better, he told me that he had a favor to ask of me.

When I answered that I should be only too happy to perform any service for him that lay at all in my power, that he had only to say what he wanted me to do and I would certainly do it, he replied: "Before I make my request there is something that I must first tell you. Please note that I am not telling you this because it is important, but because it will enable you to understand how things have come to be as they are, and will perhaps make you more inclined to grant my request. You have always been very kind to me, and I was told that you even drove to the town the other day to ask a doctor about my illness. That encourages me to approach you about this matter.

I am the son of a rich tanner in the capital of our country. My great-grandfather was a foundling from Swabia who emigrated to our city, arriving on foot with a stick in his hand. The generosity of kind friends enabled him to learn the tanner's trade; he then visited a number of workshops to practice it, and traveled to various countries to earn his living by his handiwork and also to learn how the trade is carried on in different places. Thus instructed, he returned to our city and took employment with a well-known leather merchant. Here he distinguished himself by his proficiency, and finally became foreman; his employer entrusted him with much of the business, and put him in charge of a number of experiments in new processing methods. My great-grandfather also tried his hand at small trading transactions, buying cheap raw materials and reselling them. In this way he acquired a modest fortune. As he was already advancing in years, he bought a large garden far out in the suburbs, bordering on some unused land. On this site he built a workshop and a small house; he married a poor girl and set up in business as his own master. His affairs prospered, and he died as an established merchant, respected by his associates. He had only one son, my grandfather.

My grandfather carried on his father's business and expanded it still further. He built a big house at the edge of the garden, positioned so that its windows overlooked the line of a future road where other houses would be. Behind it he built his workshops and warehouses. My grandfather was in general an enthusiastic builder. In addition to the house he built, around a large courtyard, some further workshops and other outhouses used for our business. He sold the unused pieces of land outside our garden, and as the city was being actively developed at that time, they fetched a very high price. Around the garden he put a wall which had openings at regular intervals, fitted with iron grilles. He raised the business to a high level of prosperity and built the great warehouses where we deposited our own products and those in which we traded. My grandfather too had only one son, who carried on the business and whose children were myself and my brother.

Our father's only additions to the buildings were the drying lofts above the workshops, a small wing which he added to the garden side of the house, and a conservatory. In his time our main windows already looked out over a new street which was lined with houses, paved with cobblestones, and filled with people walking and driving by. I still remember from my childhood how big and spacious our house was and how many courtyards and enclosures it had, which were needed for our work. My favorite memory is the beautiful garden full of trees and flowers and herbs and vegetables. Inside the buildings and outside in the yards the workmen in their linen clothes would be moving to and fro, with their hands and faces stained almost brown from their work; in the big storeroom on the ground floor and the two smaller ones adjoining it stood great bales of leather, hides hung from the bars in the drying loft, and were graded and arranged in the great sorting rooms. In the salesroom they lay neatly in their proper compartments. There were cows in the cattle shed and six horses in the stable and coaches and carriages in the coach house, and I even still remember Hassan, the big black dog by the gate of the main courtyard, who let everyone in through it but allowed no one out.

Father was a tall, strong man who walked around through the big rooms all over the house, inspecting everything and giving instructions about everything. He hardly ever left the house except on business or to go to church; and when he was at home and was not supervising the work he would sit at his desk and write. He was often seen in the garden too, walking along with his hands clasped behind him, or standing looking up at a tree, or gazing at the clouds. He had a passion for fruit growing, employed a gardener especially for this purpose, and had had grafts sent to him from all over Europe. He was very kind to his workmen, paid them adequately, and saw to it that each man got what was due to him but also that he did what was expected of him. When one of them was ill, he would go in person to his bedside, ask how he was, and often give him the medicine himself. He was known to everyone in the house simply as 'Father.' He disliked ostentation, to the point indeed of being too simple and modest in his appearance rather than too imposing; his living rooms were plainly furnished, and when he went out in a carriage he insisted on its looking like a perfectly ordinary vehicle.

My brother and I were twins, and our mother had died at our birth. Father had thought the world of her and therefore never married again, for he could not forget her. As there was too much noise on the street, we were put in the back wing which Father had built onto the garden side of the house. We lived in a big room with windows overlooking the garden; our room was separated from the rest of the house by a long corridor, and to avoid our having to pass through the front of the house every time we went out, Father had a stair built in the garden wing, which led straight down into the garden and thence into the open.

After our mother's death Father had entrusted the management of the household to a servant who had already been with our mother before her marriage and had indeed largely been responsible for her upbringing. Our mother had recommended her to our father on her deathbed. Her name was Luise. She managed and supervised everything connected with food and drink, linen, crockery and cutlery, the furniture, the cleaning of stairs and rooms, the heating and airing, in fact every aspect of the domestic work. The maids were all under her orders. And she looked after the needs of us two boys.

When we were older we were given a tutor, who lived with us in the house. Two fine rooms were furnished for him, they were next to ours and together with it they occupied the whole back part of the so-called garden wing. From him we learned what all children must first be taught: our letters, reading, writing, and arithmetic. My brother was much quicker at it than I was, he could memorize the letters and combine them into syllables, he could read long sentences clearly, his sums always came out right, his written letters were even and ran in a straight line. In my case it was different. I could not keep the names of the letters in my mind, and then I could not say the syllable they represented, and I found the long words very difficult to read and suffered agonies when there was a long passage without a comma. In arithmetic I followed the rules, but the figures I brought out at the end were usually quite different from what they should have been. When I wrote I held my pen with great care, looked hard at the line, made even movements upwards and downwards, and nevertheless the letters did not stand evenly, they dipped below the line and pointed in different directions, and I could not get the pen to draw the thin strokes. Our tutor was very persevering, and my brother also showed me how to do a great many things, until I could manage them myself. Our room contained a large oak table at which we did our lessons. Each of its two longer sides was fitted with several drawers, my brother used one row of these to put his school things in and I used the other. In each of the far corners of the room was a bed with a bed table beside it. At night the door stood open between our room and our tutor's bedroom.

We frequently went out into the garden and employed ourselves there. We often drove with our pair of grays through the city, or out into the country or on some other expedition, and our tutor always sat with us in the carriage. We also went out walking with him, we would take a walk along the top of the city wall or down an avenue, and if something took place in town that was particularly well worth seeing, and our father gave permission, we would go with our tutor to see it.

When we had been well grounded in our primary school subjects we went on to those that were taught in the grammar school, and our tutor told us that we should have to be examined in these subjects by the headmaster and the other teachers. We studied Latin and Greek, we studied natural history and geography, mathematics, essay writing, and other things. The worthy chaplain of our parish church came to our house to give us religious instruction, and in matters of religion and morals we had our father's good example before us. But as it had been in our earlier studies, so it was again now. My brother learned everything easily, he did his exercises well, he could say the Latin and Greek sentences in German, he could do algebra, and his letters and essays might have been written by a grown man. I could do none of this. I of course worked very hard too, and at the initial stage of every subject I did not do too badly, I could understand it and say and do what was expected; but when we advanced further I would become confused, everything got mixed up, I did not know where I was, and could not see the solution. In my translations from German I followed all the rules very carefully, but there was always a word to which several contradictory rules applied, and when my work was finished it was full of mistakes. The same thing happened with my translations into German. In the

Latin or Greek text there were always such strange intractable words, which I could not find in the dictionary when I looked them up, and the Greek and Latin books did not obey the rules of grammar that we had learned. I managed a little better in two subsidiary subjects which our father had ordered that we should learn because they might be useful to us later, namely French and Italian, which we studied with a teacher who came to the house twice a week. My brother and our tutor took a great deal of trouble with me and tried to help me. But when the examinations came I did not pass them, and my reports were not good.

Thus several years went by. When the period which our father had allotted for these studies came to an end, he told us that we must now learn our family business, which he would hand over to us at his death and which he expected the two of us to carry on in the same honorable and imposing fashion as our forefathers and his had done. He said that we must receive the same training as they had had, in order to be able to act just as they had acted. We must acquaint ourselves thoroughly with all the techniques and facts of our trade, we must first qualify ourselves to work at it as well as any good workman in our employ, indeed as well as the best of them, in order to be able to judge a workman and his work, to know how the workmen should be treated and to earn their respect. Not until we had done this were we to proceed to the further studies necessary for the conducting of the business.

Father also wanted us to live just as our workmen did, so that we should understand their situation and not be strangers to them. It was therefore his wish that we should eat with them, lodge with them, and sleep with them. The tutor hitherto in charge of us left, giving each of us a book as a farewell present; we moved out of our schoolroom and over into the workmen's quarters.

Father had selected the best man in our employ, who was also foreman, to be our instructor and generally look after us. We were each assigned a place in his workshop, provided with a set of tools, and made to begin at the beginning like any apprentice. For our meals we sat at the same table as all our workmen, but were given seats right at the foot of it where the apprentices were. We also shared the apprentices' bedroom; next door to it was the foreman's, and he was the only person who had a room of his own. This meant that he had to be not only a highly skilled workman, but also distinguished for his integrity, respectability, and good character. We never gave his job to anyone who was not. He was specially appointed to look after the apprentices, since they were still in need of training. We were given beds like the rest of them, and clothes such as all our workmen wore.

That was how it began. But here too things were again exactly as they had been in all our previous activities. My brother worked fast and produced good results. I followed our instructor's directions exactly, but my pieces of work did not turn out as they should have done and were not as good as my brother's. And yet I worked extraordinarily hard. In the evening we would often sit in the big parlor with the other workmen and listen to their talk. Occasionally some of them were a bad example to us, but this did not lead us astray, on the contrary it served to make us more steadfast and fill us with abhorrence. Father would say that in order to live one must know life, the good and the evil of it, but be strengthened and not tainted by the latter. On such evenings the workmen used to send me to fetch them wine and cheese and other things; I would gladly do so, and this greatly endeared me to them.

When we had finished our training in one workshop and could do what we had been taught there, we were moved to another, until in the end we were discharged from these tasks and entered the trade as apprentices. When we had passed through this stage too, we were put in the office to learn the clerical work involved in our business.

When at last after a number of years our period of apprenticeship was over, we took up residence as sons of the house and were given the same kind of simple clothes as it was our father's custom to wear.

Not long after we had ceased to be apprentices, and when my brother was already playing an active part in all branches of the business, our father fell ill. His illness was not so serious as to make us fear that he was in danger, nor did he have to keep to his bed, but his powerful figure became less powerful, he looked frailer, he walked about a great deal in the house and in the garden, and no longer concerned himself so actively with the business as it had hitherto been his habit and his pleasure to do.

My brother took over the leadership of the firm, there was no need for me to be involved, and in the end Father, when he was not in the garden, spent most of the day in his room.

At about that time I requested to be allowed to move back into our old schoolroom and live there. Permission was given, and I carried my belongings across to the room at the end of the long corridor. Father now no longer gave any orders or instructions in the firm, and my brother gave me no work to do, and so I was able to pass my time as I pleased. I remembered that I had never been reproached for my unsatisfactory reports in the subjects we had studied, and I decided that I would now make up for all I had left undone, and learn everything properly. I took a book out of the drawer, sat down in front of it, and read the beginning. I understood it all and learned it and took note of it. On the following day I repeated what I had learned the day before, tested myself to see whether I still knew it, and learned a new portion. I set myself only short tests, but tried to understand the material and to impress it thoroughly on my memory. I set myself exercises to compose, and they turned out successfully. I looked up the exercises our tutor had once given us and did them again, and this time I made no mistakes. I did the same with the other books as I had done with the first. I studied very diligently, and gradually I found myself spending the whole day working in the schoolroom. When I had some time to spare, I liked to sit down and read the book my tutor had given me to remember him by, and I would think of this man who had once lived with us.

In the schoolroom everything was still just as it had been. The big oak table still stood in the middle of the room, it still bore the marks we had made in its wooden surface either on purpose with our penknives or accidentally with other instruments, it still showed the dried meandering inkstains which had formed when one of us had upset the inkwell and all washing and scrubbing had been in vain. I opened the drawers. There, in those that had been mine, my schoolbooks still lay, with the red or black pencil marks on their pages indicating how far we had had to learn; the exercise books in which we had written our essays were still there, prominently scored with red ink where our tutor had marked our mistakes; and the drawers still contained our old dusty pens and pencils. The same was true of those on my brother's side of the table. Here too were his old reading and writing materials, all neatly arranged. I sat now studying my lessons at this same table where I had sat over them so many years ago. I slept in the same bed, and the bedside table with the candle stood by it. But my brother's bed remained empty and its coverlet was never removed. In the two rooms in which our former tutor had lived I had a few cupboards containing clothes and other things, but apart from this they were unused and their old furniture was still there. So I was the sole inhabitant of the garden wing at the back of the house, and thus things continued for several years.

Suddenly our father died. It was a terrible shock to me. It had occurred to no one that his death was so imminent, or indeed that his life could be in danger at all. To be sure, he had recently become more and more withdrawn and rather frailer-looking, and he often spent several days in bed; but we had grown so used to this state of affairs that in the end we had come to regard it as normal; everyone who lived in the house looked on him as a father, and our father was so necessary a member of the household that his departure was unimaginable, indeed it really never entered my mind that he might die and that he was so ill. At first all was confusion, but then the funeral preparations were made. All the poor people of the district joined in the procession, his coffin was followed by his office employees, by his friends, by many strangers, his workmen, and his two sons. Many tears were shed, he was mourned like few of his fellow countrymen, and those present declared that one of the finest of men, a noble citizen and an honorable man of business, had been laid to his rest. A few days later the will was opened, and by its dispositions my brother and I found ourselves appointed as heirs and joint proprietors of the firm.

After a time my brother said to me that the whole responsibility for the business now rested on our shoulders, whereupon I informed him that I had revised all the studies in which I had made so little progress when we were pupils together, Latin and Greek and natural history and geography and arithmetic, and that I had now almost perfectly mastered these subjects. But he answered that Latin, Greek, and all the rest were not exactly necessary qualifications in our walk of life, and that my efforts in acquiring them had been too late. I replied that just as I had done these studies over again, so too I should gradually be able to revise all the technical training that was directly required for our business. To this he answered that if the firm had to wait for me, it would have gone to ruin by the time I was ready. He declared, however, that he would manage it himself to the best of his ability, and that he would leave me free to do as I pleased, that I could watch how he was getting on, help him in this and that, learn a few more things, but that in any case I should be guaranteed my full share of the inheritance.

I returned to my schoolroom, making no attempt to intervene in the firm's affairs, which I was probably incompetent to do, and my brother let me stay there. Indeed, he even sent me some better furniture and supplied me with various comforts to make the study agreeable for me to live in. When some time had elapsed he appeared with our family lawyer, some officers of the court, and some witnesses who had been friends of our father's and presented me with a legal document which set out my claims to the inheritance, defined my share, and stated what sums were due to me in the future. My brother, the witnesses, and I put our signatures to the paper.

I now continued with my studies, and my brother took complete charge of the firm's affairs. Three months later he brought me a sum of money and told me that this was the interest due to me on my share of the inheritance, which was invested in the business. He said that he would hand over this sum to me every quarter. He asked if I was satisfied with this arrangement and I answered that I was entirely satisfied.

After some time had passed he remarked to me one day that my studies really ought to be serving some purpose, and asked me whether I did not feel inclined to work my way into one of the learned professions for which my present occupations could prepare me. When I replied that I had never considered this and had no idea which profession might suit me, he said that that did not matter for the time being; what I should do was merely in due course to take examinations in the subjects I had now taught myself, and thus acquire written certificates of my qualifications. I ought also to try to master the subjects I had not yet studied and take examinations in them as well, so that when the time came for me to choose a particular profession I should then have still further increased my experience and should find it easier to decide in what direction to turn.

I found this proposition very acceptable, and consented. After a while I entered for the first examinations in the preliminary subjects, and my results were extraordinarily good. This encouraged me, and I eagerly set to work on the other disciplines. My heart trembled with joy at the thought that I should one day belong to one of those professions which serve the world with their knowledge and skill and which I had always so revered. I worked very hard, I husbanded my time, I hardly ever set foot in the rest of the house, and after a few more months I was again able to pass an examination successfully.

I had thus become a full-time occupant of our rear wing overlooking the garden, and here I was permitted to remain and could devote myself with a good conscience to my studious pursuits.

Down beyond the end of our garden lay another, which however was not really so much a garden as a meadow with nothing on it but an occasional untended tree. The path through this neighboring garden passed close to the wrought-iron gate at the foot of our own. In that garden I always saw beautiful white linen sheets and other laundry hanging up to dry on long clotheslines. I would often look at it, either from my window or through the gate if I happened to be in the garden. When the linen was dry it was collected in a basket, under the supervision of a woman who stood by. Other wet linen was then hung up, after the woman had taken a cloth and wiped the rope between the poles. This woman was a widow. Her husband had been in an employment which adequately provided for his needs. Shortly after his death his kindly old master had also died, and this man's son was so hard-hearted that he gave the widow only just enough to keep her from starving. She therefore rented this small piece of land next to our garden, and rented the little house that stood on it. With the money that her husband had left her she then set up the house and garden as a laundry for clients who would entrust their fine linen or any other washing to her. In the house she installed the vats and other equipment needed for boiling and chemical soaking. She set up washrooms, and places for ironing and folding the linen, and a drying room for use during bad weather and in winter. In the garden she had poles inserted at equal distances, rings fitted to the poles, and ropes drawn through the rings, ropes which were often changed. Close behind the house ran a stream, which was what had led the widow to select this spot for her laundry. Water from the stream was pumped along conduits into the vats, and a small washhouse had been built directly over it. The woman employed many maids to carry out the work and make the necessary preparations, she stood by and supervised them, showed them the right way to do everything, and as she never let the linen be scrubbed or treated roughly, insisted on a beautifully white finish and on any repairs that might be needed, her clients were very numerous. She had to enlarge her establishment and take on more assistants, and quite often some lady of high society would come and sit with her under the big pear tree in the garden.

This woman also had a young daughter, a child—no, she was no longer a child—at the time I really did not know whether she was a child or not. This girl had very delicate rosy cheeks and delicate red lips and she gazed about her with innocent brown kindly eyes. Her eyelids were big and gentle and had long lashes that looked delicate and modest. Her dark hair had been neatly parted and combed by her mother and lay smoothly and beautifully over her head. Often she would be carrying a little basket, long in shape and finely wrought; over it was fastened a coverlet of very fine white material, and this basket no doubt contained linen of quite exceptional quality which the girl had been sent to deliver to some lady.

I loved to watch her. Often I would stand at my window and look over into her garden, where always, with never a break, except at night or in bad weather, linen hung from the lines, the white linen of which I was so fond. Then sometimes the girl would come out and walk to and fro over the grass, busy with this and that; or I would see her, although her house was very much hidden among branches, standing at her window reading her lessons. And soon I got to know the time at which she went out to deliver laundry, and then I would often go down into the garden and stand by the wrought-iron gate. As the path came close to our gate, the girl would have to walk right past me. She knew quite well that I was standing there; for she always cast her eyes down and walked quickly and modestly by.

One day, when I saw her approaching from some way off with her laundry basket, I took a beautiful big peach which I had already picked for this purpose, and quickly put it out between the bars of the gate onto her path, then retreated into the bushes. I hid myself so deeply among them that I could not see her. When I had waited long enough to be sure that she had gone by, I came out again; but the peach was still lying on the path. I then waited until the time of her return. But when she had already come by again, and I looked out through the gate, the peach was still there on the path. I took it back again. On the third occasion I stood waiting as the peach with its soft pink skin lay there on the sand, and when she approached I said: 'Take it.' She looked at me, hesitated for a moment, then stooped and picked up the fruit. I no longer remember where she put it, but I know for sure that she took it. After some time I again did the same thing, and she again took the fruit. This happened on several occasions, and finally I gave her the peach with my hand through the gate.

In the end we even began speaking to each other. I no longer remember what we said. We must have talked of commonplace things. We would take each other by the hand as well.

As time went on I could no longer wait until she came with her basket. I stood continually at the gate. She stopped when she came up to me and we talked. Once I asked her to show me the things in her basket. She undid the linen cover with its little tapes and showed me the contents. I saw fine sleeves and ruffs and other articles, all smoothed and ironed. She told me what each of them was, and when I remarked on their beauty she replied: 'This laundry belongs to an old countess, a lady of rank, and I always have to deliver it to her myself so that no harm shall come to it, because it is so fine.' When I said again: 'Yes, it is beautiful, it is really beautiful,' she answered: 'Indeed it is beautiful; my mother says that a household's linen is its most precious possession after the silver, and that linen itself is fine white silver which can always be cleaned when it is dirty and turned into fine white silver again. Our best and innermost garments are made of it. That is why Mother stored up so much linen that we had enough after Father's death, and that is why she has undertaken to wash other people's linen for them and never lets it be handled roughly or wrongly treated. Gold is precious too of course, but gold is not a household article, only an ornament.' And as she spoke I indeed remembered that I had never seen this girl wear, around her neck or wrists, anything but the finest white linen, and that her mother's face was always surrounded by a snow-white bonnet with a fine ruff.

From that moment on, with the money my brother paid over to me every quarter, I began to collect exquisite pieces of linen like those of the old Countess, and to buy all kinds of household silver.

One day, when we were standing together as usual, her mother passed quite close to us and called out: 'Johanna, you should be ashamed of yourself.' We were indeed ashamed and parted company at once. My face was blushing scarlet and I should have started with fright if anyone had met me in the garden.

After that we no longer met at the gate. I always went into the garden when she came past, but I stayed hidden in the bushes where she could not see me. She would walk past blushing and with downcast eyes.

In the two rooms next to my living room I now had chests of drawers installed, made according to my directions with narrow drawers at the top, where I put the silver, and wide ones lower down in which I stored the linen. I laid everything in its proper place, with red silk ribbons tied around the pieces that belonged together.

Some months later I noticed for a long time that the girl no longer walked past the iron gate. I did not dare inquire, and when finally I did, I was told that she had been sent to another town and was to be married to a distant relative.

I thought at the time that I would weep the very soul out of my body.

But after a while a terrible thing happened. My brother was the client of an eminent banker, who would always give him credit to finance his current expenditure up to a certain agreed sum, recalling these loans from time to time as circumstances permitted. I do not know whether my brother's credit had been undermined by other people's reports, or whether the banker himself had become suspicious because two firms heavily in our debt had gone bankrupt and deprived us of our prosperity: at all events he refused to honor our bills of exchange any longer, and insisted that my brother should back several of them with cash. My brother did not have enough ready money to do so, the friends whose assistance he sought became suspicious too, and thus it came about that the holders of our bills went to law, our house and our other property and our merchandise were submitted to assessment, to find out whether their value would suffice without recourse to our understanding claims. But when this became known, everyone to whom we owed anything came forward and demanded payment, whereas no one who owed money to us showed his face. My brother wanted to keep me in ignorance of all this in order to spare my feelings, and he still had hopes of surmounting the crisis. But when the court decreed the immediate sale of our house to cover our bills of exchange, it was impossible for him to conceal it from me any longer. He came to my room and told me everything. I gave him the money I had; for my needs had been very modest and I had been able to save a large part of my income. I opened the narrow upper drawers of my storage chests and laid out all my silver on our old schoolroom table, and offered it to him. He said that this was not enough to save the house and the business, and he refused to accept it. Nor did the court direct me to contribute anything; but I could not bear that my brother should burden his conscience with any unpaid debt, and so I added everything I had to the other assets. The total enabled us to meet the demands of all our creditors and satisfy them to the last penny. But our beautiful house with its back wing, and our beautiful garden, were lost.

I do not remember what further blows struck us; but even the hope of starting another small business with such money as was left, and gradually re-establishing ourselves, very soon proved vain.

My brother, who was unmarried, took it all so much to heart that he fell into a fever and died. His funeral was attended only by myself and a few other people to whom he had shown kindness. Since our great-grandfather's time there had always been only one son and heir and no other children until my brother and I were born; our old housekeeper Luise had also died some time ago, and I therefore had no remaining relatives or friends.

I had conceived the idea of becoming a preacher of the Lord's word, of entering the priesthood. I hoped that, unworthy as I was, God might nevertheless give me grace and strength enough to become a not wholly discreditable servant and representative of His gospel and His works.

I collected my examination certificates and other papers, went to the theological seminary, and anxiously applied for admission. I was accepted. On the appointed date I took up residence and began my training. I completed it successfully and was in due course ordained as a servant of God. At first I served under older priests, assisting them in the care of the souls committed to their charge. This involved me in a variety of experiences and taught me to know my fellow men. From the priests I learned many things, both spiritual and secular. When enough years had passed to enable me to apply for a parish without seeming too presumptuous, I asked for my present parish and it was allotted to me. I have been here now for more than twenty-seven years and I shall never leave. People say it is a poor parish, but it yields enough for a minister of the gospel to live on. They call it an ugly district, but that is not true either, one must merely look at it with the right eyes. My predecessors here were transferred to other parishes. But since those of my colleagues now living who are my age or younger attained considerable distinction during their training, and are in all respect my superiors, I shall never ask to be promoted from here to another charge. My parishioners are good people, they have had ears to hear many of my words of instruction, and they will go on listening to me now.

In addition I have another more worldly and more particular reason for staying in this place. You will learn it in due course, that is, if you consent to perform the service that I want to ask of you. I am coming to this request now, but there is still something else I must tell you before I make it. In this house I began saving up money for a purpose. It is not an unworthy purpose, it involves not only a temporal good but a good of another kind also. I will not tell you now what it is, it will be made known at a later time; but it is because of this purpose that I began to save. I was not able to bring any money with me from home; the little that I recovered was spent on various things, and the income ceased altogether years ago. All I have left of my inheritance is that one crucifix which you see hanging by my door over the stoup; my grandfather once bought it in Nuremberg, and my father gave it to me because I always liked it. So I began to save out of my parish stipend. I put on simple clothes and tried to make them last a long time, I got rid of my bed and lay on the bench in the hall and put the Bible under my head to bear witness and to help me. I no longer kept a servant but paid old Sabina for a few domestic tasks which are all that I need. I eat what is good and wholesome for the human body. I have let the upper floor of the presbytery. This has already twice earned me a reprimand from the Bishop's consistory, but now they tolerate it. People suspected that I had cash in the house, as indeed I had, and as result it has been stolen from me three times, but each time I began again. The thieves had only taken the money, so I tried to put it out of their reach. I invested it in absolutely safe securities, and when a little interest accumulates I always add it to the capital. So no one has interfered with me now for many years. In the long course of time my way of living has become a habit and I have grown attached to it. But one sin against these economies lies on my conscience: for I still have the beautiful linen which I bought when I lived in our schoolroom overlooking the garden. This is a grievous fault, but I have tried to make amends for it by being still more frugal in bodily and other matters. I am too weak to refrain from this one indulgence. It would be too heartbreaking to have to give that linen away. After all, it will also bring in some money after my death, and the greater part of it I never use anyway."

I now understand why he felt ashamed of his splendid linen.

"I regret," he continued, "my inability to help the people here as much as I should like to; but I must use all the money for my main purpose, and after all no one can be a benefactor on as large a scale as he would wish, that is something for which even the greatest wealth would not suffice.

Well, now I have told you all about my past and present situation. Now comes my request. It may be that when you reflect on my whole story you will be willing to grant it. But to do so involves some trouble, and only your kindheartedness and good will make it possible for me to ask this of you. I have deposited my will with the court at Schloss Karsberg. I presume it is safe there, and I have their receipt for it here in the house. But human life is beset by uncertainties, there might be a fire, devastation, enemy invasion, or some other misfortune which would endanger the will. I have therefore made two further identical copies which I want to have deposited as securely as possible, so that they may come to light after my death and their purpose be fulfilled. My request to you therefore is to let me hand over one of these copies to you for safekeeping. The other I shall either keep here, or give it to someone else so that he too may keep it safe to serve its purpose. Of course I should also have to ask you to allow me, when you leave this district, to write a few lines to you from time to time to let you know that I am still alive. When my letters cease you will know that I have died. Then you would have to have the will conveyed by someone absolutely reliable, and against a written receipt, to Karsberg or to wherever else its execution can be officially put in hand. All this is merely a precaution in case the one already in legal safe custody there should be lost. The will is sealed, and you will learn its contents after my death, that is to say if you are willing to consent to my request."

I told the priest that I should be delighted to do as he asked, that I would preserve the document as carefully as I did my own most prized possessions which would be irreplaceable if destroyed, and that I should be only too glad to follow all his instructions. I added, however, that I hoped the occasion for the unsealing of the will and its twin companions would not arise for many a long year yet.

"We are all in God's hands," he said. "It may be today, it may be tomorrow, it may not be for many years. For the sake of the purpose which in addition to my parish duties I am pursuing, I in fact hope that it will not be soon; but God knows what is best, and in any case He can finish this work without my help."

"But since I might also die before you do," I replied, "I shall as a precaution put written instructions beside your will, by which in that event my responsibility will be transferred to other hands."

"You are very kind," he answered. "I knew I could rely on your friendship, I was sure I could. Here is the paper."

So saying, he drew out a document from under the pillow. It was folded and sealed with three seals. He handed it to me. I looked at the seals; they were perfect and unbroken and marked with a single cross. On the front of the document were the words: "Last will and testament of the priest of the parish of Kar." I went to the table, took a piece of paper from my pocketbook, and wrote on it that on the date stated I had received from the priest of the parish of Kar a document sealed with three seals each bearing a cross, and on which was written: "Last will and testament of the priest of the parish of Kar." I handed him this receipt and he placed it under his pillow where the will had been. The latter I put for the time being in the case in which I kept my drawings and other work.

After the conversation I stayed on with the priest for some time and we talked of other less important matters. Sabina came in bringing him food, the girl from the floor above came down to ask how he was. Under a sky full of stars I walked back to my hut through the pale rocks and the soft sand, thinking of the priest. The will I put for the time being in the trunk in which I kept my best things, intending later to put it in a safe place in my house.

My time, after that evening on which the priest told me his story, was spent in my rocky wilderness as busily as before. We measured and worked and prepared drawings; during the day I would collect material, visit the priest toward sundown, and sit an hour or two by his bedside, and then work at night in my hut, where one of my assistants would manage to get a fire going and roast me a little meat.

Gradually the priest's health improved, in the end he was able to get up, as the doctor in the town had predicted, then he could sit in front of his house, and go to church again, and finally he came out again into the Steinkar too, and walked about among the hills or stood beside us watching our work.

But all things come at last to an end, and so too did our long stay in the Steinkar. We had advanced farther and farther, getting nearer and nearer to the boundary line of the area assigned to us, and finally our marking-posts stood along this line: our measurements up to that point were finished, and after a little more pen-work we had the entire Steinkar in our portfolio, fully surveyed in a complete set of sheets. Our various poles and posts and other working materials were immediately removed, our huts were demolished, my assistants dispersed and went about their own business, and the Steinkar, liberated from these invaders, stood empty once more.

I packed my trunk, said good-bye to the priest, the schoolmaster, Sabina, the lodger and his daughter, and to others; I had the trunk taken to the Highway Inn, went there myself on foot, ordered post horses, and when they arrived I left this place which had been the scene of my activities for so long.

I must mention that it was with the strangest of feelings that I did so. I was in fact almost overcome by a deep sadness as I took leave of this district which on my first arrival in it had seemed so hideous. As my journey took me farther and farther away into more populous country, I felt impelled to turn around in my carriage and gaze back at those rocks, at their lighted surfaces gleaming so softly and wanly, their clefts full of sweet blue shadow in which I had so often sat, whereas now I was driving out into a land of green meadows, checkered fields, and soaring trees.

Five years later a journey brought me not far from the Steinkar, and I took the opportunity of revisiting it. I found the priest still sometimes walking about in it as he had formerly done, or occasionally sitting on a rock and looking around. His clear blue eyes were quite unchanged.

I showed him the letters he had sent me, and which I had kept. He thanked me warmly for having answered all of them, saying that he enjoyed my letters and often reread them. He showed them to me as we sat together again at the pinewood table in his room.

The Zirder, like a pale blue ribbon, still wound its way between the rocks, the latter were still gray and ringed with sand at the foot.

The strips of green and the scanty shrubs were all as I had remembered them. At the Highway Inn the landlord and his wife and even their children looked almost exactly as before, indeed the same guests seemed to be sitting at the tables; so unchanging are the people in those parts who travel about their business over the hills.

After that visit to the Kar district I no longer had occasion to go there professionally and no time to visit it on my own account. Many years passed, and the priest's hope that God would grant him a long life for the achievement of his purpose seemed likely to be fulfilled. Every year I got several letters from him, which I regularly answered, and regularly they came again in the following year. Only one thing I noticed, that his writing perhaps showed signs of a tremulous hand.

One day, years and years later, I got a letter from the schoolmaster. He wrote that the priest had fallen ill, that he was talking of me, and that he had said: "If only he knew that I am ill." He was therefore taking the liberty of informing me of this, begging my pardon for such presumption, since for all he knew it might serve some good purpose.

I replied that so far from being presumptuous he had done me a service in writing to me, since I felt a sincere affection for the priest. I asked him to send me frequent reports of the latter's health, and if he got worse to let me know at once. And I added that if against expectation God should suddenly call him away, I should also like to be notified of this instantly.

To set the priest's mind at ease I wrote to him too, saying that I had heard of his illness, and that I had asked the schoolmaster to send me frequent reports of how he was; I begged him to spare himself the effort of writing to me, and to have a bed made up for him in the little room. I pointed out that he might well recover from his indisposition before long, as he had done in previous years. I said that for the moment I was prevented by my professional duties from visiting him.

He nevertheless sent a few lines in reply, saying that he was very, very old, that he was waiting in patience and was not afraid.

The schoolmaster wrote me two letters saying that the priest's condition was unchanged, then came a third which informed me that he had passed away after receiving the last sacraments.

At this I reproached myself, set everything else aside, and packed for the journey. I took the sealed document from my cupboard, took the priest's letters with me as well in case they should be needed to prove his handwriting, and set out for Karsberg.

On my arrival there I was informed that a will executed by the priest had been deposited with the court, that a second such will had been found among his effects, and that I should present my copy at the castle in two days' time, whereupon the opening and proving of the wills would take place.

During these two days I went to the Kar. The schoolmaster told me about the last days of the priest's life. He had lain quietly suffering his illness, just as he had suffered the previous one during which I had so often visited him. He had again refused to take any medicines, until the priest from the neighboring parish of Wenn, who had administered the last sacraments to him, had pointed out to him that he must use earthly remedies as well and leave their effectiveness or otherwise in the hands of God. From that time on he took everything he was given and let them do with him as they pleased. He again lay in his room, where they had made a bed for him again with the blankets. Sabina stayed by him constantly. When his death approached he made no special preparation but lay there just as he always did. It was impossible to tell whether or not he knew that he was now dying. He behaved as usual and spoke of everyday things. Finally he fell peacefully asleep, and it was over.

They changed his clothes for laying him out. They dressed him in his finest linen, then they put on his threadbare suit and his priest's habit over it. It was thus that he lay on his bier. A great many people came to look at him; they had never before seen such a thing, as he was the first priest to have died in the Kar. There he lay with his white hair, his face looked peaceful but much paler than usual, and the lids were closed over his blue eyes. Many of his colleagues came to his funeral. As he was laid in the earth many bystanders wept.

I now also asked after the lodger on the first floor of the presbytery. He himself came down into the front hall where I was, and spoke to me. He was now almost completely bald and therefore wore a black skullcap. I asked after his beautiful daughter, who at the time of her visits to the priest's sickroom in my presence had been a young and lively girl. She had moved to the capital to be married and was the mother of children who were now almost grown-up. She too had not been with the priest during his last days.

Her father told me that he would probably have to move to his daughter's house now, as when the priest's successor took up residence in the presbytery he would certainly lose his lodging and would not be able to find another in the Kar.

Old Sabina was the only person who had not changed. She looked exactly the same as when she had first tended the priest in his illness during my first stay in the district. No one knew how old she was, even she herself had no idea.

I could get no farther than the hall of the presbytery, as the little sitting room and the vaulted room near the entrance had been put under seal. Only the wooden bench on which the priest had slept was still in its place, and it had occurred to no one to move it. The Bible, however, was no longer there, I was told it had been taken into the bedroom.

When the two days had passed and the time came for the opening of the will, I proceeded to Schloss Karsberg and presented myself in the courtroom at the appointed hour. There was quite a small gathering there; the local parish authorities from the Kar, and the witnesses, had also been asked to attend. On the table lay the two wills and the inventory of the priest's effects. Among them had been found my receipt for a copy of his will, and I was now shown this receipt and asked to produce the document. I handed it over. The writing and seals were examined and the will found to be genuine.

In accordance with traditional practice, the will deposited with the court was now the first to be opened and read. Then followed the one which I had delivered. The text was word for word the same as that of the first. Finally the will which had been found in the priest's house was opened, and it too was identical in every word with the first two. The date and signature were the same in all three documents. All three wills were at once declared to be one and the same will existing in three copies.

But the contents of the will were a surprise to everyone.

The priest, after a preamble invoking God's help, placing his dispositions under His protection, and declaring himself to be of sound mind and in full use of his faculties, had written as follows: "Whereas every man finds, in addition to his livelihood or calling, some further task to perform, or should strive to find one, in order that he may in his lifetime do all that he is called upon to do: so I too have found, in addition to my pastoral work, a task which I must perform. The children from the outlying houses of the Steinkar neighborhood are in danger, and I must put an end to that danger. The Zirder often rises and can at such times become a rapid, rushing torrent; this happened twice during my first years in the parish, when it was in spate after cloudbursts and swept away all the bridges and footbridges. Its banks are low, and that on the Kar village side is even lower than that on the outlying side. There are three possibilities: either the Kar side is flooded, or the farther side is flooded as well, or the water even carries away the footbridge. But the children from the outlying houses have to cross this footbridge to get to the Kar school. So when the Kar side is flooded and they step from the bridge into the water, a number of them may come to grief by falling into some pit or hollow, for it is impossible to see the ground through the muddy floodwater. Or the water may rise so rapidly while the children are wading across it that they fail to reach the dry side and are all drowned. Or else they may be able to get onto the bridge from the farther side, which they reach from their houses, but then find that the water on the Kar side is too deep, and they may stand arguing and hesitating for so long that in the meantime the farther bank gets too deeply flooded as well; the bridge thus becomes an island, the children are standing on it and may be swept away with it. And even if none of this happens, their poor little feet are still wading in winter through this water full of melted snow and icicles, and this is very bad for their health.

"In order that they may in future be spared this danger, I have begun to save money, and I appoint as follows: that sum which after my death shall be found to be my property, together with the sum that shall be realized by the sale of my other effects, shall be used for the construction of a school building to be situated in the middle of the outlying neighborhood where these schoolchildren live. From the said sum there shall further be invested such a portion as shall yield income sufficient to maintain teachers at the said school; and in addition such a portion as shall yield for the schoolmaster in the Kar village an annuity sufficient to compensate him for the loss of the said pupils. And further if any part of the money shall still remain it shall be given to my servant Sabina.

"For greater security I have written three identical wills; and if there shall be found among my effects any disposition or statement whatsoever that shall not have the same sense and bear the same date as these my wills, it shall be invalid.

"But in order to lessen the peril to the children for the time being as well, I go every day to the meadow on the Kar side of the river to see if there are any ditches or pits or hollows there, and mark with a rod any that I find. I request the owner of the meadow, if there are any new pits or hollows, to have them filled in as speedily as may be, and he has always done as I asked. When the meadow is flooded I go out onto it and try to help the children. I am learning the signs of the weather in order to be able to foresee a flood and warn the children. To avoid any negligence in this, I never go any distance from my parish. And I intend always so to act in the future."

To these wills the priest had added the written record of his savings up to the date of their execution. The record from that date to the time of his death was found among his papers. These accounts had been kept with great precision. It was evident from them how meticulously the priest had saved. He had entered the tiniest sums, even pennies, and started the most modest of further economies if they would yield an additional mite.

The fifth day after the reading of the will was appointed for the auctioning of the priest's effects.

As we left the courtroom, his lodger said to me, with tears in his eyes: "Oh, how I misjudged him! I thought him almost a miser. My daughter knew him much better; she was always very fond of the man. I must write to her at once and tell her about this."

The Kar schoolmaster blessed the priest's memory, recalling how kind he had always been to him and how pleased he had always been to visit the school.

The rest of the local people also learned the contents of the will.

Only those whom it most directly concerned, the children of the outlying Steinkar neighborhood, knew nothing about it, or if they were told they did not understand, and knew nothing of what the priest's intentions for them had been.

As I wished to be present at the auction as well, I went back to the village and decided to spend the intervening four days revisiting various parts of the Steinkar district and other places where I had once worked. They were all unchanged; it was as if this area had been endowed with a character not only of simplicity but also of changelessness.

When the fifth day came, the doors on the ground floor of the presbytery were unsealed and the priest's remaining effects auctioned. Many people had come for the sale, and in view of the known contents of the will it turned out to be a remarkable one, during which some striking incidents took place. Among the clothes of the deceased a coat was found, in as poor a condition as a garment can be that is not actually in rags, and it was bought by a priest for a considerable sum. The parish of Kar bought his Bible to place it in the church. A purchaser was found even for the wooden bench, which they had not so much as troubled to put under lock and key.

I too acquired something in the auction, namely, the little carved wooden crucifix from Nuremberg, and all the remaining beautiful sheets and tablecloths and other pieces of fine linen. My wife and I still possess them to this day and have very seldom used them. We preserve them in memory of the poor priest and of the deep and lasting and tender emotion which led him to keep them, unused, all his life. Sometimes my wife has them washed and ironed, and gazes in delight at their indescribable beauty and purity: then the sheets are laid together in bundles, still tied with the same old faded red silk ribbons, and put back in the linen cupboard.

The outcome of all these events still remains to be told.

The sum saved up by the priest, and the sum realized by the sale of his effects, were together far too small to pay for the founding of a school. They were too small even to build a medium-sized house of the type normal in those parts, still less a schoolhouse with classrooms and apartments for the teachers, not to mention the endowment of the teachers' salaries and the existing schoolmaster's compensation.

It was in keeping with the priest's character that he did not understand worldly matters, and that he had had to be robbed three times before beginning to invest his savings.

But just as evil deeds are always intrinsically purposeless, and ineffective in the general plan of the world, whereas a good enterprise bears fruit even if undertaken with inadequate means, so too it fell out in the present case. God did not need the priest's help to finish this work. When the story of his will and the inadequacy of its provisions became generally known, the rich and prosperous people of that area at once made common cause and before long they had collectively subscribed a sum that seemed quite large enough to fulfill the priest's intentions. And in the event of more money being needed, every one of them undertook to make a further payment. I too added my modest contribution.

If my first departure from the district had been sad, tears now ran from my eyes as I left those lonely rocks.—

And now, at the time of speaking, the school has long stood among the outlying Steinkar houses, it stands within easy reach of all the schoolchildren, on a fresh and healthy site. The teacher lives in the schoolhouse with his family and his assistant, the teacher at the Kar school receives his annual compensation, and even Sabina has been awarded a further share. She has declined to accept it, however, declaring from the outset that it must be paid to the schoolmaster's daughter, of whom she had always been fond.

On the grave of the school's founder stands the one and only cross that has been erected in the Kar for a priest of that parish. I daresay many prayers are uttered before it, and that many who visit it are filled with an emotion which the priest did not inspire in them during his lifetime.

Translated by David Luke

The Jew's Beech

Annette von Droste-Hülshoff

A Picture of Life among the Hills of Westphalia

Where is the hand so fraught with gentle art
That tangled skein of narrow mind may part,
So steadfast that untrembling it may throw
The stone upon a wretched creature's woe?
Who dares to measure surge of vain ambition,
To ponder prejudice, the soul's perdition,
To weigh each word which, still retained,
Its power o'er youthful heart has gained?
Thou happy man, thou being born in light,
Cherished and guided piously toward right,
Judgment is not thy task, lay scales aside!
Take up no stone—lest it toward thee should glide!

B orn in 1738, Friedrich Mergel was the only son of a small farmer or freeholder of the humbler kind in the village of B., which, despite its smoky and poorly constructed buildings, caught the traveller's eye because of the picturesque beauty of its situation in a green forest glen among an imposing range of hills remarkable for their historical associations.* The province to which it belonged was then one of those remote areas without industry, commerce or main roads, where a strange face still created a sensation and a journey of a hundred miles made even a man of rank the local Ulysses—in short a place once common in Germany, and with all the faults and virtues, all the eccentricity and narrow-mindedness that can only flourish under such conditions.

*The reference is to the Teutoburg Forest in northwest Germany, where the Cheruscan chieftain Arminius defeated the Roman legion of Quintilius Varus in 9 AD, a date that came to be of great resonance in the historical memory of the Germans. A number of place names mentioned in the story, such as Telge Glen (Telgengrund) and Rode Wood (Rodenholz), are locales in this area.

As a result of primitive and often inadequate legislature, the ideas of the inhabitants as to right and wrong had become somewhat confused, or rather beside the official legal system there had grown up a second law based on public opinion, usage and superannuation arising from neglect. The landowners, who had the privileges of magistrates in the courts of petty sessions, punished or rewarded in accordance with motives which were honest for the most part; the peasants acted as seemed feasible and compatible with a somewhat elastic interpretation of what could be reconciled with conscience, and it only occurred sometimes to the loser in a law-suit to consult the ancient and dusty records.

It is difficult to view that time impartially, for since its passing either arrogant censure or fatuous praise have been bestowed on it, while the witness who has first-hand experience is blinded by too many familiar memories and the later generation is not capable of comprehending it. This much may be said, however: legal form mattered less, the spirit was adhered to more strictly, infringements occurred more often, but complete unscrupulousness was rarer. For a person who acts according to his convictions, however imperfect they may be, can never perish entirely, whereas nothing destroys the soul more surely than an appeal to external legal forms in contradiction to one's inner sense of justice.

Many of the actions of the inhabitants, a race more restless and enterprising than their neighbors, attained far greater prominence in the little country of which we are speaking than they would have done elsewhere in similar circumstances. Violation of the forest and game laws was the order of the day and, since brawls often took place, everyone had to console himself as best he could for a broken head. However, since the chief wealth of the country lay in the extensive and profitable woodlands, the timber was carefully patrolled, but less by lawful means than by continually renewed attempts to overcome violence and cunning with the same weapons.

The inhabitants of B. were reputed to be the most stiff-necked, wily and spirited community in the whole principality. The situation of the village, secluded amidst dense, proud forests, may have nourished early their inborn stubbornness of temperament; the vicinity of a river flowing to the sea and bearing covered barges large enough to carry timber for ship building conveniently and safely out of the country did much to stimulate the natural boldness of the timber thieves. It was merely an incentive to them that the district was swarming with foresters, for in the skirmishes which frequently occurred the advantage usually lay with the peasants. On fine, moonlit nights thirty or forty carts set out together, carrying about twice that number of persons of every age from the half-grown youth to the seventy-year-old headman who, as an experienced ringleader, led the procession with as much conscious pride as he displayed taking his seat in the courtroom. Those who remained behind listened without anxiety as the noise of the wheels creaking and jolting down the glen gradually died away, then they calmly resumed their slumbers. It is true that an occasional shot or feeble cry sometimes caused a young woman, married or betrothed, to start up in her sleep, but no one else took any notice. With the first light of dawn the procession returned home as silently as it had departed, faces glowed like bronze, here and there a bandaged head was to be seen, but this was a matter of no account, and a few hours later everyone in the district was talking about a mishap to one or more of the foresters, who were carried out of the woods battered, bruised, blinded by snuff and unable to perform their duties for some time.

It was in this environment that Friedrich Mergel was born, in a house which, boasting a chimney and window panes rather larger than usual, testified to the pretensions of its builder, while its dilapidated state indicated the miserable circumstances of the present owner. The wooden railings which had formerly encircled garden and yard had given way to a neglected fence, the roof was defective, the cattle grazing on the pastures and the corn growing on the land adjoining the yard did not belong to the owner, and, apart from a few gnarled rose-trees—relics of a better time—the garden contained more weeds than cultivated plants. Admittedly misfortune had been responsible for much of this, but considerable disorder and bad management had also played their part. As a bachelor Friedrich's father, old Hermann Mergel, had been a so-called "regular" drinker, that is one who only lay in the gutter on Sundays and feast-days, while he was as respectable as anyone else throughout the week. Thus he found no difficulty in courting a girl who was both handsome and well-to-do. They had a merry time of it at the wedding. Mergel was not too badly drunk and in the evening the bride's parents went home in good spirits. On the following Sunday, however, the young wife was seen running through the village to her people, screaming, covered in blood, abandoning all her new household utensils. That was indeed a great scandal and vexation for Mergel who was badly in need of consolation. Thus it was to be expected that by the afternoon not a window pane in his house should be still intact and that, till late into the night, he should be seen lying in front of his door, raising a broken bottleneck to his lips from time to time and woefully cutting hands and face. The young wife stayed with her parents, until she soon pined away and died. Whether it was remorse or shame which now tormented Mergel, suffice it to say that he seemed ever more in need of a source of consolation and was soon numbered among those who had gone irretrievably to the dogs.

House and farm fell into decay; hired maids brought it loss and discredit, as the years passed. Mergel was, and remained, a lazy widower living in rather poor circumstances, until he suddenly appeared once more as a bridegroom. If the event itself was unexpected, the character of the bride caused even greater astonishment. Margret Semmler was an honest, decent woman in her forties, who had been a village beauty in her youth and was still respected for her shrewdness and thrift; at the same time she was not without means of her own, and thus nobody could understand what had driven her to this step. We believe that the motive for her action lay in that very consciousness of her own perfection. On the evening before the wedding ceremony she is said to have declared: "A woman who is ill-treated by her husband is stupid or worthless; if I live to regret it, say it's my own fault." What followed unfortunately showed that she had over-estimated her powers. At first she overawed her husband; whenever he had drunk too freely, he did not come home or crawled into the barn; but the yoke was too heavy to be borne long, and soon he was to be seen often enough staggering across the road into the house, making a deafening noise inside so that Margret hurriedly closed doors and windows. On one such evening—now no longer a Sunday—she was seen rushing out of the house without cap or neckerchief, her hair hanging wildly about her head; she threw herself down in the garden beside a vegetable bed and dug up the earth with her bare hands. Then, looking fearfully about her, she quickly gathered a bundle of herbs and went back slowly towards the house with them, finally entering not the house but the barn. Although a confession never passed her lips it was said that Mergel had first laid hands on her that day.

The second year of this unhappy union was—one cannot say gladdened—by the birth of a son, for Margret is believed to have wept a great deal when the child was handed to her. However, although borne under a heart full of grief, Friedrich was a healthy, handsome child who thrived in the fresh air. His father was very fond of him and never came home without bringing him a piece of fine wheaten bread or something of the kind, and people were even of the opinion that he had grown steadier since the birth of the child; at least there was less noise in the house.

Friedrich was now in his ninth year. It was a cold stormy winter night in Epiphany. Hermann had gone to a wedding, having already started early, because the house of the bride was about four miles away. Although he had promised to come back in the evening, Frau Mergel was not counting on this, particularly since a dense snowstorm had set in after sunset. Towards ten o'clock she raked the ashes together on the hearth and prepared to go to bed. Friedrich, already half undressed, stood beside her, listening to the howling of the wind and the rattling of the attic window.

"Mother, isn't Father coming home tonight?" he asked.

"No, child, tomorrow."

"But why not, Mother? He promised."

"Goodness, if he kept all his promises! Get along with you, off to bed."

They had scarcely lain down when a gale arose, threatening to sweep the house away. The bedstead shook and there was a rattling in the chimney as though a goblin were there.

"Mother—there's someone knocking outside!"

"Quiet, Fritz, that's the loose board on the gable blown by the wind."

"No, Mother, at the door!"

"It doesn't close properly, the latch is broken. Goodness, go to sleep! Don't rob me of the little rest I get at night."

"But supposing Father comes now?"

His mother turned violently in the bed.

"The devil will look after him!"

"Where is the devil, Mother?"

"Just wait, you fidget! He's at the door and will fetch you if you don't be quiet!"

Friedrich fell silent, listened for a short while longer and then went to sleep. He awoke a few hours later. The wind had turned and now hissed like a snake past his ear through the crack in the window. His shoulder had grown numb with cold and, in his fear, he crept deeper under the cover and lay quite still. After some time he noticed that his mother too was not sleeping. He heard her weeping and praying at intervals, "Hail, Mary!" and "Pray for us sinners!" The beads of the rosary slid past his face, and he was unable to suppress a sigh.

"Are you awake, Friedrich?"

"Yes, Mother."

"Pray a little, child, that God may keep us from flood and fire. You already know half the Lord's Prayer."

Friedrich thought of the devil and what he might look like. The many different sounds and noises in the house seemed strange to him. He thought there must be something alive, both inside and outside.

"Listen, Mother, isn't that someone knocking?"

"No, child, but there's no old board in the house that isn't rattling!"

"Listen! Don't you hear? Someone's calling! Listen!"

His mother sat up in bed; when the raging of the storm abated for an instant, a knocking at the window shutters and the sound of several voices could be heard distinctly.

"Margret, Frau Margret! Hey, open up!"

Margret uttered a violent cry: "They're bringing me back the swine again!"

The rosary flew rattling on to the yarn-winder, clothes were snatched up. She ran to the hearth and soon afterwards Friedrich heard her striding defiantly over the threshing-floor. Margret never came back to bed, but in the kitchen there was much murmuring and the sound of strange voices. Twice an unknown man came into the room and seemed anxious to find something. Suddenly a lamp was brought in, followed by two men supporting his mother. She was as white as chalk and her eyes were closed. Friedrich thought she was dead; he gave a fearful scream, whereupon someone boxed his ears; this quietened him and now he gradually realized from what was said by those around him that his father had been found dead in the wood by Uncle Franz Semmler and Hülsmeyer and was now lying in the kitchen.

As soon as Margret regained consciousness, she tried to get rid of the strangers present. Her brother stayed with her, and Friedrich, threatened with severe punishment if he left the bed, heard the whole night through the fire crackling in the kitchen and a noise like scuffling of feet and brushing. Little was spoken, and that softly, but sometimes the boy could hear sighs which, young as he was, went to the very marrow of his bones. At one point he understood his uncle to say: "Margret, don't take on so, we'll each have three masses said for his soul and at Easter we'll make a pilgrimage to the Mother of God at Werl."*

When, two days later, the body was taken away, Margret sat by the hearth, covering her face with her apron. After some minutes, when all was quiet once more, she muttered to herself: "Ten years, every one a cross. Yet we bore them together, and now I am alone." Then she said louder: "Come here, Fritz!" Friedrich approached shyly; his mother seemed alien to him in her black ribbons and with her troubled expression. "Fritz," she said, "are you going to be good now and make me happy, or are you going to be wicked and tell lies or drink and steal?"

"Hülsmeyer steals, Mother."

"Hülsmeyer? God forbid! Do I have to whip you? Who tells you such wicked stories?"

"Not long ago he beat Aaron and took sixpence from him."

"If he took money from Aaron, the wretched Jew had certainly swindled him out of it earlier. Hülsmeyer is a respectable man, one of us, and Jews are all rogues."

"But, Mother, Brandis too says that he steals wood and game."

"Child, Brandis is a forester."

"Mother, do foresters tell lies?"

Margret was silent for a while; then she said: "Listen, Fritz, God makes wood grow in freedom and the game changes its haunts from the land of one master to that of another, it can't belong to anybody. But you can't understand that yet, now go to the shed and fetch firewood for me."

*Westphalian town near Soest with an image of the Virgin believed capable of miracles.

Friedrich had seen his father lying on straw, where, it was said, he had looked blue in the face, a terrible sight. However, he never spoke of it and seemed unwilling even to think of it. The memory of his father had left in him a tenderness mixed with horror, for nothing is so captivating as love and care from a person who seems hardened against everything else, and with the years this feeling grew through the sense of many a slight suffered from others. Throughout his childhood he was extremely sensitive to any allusion to the dead man phrased in none too praiseworthy terms, an unhappiness not spared him by any consideration on the part of the neighbours. In those districts it is the customary belief that victims of disaster enjoy no rest in the grave. Old Mergel had become the ghost of Brede Wood. In the form of a will-o'-the-wisp he had almost led a drunken man into Zelle Pond. The shepherd boys, whenever they huddled over their fires at night and the owls hooted in the glens, sometimes heard quite distinctly in the intervals the disconnected notes of his song, "Listen, pretty Lizzie," and an unauthorized woodcutter who had fallen asleep under the Broad Oak as night had come on, had, on awakening, seen his swollen blue face peeping through the branches. Friedrich had to hear a good deal about this from other boys, whereupon he howled, struck out at those around him, sometimes stabbed at his enemies with his little knife and was lamentably beaten on these occasions. Since that time he drove his mother's cows alone to the other end of the valley, where he was often to be seen, lying in the grass for hours on end in the same position and plucking the thyme from the ground.

He was twelve years old, when his mother received a visit from her younger brother who lived in Brede and had not crossed her threshold since her foolish marriage. Simon Semmler was a small, restless, spare man with bulging, fishlike eyes and a face just like a pike's, an eerie fellow in whom pompous reserve often alternated with a candor just as affected; he fancied himself as a man of enlightenment, but was reckoned to be a malicious trouble-seeker whom everyone preferred to avoid, the more he approached an age at which men who are in any case limited in intelligence easily gain in pretensions what they lose in usefulness. However, Margret, who had no other relatives still alive, was pleased to see him.

"Is that you, Simon?" she said, trembling so much that she had to hold on to a chair. "Have you come to see how I and my grubby boy are getting on?"

Simon looked at her earnestly and held out his hand. "You have grown old, Margret!"

Margret sighed: "Since you saw me last, I've often had a bitter time of it, with all kinds of misfortunes."

"Yes, my girl, marry too late and repent ever after! Now you are old and the child still small: everything has its own time, but when an old house catches fire, there's no use in trying to put it out."

A flame, red as blood, shot across Margret's careworn face.

"But I hear that your boy is sly and smart," Simon continued.

"Yes, he is rather, but he is pious too."

"Hm, there was once a chap stole a cow who was also called Pius. But he is quiet and thoughtful, isn't he? He doesn't run around with other boys?"

"He's an odd child," Margret said, as though to herself; "that isn't a good thing."

Simon burst into a hearty laugh. "Your boy is shy because the others have tanned his hide a few times; he'll pay them back all right. A little while ago Hülsmeyer was at my place and he said 'Friedrich is as nimble as a deer.'"

What mother's heart is not gladdened, when she hears her child praised? Poor Margret had seldom felt so happy. Everyone else called her boy artful and sulky. The tears started to her eyes. "Yes, he has straight limbs, thank God."

"What does he look like?" Simon went on.

"He has much of you in him, Simon, very much."

Simon laughed: "Well, he must be a fine fellow, for I get handsomer every day. He must be careful not to get his fingers burnt at school. Do you make him mind the cows? That's just as good as going to school. Not half of what the schoolmaster says is true. But where does he mind the cows, in Telge Glen or in Rode Wood? In the Teutoburg forest? Nights too and early in the morning?"

"Whole nights through; but why do you ask?"

Simon seemed not to hear her question; he stretched his neck towards the door. "Well, here comes the lad! He's the son of his father and swings his arms just like your dead husband. And just look! The boy really has my fair hair!"

A fleeting smile of pride lit up the mother's features; the fair curls of her Friedrich compared with Simon's ginger bristles! Without answering, she broke off a branch in a nearby hedge and went to meet her son, apparently to drive on a lazy cow, but really to whisper to him a few quick, half-threatening words, for she knew his stubborn nature and Simon's manner had seemed to her today more intimidating than ever. But all went far better than she had expected: Friedrich was neither stubborn nor insolent in his behavior, but rather somewhat bashful and very eager to please his uncle. Thus it happened that, after a half-hour's talk, Simon proposed a kind of adoption of the boy by which he would not deprive his mother of him completely, but would have him at his disposal for the greater part of the time, in return for which he was to inherit the old bachelor's possessions (these would certainly have come to him in any case). Patiently Margret listened to the explanation of how much she would stand to gain, how little to lose through the bargain. She knew best how much an ailing widow would miss the help of a twelve-year-old son whom she had already trained to take the place of a daughter. Yet she kept silent and gave way in every respect. She only begged her brother to be strict but not hard in his treatment of the boy.

"He is a good lad," she said, "but I'm a lonely woman and my son is not like one ruled by a father's hand."

Simon nodded slyly: "Just leave it to me, we'll soon get along. I'll tell you what. Let me have the boy straight away. I have to fetch two sacks from the mill; the smallest is just right for him and he'll learn to lend a hand. Come, Fritz, put on your clogs!"

And soon Margret was looking after them both as they walked away, Simon in front, cleaving the air with his face, while the tails of his red coat trailed behind him like flames of fire. Thus he looked rather like a "fiery man," atoning for his guilt beneath his stolen sack, Friedrich following him, slim and well-made for his years with delicate, almost noble features and long fair curls which were better cared for than one might otherwise have expected from his appearance; for the rest he looked ragged, sun-burnt and neglected, while his expression reflected a certain rude melancholy. Nevertheless one could not fail to recognize a great family likeness between them and, as Friedrich thus walked slowly after his leader, his gaze firmly fixed on his uncle, who attracted him just because of the strangeness of his appearance, he called to mind someone who regards with troubled concentration the image of his future in a magic mirror.

Now they both approached the place in the Teutoburg forest where Brede Wood stretches down the side of the mountain and covers a very dark ravine. Up to this point little had been said. Simon seemed thoughtful, the boy absent-minded, and both panted under their sacks. Suddenly Simon asked: "Do you like brandy?" The boy did not reply. "I'm asking if you like brandy? Does Mother sometimes give you some?"

"Mother herself has none," said Friedrich.

"Really, all the better! Do you recognize that wood in front of us?"

"That is Brede Wood."

"And do you know what happened there?"

Friedrich was silent. Meanwhile they drew ever nearer to the gloomy ravine.

"Does your mother still pray so much?" Simon went on.

"Yes, two rosaries every night."

"Really? and you pray with her?"

With a knowing look, the boy laughed, half-embarrassed by the question. "Mother prays one rosary at dusk before supper—I'm usually still away with the cows then—and the other in bed when I mostly fall asleep."

"Really, my lad!"

These last words were spoken under the shade of a wide-spreading beech which arched over the entrance to the ravine. It was now quite dark; the first quarter of the moon was in the sky, but its faint gleams only served to give a weird appearance to the objects on which they sometimes shone through a gap in the branches. Friedrich, breathing quickly, kept close behind his uncle and, if anyone had been able to see his face, he would have noticed the expression of an intense excitement which was more the result of imagination than real fear. Both strode on vigorously, Simon with the firm tread of the hardened walker, Friedrich staggering and as if in a dream. It seemed to him as though everything were moving, the trees, lit up by occasional moonbeams, swaying sometimes together, sometimes one away from the other. Tree-roots and slippery places, where water had collected on the path, made his steps uncertain, at times he nearly fell. Now, some distance away, the darkness seemed to part and soon they stepped into a fairly large clearing. The bright moonlight showed that only recently the axe had raged here pitilessly. Everywhere tree-stumps projected, many several feet above the ground, just as they could be cut most conveniently by somebody in a hurry; the furtive labor must have been interrupted unexpectedly, for a beech in full leaf lay right across the path, its branches stretching high above, its foliage, still fresh, trembling in the night wind. Simon stopped for a moment and regarded the felled trunk attentively. In the middle of the clearing stood an old oak, broad rather than high; a pale beam, falling through the branches on to its trunk, revealed that it was hollow—this was probably why it had been preserved from the general destruction. At this point Simon suddenly grasped the boy's arm.

"Friedrich, do you recognize the tree? That is the Broad Oak." Friedrich started and clung with cold hands to his uncle. "Look," Simon went on, "here Uncle Franz and Hülsmeyer found your father, after he had gone to the devil in his drunkenness without confession and extreme unction."

"Uncle, Uncle!" gasped Friedrich.

"What's the matter? Surely you are not afraid? You're pinching my arm, you young devil! Let go! Let go!" He tried to shake off the boy. "Otherwise your father was a good chap and God won't be too hard on him. I loved him like my own brother."

Friedrich let go the arm of his uncle; both went in silence through the rest of the wood and then Brede village lay before them, with its clay huts and the few better houses of brick of which Simon's home was one.

The next evening, Margret had already been sitting with her distaff for an hour in front of the door, waiting for her boy. It was the first night that she had spent without hearing the breathing of her son beside her and Friedrich still did not come. She was annoyed and anxious, and knew that she was both without reason. The clock in the tower struck seven, the cattle returned home; he was still not back, and she had to get up to look after the cows. When she entered the dark kitchen, Friedrich was standing by the hearth; he had bent forward and was warming his hands at the coals. The firelight played on his features and gave them a repulsive appearance, stressing their leanness and nervous twitching. Margret stopped at the door of the threshing-floor, so strangely altered did the boy seem to her.

"Friedrich, how is your uncle?" The boy muttered inaudibly and pressed close to the chimney. "Friedrich, have you lost your tongue? Speak up, boy! You know that I'm deaf in my right ear." The boy raised his voice and began to stammer so violently that Margret understood no better than before. "What are you saying? Master Semmler sends his greetings? Gone away again? Where to? The cows are already home. Wretched boy, I can't understand you. Wait, let's see if you still have a tongue in your head!" She advanced a few quick steps towards him. The boy looked up at her with the woeful glance of a poor, half-grown creature being trained as a watchdog and in his fear began to stamp his feet and rub his back against the chimney.

With an anxious glance, Margret halted. The boy seemed shrunken to her, even his clothes were not the same, no, that wasn't her child! And yet—"Friedrich, Friedrich!" she cried.

A cupboard door banged in the bedroom and he whom she had called stepped forward, in one hand a so-called "Holschen fiddle," that is an old clog with three or four frayed violin strings stretched over it, in the other a bow equally battered. He went straight up to his stunted double with a bearing of conscious dignity and independence which at this moment threw into bold relief the difference between two boys who were otherwise remarkably alike.

"There you are, Johannes!" he said and handed him the work of art with the air of a patron, "there is the violin I promised you. I must give up playing, now that I must earn money." Johannes darted another shy glance at Margret, then slowly stretched out his hand, until he had firmly grasped what was offered him and slipped it as though in stealth beneath the flaps of his shabby jacket.

Margret stood quite still and did not interfere. Her thoughts had taken another far more serious turn and she looked restlessly from one to the other. The strange boy had bent over the coals again with an expression of momentary well-being which bordered on idiocy, while Friedrich's features reflected an interest patently more selfish than good-natured and his eyes revealed for the first time in their almost glasslike clarity the unbridled ambition and inclination to give himself airs which afterwards appeared as such a strong motive for most of his actions. A call from his mother wrenched him away from thoughts which were as novel as they were pleasant to him. She was sitting again at the spinning-wheel.

"Friedrich," she said hesitantly, "tell me——" and then fell silent.

Friedrich looked up and, when he heard nothing further, turned back to his protégé. "No, listen——" she said and then more softly: "Who is the boy? What's his name?"

Friedrich answered just as softly: "That's Uncle Simon's swineherd and he's taking a message for Hülsmeyer. Uncle gave me a pair of shoes and a canvas waistcoat which the boy carried for me on the way; in return I promised him my violin, he's only a poor lad and called Johannes."

"Well?" said Margret.

"What do you want, Mother?"

"What's his other name?"

"No other name—but wait a minute—yes—it's Niemand (Nobody), he's called Johannes Niemand—he hasn't got a father," he added in an undertone.

Margret stood up and went into another room. After a while she came out with a hard, gloomy expression on her face. "Very well, Friedrich," she said, "let the lad go on his errand. Boy, why are you lying there in the cinders? Haven't you anything to do at home?"

The boy, with the mien of a fugitive, rose so hurriedly that all his limbs got tangled and the "Holschen fiddle" missed falling into the fire by a hair's breadth.

"Wait, Johannes," Friedrich said proudly, "I'll give you half of my bread and butter, it's too big for me, Mother always cuts a whole slice."

"Never mind," said Margret, "he's going home anyway."

"Yes, but he won't get anything. Uncle Simon eats at seven."

Margret turned to the boy. "Don't they keep anything for you? Who looks after you?"

"Nobody," the child stuttered.

"Nobody?" she repeated; "here, take this, take it!" she added angrily. "You're called Niemand and nobody cares for you, God knows! And now go about your business! Friedrich, don't go with him, do you hear, don't go through the village together."

"I only want to fetch wood from the shed," Friedrich answered.

When the two boys had gone, Margret threw herself on to a chair, clapping her hands together as an expression of deepest grief. Her face was as white as a sheet. "A false oath! A false oath!" she groaned. "Simon, Simon, how will you answer for it before God!"

Thus she sat for a time, unmoving, with compressed lips and in a state of complete abstraction. Friedrich was standing before her and had already spoken to her twice before she replied. "What is it, what do you want?" she cried, starting up.

"I've brought you money," he said, more astonished than frightened.

"Money? Where?" She made a slight movement and a small coin fell with a ring to the floor. Friedrich picked it up.

"Money from Uncle Simon, because I helped him with his work. I can earn something myself now."

"Money from Simon? Throw it away, throw it away! No, give it to the poor. But no, keep it," she whispered, scarcely audible; "we are poor ourselves. Who knows if we'll get along without begging!"

"I am to go back to Uncle on Monday and help him with the sowing."

"You go back to him? No, no, never!" She embraced her son passionately. "Never mind," she added and the tears streamed suddenly down her sunken cheeks. "Go to him, he is my only brother and there's a great deal of wicked gossip about these days! But keep God in your sight and don't forget your daily prayers!"

Margret laid her face against the wall and wept aloud. She had borne many a hard burden, ill treatment by her husband or, even worse, his death. It was a bitter moment when the widow had to relinquish to a creditor the last piece of her land and the plow stood idle before the house. But she had never felt as she did now. However, after she had wept for a whole evening and passed a whole night without sleep, she had come to the conclusion that her brother Simon could not be so godless after all—the boy certainly wasn't his and likeness proved nothing. Had she not herself, forty years ago, lost a little sister who looked just like the foreign pedlar! What isn't one ready to believe when one has so little and is to lose even that through lack of faith!

From this time onwards Friedrich was seldom at home any longer. Simon seemed to have bestowed upon his nephew all the warmer feelings of which he was capable; at any rate he missed him in his absence and continually sent messages when a domestic matter kept Friedrich with his mother for any length of time. Since then the boy had been quite changed, he had completely lost his dreamy ways, as his resolute step indicated; he began to pay attention to his appearance and soon became known as a handsome and resourceful youth. His uncle, who could not live without his pet schemes, occasionally undertook quite important public works, e.g. road-building, in which Friedrich gained a reputation as one of his best workers and was regarded by everyone as his right-hand man; for although his physical strength had not yet reached maturity, there were few who had as much endurance. Till then Margret had only loved her son; now she began to be proud of him and even to feel a kind of respect for him as she saw him growing up quite independent of her help or even her counsel. Like most people she considered the latter to be priceless and therefore could not value highly enough his ability to dispense with such inestimable support.

In his eighteenth year Friedrich had already secured a notable reputation among the young people of the village through the outcome of a bet, as a result of which he carried a boar slain in the hunt on his back for over nine miles without resting. Sharing his glory, however, was just about the only advantage which Margret gained from this state of affairs, for Friedrich became ever more interested in his appearance and found it more and more difficult to pocket his pride whenever a lack of funds forced him to play second fiddle to anyone else in the village. Moreover, all his powers were directed to earning money outside the house; at home, in absolute contrast to his usual reputation, all regular work was irksome to him and he preferred to submit to short periods of hard labor which soon permitted him to resume his former occupation as herdsman. This had already become unsuited to his age and exposed him to occasional ridicule which he, however, soon silenced by a few hearty blows from his fist. Thus people grew used to seeing him, sometimes the acknowledged dandy of the village, dressed up and in a happy mood at the head of the young people, sometimes a ragged herdsman, stealing along behind the cows or, a lonely dreamer, lying apparently absent-minded in a forest clearing and plucking the moss from the trees.

About this time the slumbering laws were given a somewhat rude jolt by a band of timber thieves which, under the name of the "Blue-Smocks", so far surpassed all their predecessors in cunning and impudence that it became intolerable, even to the most forbearing of men. In direct contrast to the usual state of affairs, when the leaders of the flock can be pointed out, it had not been possible on this occasion, in spite of every vigilance, to name even a single individual.

They received their name from their identically uniform dress, by which they made it difficult for them to be recognized if a forester should see a few isolated stragglers disappearing into a thicket. They laid waste the countryside like a swarm of pine looper caterpillars; whole areas of the forest were felled in a night and moved away at once so that next morning nothing was found except chips of wood and tangled piles of unwanted top branches. The fact that cart tracks never led to a village, but always from the river and back again, proved that the thieves acted under the protection of—and perhaps with the help of—the shipowners. There must have been remarkably clever spies in the band, for the foresters could stay awake at night for weeks on end without discovering anything, but, on the first night that they gave up their watch from sheer fatigue, no matter whether it was stormy or clear and moonlit, the destruction started again. It was strange that the people of the country around seemed as ignorant and nervous of the Blue-Smocks' activities as the foresters themselves. Some villages declared positively that they did not belong to the Blue-Smocks, but then no village could be strongly suspected since the most doubtful of all, the village B., had proved its innocence. Chance had brought this about, a wedding at which almost all the inhabitants of this village had been conspicuously present during the night, while at just this time the Blue-Smocks had carried out one of their strongest expeditions.

The damage caused in the forests was, however, becoming intolerable and therefore the measures against the evil were tightened up to an almost unprecedented degree. Patrols went out day and night, farm-workers and servants were armed and drafted to foresters' groups. Nevertheless, success was only small and the guards had scarcely left one end of the forest, when the Blue-Smocks entered from the other side. This lasted more than a year, guards and Blue-Smocks, Blue-Smocks and guards, always changing places like the sun and the moon, in possession of the terrain and never meeting.

It was in July 1756 at three in the morning. The moon shone in a clear sky but its light began to wane and in the east there already appeared a narrow yellow strip which lined the horizon and sealed the entrance to a narrow valley ravine as though with a golden ribbon. Friedrich lay in the grass, as was his custom, and whittled a willow rod, to whose gnarled end he tried to give a crude animal-like shape. He looked overtired, yawned, at times rested his head on a weather-beaten trunk and let his gaze, mistier than the horizon, roam over the entrance to the glen which was almost overgrown with brushwood and young trees. His eyes lit up once or twice and then assumed the glasslike glitter peculiar to them, but immediately afterwards he half-shut them again and yawned and stretched himself, as only lazy herdsmen may do. His dog lay some distance away close to the cows, which, unconcerned about the forest laws, nibbled at the young tender tree-tops as often as the grass, and blew into the fresh morning air. From the forest a dull crash was sometimes to be heard; the sound, accompanied by a long echo from the mountain slopes, lasted only a few seconds and was repeated about every five to eight minutes. Friedrich paid no heed to it; only occasionally, when the noise was unusually loud and prolonged, he raised his head and let his gaze slowly glide over the different paths which ended at the bottom of the valley.

Already daybreak was fast approaching, the birds were beginning to twitter softly and one could feel the dew rising from the earth. Friedrich had lowered himself down the trunk, and, hands clasped over his head, was gazing at the gently spreading flush of dawn. Suddenly he started, his expression changed abruptly, and, bending forward, he listened for a moment like a hound scenting the trail. Then he quickly put two fingers to his mouth and gave a shrill, prolonged whistle. "Fidel, you wretched beast!" A hurtled stone struck the flanks of the unsuspecting animal which, roused from sleep, first snapped in all directions and then ran howling on three legs to seek consolation at the very source of its discomfiture.

At that instant, the branches in a nearby thicket were thrust apart almost noiselessly to reveal a man dressed in a green hunting jacket with a silver coat-of-arms on the sleeve and holding a loaded shotgun. His gaze, roaming swiftly over the glen, came to rest with peculiar keenness on the youth; then he came forward, making signs in the direction of the thicket, and gradually seven or eight men came into view, all in similar clothing, hunting-knives at their belts and cocked firearms in their hands.

"What was that, Friedrich?" asked the man who had first appeared.

"I wish this damned cur would fall dead here and now. He wouldn't mind if the cows nibbled the ears off my head."

"The swine saw us," another man said.

"Tomorrow I'll send you somewhere with a stone round your neck," Friedrich continued and kicked at the dog.

"Don't play the fool, Friedrich! You know me and get my meaning!" These words were accompanied by a look which had a rapid effect.

"Think of my mother, sir!"

"I am thinking. Didn't you hear anything in the forest?"

"In the forest?" The youth shot a swift glance at the forester's face. "Only your wood-cutters."

"My wood-cutters!"

The complexion of the forester, normally dusky, now changed to a deep purple. "How many of them are there, and where are they busy?"

"I don't know, sir; where you've sent them."

Brandis turned to his companions: "You go ahead, I'll be coming presently."

When, one after the other, they had disappeared into the thicket, Brandis came up close to the youth; "Friedrich," he said, struggling to master his fury, "my patience is at an end; I feel like whipping you like a dog, and that's what you deserve! You riffraff without a penny to call your own! Soon you'll have to go begging, thank God, and that old witch, your mother, won't get even a moldy crust at my door. But before that I'll have you both in jail."

With a convulsive movement Friedrich reached for a branch. He was as pale as death and his eyes seemed to start from his head like crystal balls. But only for a moment. Then he assumed once more an expression of deep calm which almost suggested complete exhaustion.

"Sir," he said firmly, almost gently, "you've said things you can't answer for and so have I, maybe. We'll call it quits and now I'll tell you what you want to know. If you yourself didn't arrange for woodcutters to be there, it must be the Blue-Smocks, for no cart came from the village; I can see the road and there were four carts. I didn't see them, but heard them going up the glen." He faltered for a moment. "Could you really say that I have ever felled a tree in your district? Or that I have ever cut wood anywhere except when ordered? Just think whether you can say that."

An embarrassed mutter was the only answer from the forester who, like most blunt men, was quick to repent his hot temper. He turned round irritably and walked towards the bushes.

"No, sir," Friedrich shouted, "if you want to join the other foresters, they have gone up past the beech."

"By the beech?" said Brandis doubtfully. "No, they went that way, to the Maste Gorge."

"I tell you, past the beech; Big Henry's gun-sling got caught on the crooked branch there; I saw it!"

The forester set out on the path indicated. All this time Friedrich had not left his place; half-lying with his arm round a dead branch, he looked steadily after the forester as he stalked down the partly overgrown footpath with the long cautious stride peculiar to his calling, as noiselessly as a fox climbs into a chicken-roost. Here one branch sank behind him, there another; the outlines of his figure became ever more blurred. There was one last glint among the foliage—a steel button on his hunting jacket—and he was gone. While the forester was gradually disappearing, Friedrich's face lost its cold expression and finally mirrored his anxiety. Did he perhaps regret that he had not asked the forester to keep quiet about what he had said? He took a few steps towards the path, but soon stopped. "It's too late," he said to himself and reached for his hat. The sound of light strokes came from the bushes, not twenty paces away. It was the forester, sharpening his gun-flint. Friedrich listened. "No!" he then said resolutely, collected his belongings and hastily drove the cattle along the glen.

About midday Margret was sitting by the hearth making tea. Friedrich had come home ill, complaining of a violent headache, and, in reply to her worried inquiry, had told her how the forester had angered him, in short the whole incident just described with the exception of some minor details which he thought it best to keep to himself. Margret gazed silently and dejectedly into the boiling water. She was accustomed to hearing her son complain now and then, but today he seemed worn out as never before. Was he perhaps sickening for something? She sighed deeply and dropped a block of wood which she had just picked up.

"Mother!" called Friedrich from the bedroom.

"What do you want?"

"Was that a shot?"

"No, I don't know what you mean."

"Perhaps it's only the throbbing in my head," he replied.

The woman from next door came in and in a soft whisper retailed some trivial gossip to which Margret listened without interest. Then she left.

"Mother!" called Friedrich.

Margret went to him.

"What did Frau Hülsmeyer say?"

"Oh nothing, some rubbish or other!"

Friedrich sat up in bed.

"About Gretchen Siemers; you know, the old story, and there's not a grain of truth in it."

Friedrich lay down again. "I'll try to sleep," he said.

Margret sat by the hearth, she was spinning and had thoughts which were far from pleasant. In the village the clock struck half-past eleven; the latch of the door was lifted and Kapp, the clerk of the court, came in.

"Good day, Frau Mergel," he said. "Could you give me a drink of milk? I've just come from M."

When Frau Mergel brought what he wanted, he asked, "Where's Friedrich?"

She was just fetching a plate and missed the question. He drank hesitantly and with short pauses. "Do you know," he then said, "the Blue-Smocks last night again swept a whole piece of Maste Wood as bare as my hand."

"Goodness gracious!" she replied indifferently.

"The scoundrels ruin everything," the clerk went on, "if only they'd spare the young wood, but to cut oak saplings no thicker than my arm, not big enough for oars even! It's as though they liked doing harm to others as much as making a profit!"

"It's a shame!" Margret said.

The clerk had finished his drink, but still did not go. He seemed to have something on his mind. "Haven't you heard about Brandis?" he suddenly asked.

"No, he never comes here."

"You don't know then what has happened to him?"

"What happened?" Margret asked in suspense.

"He's dead!"

"Dead!" she cried, "dead? Good Heavens! This very morning he went past here, perfectly well, with his gun on his back!"

"He's dead," the clerk repeated, watching her closely; "killed by the Blue-Smocks. The corpse was brought into the village a quarter of an hour ago."

Margret clapped her hands in horror. "God above, don't judge him. He didn't know what he was doing!"

"Him!" cried the clerk, "the damned murderer, you mean?"

From the bedroom deep groans were heard. Margret hurried in and the clerk followed her. Friedrich was sitting up in bed, his face buried in his hands, moaning like a dying man.

"Friedrich, what's the matter?" said his mother.

"What's the matter?" the clerk repeated.

"Oh my stomach, my head," he wailed.

"What's wrong with him?"

"God only knows," she replied, "he came home with the cows at about four o'clock because he felt so unwell."

"Friedrich, Friedrich, tell me, shall I go for the doctor?"

"No, no," he groaned, "it's only colic and I'll soon get over it."

He lay back, his face twitching convulsively with pain, then his color returned. "Go," he said feebly, "I must sleep, and then it'll pass."

"Frau Mergel," the clerk said earnestly, "are you certain that Friedrich came home at four and didn't go out again?"

She stared at him. "Ask any child in the street. Go out again—would to God he could!"

"Has he said nothing to you about Brandis?"

"Yes, to tell the truth, he said that Brandis abused him in the forest and jeered at our poverty, the blackguard! But God forgive me, he's dead! Go," she continued vehemently. "Did you come to insult honest people? Go!" She turned back to her son and the clerk left.

"Friedrich, what's the matter?" his mother said. "You heard, I suppose. It's terrible, terrible—he died without confession and absolution!"

"Mother, Mother, for God's sake let me sleep; I can't stand any more!"

At this moment Johannes Niemand entered the room, long and thin as a hop-pole, but ragged and shy, as we saw him five years before. His face was even paler than usual.

"Friedrich," he stuttered, "you are to come to your uncle straight away, he has work for you, but straight away."

Friedrich turned towards the wall. "I'm not coming," he said roughly, "I'm ill."

"But you must come," Johannes panted; "he said I must bring you back."

Friedrich burst into a scornful laugh. "I'd like to see that!"

"Let him be, he can't," sighed Margret, "you can see how it is."
She went out for a few minutes; when she came back, Friedrich
was already dressed.

"What are you thinking of?" she cried, "you can't, you shan't go!"

"What must be, must be," he replied, already going out through
the door with Johannes.

"Oh God," sighed his mother, "when children are small, they
trample on our laps, when they are big, on our hearts!"

The inquest had begun. That a crime had been committed was
obvious; however, the evidence incriminating any actual person was
so weak, that, although all known facts cast the deepest suspicion on
the Blue-Smocks, only conjectures could be advanced. One clue
seemed to throw some light on the case, but for various reasons it
was scarcely heeded. The absence of the squire had obliged the clerk
to begin the proceedings himself. He was sitting at the table; the
room was crammed with peasants, some who had come from
curiosity, some from whom, in the absence of actual witnesses, it
was hoped to obtain information. Herdsmen who had been on
watch that night, farm laborers who worked on the fields in the
vicinity, all stood solidly and sturdily, their hands in their pockets,
as though giving a silent demonstration that they were not prepared
to have anything to do with the affair. Eight foresters, whose statements tallied exactly, were questioned. On the evening of the tenth,
Brandis had ordered them out as guards, for he must have got wind
of the Blue-Smocks' plans, but he only spoke about this in a vague
way. They had gone out at two o'clock in the morning and come
across many signs of destruction which had put the head forester in
a bad temper, otherwise everything had been quiet. Towards four
o'clock Brandis had said: "They're making fools of us, let's go
home." When they had turned the corner of Breme Mountain and
the wind had changed direction at the same time, the felling of trees
in Maste Wood was heard distinctly and it was concluded from the
quick sequence of the strokes that the Blue-Smocks were at work.
Now they had taken counsel for a while as to whether it would be
feasible to attack the daring band with so much smaller numbers,
and then, without coming to a definite decision, they had moved
slowly towards the noise. Next followed the scene with Friedrich.
After Brandis had sent them on without instructions, they had

proceeded for a little while, and then, when they noticed that the noise, still some distance away, had ceased altogether, they halted to wait for the head forester. The delay had annoyed them, and after about ten minutes they had gone on until they reached the scene of destruction. All was now over, no further sound could be heard in the forest; of twenty felled trunks eight were still there, the others having already been taken away. It was inexplicable to them how this had been done, as no cart-tracks were to be found. At the same time the dryness of the season and the fact that the ground was strewn with pine needles prevented footmarks from being detected, although the soil around looked as though it had been stamped firm. As it was now considered useless to await the head forester, they went quickly to the other end of the forest, in the hope that they might catch a glimpse of the thieves. Here, on leaving the woods, the cord on one of forester's bottle had caught in the brambles, and, on looking round, he saw something glinting in the undergrowth; it was the belt buckle of the head forester, who was found lying behind the brambles, stretched out rigid, his right hand clutching his gun barrel, the other clenched and his forehead split open by an axe.

This was the statement of the foresters; now it was the turn of the peasants from whom, however, no information was to be obtained. Many said they had been still at home or busy elsewhere at about four o'clock and one and all claimed to have seen nothing. What was to be done? They were all people of good repute living in the district, and their negative testimony had to be accepted.

Friedrich was called in. He behaved in a manner no different from what was usual in him, showing neither nervousness nor impudence. The examination lasted quite a long time and the questions were sometimes phrased rather slyly; however, he answered them all openly and positively, describing the scene between the forester and himself fairly truthfully except for the end which he considered it wiser not to mention. His alibi at the time of the murder was easily proved. The forester's body was lying on the edge of Maste Wood, over three-quarters of an hour's walk away from the ravine in which he had spoken to Friedrich at about four o'clock and from which Friedrich had driven his herd into the village only ten minutes later. Everyone had seen this; all the peasants present were eager to testify to it; he had spoken to one and nodded in greeting to another.

The clerk sat in his place, ill-humored and embarrassed. Suddenly he reached behind him and placed something sparkling within Friedrich's vision. "Whose is this?"

Friedrich jumped back several paces. "Good Lord! I thought you meant to smash my skull in." His eyes had quickly alighted on the deadly instrument and seemed fixed momentarily on a spot where a splinter had been broken off from the handle. "I don't know," he said firmly. It was the axe which had been found wedged in the skull of the head forester.

"Look at it carefully," continued the clerk of the court.

Friedrich took it in his hand, looked at it, at both top and bottom, and turned it over. Laying it indifferently on the table, he then said, "It is an axe like any other." A blood stain was visible; he seemed to shudder, but he repeated once more in a determined tone: "I don't recognize it."

The clerk sighed with vexation, for he didn't know how to proceed and had only tried an experiment in the hope of discovering the murderer by surprise tactics. There was nothing for it but to end the inquiry.

For the sake of those readers who are perhaps eager to learn the outcome of this affair, I must mention that it was never cleared up, although much was done to that end and several other official inquiries succeeded this one. The Blue-Smocks seemed to have lost their courage through the stir that the incident caused and the stringent measures which followed; it was as though they had disappeared completely from this time forth, and although later many wood-stealers were caught, no reason was ever found for connecting any of them with the notorious band. For twenty years afterwards the axe lay as a useless piece of evidence in the legal archives, where it is probably still to be found, complete with rust marks. It would be unfair to leave the reader's curiosity unsatisfied in a tale of fiction, but all this really happened*—I cannot subtract or add anything.

Next Sunday Friedrich got up very early to go to confession. It was the Feast of the Assumption and the priests were already at their confessionals before dawn. After having dressed in the dark,

---

*Droste's source was the *History of an Algerian Slave* by August, Baron von Haxthausen, published in 1818.

Friedrich left the small closet furnished for him in Simon's house as noiselessly as possible. His prayer-book, he thought, must be lying on the window-sill in the kitchen, and he hoped to find it with the help of the feeble light from the moon; it was not there. In his search he cast his eyes all around and suddenly started. Simon was standing at the door, almost unclothed; his gaunt form, unkempt, tangled hair and the pallor of his face caused by the moonlight made him seem weirdly changed. "Is he sleepwalking, maybe?" Friedrich thought and remained quite still.

"Friedrich, where are you going?" whispered the old man.

"Oh, it's you, uncle? I'm going to confession."

"That's what I thought, go in God's name, but confess like a good Christian."

"So I will," said Friedrich.

"Remember the Ten Commandments; thou shalt not bear witness against thy neighbor."

"False witness!"

"No, none at all: you've got it wrong. Anyone who denounces somebody else in confession is unworthy to receive the sacrament."

Both remained silent. "Uncle, how do you come to speak of that?" Friedrich then said. "Your conscience is not clear, you have lied to me."

"I? What?"

"Where is your axe?"

"My axe? On the threshing floor."

"Did you give it a new handle? Where is the old one?"

"You'll find it in the woodshed this morning. Go," he continued, "I thought you were a man, but you're just an old woman who thinks the house is on fire when her stove is smoking. Look," he went on, "on my hope of salvation, I don't know any more of the affair than that doorpost. I was long home by then," he added.

Friedrich stood there dubious and uneasy. He would have given much to have been able to see his uncle's face. But while they had been whispering, the sky had clouded over.

"I am guilty of a great sin," Friedrich sighed, "in having sent him the wrong way—although—but I never thought of that, really not. Uncle, I have you to thank for a guilty conscience."

"Go on then, confess!" Simon whispered, his voice shaking,

"dishonor the sacrament by tale-bearing and put a spy on the track of poor wretches; if he doesn't talk straight away, he will soon find ways of snatching crusts of bread from their very mouths—go!"

Friedrich stood irresolute; he heard a slight sound. The clouds passed over, the moonlight again fell on the door: it was closed. Friedrich did not go to confession that morning.

Unfortunately the impression which this incident made on Friedrich died away all too quickly. Who can doubt that Simon did all he could to lead his adopted son along the paths that he took himself? And in Friedrich were characteristics which made this all too easy, frivolity, fiery temper and above all a boundless arrogance. Thus he did not always scorn mere outward pretense and then moved heaven and earth to escape possible shame by providing a foundation for his claims. His nature was not ignoble, but he accustomed himself to preferring inner to outer shame. One can only say that he got used to making a show, while his mother lived in want.

This unhappy change in his character developed, however, over several years, during which it was noticed that Margret spoke less and less of her son, gradually sinking into a state of neglect such as would earlier never have been considered possible. She became timid, dilatory, even untidy, and many thought that she was no longer right in the head. Friedrich became even louder in consequence; he never missed a fair or a wedding and, since his extremely touchy sense of honor did not allow him to ignore silent disapproval from others, he was as though always on the defensive, not so much to defy public opinion as to guide it along a path which suited him. In outer appearance he was neat, sober, apparently candid, but actually he was cunning, boastful and often brutal, a man who gave pleasure to nobody, least of all to his mother and who nevertheless had acquired through his dreaded boldness and still more dreaded malice a certain power in the village, as people came to realize that they could neither really fathom him nor foresee how he might turn out in the end. Only one lad in the village, Wilm Hülsmeyer, conscious of his power and easy circumstances, dared to oppose him; and since he could use words with greater skill than Friedrich and always knew how to make a joke out of it when a thrust went home, he was the only person whom Friedrich tried to avoid.

* * *

Four years went by; it was October, and the mild autumn of 1760, which filled all the barns with corn and all the cellars with wine, had also covered this corner of the earth with its riches, and one saw more drunken men, heard of more brawls and stupid pranks than ever. Merrymaking went on everywhere; a "long week-end" came into fashion and, as soon as anybody had a few shillings to spare, he wanted to have a wife as well who would help him to eat today and starve tomorrow. Now there took place in the village a fine, respectable wedding at which the guests could expect more than a badly tuned fiddle, a glass of brandy and the high spirits which they brought with them. Everybody had been up since an early hour, clothes were aired in front of every door and the village had looked like an old-clothes shop all day long. Since many people from other parts were expected, all the inhabitants wanted to uphold the honor of their village.

It was seven in the evening and the celebrations were in full swing; shouts of merriment and laughter everywhere, the low-ceilinged rooms crammed to suffocation with figures in blue, red, and yellow, like cattle-pens into which too large a herd has been huddled. On the threshing-floor there was dancing, that is, whoever had captured two feet of space for himself, whirled around on it and tried by shrieking to make up for lack of movement. The orchestra was brilliant, the first fiddle predominating as a recognized virtuoso, the second and a double-bass with three strings played *ad lib.* by amateurs; there was brandy and coffee in abundance, all the guests were dripping with sweat, in short it was a memorable occasion. Friedrich swaggered around like a peacock in his new sky-blue coat and staked his claim as the local dandy. When the squire and his family also arrived, he was sitting bolt upright behind the double-bass, playing on the lowest string with great vigor and much dignity. "Johannes!" he shouted imperiously and his protégé came forward from the dance floor where he too had tried to fling about his clumsy legs and to whoop. Friedrich handed him the bow and, indicating his desire by a proud movement of his head, he joined the dancers. "Now, you fiddlers, play the 'Monk of Istrup'!"* The favorite dance was played, and Friedrich made such leaps, in full view of his master, that the cows close by drew in their horns, lowing

---

*A peasant dance, named for the Westphalian town of Istrup.

loudly and rattling their chains. High above the others Friedrich's fair head shot up and down like a pike turning somersaults in the water; from every corner there came the shrieking of girls to whom he, as he tossed his head, paid homage by flicking his long flaxen hair in their faces.

"That will do now!" he said at last and, dripping with sweat, went over to the refreshment table; "long live our gracious Lord and Lady and all the highborn princes and princesses and if anyone won't drink to them, I'll smack his ears till he hears the angels singing!" A loud cheer greeted the gallant toast, and Friedrich made his bow. "Don't take offense, Lord and Lady, for we are only simple peasants!" At this moment there arose a tumult at the other end of the threshing floor, shouts, scolding, laughter all mingling in confusion. "Butter thief, butter thief!" cried a few of the children and somebody made his way or rather was pushed through the crowd—Johannes Niemand, cowering and struggling for all he was worth to reach the exit.

"What is it? What's Johannes done?" shouted Friedrich imperiously.

"You'll see that soon enough," panted an old woman, holding an apron and a dishcloth. What a disgrace! Johannes, poor devil, who had to be content with the very worst at home, had tried to help himself to half a pound of butter to provide for hard times to come; forgetting that he had hidden it in his pocket after having wrapped it neatly in his handkerchief, he had stood in front of the kitchen fire and now he was put to shame by the fat running down his coat tails. There was a general uproar; the girls jumped away, for fear of soiling their dresses, or pushed the offender forwards. Others made room for him, from pity as well as foresight. Friedrich, however, moved towards him: "You miserable hound!" he cried, slapped his patient protégé hard in the face several times, pushed him towards the door and gave him a good kick from behind to help him on his way.

He returned crestfallen; his dignity had been injured, the laughter he heard on all sides cut him to the quick, and although he tried to get back into his stride with a valiant whoop, it did not work any longer. He was about to take refuge again behind the double-bass, but first he sought to create a sensation by taking out his silver pocket watch, at that time a rare and costly adornment. "It's nearly ten," he said. "Now for the bridal minuet! I'll play for it."

"A fine-looking watch!" said the swineherd, thrusting his face forward in respectful curiosity.

"What did it cost?" asked Wilm Hülsmeyer, Friedrich's rival.

"Do you want to pay for it?" asked Friedrich.

"Have *you* paid for it?" Wilm answered.

Friedrich gave him a proud look and reached in silent majesty for the fiddle-bow.

"Well," said Hülsmeyer, "it's happened before. You know very well, Franz Ebel had a fine watch too, before Aaron the Jew took it off him again."

Friedrich did not answer but signed proudly to the first violin and they began to play with all their might.

In the meantime the squire and his family had entered the room where women from the neighborhood had placed the head-band round the bride's forehead as a symbol of her married state. The young girl wept a good deal, partly because the custom required it, partly from genuine anxiety. She was to take charge of a disorderly household under the supervision of an ill-humored old man whom she was supposed to love into the bargain. He stood beside her, quite unlike the bridegroom of the Song of Solomon who "cometh into the room like the morning sun." "You've cried enough now," he said crossly. "Remember that I'm making you happy, not you me!" She looked humbly up at him and vaguely felt that he was right. The ceremony was at an end; the young bride had drunk her husband's health, young wags had followed the old custom of looking through the tripod to see if her head-band was straight and they all jostled their way back to the threshing-floor from which noise and ceaseless peals of laughter could be heard. Friedrich was no longer there. He had been thoroughly, even intolerably discredited, when Aaron the Jew, a butcher and occasional second-hand dealer from the town near by, had suddenly appeared and, after a short unsatisfactory exchange of words, had loudly pressed him, in the presence of all the guests, to pay thirty shillings for a watch already delivered to him on the previous Easter. Friedrich had gone away seeming utterly crushed, followed by the Jew who kept on shouting: "Alas! Why didn't I listen to sensible people! Didn't they tell me a hundred times that you wore all you had on your back and hadn't a crust of bread in the larder!" The threshing-floor rocked with laughter; many guests had pushed their way out into the yard in pursuit. "Get hold of the Jew! He'll outweigh a pig, you'll see!" some shouted, while others had grown serious. "Friedrich looked as white as a sheet," said an old woman, and the crowd parted as the squire's carriage turned into the yard.

Herr von S. was in an ill humor on the way home, as invariably happened when his wish to maintain his popularity made him attend such festivities. He was gazing silently out of the carriage. "What are those two figures?" he indicated two shadowlike forms, running like ostriches in front of the carriage. Now they slipped into the manor house. "So we have the ghosts of a couple of pigs from our own sty as well!" sighed Herr von S. Having arrived home, he found the large hall filled with all the servants, surrounding two farm hands, who had collapsed pale and breathless on the stairs. They said they had been pursued by the spirit of old Mergel when they were returning home through Brede Wood. At first there had been a rustling and crackling on the heights above them, after that a rattling high up in the air like two sticks struck together, then suddenly a shriek and the words, heard quite distinctly: "Have mercy on my poor soul!" coming down from far above. One claimed to have also seen glittering eyes sparkling through the branches and both had run as fast as their legs would carry them.

"Rubbish!" said the squire irritably and went to his room to change his clothes. Next morning the fountain in the garden would not work and it was found that somebody had moved a pipe, apparently to look for the head of a horse which had been buried there many years before—this was reckoned to be a guaranteed protection against witches and apparitions. "Hm," said the squire, "what the rascals don't steal, the fools spoil."

Three days later a fearful storm was raging. It was midnight, but everyone at the manor house was up. The squire was standing at the window, looking anxiously into the darkness, across his fields. The leaves and branches were flying past the window panes; sometimes a tile came down and smashed on the paved courtyard.

"Terrible weather!" said Herr von S.

His wife looked frightened. "Has somebody really seen to the fire?" she said; "Gretchen, have another look at it, it's best to put it out altogether. Come, let us say the Gospel of St. John as a prayer."

All knelt down and the lady of the house began: "In the beginning

was the Word and the Word was with God, and God was the Word."
A fearful clap of thunder sounded. Everyone shrank; then there was
a terrible screaming and tumult drawing ever nearer. "What, in
God's name? Is the house on fire?" cried Frau von S. and buried her
face in a chair. The door was flung open and the wife of Aaron the
Jew rushed in, pale as death, her hair wind-swept about her head,
dripping with rain. She threw herself on her knees before the squire.
"Justice!" she cried, "Justice! my husband has been killed!" and she
collapsed unconscious.

It was only too true, and the investigation which followed proved
that Aaron the Jew had died from a single blow on the temple with a
blunt instrument, probably a stick. On the left temple was a bruise,
but no other injury. The statements of the Jew's wife and her servant
Samuel ran as follows: three days before, Aaron had gone out in the
afternoon in order to buy cattle, and had said at the time that he
would probably be away overnight, as some long outstanding debts
in B. and S. had to be collected. He said that he would stay the night
in B. with the butcher Salomon. When he had not returned home on
the following day, his wife had become very anxious and had finally
set out too look for him on that day at three o'clock in the afternoon, accompanied by her servant and the big butcher's dog. At
Salomon's nobody knew where Aaron was, he had not been there at
all. Now they had gone to all the peasants with whom they knew
Aaron to have contemplated business deals. Only two had seen him,
and these actually on the same day on which he had left. Meanwhile
it had grown very late. The woman's apprehension drove her home,
for she nourished a faint hope of meeting him there. And so they
had been overtaken in Brede Wood by the thunderstorm and had
sought shelter under a large beech tree standing on the mountain
side; while they were there, the dog had been sniffing about in a
strange way likely to arouse attention and finally, ignoring all calls,
had run away in the forest. Then suddenly during a flash of lightning
the woman saw something white beside her on the moss. It was her
husband's stick; almost at the same moment the dog broke through
a thicket, carrying something in its mouth—her husband's shoe.
Soon they found the corpse of the Jew in a ditch filled with dead
leaves. This was the statement by the servant, supported only in a
general way by the wife's evidence; her excessive excitement had

abated and she now seemed half bewildered, or rather in a stupor. "An eye for an eye, a tooth for a tooth!" These were the only words that she sometimes muttered.

That same night the police were summoned to arrest Friedrich. A warrant was not required, for Herr von S. himself had witnessed a scene which inevitably threw the strongest suspicion on Friedrich. In addition there was the ghost story of that evening, the knocking together of sticks in Brede Wood, the cry from above. Since the clerk was absent just then, Herr von S. directed the proceedings, and indeed with greater speed than would otherwise have been the case. However, dawn had already begun to break before the police had surrounded, as quietly as possible, poor Margret's home. The squire himself knocked at the door, and scarcely a minute elapsed before it was opened and Margret appeared, fully dressed. Herr von S. started back; because of her deathly pallor and stony expression, he almost failed to recognize her.

"Where is Friedrich?" he asked in an unsteady voice.

"Look for him," she said and sat down on a chair.

The squire still hesitated for a moment. Then he said roughly, "Come in, come in! What are we waiting for?"

They entered Friedrich's room. He was not there, but his bed was still warm. They went up into the loft, down into the cellar, poked about in the straw, looked behind every barrel, even in the baking oven; he was not there. Some men went into the garden, looked behind the fence and up into the apple trees; he was not to be found.

"He's got clean away!" said the squire with very mixed feelings; the sight of the old woman had a powerful effect on him. "Hand over the key to that chest." Margret did not answer. "Hand over the key!" the squire repeated and now he noticed for the first time that the key was in the lock. The contents of the chest came to light; the good Sunday clothes of the fugitive and the shabby finery of his mother; then two shrouds with black ribbons, one for a man, the other for a woman. Herr von S. was deeply moved. Right at the bottom of the trunk lay the silver watch and some documents in a very legible hand, one of them signed by a man strongly suspected of being connected with the timber thieves. Herr von S. took them away to look through, and they left the house without Margret giving any further sign of life, except that she ceaselessly gnawed at her lips and blinked her eyes.

Arriving at the manor house, the squire found the clerk, who had already come home on the previous evening and now said he had slept through the whole affair, since his Lordship had not sent for him.

"You always come too late," said Herr von S. irritably. "Wasn't there some old woman in the village who told your maid about it? And why didn't someone wake you then?"

"Your Lordship," replied Kapp, "it is true that my Anne Marie heard of the affair about an hour before I did, but she knew that you were conducting the proceedings yourself and also," he added with a plaintive expression, "that I was so dog-tired!"

"A fine police force!" the squire muttered, "every old hag in the village knows all about things which should be kept secret." Then he continued angrily: "He'd have to be a really stupid devil of a criminal to get caught!"

Both were silent for a while. "My driver had lost his way in the dark," the clerk began again. "We stopped for over an hour in the forest; there was a terrific storm, and I thought the wind would blow the carriage over. At last, when the rain grew less heavy, we set out again towards Zelle Field, hoping for the best, but without being able to see a hand's breadth in front of us. Then the driver said: 'If only we don't get too near to the stone-quarries!' I was frightened myself; I told him to stop and struck a light in order, at least, to draw comfort from my pipe. Suddenly we heard, quite close to us, directly beneath us, the clock striking. Your lordship will understand that I was frightened to death. I jumped out of the carriage, for one can trust one's own legs but not those of a horse. And so I stood, in mud and rain, without moving, until, thank God, it soon began to get light. And where had we halted? Close to Heerse valley, with the tower of Heerse church directly below us. If we had gone on twenty paces, we would both have been dead men."

"That was certainly no joke," replied the squire, somewhat mollified.

Meanwhile he had looked through the papers he had taken away with him. There were letters, mostly from moneylenders demanding payment of sums borrowed. "I would never have thought," he murmured, "that the Mergels were so up to their necks in trouble."

"Yes, and that it should come to light in this way," replied Kapp, "will be no small annoyance for Frau Margret."

"Good gracious, she's not thinking of that now!" With these words the squire stood up and left the room in order to make the legal post-mortem examination with Kapp. The investigation was short, and it was established that death had been caused by violence and that the probable culprit had fled; the evidence against him had been indeed incriminating, but not conclusive without personal confession, though his flight was certainly very suspicious. Thus the legal proceedings had to be brought to a close without a satisfactory outcome.

The Jews in the neighborhood had shown great interest in the affair. The house of the widow was never empty of mourners and people offering advice and help. As long as one could remember so many Jews had not been seen together in L. Embittered by the murder of their brother Jew, they had spared neither effort nor money to track down the criminal. It was even said that one of them, commonly known as Joel the Shark, had promised one of his customers who owed him several hundreds and whom he considered to be a particularly sly fellow, remission of the whole sum in return for his help in getting Mergel arrested; for it was generally believed among the Jews that the murderer could only have escaped with generous assistance and was probably still in the district. However, when all this was of no avail and the legal inquiry had been declared closed, there appeared on the following morning at the manor house a number of the most respected Israelites to make a business proposition to his Lordship. The object of this was the beech, under which Aaron's staff had been found and where the murder had probably been committed.

"Do you want to fell it, just as it is, in full leaf?" asked the squire.

"No, your Lordship, it must stand in winter and summer alike, as long as a splinter of it remains."

"But whenever I have the forest felled, the beech will hinder the growth of the saplings."

"Yes, but we don't want it at the market price."

They offered fifty pounds for it. The bargain was concluded and all foresters given strict orders not to damage the Jew's beech in any way. Soon after about sixty Jews, led by their rabbi, were to be seen walking in procession to Brede Wood, all of them silent and with their eyes on the ground. They remained over an hour in the forest and then returned, in the same grave and solemn manner, passing through the village to Zelle Field, where they dispersed. Next morning these characters were to be seen carved on the beech with an axe:

אָם תַּעֲבוֹר בַּמָּקוֹם הַזֶּה יִפְגַּע בְּךָ כַּאֲשֶׁר אַתָּה עוֹשֶׂה לִי*

And where was Friedrich? Doubtless far away, far enough to be beyond the reach of the short arms of such an impotent police force. Out of sight, out of mind—he was soon forgotten. Uncle Simon seldom spoke of him and then harshly; the Jew's widow finally took solace in another husband. Only poor Margret remained uncomforted.

About six months later, the squire was reading, in the presence of the clerk, some letters he had just received. "Strange, most peculiar!" he said. "Just think, Kapp, perhaps Mergel is innocent of the murder after all. The president of the court at P. has just written to me: *'Le vrai n'est pas toujours vraisemblable;*† I often find that true in my profession and had another example of it recently. Do you know that your faithful servant Friedrich Mergel is as unlikely to have killed the Jew as you or I? Unfortunately proof is lacking, but it is very probable that he did not. A member of the Schlemming gang (most of which, by the way, we now have under lock and key) named Rag-and-bone Moses stated when last examined that he repented in particular his murder of a fellow Jew Aaron. He had killed him in the forest and yet only found sixpence on him. Unhappily the proceedings were interrupted and while we were at table the dog of a Jew hanged himself with his garter. What do you make of it? It is true that Aaron is a common name, etc., etc.' "

"What do you make of it?" repeated the squire; "and why then did the dolt of a boy run away?"

The clerk reflected. "Well, perhaps because of timber thieving which we were looking into just then. Isn't it often said: the wicked

---

*The Hebrew inscription was faulty in the original printing of the text. It is now believed that the fifth word should be יִפְגַּע and the ninth עֹשִׂית. Transliterated the inscription would then read: *im ta'abor bammaqom hazzeh yifga bekha ka'asher attah asisa li.* The sense is given in the last sentence of the novella. An inscription carved onto a tree would naturally not have vowel points.

†"The truth is not always probable."

runs from his own shadow? Mergel's conscience was black enough, even without this stain."

With that they let the matter rest. Friedrich had gone, disappeared and—with him on the same day—Johannes Niemand, the wretched Johannes, whom nobody would miss.

Twenty-eight years had elapsed, a very long time, almost half a human life-span; the squire had grown very old and gray, his good-tempered clerk Kapp had long been buried. Men, animals and plants had come to life, matured and passed away, only the manor house of B., as gray and stately as ever, looked down on the cottages, which, like old consumptive people, seemed always on the point of collapsing and yet continued to stand. It was Christmas Eve, 1788. Snowdrifts to a depth of nearly twelve feet lay on the roads and a penetrating air frost covered the window-panes in heated rooms with rime. Midnight was near, yet faint little lights glimmered everywhere from among the mounds of snow and in each house the inhabitants knelt to await in prayer the coming of Christmas, as is, or was then at least, the custom in Catholic countries. Just then a figure was to be observed moving slowly down to the village from Brede Heights; the traveller seemed very exhausted or ill; he uttered deep groans, and dragged himself laboriously through the snow.

Halfway down the slope he stopped, leaned on his crook and stared fixedly at the points of light. It was so quiet everywhere, so cold and dead, it made one think of will-o'-the-wisps in church-yards. Now the clock in the tower struck twelve; the last stroke rumbled and died away slowly, in the nearest house some people began to sing quietly and the hymn, swelling from house to house, spread through the whole village:

> This day is born an infant rare,
> To us it hath befell,
> Of virgin pure, the tidings fair
> Rejoicing all men tell.
> And had the childling been not born,
> We all would sooth have been forlorn:
> His birth is our salvation.
> O Jesu, dearest Jesu, Lord
> Once born as Man, by us adored,
> Redeem us from damnation.

The man on the slope had sunk to his knees and with trembling voice was trying to join in the singing, but the result was only a loud sobbing, as his great, scalding tears fell on the snow. In a low voice he accompanied with a prayer the singing of the second verse, then the third and fourth verses too. The carol came to an end and the lights in the houses were moved about, whereupon the man rose painfully to his feet and crept down to the village. Panting, he toiled on his way past several houses before stopping at one and knocking softly on the door.

"What's that then?" said a woman from within; "the door rattles and yet the wind's not blowing."

He knocked harder. "For Heaven's sake let in a poor half-frozen creature, returned from Turkish slavery!"

There was whispering in the kitchen.

"Go to the inn," answered another voice; "the fifth house from here!"

"For God's sake, let me in! I have no money."

After some hesitation, the door was opened and a man shone the lamp outside. "Very well, come in," he said, "you won't cut our throats."

Besides the man there were also in the kitchen a middle-aged woman, her old mother and five children. They all crowded round the stranger as he entered and inspected him with shy curiosity. He was a wretched figure with a crooked neck, a bent back, his whole frame broken and feeble, long, snow-white hair hanging round a face disfigured by years of suffering. The woman went silently to the hearth and put a few more faggots on the fire. "We cannot give you a bed," she said, "but I'll make you a good shakedown here; you must manage as best you can."

"God bless you!" replied the stranger, "I am used to much worse."

The homecomer was recognized as Johannes Niemand, and he himself confirmed that he was the same person who had once fled with Friedrich Mergel.

The following day the village was full of the adventures of one who had been missing for so long. Everybody wanted to see the man from Turkey, and many seemed almost astonished that he still looked like other people. Of course the young ones could not remember him but the old made out his features well enough, deplorably distorted as they were.

"Johannes, Johannes, how gray you've become!" said an old woman. "And where did you get your crooked neck?"

"From carrying wood and water as a slave," he replied.

"And what became of Mergel? You ran away together, didn't you?"

"Yes, we did; but I don't know where he is, we were parted. If you think of him, pray for him," he added, "he will certainly need your prayers."

He was asked why Friedrich ran away, since he didn't kill the Jew. "Didn't?" said Johannes and listened intently to the story which the squire had spread conscientiously to wipe the stain from Mergel's name. "So it was all for nothing," he said thoughtfully. "So much endured all for nothing!" He sighed deeply and now it was his turn to ask many questions. Simon had died long ago, but not before he had become completely impoverished through lawsuits and debtors whom he could not sue because, so it was said, his business with them had been of a shady nature. He had finally eaten the bread of a beggar and died on a pile of straw in a shed which was not his own. Margret had lived longer, but in complete apathy. As she let everything given to her go to rack and ruin, the village people had soon tired of helping, for it is natural to Man to abandon those who are actually the most helpless, those cases where assistance does not have a lasting effect but is constantly needed. Nevertheless she had not suffered actual want; the squire's family took good care of her, sending her food every day and arranging for medical treatment when her ailing health had declined to complete emaciation. In her house there now lived the son of the former swineherd who had so much admired Friedrich's watch on that unfortunate evening. "All gone, all dead!" sighed Johannes.

In the evening, when darkness had fallen and the moon was shining, he was seen hobbling about the churchyard in the snow; although he did not go to any grave to offer a prayer, he seemed to stare at some of them from a distance; and that was how Brandis the forester found him. Brandis, the son of the murdered man, had been sent by the squire to fetch him to the manor house.

Entering the sitting-room, he gazed around shyly, as though dazzled by the light. The Baron was sitting in his armchair, much shrivelled by age but with the same bright eyes and little red cap on his head that he had twenty-eight years before; beside him Johannes saw her Ladyship who had also grown old, very old.

"Now, Johannes," said the squire, "give us a proper account of your adventures. But really," examining him through his spectacles, "you must have had a bad time of it in Turkey!"

Johannes began to relate how Mergel had called him away from the cattle he was minding that night and told him he must go with him.

"But why did the stupid boy run away then? You know that he was innocent?"

Johannes looked down in front of him: "I don't know exactly, I think it was something to do with timber-thieving. Simon was mixed up in all kinds of deals. I wasn't told about them, but I don't think that things were as they should be."

"What did Friedrich say to you?"

"Nothing, except that we would have to run for it, as they were after us. So we ran as far as Heerse, it was still dark when we got there and we hid behind the big cross in the churchyard until it became somewhat lighter, for we were afraid of falling into the stone-quarries at Zelle Field; when we had sat there for a while, we suddenly heard snorting and stamping above us and saw long streaks of fire in the air just over Heerse church-tower. We jumped up and ran as hard as we could straight ahead, hoping for the best, and as dawn broke, we were really on the right road to P."

Johannes still seemed to shudder at the memory and the squire thought of his dead clerk Kapp and his adventure on the slope above Heerse. "Strange!" he said with a laugh, "you were so close to one another, but go on."

Now Johannes related how they had gone through P. and over the frontier without mishap. From there they had made their way as journeying apprentices to Freiburg in Breisgau. "I had my bread-bag with me and Friedrich a little bundle as well, so that people believed our story," he said.

In Freiburg they had taken service with the Austrians,* who had not wanted Johannes, but Friedrich had insisted. And so he was sent

---

*Freiburg im Breisgau, now in southwestern Germany, was at the time of the story an Austrian possession.

to the baggage train. "We remained for the winter in Freiburg and had quite an easy time, I too, because Friedrich often reminded me of things and helped me if I did anything wrong. In the spring we had to march to Hungary and in the autumn the war with the Turks started. I can't tell you much about it, for I was captured in the first battle and have been since then in Turkish slavery for twenty-six years!"

"Good heavens, that's terrible!" said Fran von S.

"Bad enough, the Turks don't treat us Christians any better than dogs; the worst was that my strength gave way because of the hard work; also as I grew older, I was still expected to do as much as years before."

He was silent for a while. "Yes," he then said, "it was beyond human strength and patience; I too could not endure it. From there I came on board a Dutch ship."

"How did you get there?" asked the squire.

"They fished me out of the Bosphorus," replied Johannes. The Baron looked at him disapprovingly and then held up a warning finger, but Johannes went on with his story. He did not have a much better time of it on the ship. An epidemic of scurvy set in and all those who were not desperately ill had to take on more than their usual work; the rope's end ruled as harshly as the Turkish whip. "Finally," he concluded, "when we came to Holland, to Amsterdam, I was released because I couldn't be used. The merchant who owned the ship took pity on me and wanted to make me his porter, but"— he shook his head—"I preferred to beg my way here."

"That was silly enough of you," said the squire.

Johannes sighed deeply: "O sir, I had to spend my life amongst Turks and heretics; may I not at least lie in a Catholic churchyard?"

The squire had taken out his purse: "There you are, Johannes, go now and come back again soon. You must tell me more about it, today your story was somewhat confused. You're still very tired, aren't you?"

"Very tired," Johannes replied, pointing to his forehead, "and my thoughts are sometimes so queer, I can't rightly say why."

"I know," said the Baron, "that started a long time ago. Now go! The Hülsmeyers will, I hope, keep you for the night, come again tomorrow."

Herr von S. had the deepest sympathy with the poor fellow,

discussing with his family until the following day where Johannes might find lodgings. They decided that he was to eat daily at the manor house and that ways and means of clothing him could be found.

"Sir," said Johannes, "I can still do something or other; I can make wooden spoons and you can use me as a messenger."

Herr von S. shook his head sympathetically: "That wouldn't work out very well."

"O yes it would, sir, once I get started—I can't go fast but I get there, and it won't be as hard for me as one might think."

"Well," said the Baron doubtfully, "do you want to try it? Here is a letter to go to P. There is no particular hurry."

On the following day Johannes moved into his little room in the house of a widow in the village. He carved spoons, ate at the manor house and ran errands for his Lordship. On the whole he had a tolerable time of it, the squire and his family were very kind and Herr von S. often talked long with him about Turkey, service in the Austrian army and the sea.

"Johannes could tell much," he said to his wife, "if only he weren't such a downright simpleton."

"More melancholic than simple," she replied. "I'm always afraid he'll go really mad one day."

"Don't worry!" answered the Baron, "he has been a simpleton all his life, and simple people never go mad."

After some time Johannes was absent on an errand far longer than was expected. The warm-hearted wife of the squire was very concerned for him and was already about to send out people to look for him, when she heard him hobble up the stairs.

"You were away a long time, Johannes," she said, "I thought you had lost your way in Brede Wood."

"I went through Pine Valley."

"But that's a long way round, why didn't you go through Brede Wood?"

He looked up at her sadly: "People told me the wood had been felled, and that now there are so many cross-paths, so I was afraid I wouldn't get out again. I'm getting old and silly," he added slowly.

"Did you see," said Frau von S. to her husband afterwards, "how queer his eyes were, he didn't look us in the face. I tell you, Ernst, he'll come to a sad end."

Meanwhile September drew near. The fields were bare, the leaves began to fall, and many a consumptive felt the shears of fate at his life-thread. Johannes, too, seemed to suffer under the influence of the approaching equinox; those who saw him in those days say he looked strangely agitated and talked incessantly to himself in a soft voice (he sometimes did this in any case, but not often). Finally he failed to come home one evening. It was thought that the squire or his wife had sent him on an errand, but he did not return on the second day either and by the third his landlady was worried. She went to the manor house to make inquiries. "No, indeed," said the squire, "I know nothing of his whereabouts, but call the gamekeeper and the forester's son Wilhelm quickly! If the poor cripple has fallen, even into a dry ditch, he won't be able to get out again," he added with feeling. "Who knows whether he hasn't broken one of his crooked legs. Take the hounds with you," he shouted to the gamekeepers as they moved off, "and above all, look in the ditches— the quarries!" he shouted louder.

The gamekeepers returned home some hours later, having found no trace of Johannes. Herr von S. was in a state of great alarm: "To think that he would just have to lie like a log and be unable to help himself! But he may be still alive—a man can hold out without food for three days." He set out himself, inquiries were made at every house, horns were blown everywhere, men shouted, hounds were driven on to search—in vain! A child had seen him sitting at the edge of Brede Wood, whittling a spoon: "But he cut it right in two," said the little girl. That had been two days before. In the afternoon another clue was found; again it was a child who noticed him on the other side of the wood, where he had been sitting in the bushes, his face on his knees, as though he were sleeping. That had been on the day before. It seemed that he had been wandering the whole time near Brede Wood.

"If only the damned bushes weren't so thick! Nobody can get through them," said the squire. The hounds were driven among the young trees; there was blowing of horns and hallooing, but eventually they all returned home out of spirits, after having made sure that the animals had combed through the whole wood.

"Don't give up! Don't give up!" begged Frau von S.; "better a few steps for nothing than that something should be overlooked."

The Baron was almost as worried as she. His alarm even drove him to visit Johannes' room, although he was certain of not finding him there. He had his room unlocked. His bed stood unmade, as he had left it; his good coat, which her Ladyship had had made for him out of the old hunting-jacket of her husband was hanging near by; on the table lay a bowl, six new wooden spoons and a box. The squire opened it; five pennies lay in it, wrapped neatly in paper, and four silver waistcoat buttons, which the squire looked at with interest. "A souvenir from Mergel," he murmured and went out, for he felt oppressed in the close atmosphere of the tiny closet. The investigations were continued till there was no doubt that Johannes was no longer in the district, not alive, at least. So he had disappeared a second time—would he be found again?—perhaps only after many years his bones would be discovered in a dry ditch? There was little hope of seeing him again alive, certainly not if he were absent for another twenty-eight years.

A fortnight later young Brandis was returning home one morning from an inspection of his district and his path took him through Brede Wood. It was an unusually warm day for the time of year, the air seemed to quiver, not a bird was singing, only the ravens croaked wearily from the branches and turned their gaping beaks towards the air. Brandis was very tired. Sometimes he took off his cap, well heated by the sun, sometimes he put it on again. It was all equally unbearable, and pushing one's way through the young trees, which grew knee high, very laborious. All around there was no tree except the Jew's Beech. He made for it as quickly as he could and dropped under it, dead tired, onto the shady moss. The coolness penetrated his limbs so pleasantly that he closed his eyes. "Disgusting toadstools!" he muttered, half-asleep. For there is in that district a type of very succulent toadstool which only grows for a few days and then collapses in decay emitting an intolerable smell. Brandis thought that he scented such unpleasant neighbors, he turned from side to side once or twice, but could not bring himself to get up; meanwhile his dog was jumping about, scratching at the trunk of the tree and barking upwards. "What is it then, Bello, a cat?" Brandis murmured. He half-opened his eyelids and the Jew's inscription, very much deformed by bark growth, but still quite legible, caught his attention. He shut his eyes again; the dog went on barking and finally put its cold nose to the face of its master. "Leave me in peace! What's the matter then?" At this point Brandis, as he lay on his back, looked upwards, then jumped up with a start and ran out into the bushes like one possessed. Pale as death he arrived at the manor house with the news that there was a man hanging in the Jew's Beech—he had seen the legs dangling just above his head.

"And you didn't cut him down, you fool?" cried the Baron.

"Sir," panted Brandis, "if your Lordship had been there, you would have known that the man was no longer alive. I thought at first, it was the toadstools!"

Nevertheless the squire urged his men to be quick and accompanied them himself.

They had arrived under the beech. "I can't see anything," said Herr von S.

"You must stand here to see him, just here!"

It was just as Brandis had said: the squire recognized his own worn-out shoes. "My God, it's Johannes! Place the ladder against the tree—that's right—now bring him down—gently, gently! Don't let him fall! Good heavens, the worms are already at work! But undo the noose and the cravat, just the same." A broad scar came into view; the squire started back. "Good gracious!" he said; he bent over the corpse again, looked at the scar intently and fell silent for a moment, deeply shaken. Then he turned to the foresters. "It is not right that the innocent should suffer for the guilty; tell everybody that this man"—he pointed to the body—"was Friedrich Mergel." The corpse was buried in the carrion pit.

As far as all the main features are concerned, this really happened as I have related in September, 1789.* The Hebrew inscription on the tree means:

"If thou drawest nigh unto this place, it will befall thee as thou didst unto me."

Translated by Lionel and Doris Thomas

---

*Droste's original text has "September 1788." This must be a slip of the pen, for Mergel (if that is who it is) has been said to have returned at Christmas, 1788 (p. 124). Modern texts, like this translation, emend the error.

The Black Spider

Jeremias Gotthelf

The sun rose over the hills, shone with clear majesty down into a friendly, narrow valley and awakened to joyful consciousness the beings who are created to enjoy the sunlight of their life. From the sun-gilded forest's edge the thrush burst forth in her morning song, while between sparkling flowers in dew-laden grass the yearning quail could be heard joining in with its lovesong; above dark pine tops eager crows were performing their nuptial dance or cawing delicate cradle-songs over the thorny beds of their fledgeless young.

In the middle of the sun-drenched hillside nature had placed a fertile, sheltered, level piece of ground; here stood a fine house, stately and shining, surrounded by a splendid orchard, where a few tall apple trees were still displaying their finery of late blossom; the luxuriant grass, which was watered by the fountain near the house, was in part still standing, though some of it had already found its way to the fodder-store. About the house there lay a Sunday brightness which was not of the type that can be produced on a Saturday evening in the half-light with a few sweeps of the broom, but which rather testified to a valuable heritage of traditional cleanliness which has to be cherished daily, like a family's reputation, tarnished as this may become in one single hour by marks that remain, like bloodstains, indelible from generation to generation, making a mockery of all attempts to whitewash them.

Not for nothing did the earth built by God's hand and the house built by man's hand gleam in purest adornment; today a star in the blue sky, a festal holiday, shone forth upon them both. It was the day on which the Son had returned to the Father to bear witness that the heavenly ladder is still standing, where angels go up and down, and the soul of man too, when it wrenches itself from the body, that is, if its salvation and purpose have been with the Father above and not here below on earth; it was the day on which the whole plant world grows closer towards heaven, blooming in luxuriant plenty as an annually recurring symbol to man of his own destiny. Over the hills came a wonderful sound; no one knew where it came from, it sounded as if from all sides; it came from the churches in the far valleys beyond; from there the bells were bringing the message that God's temples are open to all whose hearts are open to the voice of their God.

Around the fine house there was lively movement. Near the fountain horses were being combed with special care, dignified matrons, with their spirited colts darting around them; in the broad trough cows were quenching their thirst, looking about them in a comfortable manner, and twice the farmer's lad had to use shovel and broom because he had not removed the traces of their well-being cleanly enough. Well-set maids were vigorously washing their ruddy faces with a handy facecloth, while their hair was twisted into two bunches over their ears; or with bustling industry they were carrying water through the open door; and in mighty puffs a dark column of smoke from the short chimney rose straight and high, up into the clear air.

Slowly the grandfather, a bent figure, was walking with his stick round the outside of the house, watching silently the doings of the farm-servants and the maids; now he would stroke one of the horses, or again restrain a cow in her clumsy playfulness, or point out to the careless farmer's boy wisps of straw still lying forgotten here and there, while taking his flint and steel assiduously out of the deep pocket of his long waistcoat in order to light his pipe again which he enjoyed so much in the morning in spite of the fact that it did not draw well.

The grandmother was sitting on a clean-swept bench in front of the house near the door, cutting fine bread into a large basin, every piece sliced thin and just the right size, not carelessly as cooks or maids would do it, who often hack off pieces big enough to choke a whale. Proud, well-fed hens and beautiful doves were quarrelling over the crumbs at her feet, and if a shy little dove did not get its share, the grandmother threw it a piece all to itself, consoling it with friendly words for the want of sense and the impetuosity of the others.

Inside in the big, clean kitchen a huge fire of pine wood was crackling, in a big pan could be heard the popping of coffee beans which a stately-looking woman was stirring around with a wooden ladle, while nearby the coffee-mill was grinding between the knees of a freshly washed maid; but standing by the open door of the living-room was a beautiful, rather pale woman with an open coffee-sack in her hand, and she said, "Look, midwife, don't roast the coffee so black today, or else they might think I wanted to be stingy with it. The godfather's wife is really awfully suspicious and always makes the worst of everything anybody does. Half a pound or so is neither here nor there on a day like this. Oh, and don't forget to have the mulled wine ready at the right time. Grandfather wouldn't think it was a christening if we didn't set the godparents up with some mulled wine before they went to church. Don't be stingy about what's to go in it, do you hear? Over there in the dish on the kitchen-dresser you'll find saffron and cinnamon, the sugar's on the table here, and take at least half as much wine again as you think is enough; at a christening there's never any need to worry that things won't get used up."

We hear that there is to be a christening in the house today, and the midwife delivers the food and drink as cleverly as she delivered the baby at an earlier stage, but she will have to hurry if she is to be ready in time and to cook at the simple fireplace everything demanded by custom.

A firmly built man came up from the cellar with a mighty piece of cheese in his hand, picked up from the gleaming kitchen-dresser the first plate he could find, placed the cheese on it and was going to carry it into the living-room to put on the brown walnut table. "But Benz, Benz," the beautiful, pale woman exclaimed, "how they'd laugh, if we couldn't find a better plate than this at the christening!" And she went to the gleaming cherrywood china-cupboard where the proud ornaments of the house were displayed behind the glass windows. There she took up a beautiful blue-rimmed plate with a great bunch of flowers in the middle which was surrounded by ingenious legends, such as:

> Take heed, O man:
> A pound of butter costs three Batzen.
>
> God is gracious to man,
> But I live on good grass land.

In hell it's hot,
And the potter has to work hard.

The cow eats grass;
Man ends in the grave.

Next to the cheese she placed a huge cake, that peculiar Bernese confection, coiled like the women's plaits, beautifully brown and yellow, baked with best flour, eggs and butter, as large as a one-year-old child and weighing almost as much; and on either side she placed two more plates. Piled up on them lay appetizing fritters, yeast-cakes on the one plate, pancakes on the other. Thick, warm cream was standing on the oven, covered up in a jug with lovely flowers patterned on it, and in the glistening three-legged can with its yellow lid the coffee was bubbling. In this way a breakfast was awaiting the godparents, when they should arrive, of a sort that princes seldom have and no peasant-farmers in the world except the Bernese. Thousands of English people go rushing through Switzerland, but never has one of the jaded lords or one of the stiff-legged ladies been presented with a breakfast like this.

"If only they'd come soon, it's all waiting," the midwife sighed. "Anyway, it'll be a good time before they're all ready and everybody's had what they want, and the pastor is awfully punctual and ticks you off sharply if you're not there at the right time." "Grandfather never allows the pram to be taken," the young wife said. "He believes that a child which is not carried to its christening, but is led on wheels, will grow up lazy and never learn to use its legs properly its whole life through. If only the godmother were here, she'll hold us up longest, the godfathers make shorter work of things, and if the worst came to the worst they could always hurry along behind." Anxiety about the godparents spread through the whole house. "Aren't they coming yet?" could be heard everywhere; from all corners of the house faces peered out for them, and the dog barked for all it was worth, as if it was trying to summon them too. But the grandmother said, "It used not to be like this in the old days; then you knew that you had to get up at the right time on such a day and the pastor wouldn't wait for anybody." Finally the farmer's boy rushed into the kitchen with the news that the godmother was coming.

She came bathed in sweat and loaded up as if she were the Christ-child going to give the New Year presents. In the one hand she had the black strings of a large, flower-patterned hold-all in which was a big Bernese cake wrapped in a fine white cloth, a present for the young mother. In the other hand she was carrying a second bag, and in this there was a garment for the child as well as a few articles for her own use, in particular, fine white stockings; and under the one arm she had something else, a cardboard box which contained her wreath and her laced cap with its wonderful black silk hair-trimmings. Joyfully the greeting of "Welcome in God's name" was given her from all sides, and she scarcely had time to put down one of her parcels so that she could free her own hand to meet the hands stretched towards her in friendly welcome. From all directions helpful hands reached for her burdens, and there was the young wife standing by the door, and so a new series of greetings began, until the midwife summoned them into the living-room: they could surely say to each other inside there what custom demanded on such an occasion.

And with neat gestures the midwife placed the godmother at the table, and the young wife came with the coffee, even though the godmother refused and asserted that she had already had some. Her father's sister wouldn't let her leave the house without having something to eat, that was bad for young girls, she said. But after all her aunt was getting old now, and the maids didn't like getting up early either, that was why she was so late; if it had been left to her, she would have been here long ago. Thick cream was poured into the coffee, and although the godmother protested and said she did not like it, the wife threw a lump of sugar in all the same. For a long time the godmother would not have it that the Bernese cake should be cut for her, but then she had to let a good-sized piece be placed in front of her and to eat it. She didn't want any cheese, she said; she didn't need it a bit. She'd believe it was made from skimmed milk and not think much to it on that account, said the wife, and the godmother had to give in. But she didn't want any fritters, she said; she just wouldn't know where to find room for them. It was only that she believed they were not clean and she was used to better quality, was the answer she finally received. What else could she do except eat fritters? While she was being pressed to eat in all kinds of ways, she had drunk her first cup of coffee in short measured sips; and now a real dispute started. The godmother turned the cup upside down and claimed that she had no more room for any further good things, saying people should leave her in peace, or else, what is more, she would have to refuse in even stronger language. Then the wife said she was really sorry that she didn't like the coffee, she had ordered the midwife most emphatically to make it as good as possible, it really wasn't her fault that it was so bad that nobody wanted to drink it, and there surely couldn't be anything wrong with the cream either, she had taken it off the milk in a way she certainly didn't every day. What was the poor godmother to do except to let them pour her another cup?

For some time now the midwife had been hovering around impatiently, and at last she could restrain herself no longer, but said, "If there's anything you'd like me to do for you, just tell me, I've got time for it!" "Oh, don't be rushing us!" the wife said. The poor godmother, however, who was steaming like a kettle, took the hint, despatched the hot coffee as quickly as possible, and said, during the pauses forced on her by the burning drink, "I should have been ready long ago, if I hadn't had to take more than I can get down me, but I'm coming now."

She got up, unpacked her bags, handed over the Bernese cake, the infant's garment and the godmother's own present—a shining Neutaler coin, wrapped up in a beautifully painted piece of paper which had a christening text on it—and made many an apology because everything was not as good as it might be. But the mother interrupted with many an exclamation that that really wasn't the way to go about it, putting herself to so much expense that they almost felt they couldn't accept it; and if they'd known it, they wouldn't have thought of asking her to be godmother in the first place.

Now the girl too set to work, assisted by the midwife and the lady of the house, and did her utmost to be a beautiful godmother, from shoes and stockings up to the little wreath on top of the precious lace cap. The business took its time in spite of the midwife's impatience, and the godmother kept on finding something that was not as it should be, now one thing, and now another was not in the right place. Then the grandmother came in and said, "But I want to come in as well and see how lovely our godmother is." At the same time she let out that the church bells were ringing for the second time, and that both godfathers were in the outer room.

Indeed the two godfathers, an older man and a young man, were sitting outside, scorning the newfangled coffee, which they could have any day, in favor of the steaming mulled wine, this old-fashioned but good Bernese soup, consisting of wine, toasted bread, eggs, sugar, cinnamon and saffron, that equally old-fashioned spice which has to be present at a christening feast in the soup, in the first course after the soup and in the sweetened tea. They were enjoying it, and the older godfather, who was called "Cousin," made all sorts of jokes with the father of the newborn child and said to him that they didn't want to spare him today, and judging from the mulled wine he didn't begrudge it them, and nothing had been stinted in making it, you could see that he must have given his four-gallon sack to the messenger last Tuesday to fetch his saffron from Berne. When they did not know what the cousin meant by this, he said that a little while back his neighbor had had to have a christening and had given the messenger a large sack and six Kreuzer with the request to bring him in this sack six centimes' worth of the yellow powder, a quart or a bit over, that stuff you have to have in everything at christenings, his womenfolk seemed to want it that way.

Then the godmother entered like a young morning sun and was greeted by the two godfathers and brought to the table and a big dishful of mulled wine put in front of her, and she was to get that inside her, she'd got time enough while the baby was being put straight. The poor lass resisted with might and main, and asserted that she had had enough to eat to last her for days, she really couldn't even breathe any more. But it was no use. Old folk and young were urging her, both seriously and in fun, until she picked up the spoon and, strangely enough, one spoonful after another found its way down. Now, however, the midwife appeared again, this time with the baby beautifully wrapped in his swaddling clothes, and she put his embroidered cap with its pink silk ribbon on him, wrapped him in the lovely quilt, popped the sweetened dummy into his little mouth and said that she didn't want to keep anybody waiting and had thought she'd get everything ready so that they could start whenever they wanted. Everyone stood round the baby and made complimentary remarks about it, and he was indeed a bonny little boy. The mother was pleased at the praise and said, "I should have liked to come to church too and help to recommend the child to God's care; for if you're there yourself when the baby is being christened, you can think better about what you've promised.

Besides, it's such a nuisance if I'm not allowed outside the house for a whole week, especially now when we've got our hands full with the planting." But the grandmother said it hadn't got quite that far, that her daughter-in-law had to go to be churched within the first week like a poor woman; and the midwife added that she didn't like it at all when young women went with the children to christening. They were always afraid of something going wrong at home, didn't have the proper spirit in church, and on the way home they were in too much of a hurry, so that nothing should be missed, then they got too hot and sometimes became really ill and even died.

Then the godmother took the baby in his coverlet in her arms, and the midwife laid the beautiful white christening cloth with black tassels at the corners over the child, being careful to avoid the lovely bunch of flowers on the godmother's breast, and said, "Go on now, in God's holy name!" And the grandmother put her hands together and quietly said an ardent prayer of blessing. The mother, however, accompanied the procession as far as the door and said, "My little boy, my little boy, now I shan't be seeing you for three whole hours. I don't know how I can stand it!" And at once tears came to her eyes, quickly she wiped them away with her apron and went back into the house.

With rapid steps the godmother walked down the slope along the way to the church, bearing the fine child in her strong arms, behind her the two godfathers, the father and the grandfather, none of whom thought of relieving the godmother of her burden, although the younger godfather was wearing on his hat a good sprig of may, the sign that he was a bachelor, and in his eyes was a sparkle of something like approval of the godmother, hidden though this was behind an appearance of great nonchalance.

The grandfather informed everybody how terrible the weather had been when they had carried him to church to be christened, and how the churchgoers had hardly believed they would escape with their lives from the hail and lightning. Later on people had made all kinds of prophecies to him on account of this weather, some predicting a terrible death, others great fortune in war; but things had gone quietly for him just as they had for everybody else, and now that he was seventy-five he would neither die an early death nor have great fortune in war.

They had gone more than halfway when the maid came running

after them; she had the duty of carrying the baby back home as soon as he had been christened, while relatives and godparents stayed behind, according to the grand old custom, in order to listen to the sermon. The maid had not spared any efforts so that she too might look beautiful. This considerable labor had made her late, and now she wanted to relieve the godmother of the baby; but the godmother would not allow this, however much she was pressed. This was too good an opportunity to show the handsome, unmarried godfather how strong her arms were and how much they could put up with. For a real peasant-farmer strong arms on a woman are much more acceptable than delicate, miserable little sticks of arms that every north wind can blow apart if it sets its mind to it; a mother's strong arms have been the salvation of many children whose father has died, when the mother has to rule the family alone and must lift unaided the cart of housekeeping out of all the potholes in which it might get stuck.

But all at once it is as if somebody is holding the strong godmother back by her plaits or giving her a blow on the head, she actually recoils, gives the maid the child, then stays behind and pretends that she has to see to her garter. Then she catches up, attaches herself to the men, mixes in their conversations, tries to interrupt the grandfather and distract him, now with this, now with that, from the subject which he has taken up. He, however, holds firmly on to his subject, as old people usually do, and imperturbably takes up afresh the broken thread of his narrative. Now she makes up to the father of the child and tries through all sorts of questions to lead him into private conversation; yet he is monosyllabic and keeps on letting the conversation drop. Perhaps he has his own thoughts, as every father should, when his child, and what is more the first boy, is being taken to be christened. The nearer they came to the church, the more people joined on to the procession, some were already waiting by the wayside with their psalters in their hands, others were leaping more hurriedly down the narrow footpaths, and they came into the village like a great, solemn procession.

Next to the church was the inn, for these two institutions so often stand close to one another, sharing joy and suffering together, and what is more, in all honor. There a halt was made, the baby was changed, and the father ordered three liters of wine, although everyone protested that he shouldn't do it, they'd only just had all the heart could desire, and they wanted nothing, either thick or thin. Even so, once the wine was there, they all drank, especially the maid; she presumably thought she had to drink wine whenever anybody offered it to her, and that wouldn't happen often from one year's end to the next. Only the godmother could not be persuaded to touch a drop, in spite of her being pressed as if they would never stop, until the innkeeper's wife said they ought not to force her, the girl was becoming visibly paler, and Hoffmann's Drops would do her more good than wine. But the godmother did not want anything like that, scarcely wanted even a glass of wine, in the end had to allow a few drops from a bottle of smelling salts to be shaken on to her handkerchief, attracted in her innocence many a suspicious glance and could not justify herself or say what she needed. The godmother was suffering from a ghastly fear and could not say anything about it. Nobody had told her what name the baby was to have, and according to old custom it is the godmother's duty to whisper the name to the pastor on handing the child over to him, since the pastor could easily confuse the names that have been registered with him if there are many children to be baptized.

In their hurry about the many things that had to be done and in their fear of coming too late, they had forgotten to inform her of the name, and her father's sister, her aunt, had once and for all strictly forbidden her to ask what the name was, unless she really wanted to make a child unhappy; for as soon as a godmother asked about a child's name, this child would become for his whole life—inquisitive.

Thus she did not know the child's name, might not ask about it, and if the pastor had also forgotten it and asked what it was loudly in public or else made a mistake and christened the boy Magdalena or Barbara, how people would laugh and what a humiliation this would be her whole life through! This appeared to her as ever more terrible; the strong girl's legs trembled like bean-plants in the wind, and the sweat poured off her pale face in streams.

At this point the innkeeper's wife urged them to depart, if they wanted to avoid being hauled over the coals by the pastor; but to the godmother she said, "You'll never go through with it, lass, you're as white as a newly washed shirt." That was from running, the god-mother asserted, it would get better again when she came into the fresh air. But it would not get better, in church all the people looked quite black to her, and now the baby began to scream with an increasingly murderous yell. The poor godmother began to rock him in her arms, and the louder he cried, the more vigorously she rocked him, so that the petals scattered from the flowers on her breast. Her breast felt more constricted and heavier, and her breathing could be heard loud. The higher her breast rose, the higher the child flew up in her arms, and the higher he flew, the louder he screamed, and the louder he screamed, the more forcefully the pastor read the prayers. The voices actually resounded against the walls, and the godmother no longer knew where she was; there was a whistling and roaring around her like the waves of the sea, and the church danced around with her in the air. At last the pastor said "Amen," and now the terrible moment had come, now it was to be decided whether she was to become a laughingstock for children and grandchildren; now she had to take off the covering, give the child to the pastor and whisper the name into his right ear. She removed the cloth, though trembling and shaking, handed over the child, and the pastor took him, did not look at her, did not ask her with sharp eyes, dipped his hand in the water, wetted the forehead of the suddenly silent child and did not christen him a Magdalena or a Barbara, but a Hans Uli, an honest-to-goodness-real-life Hans Uli.

At that the godmother felt not only as if all the Emmental hills were falling off her heart, but sun, moon and stars too, and as if someone were carrying her from a fiery furnace into a cool bath; but all through the sermon her limbs trembled and would not be still again. The pastor preached very finely and penetratingly, all about man's life being nothing more nor less than an ascension towards heaven; but the godmother could not arrive at a proper devotional state of mind, and by the time they left the church she had already forgotten the text. She could hardly wait to reveal her secret fear and the reason for her pale face. There was a lot of laughter, and she had to hear many a joke about inquisitiveness, and how scared the womenfolk were of this, and how all the same they saw to it that their daughters became inquisitive, although they left the boys out of it. She really needn't have worried about asking.

Soon, however, fine fields of oats and plantations of flax and the magnificent growth in meadows and fields came to be noticed and attracted everyone's attention. They found a number of reasons for going slowly and standing still, but by the time they arrived home the beautiful May sun, which was higher in the sky now, had made them all feel warm, and a glass of cool wine did everybody good, however much they resisted it. Then they sat down in front of the house, while in the kitchen busy hands were at work and the fire was crackling mightily. The midwife was gleaming like one of the three men from the fiery furnace.* Already before eleven o'clock came a summons to the meal, but only for the servants, who were given their food first, and in ample quantity of course, but all the same one was glad when the servants were out of the way.

The conversation of those sitting in front of the house flowed rather slowly, but it did not dry up completely; before a meal preoccupation with the stomach disturbs the thoughts of the soul, but nobody is pleased to reveal this inner state, rather it is cloaked over with slow words on trivial subjects. It was already past midday when the midwife appeared at the door with flaming face, though her apron was still spotless, and brought the news, welcome to all, that they could eat if they were all there. But most of the guests were still missing, and the messengers who had already been sent out after them earlier returned, like the servants in the Gospel,† with all kinds of information, with the distinction, however, that actually all were willing to come, only not just now; the one had ordered workmen to come, the other farm-servants, and the third still had to go off somewhere—but they weren't to wait for them, but just to get on with the business. It was soon agreed to follow this exhortation, for if you were going to wait for everyone, it was said, it would drag out until the moon rose; it is true that the midwife growled in passing that there was nothing sillier than keeping people waiting, when in fact everybody would like to be there, the sooner the better in fact, so long as nobody should notice it. So you have the trouble of getting everything warmed up again, you never know whether there's enough, and you never get finished.

Although it did not take long to come to a decision about the absentees, there was a certain amount of trouble with those who were present in leading them to the living-room and persuading them to sit down there, for nobody wanted to be first, at one thing

*Daniel 3:20–27.
†Matthew 22: 1–10.

any more than another. When at last they were all seated, the soup came on to the table, a beautiful meat soup, colored and spiced with saffron and so thickly covered with the beautiful white bread that the grandmother had been cutting, that there was little of the soup itself visible. Now all heads were uncovered, hands were folded together, and each one prayed to himself long and earnestly to the Giver of all good gifts. Only then did they slowly take up their metal spoons, and after wiping these on the beautiful, fine tablecloth they applied themselves to the soup, and many a wish could be heard that they could ask for no more than this, that they might have such a good soup every day. When they had finished their soup, they again wiped their spoons on the tablecloth; the Bernese cake was handed round, and everybody cut himself a piece, at the same time observing that the first meat course was being served up, which consisted of meat in saffron broth—mutton, brains and liver prepared in vinegar. When this course had been dealt with, after people had helped themselves in a slow and deliberate manner, the beef was brought in, both fresh meat and salted meat, whichever one might fancy, piled up high in dishes; with this went dried beans, slices of dried pear, fat bacon and wonderful joints from pigs that weighed three hundredweight, beautifully red and white and succulent. All this slowly took its course, and whenever a new guest arrived, the whole meal was brought on again, beginning with the soup, and each newcomer had to begin where the others had begun earlier, none was let off a single course. In between, Benz, the father of the newborn child, assiduously poured out wine from the beautiful, white bottles which held more than a gallon and were richly decorated with coats of arms and mottoes. Where his arms could not reach, he transferred to others his office of cupbearer, earnestly pressing his guests to drink and very often exhorting them: "Drink it up, that's what it's there for, to be drunk!" And whenever the midwife came in carrying a dish of food, he held out his glass to her, and others did the same too, so that things might have gone very queerly in the kitchen if she had drunk a pledge every time that one was offered her.

The younger godfather had to listen to a number of jokes to the effect that he did not know how to encourage the godmother to drink as well as he should; if he could not give toasts better than that, he would never get a wife. "Oh, Hans Uli won't want a wife," the godmother finally said; unmarried fellows these days had quite different ideas in their heads from marriage, and most of them couldn't even afford to get married now. "Huh," said Hans Uli, he wasn't so sure about that. Such slovenly creatures as most girls are nowadays make very expensive wives; most of them thought that all that was needed to make a good wife was a blue-silk piece of material to wrap round their heads, gloves in summer and embroidered slippers in winter. If you found that one of the cows in the cowshed was a poor specimen, that was certainly bad luck, but you could change it all the same; but if you are landed with a wife who does you out of a house and farm, that's the end of it, and you can't get rid of her. That's why it's more useful to think about other things rather than marriage and to let girls remain girls.

"Yes, yes, you're quite right," the older godfather said; he was an insignificant looking little man in cheap clothes, but he was respected very much and called "Cousin," for he had no children, but did possess a farm of his own without a mortgage on it and 100,000 Swiss francs in capital. "Yes, you are right," he said. "Womenfolk are just no use any more. I won't say that there isn't one here or there who would do credit to a house but such are few and far between. All they can think about is foolery and showing off; they dress up like peacocks, strut about like daft storks, and if one of them has to do half a day's work, she gets a headache that lasts three days, and spends four days lying in bed before she is herself again. When I was courting my old woman, things were different, you didn't have to fear as much as you do now that you might get, instead of a good mistress of the house, only a fool or a devil about the house."

"Now look here, godfather Uli," said the godmother who had been wanting to talk for a long time, but had not had a chance, "anyone would think that it was only in your young days that there were any decent farmers' daughters. The only thing is, you just don't know them and you don't take any notice of girls any more, which of course is quite right in an old man like you; but there are decent girls still, just as much as in the days when your old woman was still young. I don't want to blow my own trumpet, but my father has told me many a time that if I go on as I have been doing, I shall outdo my late mother yet, and she became a really famous woman. My father has never taken such fat pigs to market as last year. The butcher has often said that he'd like to see the lass who had fed those pigs. But there's plenty to complain about in young fellows today; just what on earth is wrong with them then? They can certainly smoke, sit around in the inn, wear their white hats on the slant and open their eyes as wide as city-gates, hang around all the skittle-games, all the shooting matches and all the loose girls; but if one of them is supposed to milk a cow or plow a field, he's had it, and if he takes a piece of timber in his hands, he behaves as stupidly as a gentleman or even a lawyer's clerk. I have often solemnly sworn that I won't have anybody as a husband unless I know for certain how I can get on with him, and even if one of them here or there may turn out to be something of a farmer, that doesn't help you to know at all what he would be like as a husband."

At this the others laughed heartily, making the girl blush as they joked with her; how long did she think that she would want to take a man on approval until she knew for certain what sort of a husband he would be?

In this way, laughing and joking, they ate a lot of meat and did not forget the pear-slices either, until eventually the older godfather said that he thought that they should be contented for the time being and move away a little from the table, for your legs got quite stiff beneath the table and a pipe is never more welcome than after you've been eating meat. This counsel received general acclamation, even though the father and mother tried to persuade the guests not to leave the table; once people had moved away, there was hardly a hope of bringing them back again. "Don't you worry, cousin!" said the older godfather, "as soon as you put something good on the table, you'll have us all together again without much trouble, and if we stretch our legs a bit, we shall be all the more handy at tackling the food again."

The men now made the round of the cattle-sheds, took a look at the hayloft to see if any of the old hay was still available, made compliments about the lush grass and stared up into the fruit-trees to calculate how great the blessing of this crop might be.

The cousin made a halt beneath one of the trees that was still in bloom and said that this was as good a place as any to sit down and have a pipe, it was cool here, and as soon as the womenfolk had served up something good again, they would be near at hand. Soon they were joined by the godmother who with the other women had been inspecting the vegetable garden and the plantations. The other womenfolk came after the godmother, and one after another lowered themselves onto the grass, carefully keeping their beautiful skirts safe and clean, although their petticoats with their bright red edging were exposed to the danger of receiving a souvenir on them from the green grass.

The tree around which the whole company was encamped stood above the house on the first gentle rise of the slope. The beautiful new house was what first caught the eye; beyond the house the glance could rove to the edge of the valley on the other side, looking over many a fine, prosperous farm and further away over green hills and dark valleys.

"You've got a grand house there, and everything is well planned about it too," the cousin said. "Now you can really enjoy being in it, and you've got room for everything and everybody; I never could understand how anybody could put up with such a poor house when they have enough money and timber to build for themselves, as you have, for example." "Don't tease, cousin!" the grandfather said. "There's no cause for us to boast either about money or timber; and then, building is a grim business, you know when you start, but you never know when you're going to finish, and now one thing gets in the way, now another; every place has got something else that can go wrong."

"I like the house extremely well," one of the women said. "We too ought to have had a new house for a long time now, but we always shy off at the expense. But as soon as my husband arrives, he must have a good look at this house; it seems to me that if we could have a house like this, I should be in heaven. But all the same I would like to ask—and don't take it amiss, will you?—why ever that ugly black window-post is there, just by the first window; it detracts from the appearance of the whole house."

The grandfather pulled a dubious face, drew even more vigorously at his pipe and finally said that they had run out of wood when they were building, there was nothing else just at hand, and so they had taken in their need and haste something from the old house. "But," the woman said, "the black piece of wood was too short, apart from anything else, and there are pieces joined on top and bottom; besides, any neighbor would have been only too glad to give you a really new piece." "Yes, we just didn't think it out better and we could not always be pestering our neighbors afresh, they had already given us a lot of help with gifts of timber and with the loan of horses and carts," the old man replied.

"Listen, Granddad," the cousin said, "don't beat about the bush, but tell the truth and give an honest account. I've already heard various rumors, but I've never yet been able to hear the truth exactly. Now would be a good time, you could entertain us so well with the story, until the women have got the roast ready; so you give us an honest account!" The grandfather still beat about the bush before he would consent; but the cousin and the womenfolk did not give way until he at last gave his promise, though nevertheless with the express reservation that he would prefer what he had to tell to remain a secret and not to go beyond the present company. A good many people would fight shy of anything like that about a house, and he would not like to be responsible in his old age for anything that might harm his own relatives.

"Every time that I look at this piece of wood," the venerable old man began, "I cannot but wonder how it all happened that people came as far as here from the distant East, where the human race is said to have originated, and found this spot in this narrow valley; I cannot but think of those who drifted here or else were driven here, and everything that they must have suffered, and who indeed they may have been. I have inquired a lot about it, but all I have been able to find out is that this district was inhabited very early in history, and indeed that Sumiswald* is supposed to have been a town even before our Lord was on earth; but that is not written down anywhere. However, we do know that a castle, where the hospital now is, stood there more than six hundred years ago, and apparently about the same time there would be a house here too which belonged to the castle, along with a great part of the district; the house would have to pay tithes and ground rent to the castle, and compulsory labor would have to be performed as well; for the people then were held as serfs without legal rights of their own, as everybody has now as soon as he becomes an adult. People lived in widely divergent conditions in those days, quite close together there lived serfs who had the best conditions and those who were sorely and almost unbearably oppressed and were not even sure of their lives. Their circumstances

---

*A forest in the Canton of Berne. The order of the Teutonic Knights held it from 1225 to 1698.

depended on who their lord was at the time; these lords were very different from one another and at the same time almost absolute masters over their people; the latter had no one to whom they could make their complaint easily and effectively. Those who belonged to this castle are said to have suffered worse at times than most of those who belonged to other castles. Most of the other castles belonged to one family and were passed down from father to son; here the lord and his subjects were known to each other from youth onwards, and many a one behaved like a father to his people. Now this castle came at an early stage into the hands of the Teutonic Knights, as they were called, and the one who was in charge here was known as the district commander. These superiors changed frequently, and for a time there was somebody from Saxony, and then somebody from Swabia; consequently no sense of trust could grow, and each commander brought manners and customs with him from his own country.

In fact the knights were supposed to fight with the heathen in Poland and Prussia, and in these countries they almost accustomed themselves to the heathen way of living, treated their fellow-men as if there were no God in heaven, and when they did eventually come home they continued to fancy that they were still in the heathen country and carried on with the same type of life here. Those who preferred to sit in the shade and enjoy themselves rather than to fight bloodily in grim, desert country, or those who had to nurse their wounds and strengthen their bodies came to the lands which the Order (such was called the company of the knights) possessed in Germany and in Switzerland, and each of the commanders could do as he pleased. One of the worst of them is said to have been Hans von Stoffeln* from Swabia, and it was under his rule that these things are said to have happened which you want to know about and which have been passed down in our family from father to son.

This man Hans von Stoffeln had the idea of building a great castle up over there on the Bärhegenhubel;† the castle stood on the spot where in stormy weather you can even now still see the spirits of the

---

*A Hans Ulrich von Stoffeln was commander of the Teutonic Knights in Sumiswald from 1512 to 1527. He was not a tyrant, but in fact eased the burden of the peasants. In any case the fictional time of the first inner story must be sometime in the thirteenth century. A Peter von Stoffeln is known from the fourteenth century.

†A mountain ridge about an hour and a half from Sumiswald, where traces of pagan sacrifices have been found.

castle displaying their treasures. Usually the knights built their castles near the roads, just as today inns are built by the roadside; in both cases it is a question of being able to plunder the people better, though in different ways, admittedly. But why the knight wanted to have a castle up there on the wild, bare hill in the midst of deserted country, we do not know; it is enough that he did want it, and the peasants who were attached to the castle had to do the building. The knight was indifferent to what work might be demanded by the season, whether it was haymaking-time, harvest-time or seed-time. So many teams or carts had to move, so many men had to labor, and at this or that particular time the last tile had to be in place and the last nail knocked in. What is more, he insisted on every tenth sheaf of corn that was due to him and on every measure of his ground rent; he never let them have a chicken for Shrove Tuesday nor even an egg; he had no pity, and knew nothing of the needs of the poor. He spurred them on in heathen manner with blows and curses, and if anyone became tired, or was slower in his movements or wanted to rest, the bailiff would be at his back with the whip, and neither the aged nor the weak were spared. When the wild knights were up there, they enjoyed hearing the crack of the whip and playing all sorts of unpleasant tricks on the workers; if they could maliciously compel the men to double the pace of their work, they forced them to it and then took great pleasure in their fear and sweat.

At last the castle was finished, with its walls that were five yards thick; nobody knew why it was standing up there, but the peasants were glad that it really did stand, if it had to be there at all, and that the last nail was knocked in and the last tile fixed into place up on top.

They wiped the sweat from their brows, looked round their own property with dejected hearts and sighed to see to what extent the accursed building work had held them back. But there was a long summer ahead of them all the same, and God was above them; therefore they took courage and firmly grasped their plows, consoling their wives and children who had suffered severe hunger and for whom work appeared as yet another torment.

But scarcely had they taken their plows to the fields when the message came that all the peasants were to appear one evening at a specific time in the castle at Sumiswald. They were both fearful and hopeful. It was true that they had up to now experienced nothing enjoyable at the hands of the present inhabitants of the castle, but had only suffered malice and severity, but it seemed right to them that the gentry should do something for them as a reward for the unheard-of piece of forced labor which had just been accomplished; and because the peasants thought it seemed right, many of them believed their lords would think so too, and they hoped they would that evening be given a present or a remission of some other obligations.

On the evening arranged they appeared punctually and with beating hearts, but they had to wait a long time in the courtyard of the castle where the servants could jeer at them. These servants too had been in heathen countries. What is more, it must have been the same then as it is now, when every twopenny-half-penny gentleman's lackey thinks he has a right to look down on and be scornful of property-owning peasants.

Eventually they were summoned to the hall of the knights; in front of them the heavy door was opened; inside the dark tanned knights sat round the heavy oak table, fierce dogs at their feet, and at their head was von Stoffeln, a fierce, powerful man who had a head like a three-liter measure, eyes like cartwheels and a beard like an old lion's mane. Then the knights laughed so that the wine slopped over their tankards and the dogs darted angrily forward; for as soon as dogs like these see trembling, hesitant limbs they have the idea that they belong to some prey that should be hunted down. The peasants, however, did not feel confident; they thought, if only they were back home, and each tried to hide behind the other. When at last dogs and knights were silent, von Stoffeln raised his voice, and it sounded as if it came from a hundred-year-old oak: 'My castle is finished, but there is something still missing; summer is coming, and up there there is no avenue of trees to provide a shady walk. In a month you must plant an avenue for me; you must take a hundred full-grown beech-trees from the Münneberg* root and branch, and plant them for me on Bärhegen, and if one single beech-tree is missing, I shall make you pay for it with property and life. Down below there is something to eat and drink, but the first beech must be standing on Bärhegen tomorrow.'

---

*A mountainous area near Sumiswald, difficult of access, so that in past times it served as a place of refuge.

When one of the peasants heard something about food and drink he thought that the knight might be lenient and in a good mood; and he therefore began to talk about their work at home and their hungry wives and children, and the fact that this particular task could be better done in winter. Then the knight's head seemed to become more and more puffed out with anger, and his voice exploded like a thunderclap amid steep rocks, and he told them that if he were lenient, they were indolent. If someone in Poland was allowed to keep his bare life, he would kiss your feet with gratitude, but here they had children and cattle, a roof over their heads and cupboards to put their things in, and still they were not satisfied. 'But I will make you more obedient and more contented, as sure as I am Hans von Stoffeln, and if the hundred beech-trees are not planted up there within a month, I'll have you whipped until there's not a finger's length of your skin left whole, and I'll set the dogs on your women and children.'

Then nobody dared to remonstrate further, but neither did anyone want any of the food and drink; after the angry order had been given, they pressed out to the door, and everyone of them would gladly have been the first to leave, and for a long time after they had gone they were followed by the knight's voice of thunder and the laughter of the other knights, the jeering of the servants and the howling of the hounds.

When they came to a turn in the road, where they could no longer be seen from the castle, they sat down by the roadside and wept bitterly; no one had any consolation for his neighbor, and none of them had the courage for real anger, for privation and torments had extinguished their courage, so that they had no more strength left for anger, only enough for despair. They were to transport beech-trees, complete with roots and branches, for a three hours' journey over rough tracks up the steep Münneberg, while close by this hill many fine beeches were growing, but these had to be left standing! Within a month the work had to be finished; they were to drag three trees each of the first two days and four trees every third day, and the hill was steep and their cattle already exhausted. And in addition to all this it was May, the month when the peasant has to work hard in his fields and may hardly leave them by day or night, if he wants to have bread and food for the winter.

While they were waiting there so disconsolately, none daring to look into the other's face to see his misery because his own distress already overwhelmed him, and none daring to take the bad news home to his wife and family, there suddenly appeared in front of them, they did not know where he had come from, the tall, lean figure of a green huntsman. A red feather was swaying on his bold-looking cap, a little red beard blazed in his dark face, and a mouth opened between his hooked nose and pointed chin, almost invisible like a cavern beneath overhanging rocks, and uttered the question: 'What's the matter, good people, that you are sitting and moaning like this, as if to force the rocks out of the earth and the branches down from the trees?' Twice he asked thus, and twice he received no answer.

Then the green huntsman's dark face became even darker and his little red beard became even redder, so that it seemed to be crackling and sparkling like pine wood on fire; his mouth pursed itself sharply like an arrow and then opened to ask quite pleasingly and gently: 'But good people, what use is it your sitting and moaning there? You could go on howling like that till a second Flood comes or till your shrieking brings down the stars from the sky, but that's not likely to help you very much. But when somebody asks you what's wrong, somebody who means well by you and could possibly help you, you ought to answer and say something sensible instead of crying out loud; that might be more use to you.' At that an old man shook his white head of hair and replied, 'Don't take it amiss, but no huntsman can take away the cause of our weeping, and once the heart is swollen with grief, it can find words no longer.'

Then the green huntsman shook his sharp head and said, 'Father, what you say is not stupid, but that's not the way things are. You can strike anything you please, a rock or a tree, and it will utter a sound, it will lament. A man too should lament, should lament about everything, should complain to the first person he meets, for perhaps this person can help him. I am only a huntsman, but who knows whether I haven't got an efficient team of cattle at home to transport wood and stones or beech-trees and pines?'

When the poor peasants heard the word 'team,' it went straight to their hearts and there became a spark of hope; all eyes turned towards the huntsman, and the old man opened his mouth once more; he said it was not always right to tell the first person you met what was on your mind; but since they could tell from his words that he meant well and that he might perhaps help, they wouldn't hide anything from him. They had suffered now for more than two years from the building of the new castle, and there was not a single household in the whole community which was not in bitter distress. Now they had taken fresh breath, thinking that they would at last have their hands free for their own work, the administration had just given them the order to plant within one month by the new castle a new avenue of beech-trees taken from the Münneberg. They did not know how they could accomplish this in the time with their exhausted cattle; and if they did accomplish the task, what use would it be to them? They would not then be able to plant and to sow their own fields and would have to die of starvation later, even if the hard work for the knight had not killed them before that. They were reluctant to take this news to their homes, for they did not want to pour new grief on to old misery.

Then the green huntsman made a sympathetic face, lifted up his long, thin, black hand threateningly against the castle and swore deep vengeance for such tyranny. But he would help the peasants, he said. His equipment was like none other in the country, and as many trees as they could bring to Kilchstalden ('church slope'), on this side of Sumiswald, he would transport from there to Bärhegen, as a favor to them and to spite the knights and for very little payment.

The poor men pricked up their ears on hearing this unexpected offer. If they could only make an agreement about the payment, they were saved, for they could bring the beech-trees to Kilchstalden without neglecting their farm work on account of this task and consequently without being utterly ruined. The old man therefore said, 'Well, tell us what you require, so that we can make an agreement!' Then the green huntsman showed a cunning face; his little beard crackled, and his eyes gleamed at them like snakes' eyes, and a hideous laugh came from the two corners of his mouth as he opened his lips and spoke, 'As I was saying, I don't ask for much, nothing more than an unbaptized child.'

The word flashed at the men like lightning, scales fell from their eyes, and like spray in a whirlwind they scattered in different directions.

Then the green huntsman laughed out loud, so that the fish in the stream hid themselves and the birds sought cover in the thicket, and the feather swayed horribly on his hat while his little beard went up and down.

'Think it over, or see what your womenfolk have got to say about it; you'll find me here again in three nights' time!' He called after the men in flight in a sharp, resounding voice, so that the words remained fixed in their ears as arrows with barbed hooks stay stuck in flesh.

Pale and trembling in mind as in all their limbs, the men rushed home; none looked round at one of the others, not one would have turned his head round, not for everything in the world. When the men came rushing along in this scared way, like doves that have been chased by a hawk into their dovecote, they brought terror with them into all the houses, and everybody trembled fearfully to hear what news it was that had made the men stumble and hasten in such confusion.

Quivering with curiosity the womenfolk crept after the men until they had them in some quiet place where confidences could be exchanged undisturbed. There each man had to tell his wife what had been heard in the castle, and the women received the news with curses and fury; the men had to relate whom they had met and what he had proposed to them. Then nameless fear seized hold of the women, a cry of pain resounded over hills and valley, and each woman felt as if it were her own child that the ruthless huntsman had demanded. Only one woman did not cry out like the rest. This was a terribly forceful woman, who was said to have come from Lindau and who lived here on this very farm. She had wild, black eyes and had little fear of God or man. She had already been angry with the men for not refusing the knight's demands there and then; if she had been there, she'd have told him straight, she said. When she heard about the green huntsman and his offer and how the men had rushed away, she really did become angry and reviled the men for their cowardice; if they had looked the green huntsman more boldly in the face, he might perhaps have contented himself with some other payment, and as the work was to be for the castle, it would do their souls no harm if the devil undertook it for them. She was enraged at heart because she had not been there, even if only that she could have seen the devil himself and known what he looked like. That is why this woman did not weep, but in her fury uttered hard words against her own husband and against all the other men.

On the following day, when the cry of dismay had subsided into a quiet whimpering, the men sat together, looking for wise counsel, but finding none. At first there was talk of making a fresh request to the knight, but nobody was willing to go to make a petition, for nobody wanted to risk life and limb. One man suggested sending the women and children with their crying and moaning, but he soon became silent when the women themselves began to talk; for already in those days women were not far away when the menfolk took counsel together. The women knew of no other plan except to attempt obedience in God's name; they suggested having masses sung in order to obtain God's protection, or requesting neighbors to give them secret help by night, for their lords would not have allowed outside help openly; they thought of splitting up, the one half to work at the beech-trees, while the other half should sow oats and look after the cattle. In this way they hoped with God's help to bring up to Bärhegen at least three beeches a day; nobody mentioned the green huntsman; whether anyone thought of him or not, is not recorded.

They divided themselves up and prepared their tools, and when the first May morning appeared at its threshold, the men met at the Münneberg and began the work with good heart. The beeches had to be dug up in a wide circle in order to spare the roots and then lowered carefully to the ground. The morning was still not yet far advanced when three trees lay ready to be moved, for it had been decided that they should always transport three together, so that the men could help each other out with their cattle as well as with the strength of their hands. But when midday came, they still had not got the three beech-trees out of the forest, and when the sun went down behind the mountains, the teams had still not gone further than Sumiswald. It was not until the next morning that they reached the foot of the hill on which the castle stood and where the beeches were to be planted. It was as if a special unlucky star had power over them. One misfortune after another befell them; harnesses snapped, carts broke, horses and oxen fell down or else refused obedience. On the second day matters became even worse. New distress inevitably brought new toil with it, the wretched folk were breathless with the unceasing labor, and still there was no beech-tree up at the top, and only three trees had been transported any further than Sumiswald.

Von Stoffeln reviled and cursed; the more he reviled and cursed, the greater influence the unlucky star seemed to have, and the cattle became all the more stubborn. The other knights laughed and mocked and took great pleasure in the terrified floundering of the peasants and in von Stoffeln's anger. They had laughed at von Stoffeln's new castle built on the naked hilltop. Because of that he had vowed that there must be a beautiful avenue up there within a month's time. That was why he cursed and the knights laughed, while the peasants wept.

These last were seized by a terrible despair, for they no longer had a single cart that was not damaged, nor any team of cattle that was not harmed, nor had three beech-trees been brought to the proper place within three days, and all strength had been exhausted.

Night had fallen, black clouds had gathered and there was lightning for the first time this year. The men had sat down by the roadside; it was the same turning of the road where they had sat three days earlier, but they did not realize this. There the Hornbach peasant, the husband of the woman from Lindau, was sitting with a couple of farm-servants, and some others were also seated with them. They wanted to wait at that spot for beech-trees that were supposed to be arriving from Sumiswald; they wanted to think over their misery undisturbed and to rest their bruised limbs.

Then a woman came along with a great basket on her head, moving so rapidly that there was almost a whistling, like the wind when it has been let loose out of closed spaces. It was Christine, the woman from Lindau whom the Hornbach peasant had taken on one occasion when he had gone on a warring expedition with his lord. She was not the sort of woman who is happy to be at home, to fulfill her duties in quietness and to care only for home and family. Christine wanted to know what was going on, and if she could not give her advice about something, it would turn out badly, or so she thought.

For this reason she had not sent a maid with the food, but had taken the heavy basket on her own head and had been looking for the men for a long time without success; she let fall bitter words on the subject as soon as she had found them. In the meantime, however, she had not been idle, for she could talk and work at the same time. She put down her basket, took the lid off the saucepan containing porridge, set out the bread and cheese in orderly fashion and placed the spoons in the porridge for her husband and his servants, and also told the others to set to as well, if they were still without food. Then she asked about the men's work, and how much had been accomplished in the two days. But the men had lost all appetite and all wish to talk; no one seized his spoon, and none had an answer. There was only one frivolous little farm-servant fellow who didn't care whether there was rain or sunshine at harvest-time, provided the year took its course and he had his wages and food on the table every mealtime; he seized his spoon and informed Christine that still no single beech-tree had been planted and that everything was happening as if they had been bewitched.

Then the woman from Lindau mocked and scolded them, saying that this was nothing but vain imagining and that the men were behaving with the weakness of a woman in child-bed; they would bring no beech-trees to Bärhegen, whether they toiled and wept or sat down and cried. It would be their own fault if the knight let them feel his wanton malice; but for the sake of the women and children the matter would have to be handled differently. Then a long black hand came suddenly over the woman's shoulder, and a piercing voice called, 'Yes, she's right!' And in their midst stood the green huntsman with his grinning face, and the red feather tossed on his hat. Immediately terror drove the men away from the spot; they scattered up the slope like chaff in a whirlwind.

Christine, the woman from Lindau, was the only one who could not flee; she was learning what it means to talk about the devil and then be confronted by him in person. She stood as if transfixed by magic, compelled to stare at the red feather on his cap and to watch how the little red beard moved merrily up and down in the black face. The green huntsman gave a piercing laugh as the men disappeared, but he put on an amorous expression towards Christine and took her hand with a polite gesture. Christine wanted to withdraw it, but she could no longer escape the green huntsman; it seemed to her as if flesh were spluttering between red-hot tongs. And he began to speak fine words, and as he spoke his little red beard gleamed and moved lustfully up and down. He had not seen such a handsome little woman for a long time, he said, and it made his heart glad within his breast; what is more, he liked them bold, and in particular he liked those women best who could stay behind when the menfolk ran away. As he went on speaking in this way, the green huntsman appeared to Christine to became ever less terrifying. You could talk with a man like that, all the same, she thought, and she didn't see why she should run away, she had seen far uglier men than him before now. The thought came to her more and more that something could be done with a man like that, and if you knew how to talk to him in the right way, he would surely do you a favor, or in any case you could cheat him, just as you could cheat any other men. The green huntsman went on to say that he really did not know why people were so frightened by him, his intentions were so good towards everybody, and if people were so rude towards him, they mustn't be surprised if he did not always do to people what they most wanted. Then Christine took heart and told him that after all he did frighten people so much that it was terrible. Why had he demanded an unbaptized child, he surely could have spoken of other payment, that would seem so suspect to people, after all a child was a human being, and no Christian would go so far as to give away a child that was unbaptized. 'That is my payment, to which I am accustomed, and I shan't do the work for any other, and in any case why should any notice be taken of such a child that nobody as yet knows? It is when they are so young that you can give them away most easily, after all you have had neither pleasure nor trouble from them as yet. But the younger I can have them, the better, for the earlier I can bring up a child in my own way, the further I can mold it; but for that I don't need any christening, and won't have it either.' Then indeed Christine saw that he would content himself with no other reward; however, the thought took root in her ever more firmly that this one would be unique if he could not be deceived!

Therefore she said that if someone wanted to earn something he would have to content himself with the reward which could be given to him; but at the moment they had no unbaptized child in any of their houses, nor would there be one in a month's time, and the beech-trees had to be delivered within this period. Then the green huntsman squirmed with politeness as he said, 'I am not demanding the child in advance. As soon as it is promised that the first child to be born will be handed over to me unbaptized, I shall be satisfied.' Christine was indeed very pleased at this. She knew that there would be no newborn child in the domain of her lords for some time to come. Now once the green huntsman had kept his promise and the beech-trees were planted, it would not be necessary to give him anything in return, either a child or anything else; they would have masses read both as defense and offense, and would boldly scoff at the green huntsman, or so Christine thought. She therefore expressed her gratitude for the good offer and said this needed thinking over and she would like to speak to the menfolk about it. 'Yes,' said the green huntsman, 'but there is nothing more to think about or to talk over. I made an appointment with you for today, and now I want to know your answer; I've got a lot to do still at a good many places, and I don't exist simply on account of you people. You must accept or refuse; afterwards I don't want to hear anything more about the whole business.' Christine wanted to prevaricate about the matter, for she was reluctant to take it upon herself; indeed she would have liked to be coaxing, in order to be able to postpone the issue, but the green huntsman was in no humor for this and did not waver; 'Now or never!' he said. But as soon as the agreement about one single child was made, he would be willing to bring every night up on to Bärhegen as many beech-trees as were delivered to him before midnight at the Kilchstalden down below; it was there that he would receive them. 'Now, pretty lady, don't hesitate!' the green huntsman said, and patted Christine on the cheek with irresistible charm. At that her heart did begin to beat hard, and she would have preferred to push the men forward into this, so that she could have made out afterwards that it was their fault. But time pressed, there was no man there to be the scapegoat, and she clung to the belief that she was more cunning than the green huntsman and would have an idea that would enable her to get the better of him. So Christine said that she for her part was willing to agree; but if the menfolk later were unwilling, she could do nothing about that, and he was not to take it out on her. The green huntsman said that he would be well satisfied with her promise to do what she could. At this point, however, Christine did shudder, both with body and soul; now, she thought, would come the terrible moment when she would have to sign the agreement with the green huntsman in her own blood. But the green huntsman made it easier, saying that he never demanded signatures from pretty women and that he would be satisfied with a kiss. At this he pursed up his mouth towards Christine's face, and Christine could not escape; once more she was as if transfixed by magic, stiff and rigid. Then the pointed mouth touched Christine's face, and she felt as if some sharp-pointed steel fire were piercing marrow and bone, body and soul; and a yellow flash of lightning struck between them and showed Christine the green huntsman's devilish face gleefully distorted, and thunder rolled above them as if the heavens had split apart.

The green man had disappeared, and Christine stood as if petrified, as if her feet had become rooted deep down into the ground in that terrible moment. At last she regained the use of her limbs, but there was a whistling and roaring in her mind as if mighty waters were pouring their floods over towering high rocks down into a black abyss. Just as one does not hear one's own voice for the thundering of the waters, so Christine was not capable of knowing her own thoughts in the uproar that was thundering through her mind. Instinctively she fled up to the hill, and ever more fiercely did she feel a burning on her cheek where the green huntsman's mouth had touched her; she rubbed and washed, but the burning did not decrease.

The night became wild. Up in the air and in the ravines there was a fierce uproar as if the spirits of the night were holding a marriage feast in the black clouds and the winds were playing wild music for their horrible dances, as if the flashes of lightning were the wedding-torches and the thunder the nuptial blessing. No one had ever previously experienced such a night at this time of year.

In the dark valley there was movement around one large house, and many people pressed around its sheltering roof. During a storm it usually happens that fear for his own hearth and home will drive the countryman under his own roof, where he can watch anxiously as long as the thunderstorm is in the sky above, guarding and protecting his own house. But now the common tribulation was greater than fear of the storm. The affliction brought them together in this house, which those whom the storm was driving from the Münneberg had to pass by as well as those who had taken flight from Bärhegen. Forgetting the terror of the night because of their own misery, they could be heard complaining and grumbling about their misfortune. In addition to all their misfortunes there had now come the violence of nature. Horses and oxen had become frightened and benumbed, had wrecked the carts, had hurled themselves over precipices, and many a creature groaned in deep pain from serious injuries, while others cried out loud as their shattered limbs were set and bound up.

Those who had seen the green huntsman also took flight in their terrible fear and joined in the misery of the others; here they told tremblingly of the repeated appearance of the figure. Trembling, the crowd listened to what the men told, pressed forward from the wide, dark space nearer to the fire around which the men were seated, and when the wind blew through the rafters or the thunder rolled over the house-top the crowd cried out and thought that the green huntsman was breaking through the roof to show himself in their midst. But when he did not come, when the terror of him subsided, when the old misery remained and the lamentations of the sufferers became louder, there gradually rose up those thoughts which are so prone to threaten a man's soul when he is in trouble. They began to calculate how much more worth they all were than one single unbaptized child; they increasingly forgot that guilt with regard to one soul weighs a thousand times more heavily than the rescuing of thousands upon thousands of human lives.

Gradually these thoughts made themselves heard and began to be mingled as comprehensible words into the groans of pain of the sufferers. People asked more closely about the green huntsman, grumbling that the others had not stood up to him better; he would not have taken anyone off, and the less you feared him, the less he would do to people. They might perhaps have been able to help the whole valley, if they had had their hearts in the right place. Then the men began to excuse themselves. They did not say that dealing with the devil was no joke and that if you lent him an ear you would soon have to give him your whole head; but they spoke of the green huntsman's terrible appearance, his flaming beard, the fiery feather on his hat like a castle-tower, and the terrible smell of sulfur which they had not cared to put up with. Christine's husband, however, who was used to his words becoming effective only after they had been confirmed by his wife, said that they should only ask his wife, she could tell them whether anybody could stand up to it; for everybody knew that she was a fearless woman. Then they all looked round for Christine, but nobody saw her. Each one had thought only of saving himself and no one else, and as each of them was now sitting where it was dry, he thought that all the others were too. Only now did it occur to them all that they had not seen Christine again since that terrible moment, and that she had not come into the house. Then her husband began to lament and all the others lamented with him, for it seemed to them all as if only Christine knew how to help. Suddenly the door opened, and Christine stood in their midst; her hair was dripping wet and her cheeks were red, while her eyes were burning more darkly than usual with a sinister fire. She was received with a sympathy to which she was not accustomed, and everybody wanted to tell her what had been thought and expressed and how much they had worried about her. Christine soon saw what this all meant and, hiding her inner fire behind mocking words, she reproached the men for their overhasty flight and for the way none of them had taken any trouble about a poor woman and nobody had looked round to see what the green huntsman was up to with her. Then the storm of curiosity broke out, and everybody wanted first to know what the green huntsman had been doing with her, and those who were at the back stood up as high as they could in order to hear better and to see more closely the woman who had stood so near to the green huntsman. She wasn't to say anything, Christine said at first; they hadn't deserved it of her, they had treated her badly in the valley because she was a foreigner, the women had given her a bad name, the men had left her in the lurch everywhere, and if she had not been better intentioned than them all and if she had not had more courage than the lot of them, there would be no consolation nor way out for them at this very moment. Christine went on talking a long time in this way, reproaching the womenfolk harshly, who had never been willing to believe her that Lake Constance was bigger than the castle pond, and the more she was pressed, the more obstinate she seemed to become, and she insisted that people would put a wrong interpretation on what she had to say, and if all went well, would give her no thanks on that account; but if anything went wrong, it would be her fault and the entire responsibility would be placed upon her shoulders.

When finally the whole gathering was before Christine, begging and imploring her almost on their knees, and when those who were injured cried out loud and persisted in so doing, Christine seemed to relent and began to tell how she had stood firm and come to an agreement with the green huntsman; but she said nothing about the kiss, nor about the way it had burned on her cheek and how her mind had been overwhelmed with the roaring noise. But she related what she had been considering since then in her downcast mind. The most important thing, she said, was that the beech-trees would be taken up to Bärhegen; once they were up there, you could still see what could be done, and the main thing was that up till then as far as she knew no child would be born among them.

Many felt cold shivers down their spines at this account, but they were all pleased to think that they would still be able to see what could be done.

One young woman alone wept so bitterly that you could have washed your hands under her eyes, but she did not say anything. There was, however, one old woman, tall in appearance and with a presence that commanded respect, for her face was one which required obeisance or else compelled flight. She stepped into the middle of the room and said that to act like that would be to forget God, to risk losing what was certain for the sake of something uncertain, and to play with one's eternal salvation. Whoever had to do with the evil one would never escape from him, and whoever gave him a finger would lose body and soul to him. Nobody could help them from this distress but God; but whoever forsook God in time of trouble, would himself be lost in time of trouble. But on this occasion the old woman's words were scorned and the young woman was told to be silent, for weeping and moaning would be no use here; another kind of help was needed now, they said.

It was soon agreed to try the arrangement. In the worst eventuality the business could hardly go badly; for it would not be the first time that men had deceived the most evil spirits, and if they themselves did not know what to do, a priest surely would give advice and find a way out. But in their darkness of mind many a one must have thought what he later admitted: that he would not risk much money or time on account of an unbaptized child.

When the decision was taken according to Christine's wishes, it was as if all the whirlwinds were crashing together over the house-top, as if the armies of wild huntsmen were roaring overhead; the upright posts of the house quivered, the beams bent, trees splintered against the house like spears on a knight's breastplate. The people within turned pale and were overcome with horror, but they did not rescind their decision; when the gray light of dawn appeared they set about putting their counsel into effect.

The morning was beautiful and bright, thunder and lightning and witchcraft had vanished, the axes struck twice as sharply as before, the soil was friable and every beech-tree fell straight, just as one would like it, none of the carts broke, the cattle were amenable and strong and the men were protected from all accidents as if by an invisible hand.

There was only one thing that was queer. At that time there was no track below Sumiswald leading to the lower valley; in that part there was still swampland which was watered by the uncontrollable river Grüne; one had to go up the slope and through the village past the church. As on the previous days they travelled always three teams together, so that they could help each other with advice, strength and cattle, and from that point onwards all they had to do was to go through Sumiswald, down the slope by the church on the other side of the village, and here there stood a little shrine; they had to lay out the beeches beyond the slope where the road was flat. As soon as they had come up the slope and were approaching the church on a level part of the road, the weight of the carts did not become lighter but heavier and heavier; they had to harness as many animals as they could muster, had to beat them unmercifully, had to lay hand on the spokes themselves to turn them, and what is more, even the quietest horses shied as if there were something invisible appearing from the churchyard that stood in their way, and a hollow sounding of a bell, almost like the misplaced noise of a distant death-knell, came from the church, so that a peculiar sensation of horror seized even the strongest men, and every time that they approached the church, both men and beast shook with fear. Once they had passed beyond, they could move on quietly, unload quietly, and then go quietly back for a fresh load.

On that same day the peasants unloaded six beech-trees and placed them side by side at the agreed spot; the next morning six beech-trees had been planted up on Bärhegen and throughout the whole valley nobody had heard an axle turning over on its hub, and nobody had heard the usual calling of carters, the neighing of horses or the monotonous bellowing of oxen. But there were six beech-trees standing up there, anybody could see them who wanted to, and they were the six trees which had been laid down at the foot of the slope, and no other ones.

At that there was great astonishment throughout the valley, and many people's curiosity was aroused. The knights especially wondered what kind of agreement the peasants had made and by what means the beech-trees had been transported to the spot. They would have gladly used heathenish means of forcing the secret from the peasants. However, they soon realized that the peasants too did not know all and were themselves half terrified. Furthermore, von Stoffeln resisted them. He was not only indifferent about how the trees came to Bärhegen, on the contrary, provided only that the trees did arrive there, he himself was glad that the peasants were not being exhausted in the process. He had indeed realized that the mockery of his knights had misled him to a foolish action, for if the peasants were ruined and the fields not cultivated, it was the ruling class which would suffer the greatest loss; but once von Stoffeln had given an order, it had to stand. Therefore the relief which the peasants had obtained for themselves suited him quite well, and he was wholly indifferent whether in consequence they had forsworn their souls' salvation; for what did he care about the souls of peasants, once death had taken their bodies? Now he laughed at his knights and protected the peasants from their wantonness. In spite of this the knights wanted to get to the bottom of the business and sent squires to keep watch; these were found the next morning lying half-dead in ditches, hurled there by an invisible hand.

Then two knights set off to Bärhegen. They were bold warriors, and where there had been any hazardous enterprise to be faced in heathen lands, they had faced it. They were found the next morning lying unconscious on the ground, and when they recovered their speech they said that they had been hurled down by a red knight with a fiery lance. Here and there could be found an inquisitive woman who could not refrain from looking out at midnight from a crack in the timber or from a dormer-window to the road in the valley. Immediately a poisonous wind blew up at such a one, so that the face swelled up, and for weeks afterwards nose and eyes could not be seen and her mouth could be found only with difficulty. That made people less anxious to indulge in peeping, and no single eye looked out when midnight lay over the valley.

On one occasion, however, death came suddenly upon a man; he needed the last sacraments, but nobody could fetch the priest, since it was almost midnight, and the way lay past the Kilchstalden. So an innocent little boy, dear in the sight of God and man, ran to Sumiswald without informing anybody, impelled by anxiety for his father. When he came to the Kilchstalden he saw beech-trees rising up from the ground, each one drawn by two fiery squirrels, and nearby he saw a green huntsman riding on a black ram, with a fiery whip in his hand, a fiery beard on his face and a feather swaying red hot on his hat. The transport flew high into the air over all the slopes and as quick as a flash. This is what the lad saw, and no harm came to him.

Before three weeks had passed, ninety beech-trees were standing on Bärhegen, making a beautiful shaded walk, for all the trees put out shoots luxuriantly and none of them withered. But neither the knights nor von Stoffeln himself went walking there often, for every time they were seized by a secret horror; they would rather have known nothing further about the business, but nobody made a suggestion that the work should be stopped, and each comforted himself by saying that if things went wrong, it would be somebody else's fault.

But the peasants felt easier with every beech-tree that was planted up on top, for with every tree grew the hope that their lord would be satisfied and the green huntsman deceived; after all, he had no guarantee, and once the hundredth tree was up there, what did they care about the green huntsman? Nevertheless they were still not certain about the matter; every day they were afraid that he might play them a trick and leave them in the lurch. On May 25th, St. Urban's day, they brought him the last beeches to the Kilchstalden, and neither old nor young slept much that night; it was scarcely believable that he would complete the work without making some trouble, if he were without a child or any surety.

The next morning old and young were up long before sunrise, for everyone was impelled by the same inquisitive anxiety; but it was a long time before anybody ventured to the place where the beech-trees had been put; perhaps there would be some trap there for those who wished to deceive the green huntsman.

A wild cowherd who had brought goats down from high mountain pasture finally dared to go forward; he found no beech-trees lying on the ground, nor could any trace of trickery be perceived at that spot. They still had no trust in the business; the cowherd had to go ahead of them to Bärhegen. There everything was in order, a hundred beech-trees stood in full array, none was withered, nobody's face swelled up, nobody had pains in any limb. Then their hearts became exultant, and much mockery could be heard at the expense of the green huntsman and the knights. For the third time they sent out the wild cowherd and had him inform von Stoffeln that everything was now in order on Bärhegen, and that he might like to come and count the beech-trees. But von Stoffeln felt terrified, and he sent them the message that they should see to it that they went home. He would have gladly told them to remove the whole avenue of trees, but he did not do this on account of his knights; he did not know about the peasants' compact, and who it was who might intervene in the business.

When the cowherd brought the message, hearts swelled yet more with defiance; wild youths danced in the avenue, a wild yodelling resounded from ravine to ravine, from one mountain to another, and re-echoed from the walls of Sumiswald castle. Thoughtful older people admonished and pleaded, but defiant hearts do not pay attention to the warnings of cautious old age; and then once the misfortune has come about, the old people are blamed for it on account of their hesitation and warnings. The time has not yet come when it is recognized that when defiance stamps its foot, misfortune grows forth from the ground. The rejoicing spread over hill and vale into all the houses; and wherever a finger's length of smoked meat remained, it was taken down and prepared for eating, and wherever a lump of butter as big as a hand remained in a basin, it was used for baking.

The meat was eaten, the fritters disappeared, day had gone and a new day rose in the sky. Nearer and nearer came the day when a woman should bear a child; and the nearer the day, the more urgently did the fear become renewed that the green huntsman would announce himself again and demand what was his by right, or else prepare a trap for them.

Who could measure the distress of that young woman who was to give birth to the child? Her cries of despair resounded throughout the whole house, gradually affecting all who lived there, and nobody could give any counsel, apart from saying that there was no trusting that huntsman whom they had had the dealings with. The nearer the fateful hour came, the more closely the poor woman pressed to God, embraced the Holy Mother not with her arms alone but with body and soul and whole mind, praying for protection for the sake of Her blessed Son. And it became clearer and clearer to her that in life and death in every need the greatest comfort is in God, for where He is, the evil one may not be and has no power.

Her soul was convinced ever more clearly that if a priest of the Lord were present at the birth with that holiest of all things, the sacred body of the Redeemer, and if he were armed with strong sentences of anathema, no evil spirit would dare to draw near, and at once the priest would be able to provide the newborn child with the sacrament of baptism, as was allowed by custom at that time; then the poor child would be removed for ever from the danger which the presumption of its fathers had brought upon it. This belief came to be shared by others, and the young woman's wretched plight went to their hearts, but they fought shy of confessing to the priest their pact with Satan, and since that time nobody had gone to confession nor had given an account of themselves to him. The priest was a very pious man, and even the knights of the castle did not make fun of him, though he told them the truth straight. What the peasants had thought was that once the business was over, he could do nothing to stop them; but all the same nobody now wanted to be the first to tell him, and their consciences told them why.

At last the wretchedness of the situation moved one woman to take action; she went off and disclosed to the priest the compact and what it was the poor woman wanted. The pious man was greatly shocked, but he did not waste time with empty words; he boldly took up the fight with the mighty enemy on behalf of a poor soul. He was one of those men who do not fear the hardest fight, because they wish to be crowned with the crown of eternal life, and because indeed they know that no man will be crowned unless he fights well.

He drew a consecrated circle with holy water about the house where the woman was awaiting her time, for no evil spirits might step into this circle; he blessed the threshold and the whole room, and the woman had a quiet labor and the priest baptized the child without any disturbance. Outside all was quiet, bright stars sparkled in the clear sky and gentle breezes played in the trees. Some people said they heard laughter like a horse's neighing from afar; but others thought it was only the owls at the edge of the wood.

Everyone present, however, was highly delighted, and all fear had disappeared, for ever, as they thought; for if they had fooled the green huntsman once, they could go on doing so by the same method.

A great feast was prepared, and guests were invited from far and wide. The priest of the Lord warned them in vain against feasting and rejoicing, told them to be fearful and to pray, for the enemy was not yet overcome nor God propitiated. He felt in his mind that he was not in a position to lay any act of penance upon them, and that a mighty and heavy punishment was approaching from God's own hand. But they did not listen to him and wanted to satisfy him with invitations to food and drink. He, however, went sadly away, prayed for those who did not know what they were doing, and armed himself with prayer and fasting to fight like a true shepherd for the flock entrusted to his care.

Christine too was sitting in the midst of the jubilant throng, but she sat strangely still with glowing cheeks, somber eyes, and one could see a strange twitching in her face. Christine, as an experienced midwife, had been present at the birth, and had acted as godmother during the hasty christening ceremony with an insolent, fearless heart, but when the priest sprinkled the water over the child and baptized it in the three holy names, she felt as if someone were suddenly pressing a red-hot iron on the spot where she had received the green huntsman's kiss. She had started in sudden terror, had almost dropped the child on to the ground, and since that time the pain had not decreased but became more glowing from hour to hour. At first she had sat still, had forced back the pain and kept to herself the dark thoughts which were turning in her awakened mind, but she moved her hand ever more frequently to the burning spot, on which a poisonous wasp seemed to be placed, piercing with a burning sting right into her marrow. But as there was no wasp to be chased away and as the stings became ever more burning and her thoughts ever more dreadful, Christine began to show people her cheek and ask them what could be seen on it, and she kept on asking, but nobody saw anything, and soon nobody had any wish to be diverted from the pleasures of the christening celebration by peering at her cheeks. Finally she found an old woman who was willing to look carefully; just at that moment the cock crowed, the gray of dawn came, so that what the old woman saw on Christine's cheek was an almost invisible spot. It was nothing, she said, it would go away all right; and she moved off.

And Christine tried to comfort herself that it was nothing and it would go away soon; but the pain did not lessen, and the little spot grew imperceptibly, and everybody saw it and asked her what that black thing was on her face. They did not mean anything special by it, but their remarks went to her heart like swordthrusts, rekindled her dark thoughts, and she could not avoid coming back to the thought, time and time again, that it was on this very spot that the green huntsman had kissed her, and that the same fire which on that occasion had shot through her limbs like lightning, now remained burning and consuming there. Thus she could not sleep, her food tasted like firebrand, she rushed aimlessly about, seeking consolation but finding none, for the pain increased still further, and the black spot became bigger and blacker, single dark streaks ran out from the spot, and down towards the mouth it seemed as if there was a lump planted on the round spot.

In this way Christine suffered and rushed around many a long day and many a long night without revealing to anyone the fear in her heart and what it was she had received from the green huntsman on this spot; but if she had known how she could have got rid of this pain, she would have given anything in heaven or on earth to do it. She was by nature a brazen woman, but now she was savage with angry pain.

It now happened that once again a woman was expecting a child. This time there was no great fear and people were easy in mind; so long as they saw to the priest coming at the right time, they thought they could defy the green huntsman. It was only Christine who did not share this belief. The nearer the day of the birth came, the more terrible the burning on her cheek became, the more violently the black spot extended, stretching out legs visibly, driving up short hairs, while shining points and strips appeared on its back, and the hump became a head out of which there blazed a poisonous brilliance as if from two eyes. Everyone who saw the poisonous spider on Christine's cheek shrieked aloud, and they fled full of fear and horror when they saw how this spider sat firm on her face and had grown out from her flesh. People said all kinds of things, some advised this, some advised the other, but all wished Christine joy of it, whatever it was, and all avoided her and fled from her whenever this was possible. The more people fled from her, the more Christine was driven to follow them, and she rushed from house to house; she must have felt that the devil was reminding her of the promised child; and she rushed after folk in hellish fear to persuade them in no uncertain words to make the sacrifice required by the pact. But the others were little troubled by this; what was tormenting Christine did not hurt them, and what she was suffering was in their opinion her own responsibility, and if they could no longer escape from her, they said to her: 'That's your affair! Nobody has promised a child, and therefore nobody is going to give one.' She set about her own husband with furious words. He fled like the rest, and when he could no longer avoid her he cold-bloodedly told her that it would get better all right, it was a spot such as many people had; once it had taken its course, the pain would cease, and it would be easy to disperse it.

Meanwhile, however, the pain did not cease, each leg was hellfire, the spider's body hell itself, and when the woman's appointed time came, Christine felt as if a sea of fire were surging around her, as if fiery knives were boring in her marrow, as if fiery whirlwinds were rushing through her brain. But the spider swelled and arched itself up, and its eyes glared viciously from between the short bristles. When Christine found no sympathy anywhere in her burning agony and saw that the woman in labor was strongly guarded, she burst forth like a mad woman along the road where the priest would have to come.

The latter was coming up the slope at a quick pace, accompanied by the sturdy sexton; the hot sun and the steep road did not slow down their walk, for it was a matter of saving a soul and of preventing an eternal misfortune; coming from a visit to a sick parishioner who lived a long way off, the priest was anxious on account of the fearful delay he had experienced. In desperation Christine threw herself before him in the road, clasped his knees, begged for release from her hell, for the sacrifice of the child that was not yet born, and the spider swelled still more, gleamed terrible and black in Christine's red swollen face, and with terrifying glances it glared at the priest's holy requisites. But the priest pushed Christine quickly to one side and made the holy sign; he saw the enemy well enough, but desisted from the fight in order to save a soul. But Christine started up, stormed after him and did her utmost to stop him; yet the sexton's strong hand held the woman off from the priest, and the latter could just arrive in time to protect the house, to receive the infant into his consecrated hands and to place it into the hands of Him Whom hell never overcomes.

Meanwhile Christine had been undergoing a terrible struggle outside. She wanted to have the child unbaptized in her hands and wanted to force her way into the house, but strong men prevented her. Gusts of wind buffeted against the house and yellow lightning hissed round it, but the hand of the Lord was above it; the child was baptized, and Christine circled round the house in vain and without power. Seized by ever wilder hellish torture, she emitted sounds which did not resemble sounds that might come from a human breast; the cattle quivered in their sheds and tore loose from their halters, while the tops of the oak-trees in the forest rustled in terror.

Inside the house there was rejoicing over the new victory, the impotence of the green huntsman, the vain writhings of his accessory; but Christine lay outside, thrown on to the ground by dreadful pains, and her face was seized by labor pains such as no woman in childbed has ever experienced on this earth, and the spider in her face swelled higher and higher and burned ever more searingly through her limbs.

Then Christine felt as if her face were bursting open, as if burning coals were being born, coming to life and crawling away over her face, over all her limbs, as if her whole face were coming to life and crawling away red-hot over all her body. In the pale light from the lightning she now saw black little spiders, long-legged, poisonous and innumerable, running over her limbs out into the night, and after those that had disappeared there ran others, long-legged, poisonous and innumerable. Finally she could see no more following the earlier ones, the fire in her face subsided, the spider settled down, became once more an almost invisible point and looked with weary eyes out at the hellish brood which it had borne and sent forth, as a sign that the green huntsman would not let himself be made a fool of.

Exhausted like a woman who has just given birth to a child, Christine crept into the house; although the fire no longer burned so hot on her face, the fire in her heart had not abated, even if her weary limbs longed for rest, for the green huntsman would give her no more rest; once he has got somebody, that is how he treats them.

Inside the house, however, there was jubilation and rejoicing, and for a long time they did not hear how the cattle were bellowing and raging in the cowshed. At last they did start up, and a few went out to see; when those who had gone out returned they came back pale as death with the news that the best cow lay dead and the rest of them were raging and stampeding in such a way as had never been seen before. It wasn't right, there was something unusual at the back of it, they said. At that the sounds of rejoicing were silenced; everyone ran out to the cattle, whose bellowing could be heard over hill and valley, but nobody had any suggestions. They tried both worldly and spiritual arts against magic, but all in vain; already before day broke, death had laid low all the cattle in the shed. But when it became silent in one farm, the bellowing started up on another farm, and yet another; those who were there heard how the trouble had broken into their cattle-sheds and how the animals called to their masters for help in their terrible fear.

They rushed home as if flames were leaping from their house-tops, but there was nothing they could do; on one farm as on another death laid low the cattle; cries of distress from man and beast filled hills and valleys, and the sun which had set leaving the valley so happy, rose to gaze upon scenes of awful distress. When the sun shone, people at last could see how the sheds where the cattle had been stricken were teeming with countless black spiders. These creatures crawled over the cattle, and the cattle-food which they touched became poisoned, and any living creature began to rage until soon it was felled by death. It was impossible to get rid of these spiders from any cattle-shed where they had penetrated, it was as if they grew out of the ground itself; it was impossible to protect any shed where they had not yet entered from their invasion, for unexpectedly they started creeping out of all the walls and would fall in clusters from the threshing-floor. The cattle were then driven out to pasture, but it was simply driving them into death's jaws. For wherever a cow placed her foot on to grassland, the ground began to come to life; black, long-legged spiders sprouted up, horrible Alpine flowers which crawled on to the cattle, and a fearful wailing could be heard from the hilltops down to the valley. And all these spiders resembled the spider on Christine's face as children resemble their mother, and nobody had ever seen such before.

The noise of the wretched animals had penetrated to the castle too, and soon shepherds followed with the news that their cattle had fallen because of the poisonous animals, and von Stoffeln heard with ever increasing anger how herd upon herd had been lost; now he learned what type of pact his peasants had made with the green huntsman, and how the huntsman had been deceived a second time, and how the spiders resembled, as children their mother, the spider on the face of the woman from Lindau who alone had made the compact with the green huntsman and had never given a proper account of what had happened. Then von Stoffeln rode up the hill in fierce anger and roared at the peasants that he was not going to lose herd upon herd for their sake; they would have to keep any promises that they had made; what they had done of their own free will, they would have to put up with. He wasn't going to suffer damage on their account, or if he did have to suffer, they would have to make it good to him a thousand times over. They would have to look out. In this way he spoke to them, indifferent to what it was he was expecting of them; it did not occur to him that he had driven them to it, for he only took account of what they had done.

It had already dawned upon most of the peasants that the spiders were a visitation of the evil one, a warning that they should keep the agreement; that Christine must know more about it, and that she had not told them all about her agreement with the green huntsman. Now they all trembled again at the thought of the green huntsman and no longer laughed at him, and they trembled before their temporal lord; if they did placate their overlords, what would their spiritual lord say about it, would he allow this, and would he not then lay any penance upon them? The leading peasants met in their fear in a solitary shed, and Christine was to come there and give a clear account of what exactly she had agreed with the green huntsman.

Christine came, more savage, thirsting for revenge, again racked by the growing spider.

When she saw the hesitation of the men and realized that there were no women there, she related exactly what had happened to her: how the green huntsman had quickly taken her at her word and had given her a kiss as a token to which she had not paid any attention any more than to other kisses; how the spider had now grown in hellish pain on that same spot from the moment onwards when the first child had been baptized; how the spider had given birth in hellish agonies to an innumerable host of spiders as soon as the second child had been born and the green huntsman had been fooled; for it was obvious that you could not fool him and get away with it, as she herself felt in her thousandfold pains of death. Now the spider was growing again, she said, the pain was increasing, and if the next child were not given to the green hunstman, nobody could tell how horrible a calamity might break in upon them, and how horrible the knight's vengeance might be.

This is what Christine said, and the men's hearts throbbed, and for a long time nobody was willing to speak. Gradually broken sounds pressed forth from their frightened throats, and when these sounds were pieced together, it was evident that the peasants thought exactly as Christine did, but they insisted that not one of them had given his consent to her action. One of the men stood up and said shortly and sharply that it seemed to him that the best thing was to kill Christine, for once she was dead, the green huntsman could do as he pleased with her, but would have no further claim on the living. Then Christine laughed wildly, stepped close up to him and said into his face that he could hit out at her, it was all the same to her, but the green huntsman wasn't interested in her, but in an unbaptized child, and just as he had laid his mark on her, so he could mark the hand which wrongfully seized her. Then there was a twitching in the hand of this one man who had spoken, he sat down and silently listened to the advice of the others. In tentative, fragmentary phrases, of the type where nobody says everything but each speaker only says something that is intended to mean little, an agreement was made that the next child should be sacrificed; but nobody was willing to lend a hand here by carrying the child to the Kilchstalden where the beech-trees had been laid out. Nobody had been reluctant to use the devil for what they considered to be the general good, but nobody wanted to meet him personally. Then Christine offered herself willingly for this, for if one has had to do with the devil on one occasion, it could do little further harm a second time. It was known who was to give birth to the next child, but nothing was said about it, and the father of the child was not present. After making this agreement, which was both a spoken and an unspoken one, they dispersed.

The young woman who had trembled and wept without knowing why on that dreadful night when Christine had given her account of the green huntsman was now expecting the next child. What had happened in the previous cases did not make her feel cheerful and confident, an indefinable fear lay upon her heart which she could not remove either by prayer or confession. It seemed to her as if she were encircled by a conspiracy of silence, nobody spoke about the spider any more, all eyes which looked at her seemed to her suspicious, and seemed to be calculating the hour when they might seize upon her child in order to placate the devil.

She felt so lonely and forlorn in face of the secret power around her; the only support she had was her mother-in-law, a pious woman who remained faithful to her, but what can an old woman do against a wild crowd? She had her husband who had indeed promised all good things; but how he wailed about his cattle and how little he thought of his poor wife's anxiety! The priest had promised to come as quickly and as soon as they might ask, but what could happen during the period after he had been sent for and before he arrived? And the poor woman had no reliable messenger except her husband, who should be her protection and guard; and, what is more, the poor woman lived in one house with Christine, and their husbands were brothers, and she had no relations of her own, for she had come into the house as an orphan! You can imagine the poor woman's anxiety of heart; she could find some confidence only when she prayed with her good mother-in-law, but this confidence at once disappeared again as soon as she saw the evil looks around her.

Meanwhile the sickness was still there, keeping the terror alive. It was true that it was only here or there that one of the animals died, if the spiders showed themselves. But as soon as the terror lessened at one farm or as soon as somebody said, or thought, that the bad business was becoming less serious of its own accord and that one should think twice before treating a child sinfully, Christine's hellish pains flamed up, the spider swelled high and the man who had thought or talked in this way discovered that death had returned among his herd of cattle with renewed rage. Yes, the nearer the expected hour came, the more the distress seemed to increase again, and people realized that they would have to make a definite arrangement about how they were to get hold of the child safely and without fail. They were most afraid of the husband, and they were loath to use violence against him. He said he did not want to know about the business; he was willing to do as his wife asked and fetch the priest, but he agreed not to hurry about it, and what might happen in his absence was not his business; in this way he placated his conscience; he would placate God through extra masses, and it might still be possible to do something for the poor child's soul, he thought; perhaps the pious priest would wrest the child back from the devil, and then he and the other peasants would be out of the business; they would have done their part and at the same time still cheated the evil one. That is what the husband thought, and in any case, however matters turned, he argued, he himself would have no responsibility for the whole business, since he was not taking any active part with his own hands.

In this manner the poor wife had been sold and did not know it; she anxiously went on hoping that rescue would come; the stab to her heart had been decided in the counsel of the people—but what He above had decreed was still covered by the clouds which hide the future.

It was a year of storms, and harvest-time had come; all possible strength was being mobilized, in order to bring the grain safely under cover during the bright periods. A hot afternoon had come, the clouds stretched their black heads over the dark peaks, the swallows fluttered fearfully around the roof, and the poor wife felt so constrained and anxious alone in the house; for even the grandmother was outside in the fields, helping more with good intentions than with deeds. Then the pain pierced double-edged through the woman's marrow and bones, everything went dark in front of her eyes, she felt her hour approaching and was alone. Fear drove her out of the house, with dragging feet she walked out to the field, but soon had to sit down; she wanted to call out into the distance, but her voice would not leave her heavily breathing breast. There was with her a little lad who had only just learned how to walk and who had never gone to the field on his own legs but only in his mother's arms. The poor woman had to use this boy as her messenger; she did not know whether he would be able to find the field or whether his little legs could carry him there. But the faithful lad saw how anxious his mother was, and ran, and fell down, and stood up again, and the cat chased his pet rabbit, doves and hens ran about his feet, his pet lamb jumped after him, playfully pushing; but the boy saw nothing of it, did not let himself be held up and faithfully delivered his message.

The grandmother appeared in breathless haste, but the husband delayed; he only wanted to finish stacking up the cartload, was the message. An eternity passed, at last he came, and another eternity passed, at last he set out on the long road, and the poor wife felt in deathly fear how her time was drawing more and more quickly upon her.

Christine had been gleefully watching everything outside in the field. The sun might burn hot as she worked at the heavy labor, but the spider hardly burned any more at all, and for the next few hours walking seemed easy to her. She got on with the work happily and was in no hurry to return home, for she knew how slow the messenger was going to be. It was not until the last sheaf had been loaded and gusts of wind announced the approaching storm that she made haste towards her prey which she thought was so safely hers. And as she walked home, she waved knowingly to various passers-by, and they nodded to her and quickly took the news to their own homes; there was much sinking at the knees where the news was heard, and many souls wanted to pray in their involuntary fear, but could not do so.

Inside the little room the poor woman was whimpering, and each minute became an eternity, and the grandmother could not allay the extreme distress, even though she prayed and spoke consolingly. She had locked up the room carefully and placed heavy furniture in front of the door. As long as they were alone in the house, it was still tolerable, but when they saw Christine coming home, when they heard her slinking step by the door, when they heard many another footstep outside and secret whispering, and no priest nor any faithful person showed himself, and when the moment, usually longed for so intensely, approached nearer and nearer, you can imagine how the poor women in their fear were as if swimming in boiling oil, without help and without hope. They heard how Christine would not move from the door; the poor woman could feel the fiery eyes of her wild sister-in-law piercing through the door and burning her through body and soul. Then the first whimpering sign of new life was heard through the door, stifled as quickly as possible, but too late. The door flew open from a violent lurch which Christine had been waiting to give all this time, and just as a tiger leaps upon its prey, so Christine leaps upon the poor woman in childbirth. The old woman who throws herself to meet the storm is hurled down; the woman in childbed pulls herself together in a mother's holy fear, but her weak body collapses, and the child is in Christine's hands; a ghastly cry bursts from the mother's heart, and then she is enshrouded in the black shadows of unconsciousness.

Hesitation and horror seized the men as Christine came out with the stolen child. The anticipation of a terrible future was revealed to them, but nobody had the courage to stop the deed, and fear of the devil's visitations was stronger than the fear of God. Christine alone did not hesitate; her face gleamed burning, like that of a victorious warrior after the fight, and it seemed to her as if the spider were caressing her with a soft tickling; the flashes of lightning which had licked around her on her way to the Kilchstalden now seemed to be cheerful lights, while the thunder sounded like a gentle growl, and the vengeful storm like a pleasant rustling.

Hans, the poor woman's wretched husband, had kept his word only too well. He had made his way slowly, had looked ponderingly at every field, watched every bird and waited to see how the fish in the stream leapt up to catch flies just before the storm broke. Then he started forward with rapid steps and prepared to take a jump; there was something within him which drove him to it and made his hair stand on end; it was his conscience, which told him what a father deserved if he betrayed his wife and child, it was the love which he still bore to his wife and to his own seed. But then there was something else which held him back, and that was stronger than the first thing; it was fear of other people, fear of the devil and love of those things which the devil could take from him. Then he went more slowly again, slowly as a man who is taking his last walk, the walk to the scaffold. Perhaps this really was the case, for after all many a man does not know that the walk he is taking may be his last; if he knew this, he would not set out on it, or else he would do so in another spirit.

Thus it was late before he came to Sumiswald. Black clouds raced across over the Münneberg, heavy drops of rain fell, hissing in the hot dust, and the little bell in the church-tower began its hollow ringing to admonish the people to think of God and to beg that His storm should not become a judgment upon them. The priest stood in front of his house, prepared for any journey to his parishioners, and ready to set out to a dying man, to a burning house or whatever else it might be, if his Master, Who was moving above him across the heavens, should call upon him. When he saw Hans coming he recognized that this was a call to a difficult task; he wrapped his robes firmly about him and sent word to his sexton that he should find someone else to take his place as bell-ringer. In the meantime he provided Hans with a cool drink which would be so refreshing after the quick walk in the sultry atmosphere, though Hans had no need of it; but the priest did not suspect the man's deceitfulness. Hans took his refreshment slowly and deliberately. The sexton appeared, but in no hurry, and gladly shared in the drink which Hans offered him. The priest stood accoutered before them, scorning any drink which he did not need for the walk and the struggle ahead. He did not like to tell anyone to leave the drink he had before him and to infringe a guest's privileges, but he knew a law which was higher than the law of hospitality, and this leisurely drinking made him impatient with anger.

At last he told them that he was ready, that a distressed woman was waiting and that an appalling misdeed was threatening them; he would have to come between the woman and the evil deed with his holy weapons, and therefore they were to come without further delay; up above there would still be something for the man who had not quenched his thirst here below. Then Hans, the husband of the woman who was waiting, replied that there was no particular hurry, as his wife was slow and had difficulties about everything. And at once a flash of lightning burst into the room so that they were all blinded by it, and a clap of thunder sounded over the house so that every post and beam trembled. Then after he had finished his prayer of blessing the sexton said: 'Hark at the weather outside; the heavens themselves have confirmed what Hans said, that we ought to wait, and what use would it be if we did go, we should never get there alive, and after all he said himself that there would be no need to hurry in the case of his wife.'

And truly the storm was pelting down in a way that is seldom seen more than once in a lifetime. It was raging from every cleft and valley, from all sides, and from all quarters the winds were driving in upon Sumiswald, and every cloud became an army of warriors, and one cloud stormed upon another, one cloud wanted the other cloud's life, and a battle of the clouds began, and the storm stood its ground, and flash after flash of lightning was let loose, and flash after flash was slung down to earth as if the lightning were trying to cut a passage down through the center of the earth and out on to the other side. The thunder roared without intermission, the storm howled angrily, the clouds' belly burst open, and floods poured down. When the battle of the clouds broke out so suddenly and violently, the priest had not answered the sexton, but neither had he sat down; an ever mounting anxiety seized hold of him, and an urge came upon him to plunge out into the raging of the elements, though he hesitated on account of his companions. Then he seemed to hear above the terrible voice of the thunder the piercing cry of a woman in labor. Then the thunder appeared to him all at once as God's terrible reproach for his delay; he prepared to set out, whatever the other two might say. Ready for whatever might come, he stepped out into the fiery raging of the tempest and the downpour from the clouds; the two others followed slowly and reluctantly behind him.

There was a roaring and whistling and raging, as if these sounds were to fuse into the last trump heralding the end of the world, and sheaves of fire fell upon the village, as if every house were to burst into flames; but the servant of Him Who gives His voice to the thunder and uses the lightning as His servant need have no fear of this fellow-servant of the same Lord, and whoever goes on God's errands can confidently leave God's weather to take care of itself. Hence the priest walked fearlessly through the storm to the Kilchstalden, carrying with him the hallowed holy weapons, and his heart was with God. But the others did not follow him with the same courage, for their hearts were not in the same place; they did not wish to go down the Kilchstalden, not in such weather and at such an hour, and, what is more, Hans had a special reason to be reluctant. They begged the priest to turn back, to go another way: Hans knew a nearer path, while the sexton knew a better one, and both warned him against the floods in the valley from the swollen river Grüne. But the priest did not hear and took no notice of what they said; urged on by an unaccountable impulse, he hastened towards the Kilchstalden on the wings of prayer, no stone catching his feet and no lightning blinding his eyes; Hans and the sexton followed behind trembling, and protected, as they thought, by the holy sacraments which the priest himself was carrying.

But when they arrived in view of the village, where the slope goes down to the valley below, the priest suddenly halts and puts his hand over his eyes for protection. Beyond the shrine a red feather gleams in the light of the lightning, and the priest's sharp eye sees a black head rearing up from the green hedgerow, and on the head the red feather. And as he goes on looking, he sees a wild figure coming down the opposite slope in rapid flight, as if driven by the wind's wild fury, hastening towards the dark head upon which the red feather was swaying like a flag.

At that the priest was inflamed by the sacred fighting urge which comes upon those whose hearts are dedicated to God as soon as they sense the imminence of the evil one; it comes like the growth of life upon the seed of corn or the opening flower or upon the warrior who is confronted by his opponent's drawn sword. And the priest rushed down the slope like a thirsting man towards the cool waters of a river or a hero into battle, rushed into fiercest battle, thrust himself between the green huntsman and Christine as she was about to place the child in the evil one's arms, and hurled the three holy names into their midst; he holds up the holy implement before the green huntsman's face, dashes holy water over the child and at the same time catches Christine with it. Thereupon the green huntsman makes off with a terrifying howl of pain, flashing by like a red-hot strip until the earth swallows him up; after being touched by the holy water Christine shrivels up with a frightful hissing, like wool in fire or quicklime in water, shrivels up, hissing and flame-flaying, until nothing remains but the black, swollen, ghastly spider in her own face, shrivels into it, hisses into it, and now this spider sits distended with poison and defiant, right on the child, and shoots angry flashes of lightning from her eyes at the priest. The latter throws holy water at her, which hisses like ordinary water on a hot stone; the spider grows bigger and bigger, and extends her black legs further and further over the child, glaring ever more poisonously at the priest; with the courage of his burning faith the priest now stretches out a daring hand towards her. It is as if he were plunging his hand into red-hot thorns, but he holds fast undeterred, hurls the verminous creature away, picks up the child and takes it to the mother without further delay.

And as the priest's struggle ended, the battle of the clouds abated too, and they hurried off to their dark chambers; soon the valley in which the fiercest battle had just been raging was shimmering in the quiet light of the stars, and almost breathlessly the priest reached the house where the crime had been committed against mother and child.

The mother was still lying in a faint, for she had lost consciousness after emitting her piercing cry; the old woman sat praying by her side, for she still trusted God and believed His strength was greater than the devil's wickedness. By returning the child the priest also restored life to the mother. When she saw her baby again as she awoke, she was permeated by a rapture such as is only known to the angels in heaven, and the priest baptized the child as it lay in its mother's arms in the name of God the Father, Son and Holy Spirit; and now the infant was snatched from the devil's power for ever, unless it should at some future time submit of its own accord to the evil one. But God protected the infant from this fate; the newborn soul was given into God's care, while the body lay poisoned by the spider.

Soon the soul departed from this life, and the little body was marked as if by burns. The poor mother wept indeed, but when each part returns to where it belongs, the soul to God, the body to the earth, consolation will come, more quickly to one person perhaps, and more slowly to another.

As soon as the priest had fulfilled his holy office, he began to feel a strange itching in the hand and arm with which he had hurled away the spider. He noticed small, black blotches on his hand which grew visibly larger and swelled up; the shudder of death penetrated to his heart. He gave the two women his blessing and hurried home, wishing, faithful warrior that he was, to bring back the holy weapons to the place where they belonged, so that they might be at hand for his successor. His arm became distended, and black boils swelled up more and more fiercely; he was fighting against the exhaustion of death, but did not succumb to it.

When he came to the Kilchstalden he saw Hans, the godless father whose whereabouts had been known to nobody, lying on his back in the middle of the road. His face was terribly swollen and black with burns, and there sitting right on top of him was the spider, big, black and gruesome. When the priest came, it puffed itself up, its hairs stood poisonously on end on its back, its eyes glared fiercely at him, and it was behaving like a cat which is preparing to spring at the face of a deadly enemy. Then the priest began to say a prayer and lifted up the holy implements, so that the spider cringed in terror and slunk on its long legs away from the black face until it was concealed in the hissing grass. After that the priest went on home, where he put the holy implements in their proper place, and while fierce pains were racking his body to death, his soul waited in sweet contentment for God, on Whose account it had been so valiantly fighting the good fight; and God did not let the soul wait long.

But such sweet peace which waits patiently on the will of the Lord was not to be found down in the valley or up on the hills.

From the moment when Christine had snatched the child and rushed with it down the hill towards the devil, a desperate terror had seized all hearts. During the terrible storm the people were trembling in fear of death, for they knew well enough in their hearts that if God's hand should come upon them and destroy them, it would be a visitation more than well deserved. When the storm was over, the news spread from house to house that the priest had brought back the baby and baptized it, but that neither Hans nor Christine had been seen.

The gray light of early morning revealed that all faces were pale, and the beautiful sun gave them no color, for everyone knew well enough that the worst horror was yet to come. Then people heard that the priest had died covered with black tumors, and Hans was found with his terrible face, while strangely confused reports were told of Christine's transformation into the dreadful spider.

It was a fine day for harvesting, but no hands set to work; people came together as they do on the day after the day on which a great misfortune has happened. Now for the first time they truly felt in their vacillating souls what it means to consent to buy oneself off with an immortal soul from earthly trouble and distress; now they felt that there was a God in heaven Who would avenge Himself terribly for all the injustice that is done to poor children who cannot defend themselves. So they stood together trembling and whining, and anyone who was with a group felt he could not return home; but then they would begin arguing and quarrelling, the one would blame the other, everyone claimed that he had warned them and told them so earlier, and nobody minded punishment being meted out to the guilty ones, so long as he and his house might go unscathed. And if they had known of some new, innocent victim while they stood there in their terrible suspense and quarrelsome spirit, not one of them would have hesitated to make a criminal sacrifice in the hope of saving his own skin.

Then one of them shrieked out in terror in the midst of the crowd; he felt as if he had put his foot on a searing thorn, as if a red-hot nail were being driven through his foot on to the ground, as if fire were streaming through the marrow of his bones. The crowd scattered, and all eyes gazed upon the foot towards which the screaming man was reaching down with his hand. But on the foot the spider was seated, black and gross, staring poisonously and gloatingly at the people around. Then they felt the blood freezing in their veins and their breath freezing in their lungs, while their eyes were fixed in a petrified glance; the spider stared round at them quietly and maliciously, and the man's foot became black, and his body seemed as if it were a battlefield between raging fire and hissing water; fear burst the bonds of terror, and the crowd dispersed in all directions. The spider, however, had relinquished its first seat with miraculous speed, and now it crawled over this man's foot and that man's heel, so that fire pierced their bodies and their ghastly screaming impelled the others to even more hasty flight. They rushed towards their homes with the speed of the whirlwind, in dreadful fear like that of the ghostly prey pursued by the wild hunstmen, and everyone thought that the spider was at his back; they bolted their house-doors behind them, but still did not stop trembling in unspeakable terror.

And one day the spider had disappeared; no fresh death screams were heard, people had to go out of their bolted houses to look for food for themselves and their cattle, deathly though their fear was. For where was the spider now, and might it not be just here and plant itself without warning on their feet? And he who walked most carefully and used his eyes most sharply was the one who found the spider suddenly sitting on his hand or his foot, running over his face, or sitting black and gross on his nose and leering into his eyes; blazing thorns dug into his limbs, the fire of hell swept over him and death laid him low.

Thus it was that the spider was now here, now there, now no-where, now down in the valley, now up on the hills; it hissed through the grass, fell from the roof or sprang up from the ground. When people were sitting over the midday meal of porridge, it would appear gloating at the far end of the table, and before they had had time to scatter in terror, the spider had run over all their hands and was sitting on the head of the father of the family, staring over the table at the blackening hands. It would fall upon people's faces at night, it would encounter them in the forest or descend upon them in the cattle-shed. No one could avoid it, for it was nowhere and everywhere; no one could screen himself from it while he was awake, and when he was asleep there was no protection. When someone thought himself to be safest, in the open air or in a treetop, then fire would crawl up his back, and the spider's fiery feet could be felt in his neck as it stared over his shoulder. It spared neither infant in the cradle nor the old man on his deathbed; it was a plague more deadly than any that had been known before, and it was a form of death more terrible than any that had been previously experienced, and what was still more terrible than the death-agony was the nameless fear of the spider which was everywhere and nowhere and which would suddenly be fixing its death-dealing stare on someone when he fancied that he was most secure.

The news of this terror had naturally reached the castle without delay and had brought fright and quarrelling there too, as far as such was possible within the rules of the Order. Von Stoffeln was fearful lest they themselves might receive such a visitation as had befallen their cattle earlier, and the priest who was now dead had previously said many things which now disturbed his soul. The priest had told him that all the suffering which he inflicted on the peasants would come back upon him; but he had never believed it because he thought God would know how to differentiate between a knight and a peasant, or else surely He would not have created them so differently. But in spite of this he was now afraid that things might happen as the priest had spoken; he spoke harshly to his knights and expressed the conviction that severe punishment would now befall them on account of their irresponsible words. But the knights refused to acknowledge any wrong-doing, the one passed the responsibility to the other, and even if none of them said so, they all thought that this was really von Stoffeln's affair, for if one looked at the matter straight, it was he who was answerable for everything. And after von Stoffeln, there was a young Polish knight whom they looked at askance, since he had in fact uttered the most irresponsible words about the castle and had mostly incited von Stoffeln to new building and to the presumptuous planting of the avenue of trees.

This Pole, though still very young, was the wildest of them all, and if there was a rash deed to be done, he was in the lead; he was like a heathen and feared neither God nor the devil.

He noticed clearly enough what the others thought but dared not say to him, and he noticed also their secret terror. He therefore taunted them and said, if they were afraid of a spider, what did they think they could do against dragons? Then he securely buckled on his armor and rode into the valley, swearing presumptuously that he would not return until his horse had trampled down the spider and his own fist had crushed it. Fierce hounds jumped around him, his falcon perched upon his clenched fist, his lance hung at his saddle, and the horse reared up exuberantly; those in the castle watched him ride off half-spitefully, half-fearfully, remembering the nightly watch on Bärhegen when the force of earthly weapons had proved so poor a defense against such an enemy.

He rode at the edge of a pine forest towards the nearest farm, peering about and above with sharp eyes. When he saw the house and the people round about, he called his hounds, made free the falcon's head and let his dagger rattle loose in its sheath. When the falcon turned its dazzled eyes to the knight, awaiting his signal, it bounded back from his fist and shot into the air; the hounds that had gathered round howled out loudly and made off into the distance with their tails between their legs. In vain the knight rode and called out, he did not see his creatures again. Then he rode towards the people in order to ask for information; they stood still until he came close. Then they shrieked out with ghastly sounds and fled into the forest and ravine, for there on the knight's helmet the spider sat black and in supernatural size, staring poisonously and malevolently across the countryside. The knight was carrying on his person the creature he was looking for, and did not realize it; in burning anger he called and rode after the people, cried out in ever greater rage, rode at an ever madder pace, yelled out ever more terribly until he and his horse plunged over a precipice down to the valley below. There his helmet and body were found, and the spider's feet had burned through the helmet and into his brain, starting there the most fearful agony which lasted until his death.

It was after this experience that terror entered the castle in real earnest; the knights shut themselves in and still did not feel secure;

they sought spiritual weapons, but for a long time they found no one who was capable of giving them guidance or who dared to venture there. At last a priest from a distant part allowed himself to be enticed there by fair words and the promise of money; he arrived and had the intention of setting out against the wicked enemy armed with holy water and holy prayers. He did not, however, strengthen himself in preparation for this with prayer and fasting, but dined with the knights early of a morning, not counting how many goblets of wine he drank and living well on venison and bear's meat. In between he talked a lot about his spiritual feats of heroism, while the knights talked about their worldly deeds, and nobody counted the number of drinks they had and the spider was forgotten. Then all at once all liveliness was extinguished, hands holding tankard or fork went numb, mouths stayed gaping, and all eyes were fixed staring at one point; von Stoffeln alone drained his tankard and went on recounting some heroic deed performed in heathen parts. But the spider sat large on his head and stared round at the knights at table, though von Stoffeln did not know this. Then pain began to pour through his brain and blood, he cried out hideously and felt his head with his hand; but the spider was no longer there, with its terrible speed it had run over all the knights' faces, and no one could prevent it; one after another shrieked out, consumed with fire, and the spider leered down from the priest's bald head into the scene of horror; the priest wanted to put out the fire which flared up first in his head and then through marrow and bone.

Only a few servants were spared in the castle, those who had never made fun of the peasants; it was they who related how terrible it had been. The feeling that the knights had what they deserved was no consolation for the peasants, whose terror became ever greater and more horrible. Many a one tried to escape. Some wanted to leave the valley, but it was precisely these who became the spider's victims. Their corpses were found strewn on the road. Others fled to the high hills, but the spider was up there before them, and when they thought they had saved themselves, there was the spider sitting on their necks or faces. The monster become more and more evil and devilish. It no longer came upon people unawares, injecting the fire of death unexpectedly; it would lurk in the grass for someone, or hang over him from a tree, staring poisonously at him. Then such a one would flee as far as his feet could carry him, and if he stood still in his breathlessness the spider would be squatting in front of him and staring poisonously at him. If he fled once more and once more had to slow down, it would again be in front of him; and only if he could flee no further did it crawl slowly up to him and kill him.

Then some people in their despair attempted resistance to see if it might not be possible to kill the spider; they threw huge stones at it when it sat before them in the grass, or hit out at it with club or axe; but it was all in vain, for the heaviest stone could not crush it nor the sharpest axe wound it; it would squat unawares on a man's face and crawl up to him unhurt. Flight, resistance, everything was in vain. At that all hope was lost, and despair filled the valley and brooded over the heights.

Up to that time there was one house only which the monster had spared and where he had never appeared; it was the house where Christine had lived and from which she had stolen the child. As the spider, she had attacked her own husband in lonely pastureland, where his corpse had been found mauled hideously as none other had been, the features distorted in unspeakable pain; it was he upon whom it had wreaked its most terrible wrath, it was the husband for whom it had prepared the most terrible final encounter. But nobody saw how it happened.

The spider had not yet come to the house; whether it was saving it up till last or whether it was afraid of approaching it, nobody could guess.

But fear had entered there no less than at other places.

The devout woman had recovered her health and had no fear on her own account, but was considerably afraid for her faithful little boy and his little sister; she watched over them day and night, and the faithful grandmother shared her cares and her vigilance. And together they prayed God that He might keep their eyes open as they were on the watch and that He would illumine and strengthen them so that they might save the innocent children.

As they kept watch through the long nights it often seemed to them as if they could see the spider glimmering and glittering in a dark corner, or as if it were peering in at them through the window; then their fear increased, for they knew no way of protecting the children from the spider, and so they prayed the more ardently to God for His counsel and support. They had collected all kinds of weapons to have handy, but when they heard that the stone lost its heaviness and the axe its sharpness, they put them aside again. Then the idea came to the mother more and more clearly and vividly that if someone would dare to grasp the spider with his hand, it would be possible to overcome it. She had also heard of people who, when stone-throwing proved useless, had attempted to crush the spider in their hands, though without success. A fearful stream of fire which convulsed through hand and arm destroyed all strength and brought death to the heart. It seemed to her that if she could not succeed in crushing the spider, she might well be able to grasp hold of it, and God would lend her sufficient strength to put it away in some place where it would be harmless. She had already often heard tell of knowledgeable men imprisoning demons in a hole in a cliff or in wood which they had closed with a peg, and so long as no one pulled out the peg, the demon would have to remain pinned down in the hole.

The spirit moved her more and more to attempt something similar herself. She bored a hole in the window-post which was nearest to her at her right hand as she sat by the cradle; she prepared a peg which fitted closely into the hole, blessed it with holy water, put out a hammer and prayed day and night to God for strength to accomplish the deed. But sometimes the flesh was stronger than the spirit, and heavy sleep pressed on her eyes; then she saw the spider in her dreams, leering on her little boy's golden hair, then she started up out of her dream and touched her boy's locks. But there was no spider there, and a smile played on his little face in the way children smile when they see their angel in a dream; but the mother seemed to see the spider's poisonous eyes glittering in every corner of the room, and for a long time she could not go to sleep.

In this way sleep had once overcome her after she had been keeping strict watch, and it encircled her closely. Then it appeared to her as if the pious priest, who had died in saving her child, were rushing up to her from far spaces and were calling to her from the distance: 'Wake up, woman, the enemy is here!' He called thus three times, and it was not until the third time that she wrested herself from the tight bonds of sleep; but as she wearily raised her heavy eyelids, she saw the spider, swollen with poison, crawling slowly up to the little bed towards the face of her boy. Then she thought of God and seized the spider with rapid grasp. Then streams of fire emanated from the spider, piercing the faithful mother through hand and arm to her heart; but motherly fidelity and motherly love made her keep her hand tightly closed, and God gave her strength to hold out. Amid thousandfold pains of death she forced the spider with her one hand into the hole that had been prepared, and with the other hand she pressed the peg over the hole and then hammered it fast.

Inside there was a roaring and a raging as when whirlwinds struggle with the sea, the house swayed on its foundations, but the peg held fast and the spider remained imprisoned. The faithful mother, however, was still overjoyed that she had saved her children; she thanked God for His grace, then she too died the same death as all the others, but her motherly fidelity blotted out the pains, and the angels accompanied her soul to God's throne, where all heroes are who have given their lives for others and risked everything for the sake of God and their beloved ones.

Now the Black Death was at an end. Peace and life came back to the valley. The black spider was seen no more at that time, for it stayed imprisoned in that hole, where it remains still now."

"What, in that black piece of wood there?" the godmother cried and started up from the ground in one movement as if she had been sitting on an anthill. She had been sitting against that piece of wood when she had been inside the room. And now her back was burning, she turned round, she looked behind her, felt over herself with her hand and could not escape from the fear that the black spider was sitting on her neck.

The others also felt their hearts constricted after the grandfather had finished talking. A great silence had come over them. Nobody cared to venture a joke, nor did anyone feel inclined to assent to the story; each preferred to listen for the first word of the other so that they could adjust their own remarks accordingly, for that is the easiest way to avoid making mistakes. Then the midwife came running along; she had called to them several times already without getting an answer, and her face burned deep red, it was as if the spider had been crawling about on it. She began to scold them because nobody would come, however loudly she might call. That really did seem to her to be a queer business; when the food was all ready, nobody would come to the table, and if after all it was spoiled, they would say it was all her fault; she knew well enough how these things happened. Nobody could eat fat meat like that indoors once it had gone cold; and anyway it wouldn't be good for them to do so.

Now the people did come, but quite slowly, and none of them was willing to be the first at the door; the grandfather had to go first. This time it was not so much the usual custom of not wanting to give the impression that they could not wait to get at the food; it was the hesitation which befalls all people when they stand at the entrance to a gruesome place, though really there was nothing gruesome inside. The handsome decanters of wine, freshly filled, gleamed brightly on the table; two sleek hams shone forth; mighty roast joints of veal and mutton were steaming; fresh Bernese cakes lay between the dishes of meat, plates of fritters and plates with three kinds of cake on them had been squeezed in between, and the pots of sweetened tea were not missing either. Thus it was a lovely sight, and yet they all paid little attention to it, but instead they all looked round with frightened glances, wondering if the spider might not be glittering out of some corner or even be staring down at them from the magnificent ham with its poisonous eyes. It could not be seen anywhere, and yet nobody paid the usual compliments ("What were they thinking, to go on putting so much in front of them, whoever was going to eat it, they'd already had more than enough"), but everybody crowded down to the lower end of the table and nobody wanted to be at the top.

It was useless asking the guests to come to the top end of the table and to point to the empty places there; they stood at the bottom end as if nailed there. In vain the father of the newborn child poured out the wine and called to them to come along and drink a health, it was all ready. Then he took the godmother by the arm and said, "You be the most sensible and set an example!" But the godmother resisted with all her strength, and that was not little, saying, "I'm not going to sit up there again, not for a thousand pounds! I can feel something stinging up and down my back, as if somebody was playing about it with nettles. And if I sat over there by the window-frame, I should feel the terrible spider on my neck all the time." "That's your fault, grandfather," the grandmother said. "Why do you bring up such subjects! That sort of thing does no good these days and can only do harm to the whole house and family. And if one day the children come home from school crying and complaining that the other children have been baiting them that their grandmother was a witch and was shut up in the window-post, well, that'll be your fault."

"Be quiet, grandmother!" the grandfather said. "Nowadays everything soon gets forgotten again and nobody keeps things long in their memory, as they used to. They wanted to hear about the business from me, and it is better for people to hear the exact truth rather than to make something up for themselves; truth can bring our house no dishonor. But come and sit down! Look, I'll sit down myself in front of the peg in the window-post. After all, I've sat there many thousands of days already without fear or hesitation, and therefore without danger. Only if ever evil thoughts happened to rise within me which could give the devil a hold, I had the feeling that there was a purring behind me, like a cat purring when you play with it and stroke its fur and it feels comfortable; and I had a queer, strange feeling up my back. But otherwise the spider keeps itself as still as a mouse inside there, and so long as we here outside do not forget God, it has to go on waiting within."

Then the guests took heart and sat down, but nobody moved up really close to the grandfather. Now at last the father could begin serving; he placed a mighty piece of roast meat on his neighbor's, the godmother's, plate and she cut a small piece off and placed what remained on her neighbor's plate, removing it from her fork with her thumb. In this manner the piece of meat was passed on, until someone said he thought he would keep it now, for there would certainly be more where that piece came from; a new piece now began the rounds. While the father was pouring out wine and serving, and the guests were telling him what a busy day he was having today, the midwife went round with the sweet tea, which was strongly spiced with saffron and cinnamon, and offered it to everybody, saying that if anybody was fond of it, all they had to do was to say so, it was there for everybody. And if anyone said he did like it, she poured tea into his wine, saying she was fond of it too, it made it easier to stand up to the wine and didn't give you a headache. They ate and drank. But scarcely was the noise over, which always occurs when people are sitting behind new dishes of food, when everyone became quiet again, and faces grew serious; it was clear that all thoughts were turned to the spider. Eyes glanced shyly and furtively at the peg behind the grandfather's back, and yet everyone was reluctant to take up the subject again.

Then the godmother cried out loud and almost fell off her chair. A fly had passed over the peg, she had believed that the spider's black legs were creeping out of the hole, and her whole body trembled with terror. People hardly had time to make fun of her, for her fright was a welcome reason for beginning to talk afresh about the spider, and once a matter has really touched our mind, it does not easily let it go again.

"But listen here, cousin," the elder godfather said. "Hasn't the spider ever got out of the hole since then? Has it always stayed inside all these hundreds of years?" "Oh," the grandmother said, "it would be better to be quiet about the whole business"; after all they had been talking the whole afternoon about it. "Oh, Mother," the cousin said, "you let your old man talk, he's been entertaining us very well, and nobody will hold the business up against you, after all you're not descended from Christine. And you won't succeed in turning our thoughts away from the subject; and if we're not allowed to talk about it, we shan't talk about anything else, and then we shan't be entertained any more. Now, grandfather, come and talk, your old woman won't begrudge it us!" "Oh, if you want to insist, you can, as far as I am concerned, but it would have been more sensible to have started on something different now, and specially now that night is on the way," the grandmother said.

Then the grandfather began, and all faces became tense once more. "What I know, isn't much more now, but I will tell you what I do know; perhaps somebody can take a lesson from it in our own day; it really wouldn't do any harm to quite a lot of folk.

When people knew that the spider had been shut in and that their lives were safe again, it is said that they felt as if they were in heaven and as if the dear God with His blessedness were in the midst of them; and for a long time things went well. They held fast to God and shunned the devil, and the knights who had arrived at the castle as newcomers also stood in awe of God's hand and treated the people gently and helped them to recover.

But everybody regarded this house with reverence, almost as if it were a church. Admittedly the sight of it made them shudder at first, when they saw the prison of the terrible spider and thought how easily it might break out from there and start the whole wretchedness afresh with the devil's violence. But they soon saw that God's strength was greater than the devil's, and out of gratitude to the mother who had died for them all, they helped the children and worked the farm for them for nothing, until they were able to look after it themselves. The knights were willing to allow them to build a new house so that they need have no fear of the spider, in case this latter might accidentally be set free in a house which was inhabited; and offers of help came from many neighbors who could not get rid of their fear of the monster which had made them tremble so much. But the grandmother would not hear of it. She taught her grandchildren that it was here that the spider had been imprisoned in the name of God the Father, Son and Holy Spirit; as long as the three holy names held sway in the house and as long as food and drink were blessed in the three holy names at this table, they would be safe from the spider and the spider would be secure in the hole and no accident could make its imprisonment less secure. As they sat at the table with the spider behind them, they would never forget how necessary God was to them nor how mighty He was; in this way the spider would remind them of God, and in spite of the devil it would be a means to their salvation. But if they forsook God, even if this happened a hundred hours' walk away from there, the spider or the devil himself would be able to find them. The children understood this, remained living in the house, grew up to be godfearing, and the blessing of God was over the house.

The little boy who had been so faithful to the mother, just as his mother had been faithful to him, grew up into a fine man who was beloved of God and men and found favor with the knights. Therefore he was also blessed with worldly goods and never forgot God because of this, he never became grasping in his prosperity; he helped others in their need, just as he wished that he might be helped in the last resort; and where he was too weak to give help himself, he became all the more forceful an intercessor with God and men. He was blessed with a good wife, and between them there was a deep and secure peace, and therefore their children flourished and became virtuous; and both found a quiet death after a long life. His family continued to flourish in the fear of God and in right living.

Truly the blessing of God lay over the whole valley, and there was prosperity in the fields and the cattle-sheds and peace among men. The terrible lesson had gone to people's hearts, and they held fast to God; whatever they did, they did in His name, and where one man could help another, he did not hesitate to do so. No evil, but only good came to them from the castle. Fewer and fewer knights lived there, for the fighting in heathen parts became ever harder, and every hand that could wield a sword became more and more essential; but those who were in the castle were reminded daily by the great hall of death, where the spider had asserted its power over knights just as elsewhere over peasants, that God rules with the same strength over all who fall away from Him, whether they are knights or peasants.

In this way many years passed in happiness and blessing, and this valley became celebrated above all others. Its houses were impressive, its stocks were large, many a gold coin lay in the coffers, its cattle were the finest over hill and dale, its daughters were renowned up and down the country and its sons welcomed everywhere. But just as the pear-tree which is best nourished and has the strongest growth is the one into which the canker penetrates, consuming it until it withers and dies, so it happens that where God's stream of blessing flows most richly over men, canker comes into the blessing, puffs the people up and makes them blind, until they forget God because of the blessing, forget Him Who has given the wealth on account of the wealth itself, until they become like the Israelites who forgot God, after He had helped them, on account of the golden calf.*

Thus after many generations had passed, pride and arrogance made their home in the valley, brought there and increased by women from other parts. Clothes became more pretentious, jewels could be seen gleaming on them, and indeed pride dared to display itself even on the holy implements themselves, and instead of people's hearts being directed in prayer fervently to God, their eyes lingered arrogantly on the golden beads of their rosaries. Thus their public worship became pomp and pride, though their hearts became hardened towards God and man. There was little concern for God's commandments, and His service and His servants were scorned; for where there is much arrogance or much money the delusion willingly enters which thinks selfish desires to be wisdom and values this worldly wisdom higher than God's wisdom. Just as the peasants had in earlier days been ill-treated by the knights, now they in their turn became hard towards their servants and ill-treated

*Exodus 32: 1–24.

them, and the less they themselves worked, the more they expected from their servants, and the more work they demanded from farm-hands and maids, the more they treated them like senseless cattle, not thinking that their servants too had souls to be taken care of. Where there is much money and pride, people start building, one farmer vying with another, and just as the knights had used to build earlier, the peasant-farmers were now building, and just as the knights had ill-used them in earlier times, now they were merciless to their servants and their cattle, once the craze for building came over them. This change of outlook had also come over this house, although the old wealth had remained.

Almost two hundred years had passed since the spider had been made prisoner in the hole. At that time a cunning and overbearing woman was mistress here; she did not come from Lindau, but all the same resembled Christine in many respects. She too came from a distant part and was addicted to vanity and pride, and she had an only son; her husband had died through her domineering spirit. This son was a handsome fellow, good-natured and friendly to man and beast; she in her turn was very fond of him, but she did not let him notice it. She domineered over him at every step he took, and none of his friends would be tolerated by her unless she had first given her approval, and he had long been grown up, but still was not allowed to go with the village youth or to go to a local fair without his mother's company. When at last she thought he was old enough, she gave him as a wife one of her relations, a woman after her own heart. Now he had two masters instead of only one, and both were equally proud and arrogant, and because they were like this, they wanted Christen to be like this too, and whenever he was friendly and humble, as suited him so well, he soon learned who was master.

For a long time the old house had been a thorn in their eyes and they were ashamed of it, since the neighbors had new houses al-though they were scarcely as rich as they were. The legend of the spider and what the grandmother had said was at that time still in everyone's memory, otherwise the old house would have been torn down long ago, but everybody resisted the two women in this. The latter, however, came more and more to interpret this resistance as envy which begrudged them a new house. In addition, they came to feel more and more uneasy in the old house. Whenever they sat at the table here, they felt either as if the cat were purring complacently behind them or else as if the hole were gradually opening and the spider taking aim at their necks. They lacked the faithful spirit which had closed up the hole, and therefore they were more and more afraid that the hole might open. Consequently they thought they had found a good reason for building a new house, since in the new house they would not have to be afraid of the spider. They wanted to hand over the old house to the servants, who often were an obstacle to their vanity; and in this way they came to their decision.

Christen was very unwilling to do this; he knew what the old grandmother had said and believed that the family blessing was linked to the family house, and he was not afraid of the spider, and when he sat up here at the table, it seemed to him as if he could pray most reverently. He said how he felt, but his womenfolk told him to be quiet, and because he was their servant, he did keep quiet, but he often wept bitterly when they were not there to see him.

Up there, beyond the tree under which we were sitting, a house was to be built, a house the like of which nobody else in the district possessed.

In presumptuous impatience, because they knew nothing about building and could not wait to show off with their new house, they maltreated workmen and animals during the building process and did not even rest on holy feast-days and begrudged the workers their rest even at night; there was no neighbor with whom they were satisfied, however much help he might give them, no neighbor whom they did not wish ill when he went home to look after his own affairs after he had given them free assistance, as was the custom even at that time.

When they started building and drove the first peg into the threshold, smoke rose from the hole like damp straw when it is set alight; at that the workpeople shook their heads with misgiving and said, both secretly and aloud, that the new building would not become old; but the women laughed at this and took no notice of the sign that had been given. When finally the house had been built, they moved in and furnished the house with unheard-of luxury, and for a housewarming gave a party that lasted three days, so that children and grandchildren still talked about it throughout the whole Emmental.

But it is said that all the three days long a strange humming could be heard in the whole house like the purring of a cat that is contented to have its fur stroked. But they could not find the cat from which the purring came, for all they searched everywhere; then many a one felt ill at ease, and in spite of all the munificence he would slip off in the midst of the celebrations. It was only the two women who heard nothing or else took notice of nothing; they thought that now the new house was there they had nothing to lose.

Yes, a blind man does not even see the sun, nor does a deaf man hear thunder. Consequently the women of the house were delighted, grew more presumptuous every day, did not think of the spider, but lived in the new house a luxurious, indolent life, dolling themselves up and overeating; there was nobody like them, they thought, and they did not think of God.

The servants stayed on by themselves in the old house, living as they liked, and when Christen wanted to keep the old house under his surveillance, the women would not tolerate this and railed at him, the mother chiefly out of vanity, the wife mainly out of jealousy. Consequently there was no order down there in the old house and soon no fear of God either, and where there is no master in control, that is what usually happens. If there is no master sitting at the head of the table, no master listening alertly in the house, no master holding the reins both within and outside, then the fellow who behaves most wildly thinks he is the greatest and the man who talks most recklessly thinks he is the best.

That is how things went in the house down below, and all the servants soon resembled a pack of cats when they are at their wildest. Nobody knew anything more about praying, and therefore there was respect neither for God's will nor God's gifts. Just as the arrogance of the two mistresses no longer knew any bounds, so the animal insolence of the servants knew no limits. They audaciously spoiled the bread, they threw porridge over the table with spoons at each other's heads and they even defiled the food in bestial manner in order maliciously to take away the others' enjoyment of their food. They provoked the neighbors, tormented the cattle, jeered at all divine worship, denied all higher authority and abused in all manner of ways the priest who had spoken to them admonishingly; in short, they no longer had any fear of God or man and behaved more wildly every day. The farm-hands and the maids lived most dissolutely, and yet they tormented one another wherever possible, and when the farm-hands could not think of any new way of tormenting the maids, one of them had the idea of terrifying or taming the maids with the threat of the spider in the hole. He slung spoonfuls of porridge or milk up against the peg and shouted out that the spider inside must be hungry as it had had nothing to eat for so many centuries. At that the maids shrieked aloud and promised everything that they could, and even the other farm-hands felt a shudder of horror.

As the game was repeated without any punishment ensuing, it lost its effect; the maids no longer cried out or made any promises, and the other farm-hands also began the same game. Now this particular fellow began to go at the hole with his knife, swearing the most horrible oaths that he would loosen the peg and see what was inside, for it was time they had something new to see. This aroused new horror, and the fellow who did this was master of them all and could compel them, especially the maids, to do whatever he wanted.

Indeed this man is said to have been a really strange fellow, and nobody knew where he came from. He could behave as gently as a lamb and as fiercely as a wolf; if he were on his own with a woman he was a gentle lamb, but in the company at large he was like a ravening wolf and behaved as if he hated everyone, as if he wanted to outdo them all in wild deeds and words; but men like that are supposed to be just the most attractive ones to women. That is why the maids were shocked at him in public, but are said to have liked him best of all when alone with him. His eyes were uneven, but it was impossible to say what color they were, and the two eyes disliked one another, for they never looked in the same direction, but he knew how to conceal this with long hair over his eyes and by humbly looking down to the ground. His hair was beautifully waved, but it was difficult to say whether it was red or blonde; in the shade it was the most beautiful flaxen hair, but when the sun shone on it, no squirrel's coat was redder. He tormented the cattle worse than anybody else. The cattle in their turn hated him also. Each of the farm-hands thought that he was his friend, and yet he would set them up one against the other. He was the only one of them who suited the two mistresses, and was the only one who was often in the upper house; then the maids behaved wildly in the house below; as soon as he observed this, he would stick his knife into the peg and begin his threatening, until the maids ate humble pie.

However, this game too did not continue to be effective for long. The maids became used to it and finally said: 'Do it then, if you dare; but you daren't!'

The holy eve of Christmas was approaching. They had no thought for the meaning of Christmas and had planned to have a wildly merry time. In the castle over yonder only an old knight lived now; a rogue of a bailiff administered everything to his own advantage. They had procured a noble Hungarian wine from him by means of conniving at a piece of roguery (the knights were engaged in hard fighting in Hungary), and they did not know the strength and fire of the noble wine. A terrible storm arose, with thunder and lightning, such as you very rarely see at this time of year, and it was so fierce that you could not have routed out a dog from under the stove. It did not stop them going to church, because they would not have gone there even in fine weather and would have let the master go there on his own; but this fact prevented others from visiting them, so that they now were alone in the old house with the noble wine.

They began the holy Christmas Eve with swearing and dancing and with even wilder and more wicked things; then they sat down to the meal, for which the maids had cooked meat, white sauce and any other good things they could steal. Then their coarseness became ever more repulsive, they defiled all the food and blasphemed against everything holy; the farmhand mentioned before made fun of the priest, divided out bread and drank his wine as if he were officiating at mass, baptized the dog under the stove and carried on until the others became anxious and fearful, ruthless as they might otherwise be. Then he stabbed into the hole with his knife and said with curses that he would show them very different things. When they refused to be scared by this, because he had done this sort of thing so often before and there was not much to be gained by driving the knife against the peg, he grasped a gimlet in his half-crazy fury, swore in the most terrible language until their hair stood on end that he would show them what he could do and make them regret laughing at him, then he screwed the gimlet with fierce turns into the peg. The rest fell upon him crying out loudly, but before anyone could prevent it, he laughed like the devil himself and gave the gimlet a violent wrench.

Then the whole house rocked under a monstrous thunderclap, the evildoer was flung on to his back, a red stream of fire broke out from the hole and there in the middle sat the spider, huge and black, swollen with the poison of centuries, gloating in poisonous glee over the criminals who were benumbed in deadly fear and could not move a limb to escape from the terrible monster that crept slowly and malevolently over their faces and injected into them a fiery death.

Then the house quivered with terrible howls of pain such as a hundred wolves together cannot emit even when they are gnawed by hunger. And soon a similar cry of pain sounded from the new house, and Christen, just coming up the hill from holy mass, thought that thieves must have broken in, and, trusting his strong arm, he rushed to help his family. He did not find thieves, but death; his wife and his mother were wrestling with death and already had no more voice in their heavily swollen, black faces; his children were sleeping quietly, and their carefree faces were healthy and ruddy. There arose in Christen a terrible suspicion of what had happened; he rushed into the lower house where he saw the servants all lying dead, their living-room turned into a death-chamber, the fearful hole in the window-post opened wide, and he saw the gimlet in the terribly contorted hand of the farm-servant and the dreadful peg on the point of the gimlet. Now he knew what had happened, struck his hands together above his head, and if the earth could have swallowed him up, this would have suited him well. Then something crept out from behind the stove and nestled close to him; he started in terror, but it was not the spider, it was a poor boy whom he had taken into the house out of charity and had then left among the ruthless servants, as indeed often happens even nowadays, when people take in children in the name of God and then let them go to the devil. This boy had taken no part in the evil behavior of the servants and had fled in terror behind the stove; the spider had spared him alone, and now he could relate what had happened.

But even as the boy was speaking, cries of terror sounded across from other houses, in spite of the wind and the weather. The spider sped through the valley as if with the pent-up lust of centuries, picking out first the most sumptuous houses where people thought of God least and the world most and therefore least cared to know about death.

Already before daybreak the news was in every house that the old spider had broken loose and was once more bringing death to the community; it was said that many already lay dead and that further down in the valley cry upon cry was being raised to heaven from those who had been branded and now had to die. You can imagine now what distress there was in the district, what fear in all hearts and what a Christmas this was in Sumiswald! Not a soul could think of the joy which Christmas usually brings; and such distress came from the criminal behavior of men. But every day the distress grew, for the spider was now quicker and more poisonous than the previous time. Now it was at one end of the parish, now at the other; it appeared at the same time on the hills and in the valley. If on the previous occasion it had for the most part given the mark of death here to one person and there to another, this time it seldom left a house before it had poisoned all who were living there; it was not until all the inmates were writhing in agony of death that the spider sat upon the threshold and gloated maliciously over the havoc of its poisoning, as if to say that here it was, and it had come back again, however long its term of imprisonment might have been.

It was as if the spider knew that little time was to be allowed it, or as if it wanted to save itself trouble; it killed many people off at once, wherever it could. That is why it liked to lie lurking for the passing of the processions of people who wished to accompany the dead to church. Now here, now there, for preference down at the Kilch-stalden, it appeared in the midst of a crowd of people or else suddenly gloated down from the coffin on to the mourners. Then a terrible cry of distress rose to heaven from the procession of mourners, man after man collapsed, until the whole line of mourners lay in the road wrestling with death, until there was no more life among them and a heap of dead lay around the coffin, as bold warriors lie round their flag when overcome by greater forces. After that no more dead were brought to the church, for nobody wanted to carry or escort them; where death seized them, there they were left lying.

Despair lay over the whole valley. Anger was fierce in all hearts, pouring out in terrible imprecations against poor Christen, for he was held responsible for everything. Now all at once everybody was certain that Christen should not have gone from the old house and left the servants to their own devices. All at once everybody knew that a master is more or less responsible for his servants and should set himself against godless living, godless talking and godless defilement of the gifts of God. Now all at once everybody had lost their vanity and arrogance, relegating their vices to the lowest depths of hell; they would scarcely have believed God Himself, if He had told them that until a few days ago they had borne these vices within themselves. They were all pious again, wore their poorest clothes, carried their old, despised rosaries in their hands and persuaded themselves that they had always been as pious as this and that it was not their fault if they could not persuade God in the same way. Christen alone among them all was deemed to be godless, and curses fell upon him like mountains from all sides. And yet he was perhaps the best of them, except that his will lay bound by that of his womenfolk, and such dependence is certainly a heavy sin for any man, and a man cannot escape the weight of responsibility because he is different from what God intends him to be. Christen realized this too, and therefore he was not defiant or loud, but assumed more guilt than was rightly his; but he did not reconcile people by this, for indeed it was at this point that they cried to one another how great his sin must be, since he took so much upon himself and was so submissive, indeed even confessed that he was worthless.

He, however, prayed day and night to God that He might turn the evil away; but it became more terrible from day to day. He realized that he must make good where he had fallen short, that he must sacrifice himself and that the deed which his ancestress had performed was now to fall to him. He prayed to God until the resolve grew right ardently in his heart that he must save the valley community and atone for the evil; his resolve was strengthened by steady courage that does not waver and is always ready for the same deed, in the morning as in the evening.

So he moved with his children out of the new house into the old one, cut a new peg for the hole, had it hallowed with holy water and prayers, placed the hammer by the peg, sat down by the children's beds and waited for the spider.

Seated there, he prayed, watched and wrestled with firm courage against the heaviness of sleep, and did not falter; but the spider did not come, although it was everywhere else; for the plague became more and more deadly, and the rage of the survivors ever wilder.

In the midst of these terrors a wild woman was expecting to give birth to a child. Then people were overwhelmed by the old fear that the spider might take the child unbaptized, the pledge of the old agreement. The woman behaved as if insane and had no trust in God, but had all the more hatred and revenge in her heart.

It was known how in the old days people had protected themselves against the green huntsman, and how the priest was the shield whom they had placed between themselves and the eternal fiend. It was decided now to send for the priest, but who should be the messenger? The unburied dead, whom the spider had stricken during the funeral processions, barred the roads, and would any messenger going over the deserted heights to fetch the priest be able to escape the spider who seemed to know everything? Everyone was hesitant. Then at last the woman's husband thought that if the spider would be seizing him, it would be as likely to get hold of him in his own home as on the road; if he were doomed to die, he would not escape death here any more than there.

He set out on the way, but hour after hour went by, and no messenger came back. Rage and distress became more and more terrible, and the hour of the birth drew closer and closer. Then in the fury of despair the woman raised herself from her bed, lurched out towards the house of Christen, who had been the object of thousandfold curses and who sat in prayer by his children, awaiting the encounter with the spider. Already from afar her screaming could be heard, and her imprecations thundered on Christen's door long before she wrenched it open to bring the storm of her revilement to him in his room. When she rushed in with so terrible an appearance, he started up, wondering at first whether this might not be Christine in her original shape. But as she stood in the doorway, pain held back her walk, and she clung to the doorpost, pouring out the flood of her curses upon poor Christen. He should be the messenger, she said, unless he wished to be cursed with his children and children's children for all time and eternity. At that, pain smothered her swearing, and a little son was born to the wild woman on Christen's threshold, and all who had followed her fled in all directions, expecting the worst to happen. Christen held the innocent child in his arms; the woman's eyes stared stabbing, fierce and poisonous at him from her distorted features, and he felt more and more as if she herself were the spider. Then the power of God came upon him, and a superhuman will power became mighty within him; he threw an intense, loving glance at his children, wrapped the newborn infant in his warm cloak, strode over the fiercely staring woman down the hill and along the valley towards Sumiswald. He made up his mind to take the child to its holy baptism, in expiation of the guilt which lay upon him as head of his house; the rest he would leave to God. Dead bodies hindered his progress, and he had to be careful where he put his feet. Then light-moving feet caught him up; it was the poor boy who felt afraid to be with the wild woman and who, impelled by a childish urge, had run after his master. Christen's heart felt pierced as if by thorns to think that his children were left alone with the raging woman. However, his feet did not stay still, but pressed on to their holy destination.

He had already got down to the Kilchstalden and the shrine was in sight, when there was a sudden gleaming before him in the middle of the road, there was movement in the bushes, the spider sat in the road, a feather was waving red from behind a bush, and the spider reared up high as if to spring. Then Christen called with a loud voice to God in Three Persons, and a wild shout sounded from the bushes, the red feather disappeared, he placed the infant in the boy's arms and after commending his soul to the Lord he seized with a strong hand the spider which, as if transfixed by the holy words, remained motionless in the same spot. Fire streamed through his limbs, but he held fast; the road was free, and the boy with under-standing mind hastened to the priest with the child. But Christen, with fire in his strong hand, hurried with winged course towards his own house. The burning in his hand was terrible, the spider's poison penetrated through all his limbs. His blood became fire. His strength was on the verge of being benumbed, and his breathing almost stopped, but he prayed on and on, kept God firmly before his mind's eye and held out in the fire of hell. Already now he could see his house; as the pain grew, so did his hope, and there at the door was the woman. When the latter saw him coming without her child, she rushed at him like a tigress that has been robbed of her young, believing him responsible for the most shameful betrayal. She took no notice of his gesticulations, did not hear the words coming from his heaving breast, rushed into his outstretched hands and clung on to them; in deathly fear he was compelled to drag the raging woman into the house with him. He has to fight his arms free before he succeeds in forcing the spider back into the old house and securing the peg with dying hands. With God's help he is able to do it. He throws his dying glance at his children as they lie sweetly smiling in their sleep. Then he feels at rest, a higher hand seems to extinguish the fire within him, and praying aloud he closes his eyes in readiness for death. Those who ventured in, cautiously and fearfully, to see what had happened to the woman, found serenity and joy on his face. They were astonished to see the hole closed up, but they found the woman lying burned and distorted in death; she had found fiery death from Christen's hand. While they were standing by without knowing what had happened, the boy came back carrying the child, and with him was the priest who had quickly christened the child according to the custom of the time and was ready to go, well-armed and courageously, to the same struggle in which his predecessor had given up his life in victory. But God did not require such a sacrifice from this priest, for another man had already fought the fight.

For a long time people did not understand what a great deed Christen had accomplished. When at last faith and insight came to them, they prayed joyfully with the priest and thanked God for the life given to them anew and for the strength which He had given to Christen. They begged Christen's forgiveness for their injustice towards him, although he was now dead, and resolved to bury him with high honors, and his memory became gloriously enshrined in their souls like that of a saint. They hardly knew how they felt when this so fearful terror which had been coursing through their limbs suddenly disappeared and they could look joyously up again into the blue sky without fear that the spider was meanwhile crawling on their feet. They decided to have many masses sung and to hold a general procession to the church; above all they wanted to perform the funeral obsequies for the two bodies of Christen and the woman who had pressed upon him, and after that the other corpses were also to find a resting ground, as far as possible.

It was a solemn day when the whole valley walked to the church, and there were solemn feelings in many hearts, many sins were confessed, many vows were sworn, and from that day on much of the old pretentiousness disappeared from people's faces and clothes.

After many tears had been shed in the church and in the churchyard, and after many prayers had been offered, all the people from the valley community who had come to the funeral—and all had come who had the use of their limbs—went to the inn for the customary refreshment. It now happened there that, as usual, women and children sat at their own table, while all the grown men could be seated round the famous round table which may still now be seen at the 'Bear' Inn at Sumiswald. This table was preserved in remembrance of the fact that once there were only a couple of dozen men in a community where now nearly two thousand live, in remembrance of the fact that the lives of the two thousand are also kept in the hand of Him Who saved the two dozen. On that occasion people did not linger at the funeral meal; hearts were too full for there to be room for much food and drink. When they came out of the village on to the open heights above, they saw a red glow in the sky, and when they came home they found the new house burned to the ground; how it happened, they never found out.

But people did not forget what Christen had done for them, and they repaid his deed to his children. They brought these children up piously and sturdily in the most God-fearing household; nobody took any liberties with the children's property, although no legal account was to be seen. Their property was increased and well looked after, and when the children had grown up, they had been cheated neither of their worldly goods nor of their souls. They became righteous, God-fearing persons who enjoyed both the grace of God and the favor of men, and who found blessing in this life and even more in the sight of heaven. And so it remained in the family, and there was no fear of the spider, since there was fear of God, and as it was, so may it remain, if God wills it, as long as there is a house standing here and as long as children follow their parents in action and in thought."

Here the grandfather was silent, and for a long time all were silent, and some were pondering over what they had heard, and the others thought he must be taking breath and then be going to continue further.

At last the elder godfather said: "I have often sat at the round table and have heard of the plague, and how after this all the men in the parish could find room to sit round it. But just how it all happened, nobody could tell me. Some talked one sort of nonsense and others another sort. But tell me, where did you hear all this?"

"Oh," the grandfather said, "it was passed down in our family from father to son, and when the memory of it was lost among other people in the valley, it was kept very dark in the family and they were reluctant to let people know anything of it. It was only talked about inside the family, so that no member should forget what it is that builds a house and destroys it, that brings blessing and takes it away. You can tell from the way my old woman talks how she dislikes it being talked about so openly. But it seems to me that the longer time goes on, the more necessary it is to talk about it to show how far people can go in arrogance and pride. That is why I don't make such a secret of the business any longer, and it isn't the first time that I have told the story to good friends. I also think that what has preserved our family in happiness for so many years, will not do harm to others either, and that it isn't right to make a secret of what brings prosperity and God's blessing."

"You are right, cousin," the godfather answered. "But there is one thing I must ask you all the same: Was the house which you pulled down seven years ago the original old one? I find it hard to believe that."

"No," the grandfather said. "The old house had already become dilapidated almost three hundred years ago, and for a long time even then there had not been room in it for God's blessings from the fields and meadows. And yet the family did not want to leave it, and they dared not build a new one, for they had not forgotten what had happened to the earlier one. Thus they came into a very embarrassing situation and finally asked the advice of a wise man who is said to have lived at Haslebach. He is said to have replied that they might certainly build a new house on the site of the old one and nowhere else, but that they must be certain to preserve two things, the old piece of wood in which the spider was kept, and the old strength of mind which had imprisoned the spider into the old piece of wood; then the old blessing would be present also in the new house.

They built the new house and with prayer and care inserted the old piece of wood into the structure, and the spider did not move, and the spirit in the family and the blessing upon it did not change.

But the new house also became old and small in its turn, its woodwork became worm-eaten and rotten, and only the post here remained firm and hard as iron. My father already should have built anew, but he could avoid doing so, and so it came to my turn. After long hesitation I ventured to take this step. I did as people earlier had done and inserted the old piece of wood into the new house, and the spider did not move. But I am willing to admit that I never prayed so ardently in my whole life as when I was holding the fateful piece of wood in my hands; my hand, my whole body was burning, and unconsciously I had to look whether black marks might not be growing on my hand and body, and a mountainous weight fell from my mind when everything was at last in its place. Then my conviction grew even stronger that neither I nor my children and my children's children would have to fear anything from the spider, so long as we fear God."

Then the grandfather was silent, and the others still felt the shudder that had run up their backs when they heard that the grandfather had had the piece of wood in his hands, and they thought how they would feel if they too would have had to take it in their hands.

At last the cousin said: "The only thing is that it's a pity you can't know how much of this sort of thing is true. You can hardly believe everything, and yet there must be some truth about the matter, or else the old piece of wood would not be there."

The younger godfather said that you could learn a lot from it, whether it was all true or not, and what was more, they had also been enthralled by the story; it seemed to him as if he had just come out of church.

They shouldn't say too much about it, the grandmother said, or else her old man would start on another story; now they should get on and have something to eat and drink, it was indeed a shame the way nobody was eating or drinking. After all it couldn't all be bad, they had done as well as they knew how with the cooking.

Now there was much eating and drinking, and in between many a sensible conversation took place, until the moon stood large and golden in the sky, the stars stepped out from their chambers to remind men that it was time for them too to go to their rooms to sleep.

Although they saw well enough the secret reminders in the sky, the people were sitting there so cosily and each of them felt his heart beating uncannily when he thought of the journey home; and even if nobody said so, it was true that none of them wanted to be the first to go.

At last the godmother stood up and with trembling heart made preparations to leave; but she was not without reliable companions, and the whole company departed together from the hospitable house with many thanks and good wishes, in spite of all requests, made to individuals and to the whole party, that they could surely stay a bit longer, it wasn't really dark yet.

Soon it was still outside the house; soon too it was still inside.

Peacefully the house lay there, gleaming the length of the valley, clean and beautiful in the light of the moon; with friendly care it concealed good people in sweet sleep, the sleep of those who have in their hearts fear of God and a good conscience, and who will never be awakened from their slumber by the black spider, but only by the friendly sun. For where such a serene spirit is present, the spider may not move, either by day or by night. But what power the spider has when men's spirits change, is known only to Him Who knows everything and allots His strength to each and all, to spiders and to mankind.

Translated by H. M. Waidson

The Poor Musician

Franz Grillparzer

E very year in Vienna, after the July full moon, Sunday and the
next day are given up to a genuine popular festival, as festive
and as popular as any ever held.* Ordinary people are to be seen
there: ordinary people make the festival. Those of higher station can
appear only as members of the crowd, for social distinctions are
quite forgotten, or at least they were some years ago.

The Brigittenau and Leopoldstadt districts, the Augarten and the
Prater are all entirely given up to rejoicing when the feastday comes
round; and working people count the days from one anniversary of
the dedication of their patron's church to another, for the festival is
held on St. Bridget's day. At last, with the arrival of the long-awaited
saturnalia, the good-natured calm of the city turns into uproar and
the streets fill with a mass of jostling humanity, while here and there
cries and shouts thrill through the noise of footsteps and the murmur of voices. Citizens and soldiers form part of the general mass,
for class barriers are down. The throng grows as it presses forward
to the city gates, which are gained, lost, and won again, until finally
the crowd passes through. But the Danube bridge presents new
difficulties. Here another victory is won as the two streams—the old
Danube and the surging wave of people—cross one above the other:
the Danube flowing along its old river-bed while the people, freed
from the restraint of the bridge, stream out, a tumultuous and all-
embracing flood. All this might appear perilous to a newly-arrived
stranger, but it is joy that breaks its bonds and the revolt is an
upsurge of pleasure.

*The festival of St. Bridget's day, originally held in a parkland between the Danube
and the Danube Canal. The same occasion is mentioned in Mörike's *Mozart on the
Way to Prague*.

Between the city and the bridge the wicker carriages are awaiting the true celebrants of this dedicatory festival: the children of servitude and labor. Though they are crammed full, the coaches gallop on through the crowd of people, which opens immediately before them and closes swiftly behind, heedless and unharmed; for in Vienna there is a tacit understanding between vehicles and men that no one will be run down, although the vehicle is travelling at full speed and those on foot seem to pay no attention at all.

The distance between one vehicle and another narrows with every second, and already, here and there, smart carriages are to be seen mingling in the often broken course of the procession. Speed becomes impossible, until at last, five or six hours before nightfall, the separate coaches with their horses merge into a dense unbroken line, holding one another back and held back by vehicles attempting to join the stream from every side street: thus making nonsense of the old saying "Never walk when you can ride." The finely dressed ladies sit in their apparently motionless carriages, to be gaped at, pitied and ridiculed. The black Holstein horse, unused to standing still for so long, rears up, as if to leap out over the plebeian carriage which blocks the way in front; and the screams of the women and children passengers show clearly that they are afraid of this. The cabdriver, used to a cracking pace, must abandon his usual practice and angrily calculate the money he has lost by taking three hours on a journey that would normally take five minutes. The drivers argue and shout, punctuating their curses with an occasional crack of the whip.

Finally, since nothing on this earth can ever be at a complete standstill but always moves forward, however imperceptibly, a ray of hope shines on this apparently immobile scene as the first trees of the Augarten and the Brigittenau come into view. Land ahead! There's land ahead! All hardship is forgotten. Those who have come by carriage get down and mingle with those on foot; the strains of distant dance music are heard and joyfully greeted by the new arrivals.

So it continues, until at last the broad haven of pleasure opens before them: woods and meadow, music and dancing, wine and good food, shadow-shows and rope-dancers, illuminations and fireworks combine to create a Cockaigne or Eldorado, a true worldly paradise that, unfortunately or luckily, depending on how you look at it—lasts for only two days, to disappear again like the dream of a summer's night, which lives on as a memory and at most a fond hope.

I would not gladly miss this festival. I am a man passionately devoted to my fellows and especially to the ordinary people; even as a dramatist, I have always found the applause of an audience as it bursts out in a packed theater, ten times more interesting and instructive than the smartly turned judgment of one of those literary critics, maimed in mind and body but grown fat like spiders on the blood of authors whom they have sucked dry. As one, then, devoted to my fellow-men, especially when they lose for a while their individual identities in a crowd and exist only as parts of the whole in which, ultimately, divine truth is to be found—indeed, God himself—as I am such a devotee, every popular festival is to me a true feast day of the soul, an occasion for pilgrimage and pious devotion.

It is as if an entire and gigantic version of Plutarch lay open before me, released from the binding that once enclosed it. I can read the lives of obscure people spelled out in the cheerful or secretly troubled faces, the lively or halting step, the behavior to one another of members of the same family and individual, half-involuntary expressions. It is very true that you must penetrate the feelings of humble people before you can understand the famous. An invisible but unbroken thread stretches from a dispute between tipsy porters to strife among the demigods; and the young girl who, half unwillingly, is persuaded by her lover to leave the throng of dancers and follow him, is a Juliet, Dido or Medea in embryo.

Two years ago, as usual, I had walked to join the crowd of those in search of pleasure at the fair. The main obstacles had already been passed and I now found myself at the end of the Augarten, with the long-awaited Brigittenau, where the final battle was to be met with, just ahead. A narrow causeway with impenetrable hedges on either side is the only connection between the two places of amusement, and a common boundary is formed by a wooden lattice-work gate in the middle. As a connecting road it offers adequate space to any ordinary set of strollers to be found there on a normal day; but during the festival, four times its width could not accommodate the unending crowd. They press along eagerly while those returning in the opposite direction block their way: only by the general goodwill of all those on foot are these difficulties eventually overcome.

I had joined the throng and found myself halfway along the road, already on hallowed ground, but unfortunately forced again and again to halt, step aside and wait. I thus had enough time to observe what was happening at the roadside. The crowd was eager for amusement, and, to allow them a foretaste of the bliss to come, a few musicians had taken up positions on the slope of the raised causeway to the left. I imagine they wished to avoid the major competition and to harvest here at the entrance the first fruits of the as yet unexhausted generosity of the pleasure-seekers. There was a harpist (a woman whose eyes were fixed in a repellent stare) and an old veteran with a wooden leg, who sought to make the pain of his affliction apparent to passers-by, awakening general pity by offending their ears as he played a horrible instrument, half dulcimer and half barrel-organ, that he had obviously manufactured himself. A lame and deformed boy seemed inextricably tangled in one knot with his violin, and played a continuous medley of waltzes with all the feverish vehemence of his misshapen body. Finally, my attention was completely drawn to an old man, well into his seventies, whose expression was cheerful and complacent; he was bald and bareheaded, was dressed in a threadbare but clean beaverteen frock-coat, and stood there as these fellows do, with his hat as a collecting-box on the ground before him. As he worked away on his old and very cracked violin, he kept time with his foot and also by moving the whole of his bent frame in the same rhythm. But all the trouble he took to give unity to his performance was fruitless, for his playing seemed merely an incoherent sequence of sounds without either measure or melody. Nevertheless, he was completely taken up by his work: his lips quivered and his gaze was—I assure you—fixed on the score before him, whereas all the other musicians, though they played from memory, proved far more popular. In the midst of all the turmoil the old man had placed a small, portable stand in front of him: this held the soiled and dog-eared sheet music where the notes that he so completely distorted were probably in neat array. This unconventional equipment itself attracted my attention, and it was held even more firmly by the merriment of the crowd as it streamed past, mocking the old man and leaving the upturned hat empty while the other members of this orchestra were collecting hoards of treasure in coppers. I stood a little apart on the slope of the roadway to observe this eccentric undisturbed. He played on for a while and then stopped. As if coming to after a lengthy reverie he looked at the sky, which showed that dusk was already approaching; peered down into the hat; found it empty; put it on with undiminished serenity and placed the violin bow between the strings. "*Sunt certi denique fines,*"* he said, took up his music stand, and, as if returning home, made his way with difficulty in the opposite direction through the crowd streaming on to the amusements ahead.

The whole nature of the old man seemed exactly made to whet to the full my insatiable appetite for the study of human behavior: the shabby yet noble figure, his invincible serenity, so much artistic zeal together with such extreme clumsiness; the fact that he went home when for others like him the real harvest was only just under way; and, finally, the Latin words—only a tag, but pronounced with exactly the right intonation and complete fluency. This meant that he had been well educated, had acquired knowledge and become—a fiddler begging his living! I was in a fever of excitement to find out the whole story.

But there was already a thick wall of humanity between the pair of us. Because of his small stature and the annoyance occasioned by the music stand in his hand, he was pushed from one person to another, and he had already passed through the exit gate, while I was still in the middle of the causeway, struggling against the onrush of people. Thus he disappeared from my sight: when I emerged at last into the quiet of the open air, there was no musician to be seen far and wide, wherever I might look.

The frustration of missing such an experience had taken away all the pleasure which the festivity held for me. After searching the Augarten in several directions, I eventually decided to go home.

As I approached the little wicket gate that opens out from the Augarten on to the Taborstrasse, I suddenly heard the familiar sound of the cracked violin. I quickened my pace, and, lo and behold, there was the object of my curiosity playing with all his might for a circle of urchins, who impatiently demanded a waltz from him! "Play a waltz," they cried. "Can't you hear? We want a waltz!" The old man fiddled away, apparently without paying any attention to them, until the young audience departed, shouting

*Horace, *Satires*, I, 1, 106. The full phrase reads: *est modus in rebus, sunt certi denique fines* ("there is a measure in things, ultimately certain limits").

abuse and mocking him, only to collect round an organ grinder who had set up his barrel-organ nearby.

"They don't want to dance," the old man said sadly, as he gathered up his equipment. I had come up quite close to him; "Why," I said, "the waltz seems to be the only dance these children know."

"I was playing a waltz," was his reply, and he used his violin bow to indicate on the music sheet the piece he had just played.

"You must have these in your repertoire as well, for the sake of the crowd. But the children have no ear for music," he said as he shook his head mournfully.

"Well, at least allow me to make up for their lack of appreciation," I interjected, drawing a silver coin from my pocket and holding it out to him. "Please, please!" cried the old man, motioning anxiously with his hands: "In the hat! In the hat!" I placed the coin in the hat that was before him, whereupon he at once took it out and pocketed it contentedly. "That means that I go home with a good day's earnings, for once," he said, with a satisfied smile. "Just now," I said, "you reminded me of a circumstance that aroused my interest earlier on. Your takings do not seem to have been too good today and yet you are leaving just when the real money can be made. You know quite well that the festivity will go on all night and that you could easily earn more than you would usually get in a week. What might your reason be?"

"The reason?" replied the old man. "You must forgive me, I have no idea who you are, but you must be a well-wisher and a music-lover"; and he took out the silver coin and pressed it between his hands as he held them to his breast. "I shall just tell you how it all came about, although people have often laughed at what I have done. In the first place, I have never been a night-owl; I do not approve of encouraging others with music and song to take part in such distasteful behavior; secondly, a man is bound to establish a certain degree of order in all things, or he will lose all restraint and lapse into dissolute ways. Thirdly and finally, sir, I play the whole day long for these noisy people and hardly get my daily bread in return; but the evening belongs to me and my poor art. In the evenings I remain at home, and"—at this his voice dropped lower and lower, a flush came over his face and his gaze became fixed upon the ground—"then I play from inspiration, without any score and for myself alone. *Improvisation,* I believe, is the term given to it in books on music."

We had both fallen silent; he, from shame that he had betrayed his innermost secret; I, from surprise that this man should speak of the highest reaches of art, when he was unable to give a clear rendering of even the simplest waltz. Meanwhile he made ready to depart. "Where do you live?" I asked. "I should dearly like to hear you practice alone at some time."

"Oh," he replied, almost beseechingly, "you must know that, when we pray, we are told to go into our own rooms, and shut the door."

"Well then," I said, "I shall visit you in the day some time."

"All day long," was his reply, "I must seek my living in the streets."

"Well, early in the morning, then."

"Indeed, sir," said the old man, with a smile, "it almost sounds as if you were the recipient of the gift and I—if I may be allowed to say so—the donor. You are so kind and I am holding back in a most unfriendly manner. I should be honored by your gracious presence at my dwelling at any time; but I must ask you only to be good enough to warn me in advance when you will come, so that you are not detained by anything unseemly and I am not forced to bring to a sudden and unbecoming stop any activity that I might be engaged upon; for my mornings are also taken up with certain appointed tasks. Nevertheless I consider it my duty to extend a not entirely valueless recompense to my patrons and benefactors. I have no desire to be a beggar, sir. I am well aware that the other musicians who frequent public places content themselves with playing a few vulgar melodies, quick-time waltzes and even tunes of coarse songs which they have learned by heart, going through the same few, over and over again, so that people reward them merely to be rid of them or because their playing revives memories of dances they once enjoyed or some other disreputable pleasure. That is why they play from memory, and sometimes, indeed quite often, badly. But I am not given to deception. Therefore, partly because my memory is certainly not of the best, and partly because it would be extremely difficult for anyone to remember complicated compositions by the best composers note for note, I wrote out these sheets in fair copies myself." He pointed to his music book and leafed through it. To my astonishment, it contained extremely difficult compositions by old and famous masters, written out carefully though in a very formal hand: black with runs and double stops. So these were the pieces that the old man played with his clumsy fingers! "By playing these pieces," he continued, "I show my respect for those masters and composers who are still honored for their achievement and great worth, but who are themselves long since dead, receive my own enjoyment and live in fond hope that the slight talent allowed me will not remain without reward, for it refines the taste and emotions of my audience, distracted and led astray as they are in so many ways. But as—to keep to what I was saying"—And at that a self-satisfied smile came over his face—"But as such pieces must be rehearsed, my mornings are entirely given up to these exercises. The first three hours of the day are devoted to practice, the main part to earning my living, and the evening to God and myself, which I take to be a fair division," he said; and with these words his eyes glistened moistly, although he continued to smile.

"Very well, then," I said, "I shall look in upon you one day in the morning. Where do you live?"

"The Gärtnergasse," he replied.

"What number?"

"Number 34 on the first floor."

"Then you really live with the high-class people, the first flight up?"

"Well, strictly speaking, there is only a ground floor to the house, but there is another little room upstairs near the attic, which I share with two journeymen."

"The three of you share one room?"

"It is partitioned off, and I have my own bed."

"It is growing late," I said, "and you must want to go home. Goodbye then!" And with that I reached into my pocket, intending to repeat the gift he had received earlier on, which now seemed inadequate. But he had seized his music stand in one hand and taken up the violin in the other, and called out hastily: "Please forgive me, but I do not wish you to do that. The fee for my performance has already been paid in full: I do not think that I deserve any further reward at present." He made a clumsy attempt at a gracious bow and departed as quickly as his elderly legs could carry him away.

As I have already said, I had lost all desire to join further in the day's festivity, so I too made my way home, taking the road which led towards the Leopoldstadt district. Exhausted by the dust and heat, I entered one of the many beer gardens to be found there; they were usually packed with people on any ordinary day, but on this occasion had lost all their customers to the Brigittenau. The quiet of the place provided a refreshing contrast to the noisy crowd, and a variety of thoughts came into my head—among which the old fiddler was foremost; it was quite dark when at last I decided to return home, placed my money on the table and walked towards the city.

The old man had said that he lived in the Gärtnergasse. "Do you know if there's a Gärtnergasse anywhere around here?" I asked a small boy, who was running across the street. "Over there, sir," he replied, pointing to a side street which led off from the packed houses of the suburb towards the open countryside. I went in the direction he had indicated and found that the street consisted of separate scattered houses, laid out between large kitchen gardens, which, indeed, betrayed clearly the occupation of the inhabitants and how the street's name had originated. In which of these miserable hovels could my extraordinary acquaintance live? As it happened, I had forgotten the number of his house and it was hardly possible to recognize any inscription in the darkness. Just then a man heavily laden with vegetables passed by in my direction. "The old chap's scraping away, again," he grumbled, "disturbing decent folk who are trying to get their night's rest." At the same time, as I walked on, I suddenly heard the soft but long-drawn-out sound of a violin, apparently coming from the open attic window of an unprepossessing dwelling a little distance away, which was distinguished from the others only by this gable window set in the framework of the roof; otherwise it was low and without a second storey. I stood there in silence. A soft sound which certainly came from a violin grew very loud, sank, and died out, immediately rising again to the shrillest of shrieks: in fact, it was always the same note repeated with a kind of joyful insistence. At last there came an interval—the fourth. Where the musician had previously revelled in the resonance of the individual note, now the almost voluptuous delight in harmonic balance was still more apparent. Quick alternation in fingering and the use of the bow were repeated and joined in a very jerky manner by the intervening part of the scale, with an accentuated third. To this was joined the fifth, first with a tremolo like soft weeping, sustained and then dying out, then repeated again and again with a rapid whirl, with the same intervals every time and the same notes. So this was what the old man called "improvisation"! It was certainly improvisation as far as the violinist was concerned, but not for the listener.

I cannot say how long this had lasted and how unpleasant it had become when the door of the house suddenly opened and a man clad only in a shirt and loosely buttoned breeches stepped from the threshold to the middle of the road and shouted up to the gable window: "Aren't you ever going to stop?" The tone of voice in which he said this was certainly irritable, but there was nothing harsh or offensive about it. The violinist stopped even before he had finished speaking. The man went back into the house, the window was closed and soon a completely unbroken silence prevailed around me. The mental improvisation in which I indulged as I set off home, making my way with difficulty through streets I had never seen before, caused no disturbance.

The morning hours have always held a special quality of their own for me. It is as if I were somehow compelled to sanctify the remainder of the day by doing something elevating and meaningful in the morning. It is only with difficulty, therefore, that I can make up my mind to leave my room early in the morning; should I do so without any valid reason, I have to spend the rest of the day in some amusement demanding no thought or in self-absorbed depression. For this reason, I put off my visit to the old man for several days: for, according to our agreement, it had to be made in the morning. Impatience got the better of me in the end, and I went. I found the street and the house without any difficulty. The violin could be heard this time, too, but I could hardly distinguish the notes through the window. I entered the house. Almost speechless with astonishment, a gardener's wife pointed out a flight of attic stairs. I knocked at the low, ill-fitting door, received no answer and finally pressed the latch and went in. I found myself in a fairly spacious but otherwise extremely wretched room, where every wall followed the outlines of the sloping roof. Right next to the door stood a soiled and disagreeably untidy bed surrounded by every possible evidence of disorder. Opposite me, by the small window, there was a second bed—shabby, but clean and very carefully made and neatly covered. Near the window was set a small table with music paper and writing implements, and a few flower pots stood on the sill. A thick chalk line was drawn across the floor of the room from wall to wall, and it would be difficult to conceive of a harsher contrast between dirt and cleanliness as met my eyes on one side and the other of this line—the equator of a miniature world.

The old man had positioned his music stand just next to the line: there he stood, fully and carefully dressed, practicing in front of it. I have written at length of the dissonances of my eccentric friend—who, I am afraid, was mine alone—therefore I shall spare the reader a description of this demonic concert. As the performance for the most part consisted of selected runs, it was impossible to recognize the pieces he was playing, which were probably not commonly performed works. After I had listened for some time, I found a thread running through this labyrinth of noise and perceived the method in his madness. The old fellow enjoyed playing. His conception of music had two simple aspects: euphony and cacophony. The first filled him with joy—or, rather, rapture—whereas he avoided the second as far as possible, even when it had a harmonic basis. Rather than emphasize a piece of music according to sense and rhythm, he stressed and prolonged the notes and intervals that were pleasing to the ear, not hesitating to repeat them capriciously, while his face would often take on a look of ecstasy. He rid himself of the dissonances in as short a time as possible, whereas, out of conscientiousness, he did not miss a note of the passages that were too difficult for him, but rendered them in a time far too slow when set against the entire piece: this will surely give a clear idea of the confusion that resulted. After a time, it became too much even for me. After trying, without success, other ruses to bring him out of his trance I deliberately dropped my hat. The old man started, his knees shook and he could hardly hold the violin he had allowed to sink to the ground. I moved towards him. "Oh, it's you, sir!" he said, as if coming to his senses. "I had not thought your Honor would keep the promise you made." He motioned me to a seat; cleared things up and put them away; looked round the room several times with an embarrassed air; suddenly seized a plate that happened to be on a table near the door and made his way out of the room. I heard him speak to the gardener's wife outside. He soon returned to the door: he looked embarrassed and concealed the plate behind his back until he had secretly replaced it. He had obviously asked for some fruit so that he could offer it me, but without success. "This is a charming little place you have," I said, to put an end to his discomfort.

"Disorder is beating a retreat and is on its way through the door, although it's not quite over the threshold yet and my dwelling reaches only to the line," said the old fellow as he pointed to the line chalked across the middle of the room. "Two journeymen live on the other side."

"Do they respect your boundary line?"

"They do not, but I do," he said. "Only the door is shared."

"Aren't you disturbed by having them so near?"

"Hardly," was his reply. "They return late at night and even if they startle me a little when I am in bed, the pleasure of getting to sleep again is all the greater for it. On the other hand, I awaken them in the morning when tidying my room. They may complain a little and then they're off."

I had observed him as he spoke. His clothes were clean and his figure good enough for his age, even if his legs were a little short. His hands and feet were exceptionally delicate. "You are looking me up and down," he said. "What are you thinking?"

"I am most eager to hear your story," I said.

"Story?" he repeated. "I have none. Today is the same as yesterday and tomorrow will be the same as today. But, of course, who can know what the day after tomorrow and the day after that will be like. But God will provide: he knows all."

"Your life now is probably monotonous enough," I continued, "but what about your previous experiences—how did it happen. . . ?"

"That I became a musician in this way?" he broke in, as I paused involuntarily. I told him how he had attracted my attention when I saw him first, and of the impression the few Latin words he had spoken had on me. "Latin," he repeated. "Latin; I certainly learned it once, or rather I should have taken the opportunity to do so. *Loqueris latine?*"* he asked as he turned to me. "But I couldn't go on with it. It is too long ago. So you call that my story: and you want to know how it happened? Well, certainly all kinds of things have

* "Do you speak Latin?"

happened to me: nothing very unusual, but quite a few things, all the same. Well, I shouldn't mind going over it again for my own sake—if I have not forgotten it all. The morning is still young," he continued, dipping into his fob pocket, where clearly no watch was to be found. I took out my own: it was scarcely nine o'clock. "We have time, and I should quite like to have a chat," he said, and became visibly more relaxed. Now his whole body seemed to loosen up as, without too much fuss, he took my hat from my hands and placed it on the bed. He sat down, crossed his legs and generally assumed the position of a man who enjoys telling his tale.

"You must have heard," he said, "of Court Counselor N." And he named a statesman who in the latter half of the previous century had exerted a far-reaching influence, almost equal to that one expects from a Minister, while in the modest position of a Departmental Head. I said that I knew of the man. "He was my father," he continued. Could *he* have been the father of the old musician? of this beggar? A man of such power and influence, his father? The old man did not show that he had noticed my surprise but, obviously content, went on with his tale. "I was the second of three sons: my two brothers gained high positions in the government service: but they are now both dead and I am the only one still alive," he said, at the same time plucking at his shabby trousers, and dropping his gaze as he picked a few traces of down from them. "My father was an ambitious and violent man. My brothers delighted him, but I was called a dunce and I really was slow. If I remember rightly," he went on, and, turning to one side, as though gazing into the distance, rested his head on his left hand, "if I remember rightly I should have found it quite easy to learn all sorts of things, if they had only given me time and arranged things properly. My brothers displayed the nimbleness of mountain goats by skipping from height to height of learning, but I could pass hardly any obstacle; if there was a single word I could not understand, I had to start all over again. So I was always in difficulties. New information was always waiting to occupy the space where the old still lingered, and I became obstinate. In this way they made me hate music, which is now the joy and mainstay of my life. When I took up my violin in the evening twilight to play for my own pleasure, without a score, they took it from me, saying that my fingering would be ruined; they complained that their ears were in torment and said that I should be content with the lessons—yet these were torture to me. I have never hated anything or anyone so much as I hated the violin at that time.

"My father was extremely displeased and used to scold me frequently, threatening to make me become an artisan. I did not dare to say how happy it would have made me to have worked as a turner or a typesetter; but his pride would never have let me take up such work. At last the matter was settled by a public examination, which they had asked my father to attend in order to appease him. A dishonest teacher told me the questions beforehand and so—at the start—everything went admirably. At last, however, I had to recite some verses of Horace by heart and missed a word. My teacher nodded his head and smiled at my father as he listened, and came to my aid by whispering the answer when I was stuck. But I did not hear him, for I was searching for the word within me—trying to connect it with the rest of the passage. He repeated it several times: but to no avail. At last my father lost all patience: 'Cachinnum!'*— for that was the word—he thundered. That did it. I now knew that word, but I had forgotten all the others. All the trouble taken to put me on the right road was in vain. I had to stand up, an object of shame, and as I made to kiss my father's hand—out of habit—he pushed me away, rose in his turn, bowed curtly to those present and left. 'Ce gueux'† he said harshly; but, whereas I was no beggar then, I have become one now. One's parents' words are often prophetic! My father, by the way, was a good man: he was merely violent and ambitious.

"From that day on he said not another word to me. His instructions came to me through the other members of the household; and thus they told me the very next day that my studies were at an end. I was very shocked, for I knew how hurt my father must have been. The whole day long I did nothing but cry, and recite those Latin verses that I now knew completely by heart, together with the preceding and following lines. I promised to make up for my lack of talent by diligent application, if he would only let me return to school; but my father never went back on a decision.

"For a time I remained in my father's house without any occupa-

---

*"Loud laughter," from a line of Horace, *Ars poetica*, 113. Grillparzer tells a similar story on himself in his autobiography.

†"This lout."

tion. At last they decided to try me out in the office of a government auditor; unfortunately arithmetic had never been my strong point. I rejected the suggestion of a military career with horror, and I still cannot look upon a uniform without an inward shudder. To protect the relatives you love and respect, although your own life is in danger, is fine and just; but to take up wounding people and shedding their blood as a career, as a profession . . . never, never!" And he let his hands travel swiftly down the length of either arm as though at that very moment he felt a wound there of his own and of all others besides.

"So I became a copy clerk in the chancery. I felt really at home there, for I had always enjoyed penmanship and I still find it difficult to think of a more enjoyable occupation than making up-and-down strokes and joining them together in words or even in letters, with good ink on good paper. Musical notation is the height of beauty. But as yet I was not interested in music.

"I was industrious: but too scrupulous. An incorrect punctuation mark, an unreadable word or one omitted on a document to be copied—even when it could be guessed from the context—gave me many hours of misery. I passed the time in anxiety and doubt whether I should keep exactly to the original or make additions of my own, and thereby gained a reputation for carelessness: although I took more pains than anyone else for the sake of my job. I spent a few years like this, without any salary: for when my turn for promotion came, my father spoke up in the Council for someone else and the others supported his opinion out of respect for him.

"About this time—as you see"; he interposed, "in fact, there is indeed something of a story, but let me continue—About this time two events occurred: one the saddest and the other the most joyful in my life. The first was my departure from my father's house, and the second my return to the beauties of music, to my violin: which has remained my support to this very day.

"I continued to live in my father's house, ignored by the members of the household, in a little room at the back which looked out upon the neighbor's courtyard. I ate with the family at first, but no one addressed a word to me. When my brothers were promoted to posts in some other place and my father dined out almost every other day—for Mother was long since dead—it was found too troublesome to prepare meals for me alone. The servants received an allowance for their food, and so did I; it was not given to me personally but paid every month to the restaurant owner. So I spent little time in my room, except in the evening: for my father insisted that I be home at the most half an hour after the chancery closed. So there I sat, and—indeed—in the dusk without a light, on account of my eyesight, which was already failing at that time. I allowed my thoughts to stray from one thing to another, in a state halfway between melancholy and happiness.

"When sitting like this, I heard someone singing in the neighboring courtyard. I heard several songs; but only one made a really deep impression on me. It was so simple, so moving and the emphasis so exactly right, that there was no need to catch the words. I believe that in general words spoil the effect of music." And with that he opened his mouth, from whence there issued a few hoarse and harsh sounds. "I have not been gifted with a musical voice," he said, and reached for his violin. This time he certainly played with the correct expression—the tune of a tender but otherwise quite ordinary song, his fingers trembling on the strings while finally a few tears rolled down his cheeks.

"That was the song," he said, laying down his violin. "My pleasure increased whenever I heard it. But despite the strong impression it had on me, I was never able to sing even two notes of it correctly. I became almost impatient with listening: then I caught sight of my violin which had hung on the wall since my youth, like a piece of disused armor. I seized it, and—the servant had probably made use of it while I was away—found it properly tuned. Sir, as I set the bow to work on the strings, I felt as if the finger of God had touched me. The music forced its way to the very quick of my being and then issued forth again. The air around me seemed deeply intoxicated: and the song in the courtyard below and the sound brought by my fingers to my ear, took on life and shared my solitude. I fell to my knees and prayed aloud, unable to understand how in my childhood I had once so despised—even hated—this divine and beautiful instrument! I kissed the violin and pressed it to my heart and then played again and continued to play.

"The song in the courtyard—a woman was singing—continued all this time without interruption: but when I tried to play it afterwards, it was not so easy.

"You see, I did not have the score for the song. It was also quite clear that I appeared to have forgotten what little I once knew of the art of playing the violin. So I could not play any particular piece—I could merely play! But I have always been rather indifferent to the individual nature of any piece of music, with the exception of that song, and have remained so to this day. They play Wolfgang Amadeus Mozart and Sebastian Bach: but no one plays God Himself. The eternal blessing and divine favor of tone and sound; the miraculous way in which it accords with the famished and thirsty ear, when," he continued more gently, blushing now—"the tonic third harmonizes with the first, and the fifth likewise, and the *Nota sensibilis** rises like a hope fulfilled, the dissonance is suppressed as if it were by some form of willful malice or presumptuous pride and the miracles of suspension and inversion are wrought, by means of which even the second succeeds to grace within the bosom of the harmony. A musician explained all this to me, although much later. And, though I do not really understand them, there are also the *fuga,* and the *punctum contra punctum,* the *canon a duo, a tre*† and so on: a complete heavenly structure, one fitting in with another, joined together without mortar and held together by the hand of God. No one—except a very few—knows anything about that. They rather disturb this inspiration and expiration of souls by superimposing words—as if wishing to show us how the sons of God were joined to the daughters of men!—making quite sure the music appeals to vulgar minds. Sir," he concluded half-exhausted, "speech is as necessary to men as food; but drink should be taken in a pure form for it comes from God."

So lively had he become that I barely recognized the man I had met before. He paused for a moment: "Where had I got to in my tale?" he said at last. "Ah yes: to the song and my attempt to render it myself. But I did not succeed. I went over to the window to hear better. The girl who had sung was just crossing the courtyard: I could see only her back and yet she seemed familiar to me. She carried a basket which appeared to contain some small, unbaked cakes. She passed through a little door in the corner of the yard where there was probably an oven to be found; she continued to

---

* "Leading note" (translator's note).
† "Fugue"; "counterpoint"; canon for two voices"; "canon for three voices" (translator's notes).

sing the whole time. I heard the clatter of wooden utensils and her voice now sounded fainter and clearer, like that of one who bends and sings within a hollow chamber, then rises again to stand upright. After a while, she returned: only then did I realize why she had appeared familiar before. I had actually known her for some time—at the chancery, in fact.

"It happened like this. Office hours began early and lasted beyond midday. Several of the young clerks, who were either really hungry by this time or wanted an excuse for half an hour to themselves, used to eat something at about eleven. The tradespeople—who know how to turn everything to their own advantage—spared these sweet-toothed fellows a journey and brought their wares into the office building, where they stationed themselves on the stairway and in the corridor. A baker sold white rolls and the fruit woman offered cherries for sale; but the favorites were some cakes that the daughter of a neighboring grocer baked and brought for sale still warm from the oven. Her customers would come out to her in the corridor; she seldom entered the office itself and if she did so, it was only in answer to a call. There the rather peevish head clerk—if he noticed her—would always show her the door: a command which she obeyed grudgingly, murmuring her annoyance as she went.

"My colleagues did not think the girl beautiful: they found her too short; they could give no particular color to her hair; some contended that her eyes were catlike; and all agreed that she was pockmarked. Her sturdy figure was all that met with general approval; whereas they found her common and one of them spun us a long yarn about a box on the ear, the traces of which he pretended still to feel eight days later.

"I was not one of her customers. This was partly because I did not have the money and partly because I have always had to think of food and drink as necessities—often, too much so, in fact: it never entered my head to think of them as sources of pleasure and delight. Therefore we took no notice of one another. On one occasion only, to tease me, my colleagues persuaded her that I had asked for her wares. She approached my desk and held out her basket to me. 'No thanks, miss,' I said. 'Well, why do you order things from people, then?' she shouted angrily. I said I was sorry; as I knew at once that a trick had been played, I explained to her as best I could. 'Well, you can at least give me a sheet of paper to put my cakes on,' she said. I explained it was official paper that did not belong to me, but that I had some at home which was my property: this I was willing to bring to her. 'I've got plenty at home myself,' she replied mockingly, giving a little laugh as she went out.

"This incident had occurred only a few days before and I decided that I could use this encounter for the sake of my immediate need. So, the next morning, I buttoned up a whole quire of paper—never in short supply in our house—under my overcoat and made my way to the chancery. There, so that I would not betray myself, I went to the considerable trouble of retaining this encumbrance until, towards midday, I knew from the coming and going of my colleagues and the sound of hearty chewing, that the cake seller had arrived and that probably the main rush of customers was already over. I then went out, drew forth my paper, plucked up my courage and approached the girl. She stood there: her basket in front of her on the ground and her right foot on a stool on which she usually sat. She was humming softly and kept time with the foot she had placed on the stool. As I approached she looked me up and down: this increased my embarrassment. 'Dear young lady,' I began at last, 'you asked me for some paper recently, when I had none of my own to hand; I have brought some from home, and . . .'—with that, I held out my paper. 'I've told you already the other day that I've paper of my own at home: but, it will all come in useful.' She took my gift with a slight bow of the head and placed it in her basket. 'You don't want any cakes do you?' she asked, rummaging around in her goods, 'the best have already gone anyway.' I thanked her and said that I should be grateful for something else. 'Well, what is it, then?' she replied, placing her arm in the handle of the basket and standing there quite straight as she glared at me rather angrily. I hastened to tell her that I was a music-lover, but only since a short while ago when I heard her sing such beautiful songs, and one in particular. 'You? Me? Songs?' she said with surprised annoyance, 'where was this?' I explained that I lived near her and had chanced to hear her sing in the courtyard as she worked. One of her songs I had found particularly attractive: so much so that I had already tried to repeat it on the violin. 'So it was you, was it,' she cried, 'scraping away on the fiddle like that?' As I have already told you I was still a beginner at that time, and only later was I able—after long application—to persuade these fingers to the necessary dexterity" (here the old man, interrupting his story, gestured in the air, moving the fingers of his left hand as if he were playing the violin). "My face," he said as he continued his tale, "had flushed quite red, and I could see that she regretted her harsh words. 'Dear young lady,' I said, 'The scraping occurred because I did not have the score of the song: so I made up my mind to ask for a copy as politely as possible.'

" 'For a copy?' she repeated. 'The song is in print and they sell it on the street corners.'

" 'The song?' I replied. 'Surely that means only the words?'

" 'Yes, of course, the words—the song . . .'

" 'But what about the music to which they are sung?'

" 'Do they write that down, too?' she asked.

" 'Naturally,' I replied, 'that is the most important part of it. How did you come to learn it?'

" 'I heard someone singing it: then I began to sing it myself.'

"I was astonished at her natural talent; but then the untutored are often the most gifted, although they have not the genuine—the true artistic genius. I despaired again. "Which song is it then?' she asked, 'I know so many of them.'

" 'All without music?'

" 'Yes, of course: well, which was it, then?'

" 'It is so very beautiful,' I explained. 'It rises to the heights at the very beginning, then returns to its most moving melody and comes quite softly to a close: it is the one you sing most often.'

" 'Oh, this is probably the one you mean,' she said. She put her basket down again, placed her foot on the stool and sang the song quite softly and yet distinctly. She bowed her head so beautifully and so sweetly that before she had finished, I made as if to seize the hand she had allowed to hang down. 'Oho!' she exclaimed and drew her arm back, for she probably imagined I intended something improper. She was wrong: although she was only a poor young girl, I wished to kiss it. Now I too am a poor man.

"As I was now beside myself with eagerness to have the song, she comforted me, saying that the organist from St. Peter's Church often came to buy nutmeg at her father's shop; she would ask him to write down the music of the song and I could come to collect it in a few days. Then she took up her basket and walked away. I went with her as far as the staircase. As I made my final bow on the topmost step, the head clerk of the chancery appeared and ordered me back to my work, saying that she couldn't be trusted at all. This incensed me. I was about to answer that, with all due respect, I was convinced the opposite was true, when I saw that he had returned to his room. I pulled myself together and went back to my desk. After that, the head clerk seized every possible opportunity to say that my work was slovenly and that I was a dissolute wretch.

"In fact, I was so preoccupied with the song that day, and on the days that followed, that I could hardly present any reasonable work. I was nearly out of my mind. Several days passed; I began to wonder if it was now time to fetch the sheet of music. The girl had said that the organist used to come to her father's shop to buy nutmeg, which he could only use for beer. But the weather had been cool for some time, so, it was likely that the worthy musician would keep to wine and not need any nutmeg for the present. I thought it would be ill-mannered and intrusive to inquire too soon about the music; on the other hand, if I waited too long, I might appear indifferent. I dared not speak to the girl in the corridor, as my colleagues had learned of our first meeting and were anxious not to miss an opportunity to play a trick on me.

"Meanwhile I had eagerly taken up the violin again and zealously practiced the basic exercises; of course, I allowed myself to improvise from time to time—but when I did this, I carefully closed the window, as I knew people did not like my playing. But even when I opened the window, I did not hear my song again. My neighbor did not sing at all, or sang behind a closed door so softly that I could not make out the tune at all.

"At last, when about three weeks had passed, I could stand it no longer. On two evenings I crept out into the street; I avoided wearing a hat, so that the servants would believe that I was in search of something in the house. But, as soon as I came near to the grocer's shop I began to tremble so violently that I had to turn back, whether I wanted to or not. At last, as I said, I could bear it no longer: so one evening I plucked up my courage, left my room and went downstairs—again without a hat. I walked resolutely along the street until I came to the grocer's shop, where I stopped for a time to consider what I should do next. A light was burning inside and I could hear voices there. After a moment's hesitation, I bent forward and glanced in from the side. I could see the girl sitting near the lamp, close to the counter: she was sorting peas or beans into a wooden trough. A well-built, sturdy man stood before her; his jacket was slung over one shoulder and he held a kind of cudgel in his hand; he looked rather like a butcher. They were talking and were evidently in a cheerful mood, for, from time to time, the girl would laugh out loud, but she did not interrupt her work, or even look up. I do not know whether it was because of the unnatural way in which I was leaning forward, or for some other reason, but I was beginning to tremble again when I suddenly felt myself seized roughly from behind and dragged forward. I was inside the shop in a moment. When I felt the grip on me relax and was able to turn round, I saw that it was the owner himself who had returned home and caught me loitering suspiciously—as he thought. 'The Devil!' he exclaimed, 'now we know what happens to the plums and the handfuls of peas and pearl barley which disappear from the open baskets when it is dark: damn you!' As he said this he made as if to set about me in real earnest.

"I was completely downcast; but the realization that he doubted my honor soon brought me to my senses. I gave a curt bow and told the impolite fellow that the object of my visit was not his plums or pearl barley, but his daughter. At this, the butcher, who was standing in the middle of the shop, laughed out loud and turned to go, after whispering a few words to the girl; she laughed, too, and slapped his back noisily with the flat of her hand. The grocer went with him as far as the door. By now I had lost all my courage: I stood there facing the girl, who continued to sort her peas with an air of complete indifference. Then her father blustered back into the room. 'Damn it, sir,' he said, 'what do you want with my daughter?' I tried to explain my acquaintance with his daughter and the reason for my visit. 'What, a song?' he answered. 'I'll teach you a song or two!' As he said this he waved his right fist in front of me most suspiciously. 'It's over there,' the girl said, leaning to one side on her chair and pointing to the counter; but she did not put away her trough of peas. I hurried over and saw a sheet of music lying there: it was the song. But the old man reached it first and crumpled the sheet of fine paper in his hand. 'I should like to know what is going on here!' he said. 'Who is this fellow?'

" 'He is a gentleman from the government office,' she answered, as she threw a maggoty pea a short distance from the others.

" 'A gentleman from the government office,' he exclaimed, 'in the dark—without a hat?' I was able to explain my lack of a hat from the fact that I lived quite close by; I mentioned the house. 'I know that house,' he exclaimed, 'but Counselor N. lives there'—he named my father—'and I know all the servants.'

" 'I am the Counselor's son,' I said softly, as though telling a lie. I have seen many changes in my life but none so sudden as came over the whole attitude of this man as I said those words. His mouth— open to insult me—remained open; the eyes were still threatening; but a kind of smile began to play about the lower part of his face and broadened gradually. The girl remained bent over her work: she seemed unconcerned. Some of her hair had come loose and she brushed it back behind her ears with her hand.

" 'The Counselor's son?' the old man cried out at last, beaming now over his whole face. 'Won't you make yourself at home, sir? Barbara: a chair!' The girl moved reluctantly on her own chair. 'Just you wait, you little hypocrite!' he said, as he lifted a basket out of the way himself and used his apron to clean the dust from the chair beneath.

" 'I am deeply honored,' he went on. 'So the Counselor—I mean the Counselor's son—is fond of music? Perhaps you sing, sir, as my daughter does; or rather—I am sure—sir, you must sing like a real virtuoso and follow written notes.' I told him that nature had not given me a good voice. 'You play the harpsichord then, sir, as fine people are in the habit of doing?' I said that I played the violin. 'When I was a young chap I used to scrape away a little on the fiddle myself,' he exclaimed. At the word 'scrape' I could not help looking at the girl, and saw a mocking smile on her lips: this irritated me very much.

" 'You should take the girl in hand, sir: I mean teach her music,' he went on. 'She has a good voice and other qualities besides; but she has had no chance to learn refined manners—how could she have?' As he said this he kept crossing and uncrossing the thumb and forefinger of his right hand. I was quite ashamed to hear him credit me with a knowledge of music I did not possess. I was about to explain the real situation when someone passing the shop called in: 'Good evening, all!' I was taken aback, for it was the voice of one of our servants. The grocer had recognized it, too. He rounded his lips, raised his shoulders and whispered: 'It was one of your papa's servants; but he couldn't recognize you—you were standing with your back to the door.' This was true; but I was tormented by the feeling that I was secretly doing something wrong. I took my leave simply, by stammering a few words. I should even have forgotten my song, if the old man had not run after me in the street and put the sheet of music into my hand.

"So I reached home, went up to my room and waited to see what turn events would take. I did not have to wait long, for the servant had recognized me. A few days later my father's secretary entered my room and announced that I must leave the family house. I protested: but in vain. They had rented me a little room in one of the outer suburbs, and thus I was exiled from my family. I saw no more of my singing neighbor, either. She had been forbidden to sell cakes in the office and I could not summon up the courage to visit her father's shop, because I knew that my own father did not wish me to go there. One day, when I chanced to meet the old grocer in the street, he turned away from me with a fierce look: I was completely disheartened. I used to sit along playing and practicing on my violin for entire mornings or afternoons at a time.

"But the worst was yet to come. The fortunes of our house were on the decline: my youngest brother, an officer in the Dragoons and a willful, wild fellow, made a reckless wager when deep in the heart of Hungary that he would swim across the Danube after a long ride, fully armed and on horseback. He paid for his bet with his life. The elder, favorite brother was a member of one of the provincial governing councils. He constantly opposed his superiors: for as they said, he was secretly encouraged by our father to the extent of making false statements to injure his opponents. An official inquiry took place and my brother left the country in secret. Our father's enemies—there were many of them—used this opportunity to ruin him. Day after day he delivered virulent speeches in the Council, attacked on all sides and deeply angry at the decline in his influence. He suffered a stroke when halfway through one of these speeches: he was carried home unconscious. At the time I was quite unaware of this; of course, I noticed at the office next day that people were whispering to one another and pointing at me; but I was already used to this kind of behavior and suspected nothing. The following Friday—my father had been taken ill on the Wednesday—a black suit with crêpe mourning bands was suddenly brought to my room. I was taken aback; in answer to my questions I learned what had happened. I usually enjoy robust health, but my natural resistance was useless on this occasion; I fell to the floor, in a swoon. They carried me to my bed, where I remained in a delirium all that day and the following night. My constitution regained strength the next morning: but my father was dead and buried.

"I had not been able to speak to him again or ask his forgiveness for all the sorrow I had caused him; I had not been able to thank him for the favors he had shown me, and which I did not deserve: yes, favors!—For his intentions had been good, and I hope one day to be reunited with him in that place where we are judged by our intentions rather than our acts.

"I remained in my room for several days; I ate hardly anything. When I finally ventured out, it was only to return home immediately after luncheon; but in the evenings I wandered about the dark streets like Cain after the murder of his brother. I was careful to avoid passing my father's house, for the very thought of it terrified me. But, one evening, while walking lost in thought, I suddenly found myself close to the dreaded house. My knees shook so violently that I had to stop there. I rested my hands on the wall behind me, and recognized the door of the grocer's shop: there was Barbara, sitting inside with a letter in her hand. There was a lamp on the counter beside her, and her father stood nearby: he seemed to be talking to her. I felt that I must enter at all costs. There was no one else to whom I could express my sorrow; there was no one else to feel sympathy for me! I knew that the old man was angry with me; but the girl—I thought—would have a kind word to say to me. The opposite happened. As I came in Barbara stood up; glanced at me haughtily, went into the next room; and locked the door behind her. The old man took me by the hand, told me to sit down, comforted me and said that I was now a rich man who need no longer care what others thought of him. He asked me how much money I had inherited, but I did not know. He told me that I should go to the courts, and this I promised to do. In his opinion, nothing was to be obtained from working in government offices: I should invest my inheritance in trade. Good profits were to be had from selling gallnuts and fruit; a partner who knew what he was about could mint money; he himself had had a lot to do with this trade in the past. He kept calling to the girl, but she showed no sign of life. Sometimes, however, I thought I could hear soft movements behind the door. Since she did not return and the old man continued to talk about money, I at last took my leave. The old man apologized for being unable to accompany me, as he was alone in the shop. I was sad that my hopes about the girl had proved false and yet I felt strangely calm. Suddenly, when I stopped on the street to look across at my father's house, I heard a voice behind me, saying in a muffled and rather exasperated tone: 'Don't trust everyone—they don't all mean well.' I turned round as quickly as I could, but I saw no one; only the sound of a window closing on the ground floor of the grocer's house told me that Barbara had given me this secret warning, although I had not recognized her voice. She must have heard what had been said in the shop; was she trying to warn me about her father, or had she learned that colleagues from the office, and even complete strangers, had approached me with requests for assistance and urgently needed support immediately after my father's death? I had, in fact, agreed to help them when I came into my money. I had to keep my promises; but I decided to be more prudent in the future. I claimed my inheritance, which was less than people had thought; nevertheless, it was a considerable amount—nearly eleven thousand gulden. People with requests for assistance filed through my room all day long; but my heart had become harder; I gave money only when their need seemed very great. Barbara's father also came, to complain that for three days I had not been to see them. I answered quite truthfully that I was afraid his daughter would not want to see me. He said that I need not worry about that, for he had now put the right ideas into her head; he quite startled me by laughing maliciously as he said this. I remembered Barbara's warning, and, when the conversation turned to my newly found wealth, I did not tell him how much I had inherited. I also took care to avoid accepting his business propositions.

"In fact, I had other plans. My job in the office—where I had been tolerated only because of my father's position—had already been filled by another. I was not very concerned about this as there was no salary attached to the post; but my father's secretary, who had found himself unemployed as a result of the recent events, informed me of his plans to start a secretarial, translating and general information bureau. He suggested that I advance the money needed to start the business which he would manage himself. At my request, the copying side of the business was to be extended to musical manuscripts:

my happiness was complete. I advanced the necessary money; but, as I had already become more cautious, I had a document drawn up, to show exactly how much I had lent. The caution money for the establishment—which I also advanced—seemed hardly worth worrying about—although a considerable amount of money was involved—as it had to be deposited with the courts; there it remained my property, as though I kept it locked away in my cupboard.

"The matter was settled, and I felt relieved and exhilarated: I was independent for the first time in my life; in short, I was a man. I hardly gave another thought to my father. I moved to better rooms; bought better clothes; and, one evening, I walked through the familiar streets to the grocer's shop. I hummed my song as I walked briskly along, although I could not get it quite right. With my voice, I have never been able to reproduce a B flat in the second half. I arrived in good spirits, but an icy glance from Barbara at once restored my former nervousness. Her father received me in the most friendly manner, but she behaved as though I were not present: she continued to make paper bags and said not a single word. Only when our conversation turned to my inheritance, she half started up to say, almost threateningly: 'Father . . .!' whereupon the old man immediately changed the subject. Apart from this she said nothing all evening and did not look at me again. When I finally left, her 'Good evening!' sounded almost like 'Thank God he's going!'

"But I went again and again, and she gradually gave in. Not that I could ever please her: on the contrary she criticized and scolded me the whole time. Everything I did was clumsy; God had given me two left hands; I looked like a scarecrow in my coat, and walked like a duck, with something of a cockerel's gait, too. She particularly disliked my politeness to customers. I was without a job until the secretarial bureau could be opened; and, thinking that I should have to deal with the public when it did open, I took an active part in the trade in the grocer's shop, in order to gain practice. I often served in the shop for an entire morning or afternoon. I weighed out spices, counted out nuts and prunes for boys, and gave change; the last task being often attended by mistakes which Barbara would always correct. She would take away whatever I had in my hand and make fun of me in front of the customers. If I bowed or said good-day to a customer, she would remark sharply before he had left the shop: 'Our goods are their own recommendation,' and turn her back to me.

"Sometimes, however, she was kindness itself. She would listen to me when I gave her news from the town or talked about my childhood and the life of the civil servants in the office where we had first met. But she always left me to do the talking and would indicate her approval—or, more often, disapproval—by a single word.

"We never talked about music or singing; she thought one should either sing or keep quiet about the subject, as there was nothing that could be said about it. But actual singing was impossible: it would have been out of place in the shop, and I was never allowed to enter the back room where she and her father lived.

"Once, when I entered unnoticed, she was standing on tiptoe with her back to me, feeling for something on one of the top shelves, with her hands raised. She was singing softly to herself as she did this: it was the song—my song! The notes came tripping out like the song of a warbler as it washes its slender neck at a stream and jerks its head from side to side, using its beak to ruffle and smooth its feathers down again. I felt as though I were walking through green meadows. I crept closer and closer until I was so near that the song seemed no longer to come from outside but from deep within me, as though it were our two souls singing. I could restrain myself no longer: she leaned back towards me with her shoulders and I clasped her about the waist. Then it happened: she spun round like a top; her face flushed with anger as she faced me; her hand flashed, and, before I could apologize . . .

"As I mentioned before, they had often spoken in the office of the occasion when Barbara slapped the face of one of the clerks who had been too forward, in the days when she still went to the office to sell cakes. What they said about the strength of the girl's hand seemed at the time to be very exaggerated and only a joke, for she was really rather small; but, in fact, all they said of her strength was more than exact. I stood there as if a thunderbolt had struck me; but in my dazed state, the stars that I saw seemed quite heavenly: they were like little angels who sing as they play hide-and-seek. I saw visions: I was entranced. She was hardly less startled than I was and passed her hand soothingly over my face where she had struck me. 'Perhaps I hit you too hard,' she said, and—like a bolt from the blue—I suddenly felt her warm breath on my cheek, and her two lips as she kissed me. It was only a light kiss and quite soft: but it was a kiss, all the same—here on my cheek!" As he said this, the old man clapped a hand to his cheek and tears came into his eyes. "What happened next, I do not know," he continued. "I know only that I rushed at her and that she fled into the living-room and held the glass-paned door firmly shut, while I tried to force it from the other side. As she bent low and pressed against the door with all her strength, I, sir, plucked up courage, and returned her kiss through the glass with all my might.

" 'Well, you are having fun here!' I heard someone call out from behind me. It was the grocer, who had just returned. 'Well, it isn't a bad sign, when you start teasing one another . . .' he said. 'Come out of there, Barbara: don't be foolish! An honest kiss can do no harm.' But she did not come.

"I stammered a few words, really not knowing what I was saying, and went out. I even took the grocer's hat instead of my own, and he changed them back with a laugh. As I said before, this was the happiest day of my life; I almost said—the only happy one—but that would have been untrue, for God bestows many favors on us.

"I did not really know how the girl felt about me. Was she more annoyed now; or was she more affectionately disposed towards me? It was not easy to decide on my next visit. But she was in a good mood; she sat at her work, humble and quiet—not excitable, as she usually was. She nodded towards a stool beside her, indicating that I should sit there to help her. We sat like this and went on working. The old man wanted to go out: 'You may as well stay here, father,' she said, 'I have already done what was needed.' He stamped his foot and remained. He walked up and down and spoke of various matters, but I did not dare join in the conversation. Then the girl cried out suddenly: she had scratched her finger as she worked; although she was not in the least squeamish by nature, she was jerking her hand backwards and forwards. I wanted to look at her hand, but she indicated that I should continue my work. 'That's really stupid!' muttered the old man, and he went up to the girl and said, in a loud voice: 'You certainly have not done what was needed!' and with that he stamped out of the room. I wanted to apologize for what had happened the day before, but she interrupted me to say: 'Let us forget that and talk about something more sensible.'

"She raised her head, looked me up and down and continued, calmly: 'I can hardly remember myself how we happened to meet; but for some time now you have been coming more and more often,

and we have grown used to you. Nobody will deny that you have a
kind heart, but you are so weak and so easily led astray, that you
would be hardly capable of looking after your own affairs. It is the
duty of your friends and acquaintances to keep an eye on you, and to
see that you come to no harm. You sit in the shop for hours on end,
counting and weighing, measuring and marking: but you get nowhere. How do you intend to earn a decent living in the future?' I
mentioned the money I had inherited from my father. 'Was it a large
amount?' she asked. I named the sum. 'That is a large amount of
money; and again, it isn't,' she replied. 'It's a good sum to make a
start with, but not a lot to live on. It is true my father made a
proposition to you, but I advised you not to take up his idea. He has
lost money before at the same kind of business, and then,' she
added, lowering her voice, 'he is so used to making a profit out of
strangers, that he might try the same thing with friends. You must
have someone honest to look after you.' I suggested that she could
be that person. 'It is true that I mean well,' she said, placing her
hand on her breast; and her eyes, which were usually tinged with
gray, shone bright blue—as blue as the sky. 'But I shall have to go my
own way: our shop does not bring in much money and my father is
toying with the idea of opening a small taproom. There would be no
room for me there; I should have to take up needlework, for I do not
want to go into service.' As she said this, she looked exactly like a
queen. 'I have already had another offer,' she went on, pulling a
letter from her apron and throwing it down, half-unwillingly, on the
counter, 'But if I accepted, I should have to go away from here.'

" 'Far away?' I asked.

" 'Why? What does it matter to you?' I declared that I should like
to move to the same place. 'Are you a child?' she asked, 'That would
be impossible, altogether impossible! But if you trust me and like to
be near me, you need only buy the milliner's shop that is for sale in
the neighborhood. I understand the trade: and you need have no
worries about making an honest profit from your money. You would
be well occupied with the accounts and letters. Whether or not
things would go any further, we shall not discuss now. But you
would have to change! I hate effeminate men.'

"I had jumped up and seized my hat. 'What has happened? Where
are you going? she asked. 'To change all my plans,' I said hurriedly.
'What do you mean?' she said. I told her now for the first time of my

plan to set up a secretarial and information bureau. 'You won't make much out of that,' she said. 'Anybody can collect information for themselves and everyone learns to write in school.' I pointed out that we also intended to copy musical manuscripts, which not everyone could do. 'So you are back to those stupid ideas, again,' she exclaimed. 'Forget about music and just think of the essentials! Anyway, you would not be able to manage a business alone.' I explained that I had found a partner. 'A partner?' she cried. 'He is bound to be someone who wants to cheat you! I hope at least that you haven't paid any money out yet.' I trembled, without knowing why. 'Have you paid out any money?' she repeated. I confessed that I had paid three thousand gulden to get the business started. 'Three thousand gulden!' she repeated, 'As much money as that!'

" 'The remainder,' I continued, 'is deposited with the courts, and so that at least is safe.'

" 'So there's more to it, is there?' she cried out. I told her about the surety. 'Did you deposit it with the courts yourself?' My partner had done so. 'At least you must have a certificate?' I had no certificate. 'And what is your fine partner called?' she asked. My mind was—to some extent—at rest, since I could tell her that he was my father's secretary.

" 'Good heavens!' she cried, jumping up and clapping her hands together in dismay. 'Father! Father!' The old man came in. 'What did you read in the newspapers today?'

" 'About the secretary?'

" 'Yes, that's it!'

" 'Well, he's absconded: he left a heap of debts and had cheated all kinds of people. There are warrants out for his arrest.'

" 'Father,' she exclaimed. 'He, too, entrusted all his money to that man: he is ruined.'

" 'What fools one meets!' shouted the old man. 'Didn't I say that this would happen? But you always found excuses for him. You either laughed or said he had an honest soul. But now I'll have my own way and show you who is master in this house. Barbara, go to your room! And you, sir, get out of here and don't come to visit us again. We don't give alms here!'

" 'Father,' said the girl, 'don't be hard on him: he is unlucky enough already.'

" 'That's just the reason,' cried the old man, 'I don't want to be unfortunate, too. Now here,' he continued, pointing to the letter which Barbara had thrown on the table earlier on, 'here is a real man! He's got his head screwed on the right way: he doesn't cheat anyone, but he doesn't let himself be cheated, either. That is what honesty really means.' I stammered that it was not yet certain that I had lost the money which I had pledged. 'Oho! So you think the secretary is a fool, do you? He's a rogue, admittedly, but a cunning one. And now, get out quickly: perhaps you'll catch up with him!'

"As he said this, he put his hand on my shoulder and pushed me towards the door. I moved to one side, away from his hand, and turned towards the girl. She stood leaning against the counter, looking down at the floor, her breast heaving all the time. I wanted to go closer to her, but she stamped her foot angrily. When I stretched out my hand to her, she half raised her own hand as if to strike me again, whereupon I went out and the old man closed the door after me.

"I stumbled through the streets to the city gate and out into the open country. Despair and hope alternated in my mind. I remembered that I had accompanied the secretary to the commercial court when he went to deposit the money as security. I had waited downstairs in the doorway and he had gone up alone. When he came down he had told me that everything was settled and that a receipt would be sent to my house. This had not, in fact, happened; but there was still a slight chance. I returned to the town at daybreak. My first call was at the secretary's house; but people laughed and asked me if I had read the papers. The commercial court was only a short distance away; there I asked them to consult the records, but neither his name nor my own appeared there. There was no trace of any money having been paid in. My loss was now certain. Indeed, things turned out to be even worse: as a company contract had been drawn up, several of his creditors wanted to take me into custody. But this the courts would not allow. How grateful I was to them! Although it would have made no difference in the end.

"As a result of all this unpleasantness, I must confess that the grocer and his daughter had quite faded from my mind. Now, when things grew quieter, and I began to consider what else would happen, I remembered clearly what had occurred the other evening. I understood the father—selfish as he was—quite well; but the girl! I often reasoned that if I had looked after my own affairs and had been able to offer her a comfortable life, she would probably . . . but she wouldn't have wanted me." And he separated his hands so that he could survey his whole shabby figure. "She also took exception to the polite way in which I treated everyone.

"Thus I spent several days in thought, considering the matter. One evening when dusk had fallen—it was the time when I was normally at the shop—I sat down again and carried myself in imagination to the usual place. I heard them speaking and abusing me; they seemed even to be laughing at me. Suddenly there was a rustling at the door: it opened, and a woman entered. It was Barbara. I sat as if nailed to my chair—as though I had seen a ghost. Her face was pale and she carried a bundle under her arm. She stood still when she reached the middle of the room; looked round the bare walls, then downwards at the poor sticks of furniture; and sighed deeply. Then she went to the clothespress where it stood to one side against the wall, untied her parcel, which contained some shirts and some linen—she had seen to my washing lately—opened the drawer and threw up her hands in dismay when she saw the poverty of its contents. Immediately afterwards, however, she began to arrange the linen and put the things she had brought with her into place. She then moved a couple of steps from the press, looked at me, and, pointing her finger to the open drawer, said: 'Five shirts and three handkerchiefs. That's what I took away: that's what I've brought back.' Then she closed the drawer slowly, supported herself on the press with one hand and began to cry aloud. She seemed almost to be sick; for she sat down on a chair near the chest, hid her face in her scarf, and I could tell from the gasping breaths she took that she was still sobbing. I had approached her slowly and now took her hand— which she willingly gave me. But, when—in order to draw her eyes towards me—I moved my hand up her limply hanging arm until I reached the elbow, she suddenly stood up, withdrew her hand, and said in a resolute voice: 'What's the use of all that? That's the way it is: once for all. It was your own doing. You have brought unhappiness to yourself and to us; but certainly to yourself more than to us. Yet you really deserve no pity.' At this point she became more and more angry: 'If you're so weak that you can't keep your own things in order: so credulous that you put your faith in everyone— whether a villain or an honest man. . . . And yet I am sorry for you. I have come to say goodbye. Yes, you may well be alarmed: it is your own doing. Now I shall have to go out among vulgar people: something that I have resisted for so long. But there is no way out of it. I have already given you my hand, so goodbye—for ever!' I saw that she was crying again; but she shook her head curtly and left. My limbs seemed to be weighted with lead.

"When she came to the door, she turned again and said: 'The washing is in order, now. Make sure that nothing is missing: hard times will soon be here.' And then she raised her hand, made something that resembled the sign of the cross in the air, cried: 'God be with you, Jacob!' and added, more softly, 'For ever. Amen.' Then she departed.

"Only then did I regain the use of my limbs. I hurried after her, and, standing on the landing, called to her: 'Barbara!' I heard her pause on the stairs, but when I was past the first step she called from below: 'Stay there!' and went down the whole flight and out through the gateway.

"I have suffered hard days since then, but none like that; even the next day was easier to bear. I really did not know where I was; and so the next day I crept near to the grocer's shop, to see if perhaps I could find some explanation. As nothing was to be seen, I at last looked into the shop from the side and saw a woman—a stranger to me—weighing out goods and preparing and giving change. I ventured in to ask if she had bought the shop. 'Not yet, exactly,' was the reply. And where were the owners? 'They left for Langenlebarn* early this morning.'

" 'The daughter, too?' I stammered. 'Why yes, of course,' she answered, 'she is to be married there.'

"The woman may well have told me then everything that I learned from others afterwards. The butcher in the village she had named— the very one whom I had encountered when I first visited the shop— had courted the girl for some time; but she had always rejected him; until, at last, in the past few days, pressed by her father and in despair at the turn events had taken, she had accepted him. That very morning the father and his daughter had set off for Langenlebarn, and at the very moment when I was speaking to the shopkeeper, Barbara was the butcher's wife. The woman whom I found in the shop may well—as I have said—have told me all this;

*A village north of Vienna (translator's note).

but I was not listening, and stood there motionless until at last some customers arrived, who pushed me to one side; while the woman asked me gruffly if there was anything else I wanted—at which I departed.

"You will believe, sir," he continued, "that I now considered myself to be the most unfortunate man alive. So it was to begin with; but when I had made my way out of the shop and turned round to regard the small windows at which Barbara had so often stood and looked out, a blissful sensation came over me. The knowledge that she was now free of all cares, was the mistress of her own household and must not bear the burden of sorrow and misery that would have been hers, had she joined her life to that of a homeless creature, was like a soothing balm to me. I blessed her and the path she had chosen.

"As I was now sinking ever lower, I decided to seek my living in music. As long as the remainder of my money held out, I practiced and studied the works of the great composers—especially the old ones, which I copied out. When my last halfpenny was gone, I set to work to put my knowledge to some practical use. At first, I performed for select gatherings—beginning with a dinner party at my landlady's house. But as the compositions I played there were not appreciated, I stationed myself in courtyards, thinking that among so many inhabitants there must be some who would value serious music; and, finally, I made my way to public footpaths, where I actually had the satisfaction of seeing some remain to listen and question me, and depart not without sympathy. I was not ashamed that they left money on these occasions. On the one hand, that was my precise intention: on the other, I realized that famous musicians—whose level I could not flatter myself I had attained—accepted fees, and sometimes very high ones, for their performances. And so I have earned my living—poor, but honorable, as it is—to this day.

"Some years later another piece of luck was to come my way: the return of Barbara. Her husband had made money and taken a butcher's shop in one of the suburbs. She had given birth to two children, the elder of whom was christened Jacob, like myself. The way in which I earned my living and the memory of times past did not allow me to be obtrusive, but at last I was asked to visit the house to give the older boy violin lessons. He has but little aptitude and can only play on Sundays, as he works in his father's shop during the week; but he can already give a good rendering of Barbara's song, which I have taught him. When we practice, his mother sometimes joins in and sings. She has changed quite considerably in the many years that have passed: she is now stout and cares little for music, but the song sounds as beautiful as it did before." With these words, the old fellow seized his violin and began to play the song, and continued to play—paying no more attention to me. Finally, when I had heard enough, I stood up, laid a few silver coins on the table nearby, and went while the old man went on playing zealously.

Soon after this I went off on a journey, from which I returned only with the onset of winter. New images had supplanted the old, and my poor musician was almost entirely forgotten. Only with the terrifying breaking-up of the ice the next spring and the resulting inundation of the low-lying suburbs* did I remember him again. The Gärtnergasse area had been transformed into a lake; but there seemed no occasion to worry about the safety of the old man, for he lived high up under the eaves, while death had only too often chosen its victims from those on the ground floors. Nevertheless, how great his need must be—deprived of all assistance as he was! There was nothing that could be done as long as the flood lasted: the authorities had already, as far as was possible, used boats to take food and other aid to those cut off. But when the waters subsided and the streets had become passable, I decided that my contribution to the collection that had been started—and which had reached an incredible sum†—should be taken in person to the address that concerned me most immediately.

The Leopoldstadt was a ghastly sight: the streets were strewn with broken-up boats and implements, and where the ground floors of the houses were still partly flooded, household goods floated on the water. When I avoided the press of the crowd and approached a courtyard door that stood ajar, it swung open to reveal a row of corpses in the passageway leading to the courtyard: they had obviously been collected together and laid out there for official identi-

---

*The flood is a historical event that occurred in the night of February 28, 1830; more than seventy persons lost their lives.
†A collection for the relief of the flood victims, raising 350,000 gulden.

fication. Indeed, here and there, bodies of dead inhabitants were still to be seen within their rooms, standing upright and clinging to the window-bars; for there was clearly no time, nor were the officials numerous enough, to see to the legal registration of so many deaths.

Thus I continued on my way. From every point came the sounds of sobbing and of bells being tolled, of mothers in search of their young, and of children who were lost. At last I came to the Gärtnergasse. There, too, the black-clad followers of a funeral train were standing, but it appeared to be some distance from the house to which I was bound. When I came nearer I noticed some coming and going between the mourners and the house I was looking for. A sturdy-looking, elderly but still vigorous man stood on the front porch. He looked just like a country butcher with his high-fitting boots, yellow leather breeches and long-skirted coat. He was giving orders, but in the intervals spoke with apparent indifference to those near him. I passed him and entered the courtyard. The old gardener's wife approached me, recognized me at once and greeted me with tears. "Are you paying us the honor, too?" she said. "Yes, our poor old man. Now he must be playing his violin to the angels in heaven, who can't be very much better than he was while still here below. The dear soul sat up there safe and sound in his room. But when the water came and he heard the children crying out, he leaped down and rescued and dragged away and carried and bore to safety, until his breath was coming and going like a smith's bellows. And—for you can't see to everything at once—when it became clear at the very last moment, that my husband had left his tax receipts and a few banknotes in the cupboard, the old man took up a hatchet, entered the water—which reached to his chest—broke open the cupboard, and brought everything faithfully to us. It was then that he probably caught cold, and, as there was no help to be had at first, he became delirious and gradually grew worse and worse, although we helped him as best we could, and suffered more by it than he did. For he continued to make music: by singing, of course, and he beat time, and lectured us about it. When the water had subsided a little and we could fetch the apothecary and the priest, he suddenly sat upright in his bed, turned his head and listened as though he could hear something exceptionally beautiful in the distance, smiled, sank back: and died. Do go up: he often spoke of you. Madam, the butcher's wife, is up there, too; we wanted to have him buried at our own expense, but she wouldn't hear of it."

She hurried me up the steep staircase until we reached the room beneath the eaves: the door stood open and the room was quite empty except for the coffin in the center, already closed and awaiting only the pallbearers. A fairly stout woman, no longer young, sat at the head; she was dressed in a brightly colored calico skirt, although she wore a black neckerchief and had a black ribbon in her bonnet. I am almost certain that she could never have been a beautiful woman. Two fairly grown-up children stood before her—a boy and a girl, whom she was clearly instructing how to behave in the funeral procession. As I entered, she pushed the boy's arm away from the coffin and carefully smoothed down the protruding corners of the pall, for the child had leaned rather clumsily upon it. The gardener's wife led me forward; but then the trumpets down below began to sound, and immediately the butcher's voice was heard in the street: "It's time, Barbara!" The bearers appeared, and I drew back to make room for them. The coffin was raised, brought down, and the procession started off. The schoolchildren with the cross and the church-banner, and the priest together with the sexton walked in front. Immediately behind the coffin were the butcher's children and behind them the butcher and his wife. The man moved his lips all the time as if in prayer, but he kept looking to right and left about him. His wife read zealously in her prayer book, except when the two children gave her some trouble: for she would urge them forward at one moment and hold them back at another, as if she thought the proper conduct of the funeral train supremely important. But she would always return to her prayer book. Thus the procession reached the cemetery. The grave lay open. The children threw in the first handfuls of earth. Their father stood there and did the same. His wife kneeled and held her prayer book close to her eyes. The grave-diggers completed their task and the procession, half-disbanded, returned. A short altercation occurred at the door when the butcher's wife found some charge made by the undertaker excessive. The mourners dispersed in all directions. The old musician was buried.

A few days later—it was Sunday—driven by my obsessive curiosity, I went to the butcher's house, and gave as my pretext for the visit a desire to have the old man's fiddle as a memento. I found the family together: no particular impression seemed to have left its

Mozart on the Way to Prague

Eduard Mörike

In the fall of the year 1787 Mozart set out on a journey to Prague in company with his wife, there to produce *Don Giovanni*.

By the third day on the road, the fourteenth of September, towards eleven in the morning, the pair were still scarce more than thirty leagues from Vienna, driving in high spirits towards the northwest, having left behind the Mannhardsberg and the German Thaya, near Schrems, where the road has all but emerged from the lovely Moravian mountains.

"The conveyance, with its team of three post-horses," writes the Baroness von T. to her friend, "an imposing orange-colored coach, was the property of a certain old Frau von Volkstett, the wife of a general, who sems for long past to have rather plumed herself upon her relations with the Mozart family and the attentions that she had shown it." This vague description of the vehicle in question can be supplemented with a few more details by one familiar with the taste of the seventeen-eighties. The orange-colored carriage was painted on either door with posies of flowers in their natural coloring, the panels being framed with a narrow gold fillet, but the paint had still nothing approaching the gloss of the mirror-surfaced varnish used in the workshops of present-day Vienna, nor had the body such full, swelling lines, though it tapered elegantly downwards in a bold curve; add to this a high roof with stiff leather curtains, which for the time being were drawn back.

A few observations may further be added about the costume of the two travellers. The clothes worn by her husband had been chosen frugally by Frau Konstanze with a view to saving the new full-dress garments packed away in the trunk; with his embroidered waistcoat of a rather faded blue he wore his usual brown frock-coat, having a row of large buttons so fashioned that a layer of red-gold tinsel gleamed through a star-patterned network, and with it black silk breeches, stockings, and gilt buckles on his shoes. For the last hour he had gone without his coat on account of the heat, which was abnormal for that month of the year, and sat bare-headed and in his shirt-sleeves, chatting contentedly. Madame Mozart wore a comfortable travelling-dress with pale green and white stripes. The mass of her beautiful light brown hair fell down, half loosed, upon her neck and shoulders. Never in her life had it been marred by powder, but her husband's thick growth, tied back in a queue, was sprinkled for the nonce even more negligently than usual.

They had ascended at a leisurely pace a gently rising slope between the fertile fields which here and there broke the wide expanse of forest, and had now reached the fringe of the wood.

"Through how many forests," remarked Mozart, "have we not already passed today, yesterday and the day before! I thought nothing of it at the time, least of all did it occur to me to set foot inside them. Let us just get down here, shan't we, dear heart, and pick some of those blue bell-flowers growing so prettily in the shade over there. Postillion, you can breathe your beasts awhile."

As the two rose to their feet a slight mishap was revealed, which cost the Master a scolding. Thanks to his heedlessness a bottle of costly perfume had come unstoppered, and emptied its contents unobserved over their clothes and the cushioned seats. "I might have known it," she wailed; "the scent had been so strong for a long time past. Alas! a whole bottle of genuine *Rosée d'Aurore*, clean empty! And I was husbanding it like gold." "Why, simpleton!" was his consoling reply, "Don't you see? In this way, if in no other, your cordial meet for noses divine has done us a good turn. At first we were sitting in a perfect oven, and all your fanning was of no avail; but soon the whole carriage seemed somehow to have grown quite cool. You put it down to the few drops I had sprinkled on my shirt-frill. We felt new life in us and our talk flowed blithely on, instead of our having to droop our heads like sheep in the butcher's cart. And the good of it will remain with us all the way. But now let us hurry and poke our two Viennese noses into these verdant wilds!"

They stepped arm in arm over the roadside ditch, and so at once deep into the gloom of the fir-wood, which soon deepened into a darkness pierced only here and there by a shaft of sunshine striking vividly down on the carpet of velvet moss. The refreshing coolness, in abrupt contrast with the blazing heat outside, might have been dangerous to the heedless fellow but for his companion's forethought. With some difficulty she pressed upon him the garment she had held in readiness. "Good God! How glorious!" he cried, gazing up at the lofty boles; "One might be in a church! I feel as though I had never been in a forest, and now I see for the first time what manner of thing it really is—this whole population of trees ranged side by side! No human hand planted them, they grew up all of their own accord, and here they stay for the simple reason that it is fun to be alive and carry on the business of life together. You see, in my young days I travelled up and down half Europe, I saw the Alps and the ocean, all that is grandest and most beautiful in creation: and now, idiot that I am, I stand by chance in an ordinary fir-wood on the borders of Bohemia, lost in wonder and rapture that such a thing should really exist, and is not, as it were, just *una finzione de' poeti,* a figment of the poets, like your nymphs and fauns and what not, or even a stage forest, either—no! but rooted in the earth and reared to full stature by moisture and the warmth of the sun. This is the home of the deer, with his wondrous branching antlers on his brow, of the tricksy squirrel, the black-cock and the jay." He stooped and pulled a fungus, praising the splendid, brilliant red of its cap and the delicate whity gills on its underside, and he pocketed an assortment of fir-cones besides.

"One would think," said his wife, "that you had never before taken a look twenty paces into the Prater,* though it must have like rarities to offer too."

"The Prater, do you say? *Saprelotte!* How can you so much as name it here? What with coaches, court swords, French dresses and fans, music and all the din in the world, who could ever see anything else there? Why, the very trees, however they may give themselves airs—I don't know how it is, but the beech-mast and acorns strewn about the ground look for all the world like own brothers and sisters to the hosts of derelict corks mixed up with them. From as far as a couple of leagues away the woods reek of waiters and sauces."

"Did you ever!" she cried. "And this is the man who knows no greater pleasure than to sup off roast chicken in the Prater!"

When both were once more seated in the carriage, and the road, after running along for a while on the level, now sloped gently

*Amusement park in Vienna.

downwards where a smiling landscape stretched away till it melted into the more distant mountains, our Master, having sat silent for a while, began once again: "Truly the earth is fair, and no man need be blamed for wishing to remain on it as long as possible. Thanks be to God, I feel as fresh and well as ever, and shall soon be ready for a thousand things, which will follow one another in due order as soon as my latest work is completed and produced. How many strange and beautiful things there are in the great world beyond, and how many here at home, of which I know simply nothing yet, in the shape of natural wonders, sciences, arts and useful crafts! Your grimy young charcoal-burner over there at his kiln is as clever a fellow as I am about some things, though I must say I feel an inclination and a longing to have a look into this, that and the other, even though it does not happen to be connected with my own particular stock-in-trade."

"The other day," was her reply, "I came across your old pocket calendar for the year 'eighty-five; at the end of it you had jotted down three or four notes. First comes this one: 'In the middle of October they cast the great lions in the Imperial foundry;' and in the second place, doubly underlined: 'Call upon Professor Gattner.' Who is he?"

"Oh yes, I know; at the observatory—the nice old gentleman who invites me there from time to time. I had long wanted to look at the moon and the little old man in it with you. They have got a mighty great telescope up there now: they say that on the vast disk one can see, so clearly and distinctly that one could almost touch them, mountains, valleys and abysses, and, on the side where the sun does not fall, the shadow cast by the mountains. For two years now I have been intending to pay him a visit, and I have never managed it yet, more's the pity—and more shame to me, too!"

"Well," she said, "the moon won't run away. We're going to catch up with lots of things we have missed."

After a pause, he went on again: "And isn't it the same with everything? Fie upon me! I dare not think of all one has omitted to do in time, or put off, or left undone—let alone one's duty to God and one's neighbor—I mean in the way of pure enjoyment, the little innocent pleasures that come everyone's way daily."

Madame Mozart either could not or would not do anything to turn his volatile emotions in a different direction from that in which they were tending more and more, and unfortunately she could only agree with all her heart as he continued with rising agitation: "Have I ever been able to enjoy a whole hour's happiness even with my children? For me it was always by snatches and *en passant!* I might give the little chaps a ride on my knee, or romp about the room with them for a minute or two, and then *basta!* that was the end of it! I can't recall ever having spent a jolly day in the country together at Easter or Whitsuntide in a garden or a bit of a wood, all to ourselves on the grass, having fun with the children and playing with flowers, so as to become a child again oneself. And all the while life goes rushing and roaring past—Good God! when one really thinks of it, one could almost break out into a cold sweat of terror!"

The self-reproaches to which he had just given utterance led unexpectedly to a most serious talk between the two, in all confidence and affection. We shall not report it in detail, but rather make a general survey of the circumstances which now formed the express and immediate subject of their discussion, now merely loomed in the background of their consciousness.

And here the painful reflection forces itself upon us that, in spite of all he experienced, enjoyed and created during his brief span of life, this fiery being, incredibly sensitive to all the charms of the world and the sublimest heights to which the boding soul can soar, none the less never in all his life arrived at an understanding with himself on any stable and entirely satisfactory footing.

Those who are not bent upon probing deeper for the causes of this phenomenon than these probably lie in reality, will find them, first and foremost, in those inveterate and apparently insuperable weaknesses which, not altogether without reason, we are so much inclined to associate, as an inevitable accompaniment, with all those qualities in Mozart that arouse our admiration.

The requirements of the man's nature were highly manifold, and his predilection for the pleasures of society, in particular, abnormally strong. Esteemed and sought after by the most distinguished houses in the city on account of his incomparable gifts, he seldom or never refused invitations to festivities, social gatherings or parties. Besides this, he also gratified his hospitable instincts to the full within his own more immediate circle. A musical evening such as had long been an institution at his house on a Sunday, or an informal midday dinner at his bounteous table with a few friends and acquaintances two or three times a week, were things which he would not willingly have gone without. Now and then, to the consternation of his wife, he would bring guests home without notice whom he had met in the street, persons of very unequal worth, amateurs, fellow artists, singers and poets. The idle flatterer, whose only merit lay in his constant flow of high spirits, his wit and his jokes, sometimes of rather a coarse variety, was as welcome as the intelligent connoisseur and the competent player. Again, Mozart was in the habit of seeking most of his recreation outside his own house. Any and every day he was to be found after meals at the billiard-table in the coffee-house, and often, too, in the evening at the inn. He was very fond of driving and riding about the country in the company of friends and, being a consummate dancer, he frequented dances, routs and masked balls, while once or twice a year he thoroughly enjoyed himself at popular festivities, and especially at the open-air ball during St. Bridget's Fair,* where he masqueraded as Pierrot.

These recreations, now exuberant and boisterous, now attuned to a more quiet mood, were calculated to provide the necessary rest for his mind after periods of tense concentration and a prodigious discharge of force; nor did they fail to convey to him incidentally, by those mysterious channels through which genius unconsciously operates, those subtle and fleeting impressions which fertilize it by the way. Yet since, unhappily, in such hours as these his great object always was to drain the glad moment to the dregs, no other considerations, whether of prudence or of duty, of self-preservation or love of home, were of any weight. Whether enjoying or creating, Mozart was equally regardless of moderation or steady purpose. Part of the night he always devoted to composition. In the early morning he rested from his labors, often lying long abed. Then from ten o'clock onwards, whether on foot or fetched by a carriage, he went the round of his lessons, which occupied, as a rule, some hours of the afternoon as well. "We toil away for dear life," as he himself writes to one of his patrons, "and often enough it is hard not to lose patience. Being a well-accredited cembalist and music master, one saddles oneself with a dozen pupils, and now and again with an extra one,

---

*A folk festival held since the eighteenth century in the Viennese district of Brigittenau on the first Sunday after the full moon in July. The largest public festival in Vienna, it is also described in Grillparzer's *The Poor Musician.*

regardless of whether there is anything more in him, so long as he pays his thaler *per marca* [that is, per lesson]. Any mustachioed Hungarian in the Engineers is welcome who may be visited by Satan with a desire to study thorough-bass and counterpoint for no earthly reason; or else the most impertinent of little countesses, who receives me scarlet with annoyance if by chance I fail to knock at her door on the stroke of the clock, just as if I were Maître Coquerel who curls her hair." And when, worn out with these and other professional labors, concerts, rehearsals and the like, he pined for fresh air, all that was usually granted to his jaded nerves was the apparent relaxation of a fresh excitement. His constitution was stealthily undermined, and a constantly recurring mood of melancholy was, if not produced, at any rate undoubtedly fostered by the selfsame cause; and thus that premonition of an early death which came at last to dog his every step, met with its inevitable fulfillment. For his part he was inured to worries of every sort and shade, not excepting a sense of remorse, and they brought a tang of bitterness into every pleasure. Yet we know that even these sorrows, too, sublimated and purified, were merged in the deep spring which, welling from a thousand conduits, poured forth inexhaustibly in his changing melodies all the anguish and the bliss of the human heart.

The evil effects of Mozart's way of living showed themselves most plainly in the state of his domestic affairs. The charge of mad and reckless extravagance can easily be understood, for it was the inevitable complement of one of his finest qualities. Anyone who came to him in urgent need, hoping to borrow a sum of money or persuade him to act as surety, generally reckoned in advance upon his omitting to make very thorough inquiries into their pledges or security; in fact, he would not have troubled about such things any more than a child. What he preferred was to give the money then and there, and always with a laughing open-handedness, especially when he believed himself at the moment to have enough and to spare.

Yet the resources required to meet such expenditure in addition to his ordinary household needs were out of all proportion to his income. His earnings from theaters and concerts, publishers and pupils, together with his pension from the Emperor, were still less adequate because public taste was as yet far from having declared definitely in favor of Mozart's music. Such pure loveliness, richness and depth was commonly found repellent by comparison with the easily assimilated fare that had hitherto been so popular. It is true that, while it was being performed, the inhabitants of Vienna could hardly have enough of *Belmonte und Konstanze* [or *Die Entführung aus dem Serail*], owing to the popular elements in that piece; yet it was certainly not due solely to the intrigues of the manager that a few years later *Figaro* unexpectedly proved a sorry fiasco in rivalry with the charming, but greatly inferior *Cosa rara**—that same *Figaro* which the more cultivated, or less prejudiced inhabitants of Prague received immediately afterwards with such enthusiasm that, touched and gratified, the Master determined to write his next grand opera specially for them. Despite the unfavorable conditions of the day and the influence of his enemies, with a little more prudence and shrewdness Mozart might still have derived very considerable profits from his art: as it was, his own personal gains were wretched even from those ventures in which the great public perforce applauded him to the echo. In short, all things worked together—fate, character and his own fault—to prevent this unique genius from prospering.

But we can easily understand in what a sad plight any housewife knowing her business must have found herself in such conditions. Though herself young and full of spirits, and, as a musician's daughter, a true-born artist, accustomed, moreover, to privations from childhood upwards, Konstanze showed the greatest good-will in checking the evil at its source, pruning away much that was amiss, and making up for losses on a large scale by economy in small matters. Yet in this last respect she lacked, perhaps, true aptitude and early experience. She had charge of the cash-box and kept the housekeeping-book: all demands, all duns, and any tiresome things that might occur, went to her alone. At times, indeed, her troubles threatened to overwhelm her, especially when, in addition to all this tribulation—to want, painful embarrassments and the dread of public dishonor—were added the low spirits in which her husband was often plunged for a whole day on end, inert and deaf to all consolation, as with sighs and laments, whether at his wife's side or

---

*Opera by Vicente Martín y Soler (1754–1806), performed in Vienna under the title *Lilla, or Beauty and Virtue*. Mozart admired Martín and quoted his opera in *The Marriage of Figaro*.

silent and absorbed all by himself in a corner, he pursued like an endless screw a single gloomy idea, the recurring thought of death. Yet she seldom lost heart, and as a rule her clear vision supplied aid and counsel, if only for a time. But essentially there was little or no improvement. Even if by jest or earnest, by prayers or cajolery, she succeeded once in a way in persuading him to have tea with her and enjoy his supper at home with the family without going out afterwards, what did it profit her? Now and then, suddenly conscience-stricken and moved by his wife's tear-stained eyes, he might in all sincerity curse his bad habit and make the finest promises, even more than she asked of him—it was all in vain; he found himself, without intending it, back again in the old ways. One is almost tempted to believe that he could not behave otherwise, and that, had some totally different line of conduct, in keeping with our ideas of what is seemly and fitting for all men, been somehow imposed upon him by force, it must surely have ruined the most essential qualities of that wondrous nature.

Yet Konstanze continued to hope for a favorable turn in the state of affairs, in so far as this could come from outside through a fundamental improvement in their economic position, such as she considered could not fail to result from her husband's growing fame. If only, she thought, there could be a relaxation of the incessant pressure, arising from this cause, which made itself felt more or less directly upon him too; if, instead of sacrificing half his time and strength to mere money-making, he were free to devote his undivided attention to his real vocation; and lastly, if his pleasures were to prove more wholesome to him, both physically and mentally, now that he no longer had to expend so much energy in pursuit of them, and could enjoy them with a far better conscience—then surely his whole condition must soon become easier and more natural and tranquil. She even considered a possible change of residence, for his marked preference for Vienna, where, however, in her opinion, no real good would come to him, might after all be overcome.

But for the first decisive step towards the realization of her ideas and wishes Madame Mozart looked to the success of the new opera with which their present journey was concerned.

The composition had now progressed well beyond the first half. Competent judges among his intimate friends who had watched the development of this remarkable work since its inception, and thus were certain to have an adequate grasp of its character and the means by which it achieved its effects, spoke of it everywhere in such terms that many, even of his adversaries, could feel sure that before six months were out this *Don Giovanni* would have convulsed the whole musical world of Germany from one end to the other, turned it topsy-turvy and taken it by storm. More cautious and guarded views were expressed in the sympathetic comments of those who, judging from the standpoint of contemporary music, scarcely hoped for a rapid and general success. The Master himself secretly shared their doubts, which proved only too well grounded.

For her part, as is always the way with women, who, once their feelings are deeply involved, and still further biased by the warmth of a perfectly just desire, will not allow themselves to be turned aside so often as men do by subsequent doubts arising out of this cause or that, Konstanze stood firmly by her conviction and had had occasion to take up the cudgels for it again just now in the carriage. She did so in her lively and exuberant way, with redoubled assiduity, for during the conversation described above, which, since it could in no way advance matters, had broken off in the most unsatisfactory way, Mozart's spirits had already drooped noticeably. She explained to her husband in great detail and with unclouded cheerfulness how, on their return home, she proposed to use the hundred ducats agreed upon by the manager of the Prague opera as the fee to be paid for the score, for meeting the most pressing items, and so forth, and further how, according to the budget she had drawn up, she hoped to get through the whole of the coming winter easily up to the early spring.

"Your Herr Boldini* will feather his nest well out of the opera, believe me; and if he is half the man of honor you always make him out to be, he will allow you a nice little extra percentage on the sums paid him one after the other by the opera-houses for their transcripts of the score; and even if he doesn't, well, God be praised, we have other chances in prospect besides, and a thousand times more solid ones, too. I have all sorts of notions in my head."

"Out with them, then!"

---

*Misspelled in the translation for Pasquale Bondini, who had commissioned *Don Giovanni* with an advance of 100 ducats.

"A little bird told me, not so long ago, that the King of Prussia*
was wanting a conductor."

"Oho!"

"I mean, a general director of music. Let me indulge my fancy a
bit! I inherit the weakness from my mother!"

"Go ahead, then! The wilder the better!"

"No, it will all be perfectly natural. To anticipate, then: supposing
that a year from now—"

"When the Pope marries Mary Ann, I suppose?"

"Be quiet, Tom Fool! I repeat that by St. Giles's day† next year
there must be no trace to be found high or low in Vienna of any
court composer to His Imperial Majesty by the name of Wolf
Mozart."

"The deuce there mustn't!"

"I can already imagine how our old friends will be talking about
us, and all the tales they will have to tell one another."

"For example?"

"Well, this one, for instance: early one morning, after nine
o'clock, our enthusiastic old Volkstett comes tacking across the
Kohlmarkt at her most furious pace, prepared to take her friends'
houses by storm. She has been away for three months, for the great
visit to her brother-in-law in Saxony, her daily topic of conversation
ever since we have known her, has at last taken place; she has been
back since the night before, and now, with her heart full to overflowing—it is fit to burst with traveller's joy and friendly impatience and
the most delicious tit-bits of news—off she goes like a shot to pour it
all out to the Colonel's wife. Up the stairs she goes, and raps at the
door without waiting for any 'Come in!' Imagine the rapture and
the mutual embraces! 'Well, my best and dearest Mrs. Colonel,' she
begins, taking breath after a few preliminary remarks, 'I have
brought you a whole budget of greetings—now guess from whom! I
have not come quite, quite straight from Stendal,** but went a little
way round, towards the left, as far as Brandenburg.'—'What! Is it

---

*Frederick William II. In 1789 he offered Mozart a position as music director at a
good salary, but Mozart declined with the explanation that he could not leave
Emperor Joseph II. This occurred after the premiere of *Don Giovanni;* Mörike has
altered the chronology.

†September 1.

**Town in Prussia, from which the French writer Stendhal took his pen name.

possible? You got as far as Berlin—and called on the Mozarts?' 'Ten heavenly days I spent there!' 'Oh, my dear, my sweet, my incomparable Mrs. General, do tell me, do describe it! How are our dear young couple? Are they still as pleased wtih things there as they were at first? It is fabulous, unbelievable, that this very day—and even more so now that you have come straight from him. Mozart as a Berliner! How is he getting on? How does he look, now?' 'Oh, Mozart! You should just see him! This summer the King sent him to Karlsbad. When would such an idea have occurred to his beloved Emperor Joseph, hey? The two of them were barely home again before I arrived. He is radiant with life and health, and as round and plump and lively as quicksilver. His eyes simply beam with happiness and comfort!' "

And now, still keeping up her assumed rôle, the speaker began to paint their new position in the most rosy colors; from his apartment on Unter den Linden and his garden and villa to the brilliant scenes of his public activity and the intimate court circles in which he had to accompany the Queen at the piano, the picture she drew of it brought the whole thing before them as though it had been real and present. She improvised whole conversations and the most glorious anecdotes. She seemed positively more at home in the royal capital, at Potsdam and Sanssouci,* than in the Palace of Schönbrunn† and the Imperial Burg.** Besides, she was sly enough to endow the person of our hero with a number of entirely novel domestic qualities which had developed on the solid foundation of his life in Prussia, and among which the above-mentioned Frau Volkstett, as the supreme marvel and proof of how extremes meet, had actually noted the beginnings of a slight touch of stinginess, which sat upon him delightfully.

" 'Yes, only imagine it, he has his three thousand thalers coming in regularly, and for what? For giving a chamber concert in the royal apartments once a week and conducting the grand opera twice. Oh, Mrs. Colonel, I saw him, our dear, precious little man, surrounded by his crack orchestra, trained by himself, which worships him! I sat

*Prussian royal palace in Potsdam.

†Austrian Imperial palace on the outskirts of Vienna.

**Literally, "castle"; a complex of buildings that is the center of government in Vienna.

with Frau Mozart in her box, immediately opposite the Royalties! And what was printed on the bills, if you please? I brought one away for you, with a little holiday present from me and the Mozarts wrapped up in it. Look here, now, only read it: there it stands printed in letters an ell high!' 'Heaven help us! What? *Tarar?** 'Yes! There now, my dear, the things one sees in life! Two years ago, when Mozart was writing *Don Giovanni,* and that accursed, venomous, sallow-faced Salieri was already scheming on the sly how he might repeat on his own territory the triumph he had carried off in Paris with his own piece, and let our good, snuff-loving public, still enchanted with *Cosa rara,* see, just for once in a way, what sort of a hawk he was, and he and his myrmidons were already colloguing and plotting how they might put *Don Giovanni* on the stage in a nicely plucked condition, neither dead nor alive, as they had done with *Figaro* before it—do you know, I vowed then and there that if the abominable piece were given, I would not go near it for anything on earth! And kept my word, too! While everybody was rushing to it as hard as they could go, and you among them, Mrs. Colonel, I sat at home by my own stove, took my cat on my lap and ate my bit of tripe; and I did the same on the next two occasions as well. But now, only think of it, *Tarar* on the stage at the Berlin opera-house, the work of his mortal enemy, conducted by Mozart! 'You really must come!' he cried, within the very first quarter of an hour, 'if only so that you can tell them in Vienna whether I have harmed a single hair of young Absalom's head. I only wish he had been there himself, so that the green-eyed monster might see that I have no need to make a botch of some other fellow's work only, after all, to remain exactly what I was before!' "

"*Brava! bravissima!*" cried Mozart at the top of his voice, and taking his little wife by the ear, he covered her with kisses, fondled and toyed with her, so that her merry sport with the gay soap-bubbles of a dream future, which was never, alas! to be realized even to the most modest extent, dissolved in the end into sheer high spirits, laughter and frolic.

Meanwhile they had long since descended into the valley and were approaching a village which had already been conspicuous

---

*Opera by Antonio Salieri (1750–1825); when it was performed in Vienna under the title *Axur, King of Ormus,* it eclipsed *Don Giovanni.*

from the high ground, and close beyond which a small country mansion in the fashionable style, the seat of a certain Count Schinzberg,* was visible in the smiling plain. It was here that they were to rest and bait the horses and have their midday meal. The inn at which they drew up stood by itself at the end of the village beside the highroad, from which a poplar avenue less than six hundred paces long branched off towards his lordship's garden.

When they had alighted, Mozart, as usual, left the ordering of dinner to his wife. Meanwhile he himself called for a glass of wine in the room downstairs, while she, after a drink of fresh water, asked no more than a quiet corner where she might take a short nap. She was shown upstairs and her husband followed, singing and whistling to himself in the best of spirits. In a clean, whitewashed room, which was quickly aired, among other old-fashioned pieces of furniture of more distinguished origin—for they had no doubt migrated there at some time or another from the bed-chambers of the Schloss†—stood a neat, light bed with a painted tester supported on slender green-lacquered columns, its silken curtains long since replaced by more ordinary stuff. Konstanze settled down comfortably, he promised to wake her in good time, she bolted the door behind him, and he forthwith betook himself to the public bar in search of entertainment. But not a soul was there save the innkeeper, and since the conversation of the latter was as little to the visitor's liking as his wine, he said he would like to take a walk as far as the Schloss garden till dinner was ready. It was open to respectable strangers, he was told, and on that day, moreover, the family were away on an excursion.

He went out, and had soon covered the short distance from there to the metal-work gates, which were standing open; he then sauntered slowly along a tall avenue of ancient lime-trees, at the end of which, on the left, he suddenly found the façade of the mansion before him a short distance away. It was built in the Italian style, washed over with a light color, and approached in front by a broad double flight of stone steps; the slate roof was adorned with a few statues of gods and goddesses in the conventional style then in vogue, together with a balustrade.

*A fictional character, as the whole episode is Möike's invention.
†"Manor house."

Issuing from between two large flower-beds, still rich with bloom, our Master walked towards the part of the grounds where the shrubberies were, passing by a few fine, somber groups of pine-trees, and, following the twists and turns of the winding paths, gradually turned his steps back in the direction of the more open parts, towards the busy plash of a flowing fountain, at which he soon arrived.

The ample breadth of its oval basin was surrounded by a carefully tended group of orange-trees in tubs, interspersed with laurels and oleanders; the whole was surrounded by a soft, sanded path, off which opened a small trellised bower. This arbor offered a most agreeable resting place; a little table stood in front of the seat, and Mozart sat down at it towards the front, near the entrance.

His ears pleasantly beguiled by the plash of water, and his eyes resting upon an orange-tree of moderate size, which stood on the ground apart from the rest close by his side, thickly hung with the most beautiful fruit, our friend was immediately carried back by this glimpse of the south to a charming memory of his boyhood's days. With a pensive smile he reached out towards the nearest orange, as though to try the feel of its splendid roundness and juicy coolness in the hollow of his hand. But closely connected with that scene from his youth which had risen up again before him was a long-effaced musical reminiscence, the faint trace of which he dreamily pursued awhile. And now his eyes lit up and wandered about him, now here, now there; he was seized by an idea, which he at once followed up eagerly. Absent-mindedly he grasped the orange a second time; it came away from the stalk, and lay there in his hand. He looked upon it, but saw it not; so lost was he, indeed, in his artistic abstraction that, as he continued to turn the fragrant fruit over and over under his nose, humming inaudibly between his lips now the beginning and now the end of a melody, at last he instinctively drew an enamelled case from the side pocket of his coat, took from it a small silver-handled knife, and slowly divided the yellow, spherical mass from top to bottom. He may have been obscurely prompted by a vague feeling of thirst, but his quickened senses were content to inhale the precious fragrance. For a whole minute he stared at the two inner surfaces, gently put them together again, then took them apart and fitted them together once more.

But now he heard footsteps close at hand; he started, and the consciousness of where he was and what he had been doing abruptly flashed upon him. Though already in the act of concealing the orange, he paused, whether out of pride or because it was too late. A big, broad-shouldered man in livery stood before him, the Count's gardener. The man must, moreover, have seen that last suspicious movement, and stood for a few seconds in shocked silence. Mozart, equally speechless, and as though riveted to his seat, fixed his blue eyes upon the man's face, blushing visibly, yet with a sort of boldness and dignity; then he laid the apparently undamaged orange in the center of the table—had any third person been present, it would have been a highly comical sight—with a sort of defiant and spirited flourish.

"Beg pardon," now began the gardener, in a covertly surly tone, having taken a good look at the stranger's not very prepossessing costume, "I do not know whom I have the . . ."

"Kapellmeister Mozart from Vienna."

"You are doubtless known to the family?"

"I am a stranger here, travelling through. Is his lordship the Count at home?"

"No."

"His lady, then?"

"She's engaged, and it's not easy to have a word with her."

Mozart rose, and made as if to depart.

"By your leave, Sir, how comes it that you have helped yourself here like this?"

"What?" cried Mozart, "helped myself? The devil! Do you suppose, fellow, that I meant to steal, and gobble the thing up?"

"Seeing is believing, Sir. These fruits have been counted, and I am responsible for them. The tree is intended by his lordship for a special occasion and is shortly to be removed. I don't let you go till I have reported the matter and you have proved to my satisfaction how this business happened."

"Very well, then, I will wait here for the present. You may depend upon that."

The gardener looked about him in some indecision, and Mozart, thinking it was, perhaps, only a matter of a tip, put his hand in his pocket, only to find that he had not so much as a copper about him.

Two under-gardeners now did, in fact, come up, lifted the tree on to a barrow and took it away. Meanwhile our Master had drawn out his wallet, taken from it a blank sheet of paper, and begun to write in pencil, the gardener still standing his ground.

"Most gracious lady, Here I sit in your paradise, though not one of the blest, like Adam of old after eating the apple. The calamity has happened, and I cannot even throw the blame on my good Eve, who at this very moment, with the Graces and Loves of a four-post bed sporting around her, is enjoying the most innocent slumber at the hotel. Command me, and I will answer in person to your ladyship for my act of sacrilege, inexplicable even to myself.

"In sincere humiliation,

"Your ladyship's most humble servant,

"W. A. Mozart, on the way to Prague."

He handed the somewhat clumsily folded note with the necessary instructions to the servant, who was waiting in painful uneasiness.

The marplot was no sooner gone than the roll of wheels was heard from the other side of the Schloss. It was the Count, escorting from the neighboring estate a niece of his with her future husband, a rich young baron. Since the latter's mother had not left the house for years, the ceremony of betrothal had taken place that day in her presence. The occasion was now to be celebrated here, too, at another merry party among a few relations; for since her childhood the Schloss had been to Eugenie a second home, where she was like a daughter of the house. The Countess had driven home a little earlier with her son Max, the lieutenant, for the purpose of completing various arrangements. And now everyone in the Schloss might have been seen in a perfect commotion about the stairs and corridors, and it was only with difficulty that the gardener did at last succeed in handing her ladyship the note in the ante-room; she did not, however, open it on the spot, but without paying much attention to the messenger's words, went fussing off again. Servant after servant hurried past him, footmen, lady's maids, and valets; he asked for his lordship—but he was changing his clothes; he then went in search of Count Max, and found him in his room, but he was talking earnestly with the Baron, and cut the man short, as though afraid he was trying to tell him something or ask some question on a subject about which not a whisper must yet be heard. "I'm just coming," he said. "Now be off." It was some time before the father and son emerged simultaneously from their rooms and heard the disastrous news.

"It really is an infernal plague!" cried the stout, good-natured, but rather peppery Count. "It really passes all comprehension! A musician from Vienna, did you say? Some low fellow, I suppose, hanging round for a tip, and ready to pick up anything he can find at the same time?"

"By your lordship's leave, he does not look quite that sort. He seems to me not quite right in the head; besides, he is very high and mighty. Moser, he calls himself. He is waiting for your decision down there. I told Franz to hang about and keep an eye on him."

"What the devil is the use of that now the harm is done? Even if I were to have the fool locked up, that would not repair the damage! I had told you a thousand times that the front gate should always be kept locked. This business would have been prevented, at any rate, if you had taken your measures in time."

At this point the Countess came hurriedly out of the adjoining boudoir in a state of joyous excitement, holding the open letter in her hand. "Do you know," she exclaimed, "who is down there? For Heaven's sake read the letter—Mozart, the composer from Vienna! Somebody must go at once and invite him up to the house. I am afraid he may already be gone. What will he think of me? You there, Velten, did you treat him politely? Now what was it that really happened?"

"Happened?" retorted her husband, whose irritation could not be altogether allayed on the spot by the prospect of a visit from a famous man, "the crazy fellow has picked one of the nine oranges from the tree I had intended for Eugenie. The—the—monster! And so the whole point of our little pleasantry is gone, and Max might just as well tear up his poem."

"Oh no!" insisted the lady, "the deficiency can easily be made good. Only leave it to me. Now go, both of you, set the good man at liberty and welcome him in the kindest and most complimentary fashion you possibly can. If we can devise any way of keeping him, he shall go no further today. If you do not find him still in the garden, go and look for him at the inn and bring him here with his wife. Chance could have brought us no finer gift or lovelier surprise for Eugenie on such an occasion."

"Of course!" replied Max, "that was my own first thought, too. Come, Papa, quick! And," he added, as they ran swiftly down the stairs, "you may set your mind at rest about the verses. The ninth

Muse shall not go short; on the contrary, I shall manage to turn this mishap to special advantage." "Impossible!" "Yes I shall, really and truly." "Well, if that is so—mind, I am taking your word for it—we will do the crazy fellow every imaginable honor."

While this was taking place in the Schloss our hero, though virtually a prisoner, had his mind reasonably at rest with regard to the upshot of the affair, and occupied himself for a considerable time in writing. But when nobody at all appeared, he began pacing restlessly to and fro, during which time an urgent message arrived from the inn to say that dinner was long since ready, and would he kindly come at once, for the postillion was urging haste. He was therefore trying to gather up his belongings and meant to start without delay, when the two gentlemen appeared before the arbor.

The Count greeted him jovially in his powerful ringing voice, almost like an old acquaintance, and gave him no time to make excuses, but at once expressed his desire to entertain both husband and wife in his family circle, at least for that afternoon and evening. "You are so little of a stranger to us, my dearest Maestro, that scarcely anywhere else, I venture to say, is the name of Mozart mentioned more often, or with greater enthusiasm than here. My niece sings and plays, she spends almost the whole day at the grand piano, she knows your works by heart, and is most anxious to have the chance of seeing you at closer quarters than was possible at one of your concerts last winter. And since we are shortly going to Vienna for a few weeks, relations had promised us an invitation to the house of Prince Galitzin,* where you are fairly often to be found. But now you are off to Prague, and will not be back for some time, and goodness knows whether you will come this way on your return journey! Do take a holiday for today and tomorrow! We will send your conveyance home at once, and you must allow me to make arrangements for the rest of your journey."

The composer, who on such occasions as this, when friendship or enjoyment was concerned, would readily have sacrificed ten times more than was asked of him now, did not take long to think it over; he joyfully conceded this one half day, but, he said, on the morrow they must proceed upon their way as early as possible. Count Max begged that he might have the pleasure of fetching Madame Mozart

*Russian ambassador to Vienna, patron of Mozart.

and making all necessary arrangements at the inn. He went off, and a carriage was to follow him immediately.

As to this young man, we may remark in passing that with the sunny temperament inherited from his father and mother, he combined talent and a love of fine literature, and, though conscious of no real vocation for the military profession, had none the less distinguished himself as an officer by his intelligence and good conduct. He had a knowledge of French literature, and at that time, when German verse was held in but small esteem in high society, had won praise and favor by the quite uncommon ease with which he handled the poetic form in his mother tongue, following such good models as he found in Hagedorn, Götz and others.* On this particular day, as we have already gathered, an especially gratifying occasion had offered itself for the exercise of his talent.

He found Madame Mozart gossiping with the innkeeper's daughter at the ready-laid table, where she had already started upon a plate of soup. She was too well used to extraordinary happenings and audacious pranks on the part of her husband to be more than mildly perturbed at the appearance of the young officer and the mission entrusted to him. With unruffled good-temper and in cool, practical fashion she settled matters then and there and gave all requisite orders in person. The luggage was repacked, the bill paid, the postillion dismissed, she got ready without any undue fuss over her toilette, and drove off cheerfully to the Schloss with her escort, never suspecting in how strange a fashion her husband had gained an entrance there.

Meanwhile he was already installed most comfortably and excellently entertained. After a time he saw Eugenie, a blooming creature of great charm and depth of feeling, with her affianced lover. She was golden-haired, her slender form festally attired in lustrous crimson silk with costly laces, and round her brow was a white fillet adorned with orient pearls. The Baron, but little older than herself, with a gentle, candid nature, seemed in every respect worthy of her.

The first brunt of the conversation was borne, if anything too bountifully, by the kindly, whimsical host, thanks to his rather exuberant way of talking, abundantly embellished with jests and

---

*Friedrich von Hagedorn (1708–54) and Johann Nikolaus Götz (1721–81), poets in the Rococo style already dated at this time.

anecdotes. Refreshments were handed round, of which our traveller was by no means chary.

Somebody had opened the pianoforte, *The Marriage of Figaro* stood open on the rack, and the young lady, accompanied by the Baron, made ready to sing Susanna's aria in the garden-scene,* from which we inhale in great streams the very spirit of tender passion, like the aromatic breezes of the summer night. The delicate flush on Eugenie's cheek changed for a breathing space to an extreme pallor; but with the first full note that passed her lips she found relief from the sense of oppression which had seemed to constrict her bosom. Smiling and confident, she rode, as it were, on the crest of the wave, and the savor of this moment, unique, perhaps, in its way, among all the days of her life, filled her with a corresponding exaltation.

Mozart was clearly surprised. When she had finished, he went up to her and, in his simple way, speaking straight from the heart, began as follows: "What is a man to say, dear child, in a case like that of the blessed sunshine, whose best praise is that everyone straightway feels well in its presence! During such singing as this the soul feels like a baby in its bath; it laughs and wonders, and can think of nothing better in the world. Then too, believe me, it is not every day that the likes of us in Vienna have the chance of listening to our very selves, so pure, so unadorned and warm—in short, so complete." And with these words he took her hand and kissed it with all his heart. The noble kindliness of the man and his goodness of heart, no less than the handsome tribute with which he had honored her talent, filled Eugenie with that overmastering emotion that is like a touch of vertigo, and her eyes must needs fill suddenly with tears.

At this point Madame Mozart entered the room, and close upon her appeared some other guests who were expected—a baron's family from the neighborhood, closely related to that of the Count and with a daughter, Franziska, who had been attached since childhood to the future bride by ties of the most tender affection, and felt quite at home in the house.

They all exchanged greetings, embraces and congratulations, the

---

* "Finally the hour draws near when I shall soon wholly possess you, oh my beloved," Act IV, Scene 10.

two visitors from Vienna were introduced, and Mozart seated himself at the grand piano. He played a movement from a concerto of his own composition, which Eugenie was practicing at the time.

The effect of such a performance in so small a party as this naturally differs from one in a public place by reason of the infinite satisfaction to be drawn from direct contact with the person and genius of the artist within the familiar walls of home.

It was one of those brilliant pieces in which, as though by some caprice, pure beauty elects of its own free will to place itself at the command of elegance, but in such a way as only, so to speak, to veil itself in this more wanton play of forms, dissembling itself behind a host of brilliant lights, yet betraying in its every movement its essential nobility, and pouring forth lavishly a splendid fullness of passion.

The Countess observed to herself that the majority of the audience, perhaps not excepting even Eugenie herself, for all their rapt attention and awed silence during this magical playing, were none the less greatly torn between the claims of eye and ear. As, in spite of themselves, they watched the composer, with the simple, almost stiff carriage of his body, his good-humored face and the circling action of his small hands, it was certainly far from easy to stem the inrush of a thousand jostling ideas on the subject of this man of wonder.

Turning towards Madame Mozart when the Master had risen from the piano, the Count remarked: "When faced with an artist of renown, for whom one feels it incumbent upon one to turn some apt and knowledgeable compliment—which is not everybody's knack, I may say—how fortunate are kings and emperors! From such lips as theirs every remark seems original and out of the common. There is nothing they may not venture to say; and how nice and easy it is to stand just behind your husband's chair, and, on the closing chord of some brilliant improvisation, to tap this modest, tip-top performer on the shoulder and say: 'You are a devil of a fellow, my dear Mozart!' No sooner is the word out of his lips than it flies round the room like wild-fire: 'What was it he said to him?' 'A devil of a fellow, he called him!' And every soul who fiddles or pipes or composes is wild with rage at this one word; in short, that is your grand style, the familiar style of emperors, the inimitable style which I have always envied your Josefs and Friedrichs, and never more than at present, when I am simply in despair because I cannot discover a doit of any wit superior to that in my pockets."

The way in which the droll old fellow brought this out was irresistible for all its bluntness, and could not fail to raise a laugh.

But now, at their hostess's bidding, the company made a move towards the round dining-parlor, which had been decorated for the occasion, so that as they entered the festal perfume of flowers floated out to meet them, with a cooler air propitious to the appetite.

Each took the place tactfully assigned to him, the distinguished visitor, for his part, being placed opposite the betrothed couple. On one side he had a little elderly lady, a maiden aunt of Franziska's, and his neighbor on the other side was the fascinating young niece herself, who soon managed to commend herself to his especial approbation by her intelligence and liveliness. Frau Konstanze sat between the master of the house and her amiable escort the lieutenant. The rest fell into place, and so they sat down to table eleven in all, each lady, so far as possible, next a gentleman, while the lower end was left empty. In the middle rose two huge great porcelain centerpieces with painted figures bearing on their heads ample dishes piled high with natural flowers and fruit. Round the walls of the room hung rich garlands. Everything else that was in the room, or was brought into it in constant succession, seemed to announce a prolonged revel. Partly on the table among the dishes and plates, partly on the sideboard in the background, there gleamed every variety of noble wine, from a red that was almost black to the yellow-tinged white whose foaming gaiety is traditionally reserved to crown the second half of a feast.

Till this point had nearly arrived the conversation had ranged over every sort of topic, being kept up by several parties with equal animation. But from the very first the Count had thrown out an occasional distant allusion to Mozart's adventure in the garden, and his references now became more and more mischievous and pointed, till some smiled mysteriously, while the others vainly racked their brains to discover what he could possibly mean, till at last our friend spoke up as follows:

"In Heaven's name!" he began, "I am ready to confess exactly how it was that I had the honor of becoming acquainted with this noble house. I do not play a particularly dignified rôle in the story, and instead of sitting here enjoying myself at table, it was touch and go that I did not find myself under arrest in some remote corner of this lordly mansion, where I might have sat with an empty stomach staring at the spiders' webs on the walls."

"There!" cried Madame Mozart, "now I shall hear a pretty story!"

He then described in detail first how he had left his wife at the White Horse, then his walk in the park, his ill-starred adventure in the arbor, his encounter with the custodians of order in the garden, in short, very much what we already know, all of which revelations were made with the utmost candor and to the high delight of his listeners. It seemed as though the laughter would never come to an end; even the self-possessed Eugenie could not help herself, but fairly shook with it.

"Well," he went on, "the proverb says that he who has the profit can face the laughter. And I have turned a little profit of my own out of the adventure, as you soon shall see. But first of all you must hear how it really came about that my old childish head managed so to forget itself. A memory of my youth had something to do with it.

"In the spring of 1770, as a lad of thirteen, I went with my father on a tour in Italy.* We travelled from Rome to Naples. I had played twice at the Conservatorio and on various occasions elsewhere too. The nobility and clergy paid us many kind attentions, and one *abbate* attached himself to us in particular who plumed himself upon his discriminating taste and had, moreover, a certain influence at court. The day before we left he drove us, in company with a few other gentlemen, to one of the royal gardens, that of the Villa Reale,† beside the magnificent road that runs along next the sea, where a troupe of Sicilian *commedianti* was performing—*figli di Nettuno*, sons of Neptune, as they called themselves among other high-sounding titles. We sat in a large and distinguished audience, among which was the charming young Queen Carolina** herself, with two princesses, on a long row of seats shaded by a low gallery with a tentlike awning, along the wall of which the waves murmured below. The sea, streaked with changing hues, reflected in a blaze of glory

---

*Mozart was fourteen at this time.
†Royal Villa.
**Queen Caroline of Naples (1752–1814), daughter of Emperor Francis I and Maria Theresa.

the blue and sunny skies above. Immediately opposite was Vesuvius, and on our left a lovely coast lay glimmering in a soft curve.

"The first part of the entertainment was over: it had been performed on the dry planks of a sort of raft floating on the water, and had nothing very remarkable about it; but the second and finer half was entirely made up of feats of boating, swimming and diving, and has always remained with all its details freshly imprinted upon my memory.

"From the far side of the raft two graceful, very lightly built barks approached and drew together, both bound, as it seemed, on a pleasure-cruise. One, a trifle the larger, was furnished with a half-deck, and equipped, next the rowers' benches, with a slender mast and sail; it was gorgeously painted besides and had a gilded prow. Five young men of ideal beauty, scantily clad and with arms, breast and legs seemingly bare, now busied themselves at the helm, now sported with their lady-loves, an equal number of pretty girls. One of these, who was seated in the middle of the deck weaving garlands of flowers, stood out among all the rest by her stature and beauty as well as her adornments. They waited on her willingly, spread an awning over her to keep off the sun, and handed her the flowers out of the basket. A girl with a flute sat at her feet, accompanying the songs of the others with its limpid notes. Nor did this surpassing beauty lack her own special protector; yet the couple bore themselves toward each other with some indifference, and the lover, it almost seemed to me, was a trifle uncouth.

"Meanwhile the other and simpler craft had drawn closer. In it could be seen none but young men. The youths in the first boat wore a vivid red, and the second band, in like fashion, were dressed in sea-green. They started at the sight of the charming girls, waved greetings to them, and showed a desire to be better acquainted. Thereupon the liveliest of the maidens took a rose from her bosom and held it roguishly on high, as though inquiring whether such gifts would be acceptable, to which answer came back from all sides in unequivocal gestures. The reds looked on in gloomy disdain, but could do nothing when several of the maidens agreed that they would at least throw the poor fellows something to relieve their hunger and thirst. There was a basket of oranges standing on deck—though most likely they were only yellow balls made to resemble the fruit. And now began an enchanting scene accompanied by the orchestra, which was posted on the sea-wall.

"One of the maidens opened fire, being the first to toss a few oranges deftly across, which were caught with equal skill and immediately returned; to and fro they went, and soon, as more and more of the girls joined in, oranges by the dozen were flying back and forth at an ever-increasing speed. The beauty amidships took no part in the fray, beyond looking on from her stool with intense curiosity. We could not wonder enough at the skill displayed by both sides. The boats circled slowly round and round each other at a distance of some thirty paces, now lying broadside on, now at an angle, one being half across the other's bows; there were some four-and-twenty balls constantly in the air, yet such was the medley that one believed one saw many more. At times a regular crossfire would spring up, while then again they would rise and fall in a lofty curve, scarce one missing its aim on either side. It was as though they fell of their own accord into the fingers opened to catch them, as though drawn by some compelling force.

"Yet agreeably though the eye was engaged, the melodies accompanied them full as sweetly to the ear: Sicilian airs, dances, *saltarelli, canzoni a ballo,** a whole miscellany, strung lightly together like a garland. The youthful princess, a sweet, ingenuous creature of about my own age, nodded her head so prettily in time to the music. I can still see before me today her smile and the long lashes fringing her eyes.

"Now let me describe shortly the rest of the merry scene, though it has no further bearing on the point of interest to me. It would be hard to imagine anything prettier. As the skirmish gradually died down, and only a few missiles were now still exchanged, while the girls collected their golden apples and returned them to the basket, a boy over yonder, as though in play, had picked up an ample green-meshed net and held it for a time under water; he drew it in, and to the astonishment of all a great fish was to be seen in it, gleaming with azure, green and gold. Those nearest him were springing eagerly forward to pull it out, when it slipped from their hands, as

*Roman folkdances; dancing songs.

though alive, and fell into the sea. But this was only a ruse arranged in order to mislead the reds and tempt them from their boat. And sure enough, as though bewitched by this marvel, they no sooner noticed that the creature would not sink, but remained playing on the surface, than, without a moment's hesitation, they all hurled themselves into the sea, and the greens likewise, till we saw twelve expert and finely-built swimmers endeavoring to catch the elusive fish as it bobbed about on the waves, at times disappearing beneath them for minutes on end, only to appear again now here, now there, between the legs of one or the breast and chin of another. All of a sudden, while the reds were hottest in pursuit of their quarry, the other party saw its chance, and, quick as lightning, boarded the other boat, now entirely abandoned to the maidens, amid a hubbub of screams from the latter. The most nobly-proportioned of the youths, built like a Mercury, with his face lit up with joy, rushed towards the loveliest maiden of them all, clasped her in his arms and kissed her, while, far from joining in the screams of the others, she threw her arms round the young man with equal ardor, for she knew him well. The crew that had been tricked swam hastily to the spot, but were driven off by those on board with oars and weapons. Their baffled rage, the frightened screams of the girls, the vehement resistance of a few of them, their prayers and supplications, almost drowned the music, which had suddenly assumed a different character. It was lovely beyond description, and the audience broke into a storm of enthusiasm.

"At this moment the sail, which till then had been loosely brailed up, was lowered: out of it stepped a rosy boy with silver wings, a bow and arrows and a quiver, and poised lightly on the bowsprit in a graceful attitude. By this time the oars were all hard at work, and the sail swelled, but, mightier than either, the presence of the god and the rushing forward sweep of his pose seemed to drive the craft onward so fast that the swimmers in almost breathless pursuit, one holding the golden fish in his left hand high above his head, soon gave up hope, and, their strength being now exhausted, were forced to seek refuge in the boat that had been abandoned. Meanwhile the greens had reached a small bush-grown peninsula, where a splendid boat appeared unexpectedly in ambush, full of armed comrades. Faced with such a threatening situation the little band ran up a white flag as a sign that they desired an amicable parley. Encouraged by a like signal from the other side, they rowed on towards that stopping-place, and soon we saw all the nice girls save the one, who willingly remained behind, climb merrily on board their own ship together with their lovers. And with this the comedy was at an end."

"It seems to me," whispered Eugenie to the Baron with shining eyes during a pause in which everybody was loud in praise of what they had just heard, "that we have just had, as it were, a symphonic picture painted from beginning to end, and, what is more, a perfect portrayal of Mozart's own spirit in all its gaiety. Am I not right? Is not the whole charm of *Figaro* to be found in it?"

Her affianced lover was on the point of repeating her remark to the composer, when the latter went on to say: "It is now seventeen years since I saw Italy. Who that has once seen it, and especially Naples, does not think about it for the rest of his life, even if, like me, he had but half grown out of his childhood's garments? But never did that last lovely evening on the Gulf rise up again before my mind so vividly as today in your garden. If I closed my eyes, the whole scene lay stretched before me, perfectly clear, bright and distinct, with the last veil of haze floating up from it into the air. Sea and shore, mountain and city, the bright-hued throng moving along the water's edge, and then the wondrous play of the criss-crossing balls! I thought the selfsame music still sounded in my ears, a whole rose-garland of joyous melodies floated through my head, my own and other people's, a perfect Babel, one for ever succeeding the other. A little dance-tune tripped out inconsequently in six-eight time, completely new to me. 'Stop!' I thought, 'What have we here? That seems a devilish pretty thing!' I looked closer—'Heavens!' I cried, 'why, there is Masetto, there is Zerlina!' "* He laughed across at Madame Mozart, who at once guessed his meaning.

"The point," he continued, "is simply this: in my first act there was one little light number still unwritten, a duet and chorus for a rustic wedding. For two months ago, when I tried to deal with this number in its proper order, the right thing simply refused to come at the first attempt. A simple childlike tune, bubbling over and over with merriment, a knot of fresh flowers with fluttering ribbons worn

---

*Characters in *Don Giovanni*. The reference is to Act I, Scene 7.

at the maiden's breast—that is what it should have been. But since one must not force anything, even in the smallest detail, and since trifles of that sort often write themselves of their own accord as one goes along, I just passed it by, and in the progress of my more important work gave it scarcely another thought. Today in the carriage, shortly before we drove into the village, the words fleeted swiftly through my mind; but at the moment nothing more came of it—at least, not to my knowledge. Very well! About an hour later, in the arbor by the fountain, I got hold of a motive, better and more apt than any I could have invented at any other time or in any other way. Art brings one odd experiences at times, but no such trick was ever played on me before. For a tune fitting the verses absolutely like a glove—but there, I must not anticipate, we have not got to that point yet; the bird had still no more than poked its head out of the shell, so I set to work on the spot to get it out complete and perfect. All the time Zerlina's dance floated vividly before my eyes, and the smiling landscape of the Gulf of Naples blended mysteriously with it all. I heard the answering voices of bridegroom and bride, and the lads and lasses in chorus."

And here Mozart trolled forth most merrily the opening bars of the ditty:

> Giovinette, che fate all'amore,
> Non lasciate che passi l'età.
> Se nel seno vi bulica il core
> Il remedio vedetelo quà. La-la-la! La-la-la! La-la-la!
> Che piacer, che piacer ci sarà. La-la-la-le-ra!*

"Meanwhile my hands had wrought the monstrous mischief. Already Nemesis was hovering behind the bushes, and now stepped

---

*The English words in Boosey's edition of *Don Giovanni* are as follows:

> Pretty maidens, it lies in your power,
> With the summer of life still in bloom,
> To preserve in each bosom life's flower,
> And be cheered by its dainty perfume. Tra! la la! etc.
> For then all will a sunshine assume. Lalalalera!

The sentiment of the Italian words bears more resemblance to that of "Gather ye roses while ye may" (translator's note).

forth in the shape of this fearsome fellow in the blue braided uniform. Had a real eruption of Vesuvius, on that godlike evening, suddenly poured down a rain of black ashes, blotting out both audience and actors and all the glory of Parthenope,* good Heavens, the catastrophe could not have been more unforeseen or horrible. A regular devil, he was! Scarcely ever has a man made me turn so hot all over. A face as of bronze—rather resembling Tiberius, the cruel Roman emperor. 'If that is what the servant looks like,' I thought to myself when he had gone, 'what ever sort of face is his lordship likely to have!' Yet, to tell the truth, I already counted a little bit on the protection of the ladies, and not without reason. For my Stanzerl there, my little wife, being a thought inquisitive by nature, had made the fat body at the inn tell her in my presence everything most worth knowing about all the persons composing this noble household; I was just standing by, and so I heard—"

At this point Madame Mozart could not refrain from interrupting him and assuring the company in the most circumstantial way that, on the contrary, it had been he who had asked the questions; whereupon a lively altercation sprang up between husband and wife, which gave rise to much laughter. "Well, be that as it may," he said, "the long and short of it is that I heard something vaguely about a charming foster-daughter, who was engaged to be married and very lovely, and, what is more goodness itself and sang like an angel. *'Per Dio!'*† the idea flashed across my mind, 'that will help you out of your scrape! You will just sit down exactly where you are, write out the little song as far as you can, explain your indiscretion precisely as it happened, and the whole thing will be a capital joke!' No sooner said than done. I had time and to spare, and another nice clean bit of green-lined paper was forthcoming—and here is the result! I place it in these fair hands as an impromptu nuptial song, if you will accept it as such."

Thus speaking he offered Eugenie across the table his most neatly written page of music, but her uncle's hand was quicker than hers, and he whisked it away, exclaiming: "Patience one instant longer, my child!"

At a sign from him the folding-doors of the drawing-room were

---

*Old name of Naples, after one of the Sirens who was supposed to be buried there.
†"By God!"

thrown open wide and some men-servants appeared, bearing into the room the fateful orange-tree noiselessly and decorously, and set it down on a bench at the lower end of the table; at the same time two slender myrtle-bushes were placed to right and left of it. An inscription attached to the stem of the orange-tree declared it to be the property of the future bride; but in front of it, on a bed of moss, lay a china plate covered with a napkin, revealing, when the cloth was removed, a halved orange, by the side of which her uncle, with a sly glance, laid the Master's autograph manuscript. The whole company broke forth at once into applause that would not end.

"I do believe," said the Countess, "that Eugenie has no idea yet what it is that stands before her. She really does not know her old favorite again in its new adornment of flowers and fruit."

Puzzled and incredulous, the young lady looked now at the tree, now at her uncle. "It is not possible," she said. "I know quite well that it was past saving."

"So you think," rejoined the latter, "that all we have done has been to look for some sort of substitute? That would have been a nice thing to do! No! Only look here! I must do as the custom is in plays, when the son or brother who had been supposed dead proves his identity by his birthmarks and scars. Look here at this excrescence! And here again, the wrinkle running crosswise; you must have noticed it a hundred times. Well, is it the same, or is it not?" She could doubt it no longer; her amazement, emotion and joy were beyond description.

This tree was associated in the minds of the family with the more than century-old memory of a distinguished woman who is well worthy to be recalled here in a few words.

The uncle's grandfather, who had won a high reputation with the government in Vienna through his services to diplomacy and had been honored with like confidence by two consecutive sovereigns, was equally fortunate in his own home on account of his remarkable wife, Renate Leonore. Her repeated visits to France had brought her into frequent contact with the brilliant court of Louis XIV and the most important men and women of that notable epoch. For all her frank participation in that unceasing round of the most intelligent pleasures of life, in no way, whether by deed or by word, did she belie her inborn German sense of honor and strict morality, of which the strongly marked features of the Countess's portrait, still in existence, bear the unmistakable impress. Thanks, indeed, to this disposition, she took up a characteristic attitude of candid opposition in that society, and the correspondence she left behind her shows many a trace of the candor and vigorously combative spirit with which this original woman was capable of defending her sound principles and views, whether on matters of faith, literature, politics or anything else, and of attacking the defects of society without making herself in the slightest degree obnoxious to it. Her lively interest in all those to be met at the house of such a woman as Ninon,* that true center of the subtlest intellectual culture, was accordingly of such a character, and so regulated by these principles, as to be perfectly compatible with the loftier bonds of friendship that united her with one of the noblest ladies of that period, Madame de Sévigné.† In addition to a number of sportive epigrams addressed to her by Chapelle,** scribbled on the spur of the moment by the poet's hand on sheets of paper bordered with silver flowers, there were discovered in an ebony casket belonging to their grandmother after her death the most affectionate letters from the Marquise and her daughter to their outspoken friend in Austria.

It was, then, Madame de Sévigné from whose hand she had received one day on the terrace in the garden, during a fête at the Trianon, an orange-twig in bloom, which she had forthwith planted in a pot on chance and, since it fortunately struck root, had taken back with her to Germany.

For full twenty-five years the little tree grew steadily beneath her eye, and was afterwards tended by her children and grandchildren with the utmost solicitude. Apart from the personal value attaching to it, it might further be regarded as a living symbol of the subtle intellectual charm inherent in that age, which was considered almost divine, though nowadays, of course, we find little in it that is truly praiseworthy, for it already bore within it the germ of a sinister future, the world-shaking onset of which was even then not so very remote from the time of our innocent narrative.

It was Eugenie who had shown the most loving devotion to this

---

*Ninon de Lenclos (1616–1706), famous beauty and wit, whose salon was a gathering place of prominent people.

†Marie de Rabutin Chantal, Marquise de Sévigné (1626–96), famous for her correspondence with her daughter.

**Claude-Emmanuel l'Huillier (1626–86), poet and critic.

heirloom handed down from her august ancestress, and for this reason her uncle had frequently remarked that it ought sooner or later to be handed over to her keeping. It was therefore all the more painful to the young lady when, in the spring of the previous year, which she had not spent at the Schloss, the tree began to droop, the leaves turned yellow, and several of its branches died. Since no especial reason could be discovered for its decay, and no remedy was of the least avail, the gardener soon gave it up for lost, though in the natural order of things it might easily have grown to twice or three times the age. The Count, however, advised by a neighbor who had special knowledge of such things, gave orders that, in accordance with a curious, and almost oracular recipe, such as is frequent among country people, it should be secretly tended in a place apart, and his hope that he might one day surprise his beloved niece with the sight of her old friend, restored to fresh strength and perfect fruitfulness, was rewarded beyond all expectation. Restraining his impatience, and not without some anxiety as to whether the fruit, some of which had lately reached an advanced state of ripeness, would really hang so long upon the branch, he postponed the happy surprise for some weeks till that day's festivities, and no further words are needed to describe what must have been the kind-hearted old nobleman's feeling when he saw such a pleasure destroyed for him at the very last moment by a stranger.

Even before the meal the lieutenant had found time and opportunity to revise the poem that was to be his contribution to the solemn ceremony of presentation, and as best he could to adapt to the circumstances the otherwise rather too serious spirit of his verses by altering the ending. He now produced his sheet of paper, and, rising from his chair and turning towards his cousin, read out the poem. The purport of his stanzas was briefly as follows:

This scion of the much-vaunted Tree of the Hesperides, sprung from the soil of a western island ages ago in the garden of Juno as her wedding gift from Mother Earth, and guarded by the three tuneful nymphs, had always hoped and longed for a like destiny, since the custom of presenting a lovely girl with a plant on her betrothal had long since descended from among the gods and become current among mortals.

After long and fruitless waiting it seemed at last that a maiden had been found to whom it might look in expectation. She showed herself well-disposed towards it, and often lingered at its side. But the laurel of the Muses, standing proudly beside it on the fountain's verge, stung it to jealousy by the threat of depriving this beauty, with her talent for the arts, of all heart or sensibility to the love of men. In vain did the myrtle console it and teach it patience by its own example; in the end it was the continued absence of the loved one that aggravated its misery, and, after a short period of wasting sickness, at last proved fatal.

Summer brings her home from afar, and with a happy change of heart. Village, Schloss and garden all receive her with a thousand tokens of delight. Roses and lilies, their luster now enhanced, gaze up at her in rapture, though abashed. Shrubs and trees wave their branches to wish her happiness; but for one—and that, alas! the noblest—she comes too late. She finds its crown withered, her fingers touch the lifeless stem and the crackling tips of its branches. No more does it either know or see her who once had tended it. What tears, what floods of tender lamentation does she now pour forth!

But Apollo hears from afar the voice of his daughter. He comes, he approaches, and looks with compassion upon her grief. At once he lays his healing hands upon the tree, till it trembles, its dried-up sap surges mightily within its bark, already young leaves sprout forth, already white blossoms open here and there in ambrosial profusion. Yea—for what is impossible to the celestial powers?—the fine globed fruits begin to swell, three times three, to match the sisters nine; they grow and grow, their infant green changing as we watch it to a golden hue. "Phœbus—" so the poem concluded—

> Phœbus reckons up the pieces,
>   Counting them with loving care;
> And his mouth begins to water
>   At the thought of what is there.
> Smilingly the god of music
>   Plucks one, rich with juicy pride:
> Let us share it, gracious fair one,
>   And for Amor's sake—divide!

The poet received his meed of tumultuous applause, and the company willingly forgave the grotesque *dénouement* by which the effect of the whole poem, which had real feeling in it, was so completely destroyed.

Franziska, whose lively mother-wit had already been roused more than once, whether by the master of the house or by Mozart, now ran swiftly off, as though suddenly reminded of something, and returned with a discolored English engraving of very large proportions, framed and glazed, which had been hanging almost disregarded in quite an out-of-the-way corner.

"So what I have always been told must be true," she cried, propping up the picture at the end of the table, "and there is nothing new under the sun! Here is a scene from the golden age—and have we not been living through it today? I hope, however, that Apollo will recognize himself in such a position."

"Capital!" cried Max in triumph, "and so all the time we really had him there, the handsome god, just bending meditatively over the sacred fount. Nor is that all—only see, there is an old satyr watching him from behind the bushes! One could almost swear that Apollo is trying to recall a long-forgotten Arcadian dance, which old Chiron taught him to play on the zither as a child!"

"So it is! It can be nothing else!" applauded Franziska, who was standing behind Mozart; "and," she continued, "don't you see the branch laden with fruit drooping down towards the god?"

"Quite right; it is his sacred plant, the olive-tree."

"Not at all! They are the most lovely oranges! Soon, in a fit of abstraction, he will be stretching out his hand for one."

"Nay!" cried Mozart, "rather will he stop these mischievous lips with a thousand kisses." And with these words he caught her by the arm and vowed not to let her go till she had yielded him her lips, which she did thereupon without very great resistance.

"But do tell us, Max," said the Countess, "what is that underneath the picture?"

"It is some verses from a famous ode of Horace. Not long ago the poet Ramler* of Berlin translated the piece into German incomparably well. The rhythm of it is splendid. How glorious is this passage, for instance:

> . . . . et
> Nunquam humeris positurus arcum,
> Qui rore puro Castaliae lavit
> Crines solutos, qui Lyciae tenet

---

*Karl Wilhelm Ramler (1725–98), prominent poet of his time and translator of Latin poetry, especially Horace.

Dumeta natalemque silvam,
Delius et Patareus Apollo.*

"That is fine! Really fine!" said the Count, "only here and there it requires a little elucidation. Thus, for instance, 'he, whose bow is never laid aside,' would of course mean 'he who has always been the most assiduous of fiddlers.' But I am bound to say, my dear Mozart, you are sowing discord between two loving hearts."

"Indeed, I hope not. How so?"

"Eugenie is envious of her friend, and with very good reason, too."

"Aha! You have already noted my weakness. But what says the future husband?"

"Well, just for once or twice—I will look the other way."

"Very good. We will profit by the opportunity. Meanwhile, never fear, my lord. There is no danger, so long as the god here does not lend me his face and long yellow locks. I only wish he would! He might take in exchange, here and now, Mozart's queue, and his best bit of ribbon too."

"But then," laughed Franziska, "Apollo would have to be careful how he went about laving his new French coiffure in Castalia's holy spring."

Amid these jests and others of the kind the fun and mischief rose higher and higher. The wine was gradually having its effect upon the men; a number of healths were drunk, and Mozart became so much uplifted that, as his habit was, he broke into verse, in which the lieutenant kept his end up bravely, too, and even his Papa refused to be out of it, one or two of his efforts being wonderfully happy. But such things are too fleeting to be permanently captured for the

---

*Horace, *Odes,* III, 5. The translator here appends Ramler's German version, used by Mörike, then adds: "An English rendering of these verses by J. Howard Deazeley runs as follows:

> . . . And he whose bow is never laid
> Aside, who in Castalia's holy spring
> His long locks laves, o'er Lycia's thickets king,
> And o'er his native sward,
> Of Patara and Delos lord.

(From *Translations of the Odes of Horace into English Verse,* ed. M. Jourdain, Messrs. J. M. Dent & Son's Temple Classics, by kind permission of the publishers.)

purpose of our story; they refuse to lend themselves to repetition, for the very qualities that make them irresistible at the time, the general elation and the sparkle and joviality of personal expression, are lacking in both word and glance.

Among other toasts, the health of the Master was proposed by the old maiden lady, who promised him a whole long series of immortal works yet. "*A la bonne heure!* I am perfectly ready," cried Mozart, clinking his wine glass vigorously with hers. And now the Count struck up a song in his powerful and true intonation, improvising as his inspiration dictated:

> The Count:
>> May the gods grant inspiration
>> For future works of your creation—
> Max (continuing):
>> But no Schikaneder,* nor
>> The Da Ponte† any more—
> Mozart:
>> No, by God, I know they're bad,
>> But what better's to be had?
> The Count:
>> And it is my earnest prayer
>> That our Signor Bonbonnière,**
>> That accurst Italian cheat,
>> Lives to see them all complete!
> Max:
>> So let him live a hundred years—
> Mozart:
>> Unless, along with all his wares—
> All three, *con forza:*††
>> Away the devil does not bear
>> Our Signor Bonbonnière.

The Count was so uncommonly fond of singing that the trio thus casually begun developed, by the repetition of the last four lines,

---

*Emmanuel Schikaneder (1751–1812), librettist of *The Magic Flute.*

†Lorenzo da Ponte (1749–1838), librettist of *The Marriage of Figaro, Don Giovanni,* and *Così fan tutte.*

**This was Mozart's nickname for the Kapellmeister Salieri (Mörike's note, as added by translator.) The note reads literally: "This is the name Mozart gave among his friends to his colleague Salieri, who, wherever he was, nibbled sweets, and also in allusion to his delicate appearance."

††"Loudly."

into what is known as a "*canon finitus*" [ending in a coda], and the maiden aunt had humor—or perhaps assurance—enough to embellish her worn soprano in the most capable fashion with all manner of roulades. Mozart then pledged his word that, when he had leisure enough, he would work out this lively trifle expressly for the company in accordance with the correct rules of composition, a promise which he afterwards fulfilled when back in Vienna.

Eugenie had for some time been quietly conning over her treasure from the bower of Tiberius, and now a general desire was voiced to hear the duet sung by her and the composer, while her uncle was glad to show off his voice once more in the chorus. So they rose from table and hastened to the piano in the large adjoining apartment.

Pure as was the delight with which this exquisite piece filled them, its subject led up naturally, by a swift transition, to the highest pitch of convivial jollity, in which the music no longer counts for its own sake; it was, indeed, our friend who gave the signal by springing up from the piano, advancing towards Franziska, and persuading her to join in a *Schleifer,* or slow gliding waltz, while Max picked up his violin with the greatest alacrity. Nor was their host behind hand in inviting Madame Mozart. In a twinkling all the portable furniture was removed by the bustling servants in order to make more room. One after the other each had to take a turn, and the maiden aunt, by no means loath, was led out by the gallant lieutenant in a minuet, during which she became quite rejuvenated. And lastly, as Mozart was dancing the final round with the future bride, he helped himself in style to his promised right from her fair lips.

Evening had now overtaken them, the sun was about to set, and now at last it was growing pleasant out of doors, so the Countess proposed to the ladies that they should take a breath of air in the garden. The Count, on the other hand, invited the gentlemen into the billiard-room, for Mozart was known to be very fond of that game. They accordingly separated into two parties, and for our part we will join the ladies.

Having sauntered once or twice at an easy pace up and down the main avenue, they ascended a rounded hillock, half surrounded by a tall vine-covered trellis, from which there was a view out over the open country, the village and highroad. The last rays of autumn sunshine glowed red through the leafy vines.

"Would this not be a nice place to sit down cosily," said the

Countess, "if Madame Mozart would be so good as to tell us some story about herself and her husband?"

She was quite ready and willing, and they all settled down most comfortably, having drawn up their chairs into a circle.

"I am going to regale you," she began, "with a story that you would in any case have been bound to hear, for there is a little joke connected with it which I am saving up for you. It has occurred to me that, in remembrance of this occasion, I might offer a wedding present of the most choice quality to her ladyship who is soon to be married. The said present is anything but an article of luxury or fashion, so it is perhaps only by reason of its history that it may be of some interest to you."

"What can it be, Eugenie?" said Franziska, "Some celebrity's inkstand, at the very least!"

"You are not so very far out! You shall see it within the very hour! The treasure is in our travelling-trunk. I will begin, and, with your permission, I will hark back a little way.

"The winter before last, the state of Mozart's health threatened to give me serious cause for alarm, by reason of his growing irritability and frequent fits of depression—a febrile state, in fact. Though still at times lively in society, often more than was really natural, at home he was generally absorbed in gloomy broodings, sighing and complaining. The doctor ordered dieting, Pyrmont water,* and exercise outside the city. But the patient did not pay much attention to this good advice; the cure was inconvenient, wasted time, and was dead against his usual daily routine. Well, the doctor made things nice and hot for him, and he had to listen to a long lecture on the composition of human blood and those corpuscle things in it, on respiration and phlogiston—I declare, you never heard the like of it all!—or again, on Nature's real intentions with regard to food, drink and digestion, a thing about which Mozart had till that time been about as innocent as his own five-year-old boy. As a matter of fact, the lecture produced a visible impression. The doctor had not been half an hour gone when I found my husband in his room gazing meditatively, though with a more cheerful face, at a walking-stick for which he had been rummaging in a press among some old things, and had successfully found it. I should never have thought

---

*Water from Bad Pyrmont, a well-known spa in Lower Saxony.

that he would even have remembered its existence. It had come down to us from my father, and was a handsome cane with an imposing knob of lapis lazuli. Never had a walking-stick been seen in Mozart's hand before. I simply had to laugh.

" 'You see,' he cried, 'I am going in for my cure thoroughly, with all its appurtenances. I intend to drink the water, take exercise every day in the open air, and, in doing so, make use of this staff. And apropos of sticks, all sorts of ideas have been passing through my head. It is not for nothing, then, I thought, that other people—I mean real, steady-going fellows—cannot go without a walking-stick. Our neighbor the commercial councilor never crosses the street to visit his old cronies, but his stick must go with him. Professional men and officials, gentlemen in government offices, tradesmen and their customers, when they take a walk outside the city on a Sunday with their families—every one of them carries his good honest cane that has seen good service. But chief of all, I have often observed how on the Stefansplatz in front of the Cathedral, about half an hour before the sermon begins, or Mass, the respectable citizens stand about chatting in groups: and there one can see quite plainly how all and sundry of their quiet virtues, their industry and sense of order, their serene courage and contentment, depend upon their trusty stick and prop themselves up by its steady support. In a word, there must be something beneficial, some special consolation to be found in this old-world and perhaps rather unfashionable custom. Believe me or not, I can hardly wait for the first occasion when I shall take this good friend for a walk across the bridge of the Rennweg as part of my certificate of health. We are already slightly acquainted, and I hope the alliance we have concluded will be for all time.'

"But the alliance proved of brief duration; the third time the two of them went out together, his companion failed to return. Another was procured, which kept faith a little longer, and at any rate it is to this fancy for walking-sticks that I put down a great deal of the assiduity with which Mozart followed out his doctor's prescription quite tolerably well for three whole weeks. Nor were good results lacking; hardly ever had we seen him so fresh and bright or so even-tempered. But in a short time, alas! he had grown far too frisky again, so that every day I had my hands full with him. About this time it happened that, wearied by the labors of an exacting day, he nonetheless went rather late to a musical party for the benefit of a few curious travellers, though he vowed by all that was holy that it should by only for an hour; but those are always the occasions when, once he is stuck down at the piano and thoroughly roused, people take the most shameful advantage of his good nature; for at such times he sits there like the little fellow in Montgolfier's air-balloon,* floating six miles up above the earth, where one cannot so much as hear the bells ring. I sent our man round twice in the middle of the night, but it was no use, he could not get at his master. About three in the morning he at last got home. So I made up my mind to sulk hard all day."

At this point certain circumstances were passed over by Madame Mozart in silence. It should be known that a young singer, Signora Malerbi, to whom Frau Konstanze took exception with good cause, was most likely to be present as well at the above-mentioned evening party. This Roman lady owed her engagement at the opera-house to Mozart's good offices; and her coquettish wiles had undoubtedly had no small share in winning the Master's favor. There were even rumors that she had had him in her toils for several months past, and kept him nicely on the rack. But whether this was altogether true, or greatly exaggerated, it is certain that she behaved later with insolence and ingratitude, and even went so far as to make fun of her benefactor. Thus it was quite in her own characteristic vein when once, in speaking to another and more fortunate admirer, she roundly called him *"un piccolo grifo raso"* (a shaven little pig's snout). This inspiration worthy of a Circe was all the more calculated to wound him because, as we are bound to admit, it contained, after all, a germ of truth.†

On the way home from this party, at which it so happened, however, that the singer had failed to appear, a friend, heated by wine, was indiscreet enough to repeat her spiteful remark to the Master. He was not best pleased at this, for, as a matter of fact, it was the first unequivocal proof he had received of his protégée's utter

---

*The famous hot-air balloon designed and flown in 1783 by Joseph-Michel Montgolfier (1740–1810) and his brother Jacques-Etienne (1745–99).

†Mörike added a footnote at this point: "We have here a rather old, small profile portrait in mind, which, well drawn and engraved, is found on the title page of a Mozartian piano work, undoubtedly the best likeness of all the portraits, including those that have recently appeared in the art trade."

heartlessness. So bitter was his indignation that at first he did not even notice the chilly reception with which he met at his wife's bedside. Without pausing to draw breath he told her of the insult, and his honesty would lead us to infer that his conscience was not so very guilty. She was almost moved to pity him. But she purposely did violence to her feelings, for she did not intend him to get off so easily as all that. When, shortly after midday, he woke from a heavy sleep, he found that both his wife and the two children had gone out, though the table was neatly laid for him alone.

Few things had ever made Mozart so unhappy as when everything was not perfectly smooth and serene between him and his better half. And had he only known, too, what further cause for anxiety she had been carrying about with her for many days past!—one of the most serious causes, indeed, the disclosure of which, according to her long-standing custom, she was sparing him as long as possible. Her ready money would quite shortly be at an end, and there was no prospect of anything coming in for some time yet. Though he had no suspicion of this domestic crisis, yet his heart, too, suffered from a sense of oppression having some affinity with her distressed and embarrassed condition. He could neither eat nor remain still. He hastily finished dressing, if only so as to escape from the stifling atmosphere of the house. On a scrap of paper, which he left unfolded, he wrote a few lines in Italian: "You have made me take my medicine, and it serves me thoroughly well right. But do be nice again and be ready to laugh once more by the time I come home. I feel I could turn Carthusian and Trappist. I declare, I could bellow like a bull of Bashan!" He promptly snatched up his hat, but not the stick with it this time; its day was now over.

Having acted as substitute for Frau Konstanze thus far in her story, we may as well proceed a little further.

Leaving his home near the Schranne (the Market hall) and turning to the right opposite the Zeughaus (the Armory), the good man, musing idly, sauntered—for it was a warm, rather cloudy summer's afternoon—across what is known as the Hof, and on past the priest's house adjoining the Church of Our Lady, in the direction of the Schottentor, where he turned off to the left and climbed up to the Mölkerbastei, thus avoiding the greetings of a number of acquaintances who were just entering the city. Though unmolested by a guard who was pacing up and down by the cannon, he paused here only a short time to enjoy the splendid view out over the green slope of the glacis and past the outskirts of the town to the Kahlenberg and southwards towards the Styrian Alps. The fair peace of Nature was out of harmony with his inward state. With a sigh he proceeded on his way across the esplanade and then through the suburb known as the Alser-Vorstadt, walking quite at random.

At the end of the Währinger Gasse stood a tavern with a skittle-alley, the proprietor of which, a rope-maker, was very well known in the neighborhood, as well as to the country-folk whose road led them past the house, both for the quality of his wares and the soundness of his liquor. The roll of skittles was to be heard, and besides, since the house could muster a dozen clients at most, the business done there was fairly quiet. An almost unconscious craving to lose himself in something external to him, among unassuming, natural people, prompted the Master to walk in. He sat down at one of the tables, sparsely shaded by trees, with a chief inspector of wells from Vienna and two other stodgy citizens, ordered a small mug of beer, and entered into every detail of their very workaday conversation, from time to time taking a stroll round or watching the game in the skittle-alley.

Not far from the latter, by the side of the house, the rope-maker's shop stood open, a narrow space stuffed full of his wares, where, in addition to the immediate products of his craft, every variety of implement for kitchen, cellar or farm stood or hung about the shop for sale, likewise train-oil and axle-grease, as well as a few varieties of seeds, dill and caraway. A young girl, who had to act as waitress to the customers as well as attend to the shop, happened at the moment to be busy serving a peasant, who had looked in, with his little son clinging to his hand, to buy a bushel-measure for fruit, a brush, a whip or something of the kind. He picked one out from among a number of them, tried it, laid it aside, took up a second and a third, then returned irresolutely to the first, and could not make an end of it all. Several times the girl went out to wait on her clients, then she came back again, and was untiring in assisting his choice and giving him satisfaction without overmuch talk.

Seated on a low bench by the skittle-alley, Mozart was watching the whole thing and listening delightedly. Though greatly pleased with the girl's good-natured, sensible bearing and the calm, serious expression of her attractive face, he was still more interested in the peasant, who afforded him much food for thought even after he had gone off in a high state of contentment. He had entered thoroughly into the man's point of view, sensing what importance he had attached to this trifling occasion, and with what conscientious care he had chaffered over the price, though the difference involved was only a few farthings. "And then, he mused, "only think when the fellow gets home to his wife, and boasts to her of his bargain, and the children all hang round till his knapsack is opened, in case there is something in it for them; but she hurries to fetch him a snack and a cool draft of this season's home-brewed cider, for which he has been saving up his appetite.

"Who would not be as happy as this man—so independent of mankind, looking only to Nature and her blessings, hardly though she makes him earn them!

"But in my art the task that is set me daily is quite different, and, when all is said and done, I would not exchange it with anyone in the world. Yet in the meantime why do I have to live under conditions in such direct contrast with this innocent, simple existence? Supposing, now, you had a bit of land, a little house near a village in a beautiful neighborhood, you really could not help gaining a new lease of life! The whole morning busy over your scores, and all the rest of the time with your family, planting trees, going round your field, and in the autumn shaking down the apples and pears with the children; a visit to town now and then for some performance, and, for the rest, a friend or so to stay from time to time—what bliss! Well, well, who knows what yet may befall?"

He walked to the front of the shop, said a few kindly words to the girl, and began to look more closely at her wares. Apart from the direct bearing of these objects upon the idyllic trend of his thoughts, as described above, he was attracted by the neat, bright, smooth quality of all these wooden utensils, and even by the smell of them. His eye was caught by the gardening tools. For at his suggestion Konstanze had leased some time ago a little piece of land outside the Kärntner Tor and grown some green-stuff there; so the first thing that now struck him as most appropriate was a large new rake and a smaller ditto, together with a spade. For the rest, it did the greatest credit to his ideas of economy that, after a short period of reflection, he relinquished, though regretfully, a butter-keg of the most inviting and appetizing aspect. On the other hand, a tall receptacle with a cover and a beautifully carved handle seemed to him the very thing for some purpose of which he did not feel quite sure. Composed of slender rods of two sorts of wood, light and dark alternately, it was broader at the bottom than at the top, and exquisitely finished with pitch inside. A fine assortment of ladles, rolling-pins, chopping-boards, and plates of all sizes seemed eminently desirable for the kitchen, as did also a salt-box of the simplest construction for hanging on the wall.

Lastly, his eye fell upon a sturdy walking-stick, the handle of which was well garnished with leather and round brass nails. And since her customer seemed rather tempted by this too, the sales-woman remarked with a smile that it was not at all the sort of thing for a gentleman to carry. "You are right, my child," he replied, "I seem to remember that butchers on their travels carry something of the kind. Away with it! I will have none of it. But on the other hand, all the rest of what we have chosen there you shall bring to my house today or tomorrow." He then told her his name and street, after which he went back to his table to finish his drink, where he found only one of the three still sitting, a master tinsmith.

"The waitress has done well today," remarked the man. "Her cousin allows her a penny in the florin on what she sells in the shop."

Mozart was now doubly pleased with his purchase; but his personal interest was to be still further heightened. For next time she came their way this same citizen called out to her: "How goes it, Kreszenz? What is the locksmith doing? Isn't he soon to be filing his own iron?"

"Oh, rubbish!" she retorted as she hurried away again, "any iron of his, I reckon, is still growing right back there in the mountains."

"She's a decent girl," said the tinsmith. "She kept house for her stepfather for a long time and nursed him when he was ill, and then, when he died, it turned out that he had squandered her portion. Since then she has been working for her kinsman here, and she is the mainstay of the whole concern, tavern, children and all. She knows a worthy fellow, and would be glad to marry him, the sooner the better. But there is a hitch in the affair."

"What sort of a hitch? I suppose he has no means?"

"Both of them have some savings, but not quite enough. Now there is a half-share in a house and workshop that will shortly be put up at auction in the town. The rope-maker could easily advance them what they still require to make up the deposit-money, but he naturally does not want to let the girl go, and he has good friends on the Council and the Guild, so that the young fellow meets with nothing but difficulties on every side."

"Damnation!" burst out Mozart, so that the other man started and looked round to see whether anybody was listening. "So there is not a soul to put in a word in the cause of justice, or shake his fist in these gentlemen's faces? The rogues! But only wait! We will trip you up yet!"

The tinsmith sat as though on thorns. He clumsily tried to tone down what he had said, and almost took the whole thing back. But Mozart refused to listen. "Shame on you," he said, "for the way you talk. That's the way you miserable fellows always go on, as soon as you are called upon to stand by what you have said." And without bidding him good day, he turned his back on the craven. As he passed by the waitress, who had her hands full with some new customers, all he did was to whisper: "Come tomorrow in good time. My greetings to your young man. I hope your affairs will turn out well." She only started, and had neither the time nor the presence of mind to thank him.

Walking at a faster pace than usual, for this incident had fairly made his blood boil, he first followed the same way as that by which he had come, as far as the glacis, after which he slackened his pace, taking a roundabout course which led in a wide semicircle round by the ramparts. Entirely absorbed in the affairs of the unhappy lovers, he ran over in his mind a number of his acquaintances and patrons who might be able to do something in the matter in one way or another. But in the meanwhile, since some more precise explanation from the girl was desirable before he made up his mind to take any steps, he resolved to wait quietly till it came, and now, his heart and mind outrunning his feet, he felt himself already at home with his wife.

He felt an inward certainty that he might count upon an amiable, and even a glad welcome, with a kiss and embrace upon the very threshold, and as he entered the Kärntner Tor longing redoubled his speed. Not far from there he was hailed by the postman, who handed him a small, but heavy packet, on which he instantly recognized a precise and honored handwriting. He stepped aside with the postman into the nearest shop to sign the receipt, but once back in the street he could not wait till he reached home; he broke the seal, and, now walking, now stopping still, devoured the letter.

"I was sitting at my work-table," said Madame Mozart, continuing her story to the ladies, "and heard my husband come upstairs and ask our man where I was. His step and his voice sounded more cheerful and assured than I had expected, or than I was really pleased to hear. First he went to his own room, but he came across to me at once. 'Good evening,' he said; and without looking up I answered in a doleful voice. Having paced up and down the room in silence once or twice, with an attempt at a yawn he took up the fly-whisk from behind the door, a thing which it had never entered his head to do before, and muttering to himself: 'Where on earth do all the flies come from, I wonder!' he began slapping to right and left, as hard as he could go, too. For that tone of voice was always one which he simply could not bear, so that I never ventured to use it in his presence. 'Hm!' I thought, 'So what one may do oneself is quite another thing when the men do it!' Besides, I had really not noticed so many flies as all that. His odd behavior really vexed me very much. 'Six at one go!' he cried. 'Only look!'—No answer. Next he laid something on my pincushion, so that I could not help seeing it even without moving my eyes from my work. It was nothing more alarming than a little pile of gold, as many ducats as one can pick up between thumb and finger. He went on with his antics behind my back, making an occasional slap and talking to himself all the while: 'The tiresome, useless, impudent brood! For whatever purpose do they exist on earth, I wonder?'—Slap! 'Just so that one may kill them, evidently!'—Slap!—'and I must say I am a pretty good hand at it, too. Natural history tells us at what an astounding rate the creatures multiply!'—Slap! slap!—'but in my house they will always be cleared out at once! *Ah maledette! Disperate!* Despair, you wretches! Another twenty again, all together! Do you like them?' He came up to me again, and did the same thing as before. Up to this point I had restrained my laughter by an effort, but I could simply do so no longer; I exploded, he fell on my neck, and we both tittered and laughed away as though for a wager.

" 'But where did the money come from?' I asked, while he shook the rest of it out of the little roll. 'From Prince Eszterhazy!* Through Haydn! Only read the letter!' And this is what I read:

*Nikolaus Joseph, Prince von Esterházy (1714–90), employer of Haydn and patron of Mozart.

" 'Eisenstadt, etc., etc. Dearest Friend, His Serene Highness, my most gracious lord, has to my very great delight commissioned me to convey to you the accompanying sixty ducats. We have recently performed your quartets again, and His Serene Highness was, if anything, even more struck with them and pleased than he was the first time, three months ago. The prince remarked to me (I must write down his very words): "When Mozart dedicated this work to you, he meant to honor you alone; but he cannot take it amiss if at the same time I see in it a compliment to myself. Tell him that I have almost as high an opinion of his genius as you have yourself, and more than that he could hardly ask." "Amen to that!" is what I say. Are you content?

" 'Postscript: a word in your charming wife's ear: kindly see to it that there is no delay in returning thanks. It would be best if this could be done in person. We should take care not to lose such a favorable wind.' "

" 'Angelic messenger! Celestial soul!' exclaimed Mozart over and over again, and it is hard to say which pleased him most, the letter, the Prince's approbation, or the money. For my own part, I frankly confess that at that precise moment the last-mentioned appeared to me extremely timely. And so we passed a most festive and happy evening.

"As to the adventure in the Alser-Vorstadt, I heard nothing that day and equally little during the next few either. The whole of the next week slipped past, no Kreszenz appeared, and in the turmoil of his affairs my husband forgot all about the matter. One Sunday evening we were entertaining company: Captain Wesselt, Count Hardegg and others were taking part in some music. During a pause I was called out of the room—and there was the whole bag of tricks! I went in and enquired 'Did you order all sorts of wooden goods from the Alser-Vorstadt?' 'Great Heavens, yes, so I did! Isn't there a girl there? Just ask her in.' So in she came as pleasant as could be, bringing her loaded basket into the room on her arm, and the rakes and spade and all. She apologized for having been such a long time coming, but she had been unable to recall the name of the street, and had failed to ascertain it exactly till that very day. Mozart took the things from her one after the other, handing them over to me as he did so, and looking so pleased with himself. I feigned delight and thanked him most heartily, praising and commending everything, but I could not help wondering why he had bought the gardening-tools.—'Why, naturally,' said he, 'for your little bit of land on the banks of the Wien.'* 'Good Heavens! But we gave that up long ago! The water always did so much damage, and besides, we never got anything whatever to grow there. I told you all about it, and you made no objection.' 'What! And so the asparagus we ate this spring?' 'All came from the market!' 'There!' he said, 'If only I had known! I only praised it so out of pure politeness, for I was really touched at you and your gardening. Such miserable little heads they were, no bigger than so many quills!'

"The gentlemen enjoyed the joke beyond words. I had promptly to hand over the superfluous objects to some of them as keepsakes. But when Mozart went on to question the girl about how matters stood with regard to her marriage, she plucked up courage to speak out quite freely, for anything that was to be done for her and her young man must be done quietly, discreetly and without giving anybody grounds for complaint—all of which she expressed with such modesty, prudence and forbearance that she quite won the approval of all present, and was finally sent off with the most encouraging promises.

" 'These people have got to be helped,' said the Captain. 'The business with the Guild is the least part of the trouble, for I know somebody who will soon set that to rights. The question is how to pay something on account for the house, the expenses of setting up business and so forth. How would it be if we were to announce a concert, among friends, at Trattner's hall, everybody paying as much as he likes for his ticket?' The idea was greeted with vigorous applause. One of the gentlemen picked up the salt-box, saying: 'Somebody ought to open proceedings with a nice historical discourse, describing Herr Mozart's purchases and explaining his humane intentions, at which point this handsome receptacle should be set on the table as a collecting box, with the two rakes to right and left, and crossed behind it as a decoration.'

"This did not happen, of course; but on the other hand the concert did take place. It brought in a nice sum and various contributions came in afterwards, so that the happy couple had enough and to spare, and the other obstacles were soon overcome. The

*A little stream that flows through Vienna into the Danube.

Duscheks* in Prague, our greatest friends there, with whom we usually stay, heard the story, and she, being a most good-natured, kind-hearted woman, asked to have one of the things too, out of curiosity; so I set aside the most suitable pieces for her, and took this opportunity of bringing them with me. But since in the meantime we have unexpectedly chanced to discover a new and delightful fellow artist, who is very shortly to set up a house of her own, and will not, I think, despise a piece of common household gear chosen by Mozart, I mean to halve what I have brought, and you have the choice between a handsome open-work chocolate-whisk and the much-talked-of salt-box, upon which the artist has indulged himself with the luxury of a tasteful tulip. I should certainly advise you to choose this piece, for salt, that noble commodity, is, I believe, a symbol of home and hospitality, to which we should like to add all our good wishes."

Thus ended Madame Mozart's story. We may imagine with what merriment the ladies heard it, and how gratefully the present was accepted. The jubilation was renewed when immediately afterwards the things were set out before them and the men upstairs, and the emblem of patriarchal simplicity was formally presented, whereupon the young lady's uncle promised it a place in its new owner's plate-chest and in that of her remotest posterity in no whit inferior to that occupied in the collection at Ambras by the Florentine master's famous work of art.†

By this time it was nearly eight o'clock, and they had tea. But soon our musician was urgently reminded of the promise he had already given at midday to make the company better acquainted with the "rake-hell" hero (*Höllenbrand*) who lay under lock and key in the travelling-trunk, though fortunately not too deep down. Without the least reluctance he declared himself in readiness. His explanation of the plot did not detain them long, the book of words was opened, and the candles stood, ready lighted, on the pianoforte.

We only wish that something, at least, might be communicated to our readers of that rare emotion which often thrills us, as though by an electric shock, and holds us, as it were, spellbound, when, as we

---

*Franz Dušek (1736–99) and his wife Josephina (1756–?), singer; friends of Mozart.

†The reference is to the famous saltcellar of Benvenuto Cellini, now in the Vienna Art Museum but at that time in a collection at Ambras, a castle in the Tyrol.

pass by a window, a single isolated chord is borne to our ears—a chord that could come from there alone; something of that sweet, yet painful suspense with which we sit facing the curtain at the theater while the orchestra is tuning up. Or is it not something in this fashion? If on the threshold of every work of sublimely tragic art, be it Macbeth, Œdipus or any other, we feel the pulsing tremor of eternal beauty, where else should this have been intenser than now, or even of equal potency? Man at once longs and dreads to be rapt out of his ordinary self; he feels the approaching contact with the infinite and how it constricts his breast, though its purpose, all the while, is to expand it and ravish his spirit by its might. Add to this his awe in the presence of consummate art; the thought that it is granted him to enjoy a godlike marvel, to assimilate it as a thing akin to himself, induces a sort of emotion, or even pride, the happiest and purest, perhaps, of which we are capable.

But added to all this, our company was now, for the first time, to become acquainted with a work which we have made entirely our own from youth upwards, a state poles apart from ours, and, if we allow for the enviable pleasure of a personal rendering by the composer himself, one by no means as favorable as that which we enjoy, for a distinct and perfect conception of the piece was really impossible for any of them, nor could they have had this, for more reasons than one, even if the whole piece could have been presented to them without abbreviation.

Of the eighteen numbers* already fully completed the composer presumably did not perform even half (in the account upon which our narrative is based we find expressly mentioned only the last piece in this series, the sextet); he rendered them it seems, for the most part, in a free version for piano only, chiming in with his voice when necessary and suitable. As for his wife, she is recorded only as performing two airs. Since her voice is said to have been as strong as it was lovely, we should like to think that these were Donna Anna's first song, *Or sai, chi l'onore*,† and one of the two sung by Zerlina. Strictly speaking, so far as intelligence and taste were concerned,

---

*At this point Mörike added a footnote: "In regard to this numbering one must know that Elvira's aria with the recitative and Leporello's 'I understand' were not originally contained in the opera."

†"Now you know who [tried to steal my] honor [from me]," Act I, Scene 13.

Eugenie and her betrothed were the only listeners of the type which the Master would naturally have desired, and the former was, without a doubt, incomparably more so than the latter. They both sat at the far end of the room, the young lady immobile as a statue, and so profoundly absorbed in the music, that, even during the brief intervals in which the interest of the others found shy expression, or their inward emotion involuntarily escaped them in a cry of admiration, she could give none but an inadequate reply to the remarks addressed to her by her betrothed.

When Mozart reached the end of the incomparably lovely sextet, which was the occasion for a prolonged discussion, he seemed to listen with special interest and gratification to certain observations of the Baron's. They were speaking of the finale of the opera, and also of the performance, which had been provisionally fixed for the beginning of November; and somebody having expressed the opinion that certain parts of the finale might yet cost the Master enormous trouble, he gave rather a cryptic smile. But Konstanze said out loud to the Countess, in such a way that he could not have helped hearing: "He has something still *in petto* that he is keeping a secret even from me."

"You are departing from your usual rôle, my love," he rejoined, "in bringing up that point; only supposing I took it into my head to start all over again! And as a matter of fact, I am itching to do so."

"Leporello!" cried the Count, springing jovially to his feet, and signing to a servant, "Wine! Sillery, three bottles!"

"Oh no, please! The time for that is past. My lord and master has not recovered from the last yet."

"May it do him good! And the same for all of us!"

"Heavens! what have I done?" lamented Konstanze with a glance at the clock. "It is already eleven, and we have to start early in the morning. How is it to be done?"

"It can't be done, dear friend, it seems to me. No it positively can't."

"Yet at times," began Mozart, "things fall out remarkably aptly. But what will my Stanzerl say, now, when she hears that the piece of work she is about to hear was born into the world at about this very time of night, and just before a journey was arranged, too?"

"Is it possible? When? Three weeks ago, I warrant, when you were going to Eisenstadt?"

"Right! And this is how it happened. After ten o'clock, when you were already sound asleep, I came home from Richter's dinner, and meant to go to bed in good time, as I had promised, so as to be up early in the morning and take my place in the carriage. Meanwhile Veit, as usual, had lighted the candles on my writing-table, so I slipped on my dressing-gown mechanically, and it occurred to me to take just a hasty peep at my last piece of work again. But alas! by ill-luck—O accursed and most untimely fussiness of women!—you had tidied up and packed my music—for of course I had to take it with me; the Prince wished me to try the opus through. I hunted about, grumbled, scolded, but in vain! In the midst of all this, my eye was caught by a sealed envelope, from the Abbate,* to judge from the appalling scrawl in which it was addressed. Yes, sure enough it was, sending me the rest of his libretto, duly revised, which I had not hoped to see for a whole month to come. I sat down at once all agog and read it through, and was enchanted to see how well the queer fish had grasped what I wanted. It was all far simpler and more concentrated, and at the same time there was more in it. Both the churchyard scene and the finale, down to where the hero descends into the underworld, were greatly improved in every way. 'But this time, my admirable, poet,' I thought, 'you shall not conjure up heaven and hell for me again and get no thanks for it!' Now as a rule it is not my custom to compose anything out of its order, however tempting it may be; it is always a bad habit, which may be punished most unpleasantly. But there are exceptions, and, to be brief, the scene before the equestrian statue of the Commendatore and the threat which, issuing from the murdered man's grave, breaks abruptly into the laughter of the nocturnal reveller with hair-raising effect, had already gone to my head. I struck a chord, and felt that I was knocking at the right door, behind which, one beside the other, lay the whole legion of terrors let loose in the finale. Well, the first to come forth was an adagio: D minor, four bars only, followed by a second phrase in five—I flatter myself it will produce an extraordinary effect in the theater, when the most powerful of the wind instruments accompany the voice.† Only listen now, as well as I can manage it here."

*Da Ponte.
†In connection with this passage it may be recalled that, as related by Jahn, *Life of*

Without more ado he put out the lights in the two branched candlesticks standing by his side, and the grim chorale *Di rider finirai pria dell'aurora** rang through the death-like stillness of the room. As though borne from the orbits of far-distant stars, the notes come dropping from trombones of silver, ice-cold and piercing through both heart and marrow, down through the blue night.

"*Chi va la?* Who goes there? Reply!" we hear Don Juan ask. Then the voice rings out again in the same monotone, ordering the impious youth to leave the dead in peace.

When these booming accents had died away on the air down to the very last vibration, Mozart went on: "You can understand that there was no stopping now. Once the ice cracks at one point of the shore, the whole surface of the lake breaks up at once and the crash echoes even unto its remotest corner. Involuntarily I gathered up the same threads later on, at Don Giovanni's supper-party, where Donna Elvira has just gone out, and the ghost appears in response to his invitation. Listen to this!"

Now followed the whole of that long and fearful dialogue by which even the most matter-of-fact of men is swept away to the farthest confines of what the human mind can conceive, yea, and beyond, to where we look upon the supernatural and hear its voice, and feel ourselves, within our inmost breast, bereft of will and hurled from one extreme to another.

Though already alien to human utterance, the deathless voice of the departed deigns once more to speak. Shortly after the first dread salutation, when, already half immortal, he scorns the proffered earthly food, with what uncanny, gruesome effect does his voice stray up and down the strange intervals of an aerial scale, as on some ladder woven of air! He calls for a speedy decision to repent; for the time accorded him is short, and far, far, far is the way! And when Don Giovanni, defying the eternal ordinances in his monstrous contumacy, struggles distractedly, grapples and writhes under the growing onslaughts of the infernal powers, and finally sinks downwards, still expressing in his every gesture the fullness of his majesty,

---

Mozart (trs. Townshend), III, 130, "The words of the Commendatore in the church-yard scene were originally, it is said, accompanied only by the trombones" (translator's note).

*"Your laughter will cease before the dawn," Act II, Scene 11.

what man is there whose heart, and whose very entrails are not stirred by mingled terror and delight? The emotion may be compared to that with which we gaze in wonder on the glorious spectacle of some ungovernable force of Nature, or a fire on board some splendid ship. In spite of ourselves we take sides, as it were, with its blind might, and gnash our teeth as we share its travail in the anguished process of its self-destruction.

The composer had reached the end. For a while none dared be first to break the general silence.

"Give us," began the Countess at last, still with a catch in her breath, "Give us, pray, some idea of what your feelings were as you laid down your pen that night."

He looked at her with shining eyes, as though roused from some tranquil reverie, rapidly collected his thoughts, and said, half to the lady and half to his wife: "Well, by the end of it all, my head was simply reeling. I had written away at this desperate *dibattimento*** down to the chorus of spirits, going straight on in a perfect fever as I sat beside the open window, till it was finished, and after a short pause I rose from my chair, intending to go to your room so that we might chat a while longer till my blood had subsided. But now an idea flashed through my mind and brought me up short in the middle of the room." At this point he glanced down at the ground for a couple of seconds, and during what followed his voice betrayed an almost imperceptible agitation. "I said to myself: 'supposing, now, you were to die tonight, and had to break off your score at this point: would it let you rest quiet in your grave?' My eye fell on the wick of the candle I was carrying, and the mountains of wax that had dripped from it. A momentary pang ran through me at this idea; then I bethought myself again: 'but supposing that some time afterwards, be it long or short, some other man, perhaps some Italian fellow, were to get hold of the opera to complete it, and found the whole thing neatly put together, from the introduction to the seventeenth number, with the exception of a single piece—fine, sound, ripe fruits shaken down into the long grass, so that all he need do was to pick them up—yet all the same, he was feeling a little bit nervous about the middle of the finale here—and then, at that very moment, he discovered that this solid mass of rock had already

* "Argument."

been moved thus far out of his way: that would give him something over which he well might chuckle! He might perhaps be tempted to cheat me of the honor and glory. But he would be sure to burn his fingers nicely if he did; for, after all, there would still be some few of my good friends able to recognize my sign manual, who would see to it that I received my due.' So I went and thanked God, with my eyes turned heavenward in heartfelt gratitude; and gave thanks, too, dear wife, to your good angel, who had kept both his hands laid softly on your brow for so long that you went on sleeping like a dormouse and could not call out to me so much as once. But when I did come to you at last and was asked what time it was, without turning a hair I mendaciously made you out an hour or two younger than you really were, for it was close on four o'clock. And now you will understand why it was that you could not get me out of bed at six, so that the coachman had to be sent home and ordered again for the next day."

"Of course," retorted Konstanze, "but the sly fellow need not imagine that a body was so dense as not to notice anything! So there was really no need for you to keep your splendid spurt forward a secret!"

"Ah, but that was not the reason."

"I know—you wanted to keep your treasure to yourself for a while, and not have everybody exclaiming over it."

"I am only glad," cried their good-natured host, "that tomorrow we need not wound the noble heart of any Viennese coachman, supposing that Herr Mozart proves quite incapable of getting up. The order: 'Hans, unharness the horses again!' always upsets people."

This indirect invitation to prolong their stay, in which all the others joined their voices in the most cordial and pressing manner, led the travellers to explain their very cogent reasons to the contrary; but one point was readily agreed upon: that they must not start too early, but must stay long enough to enjoy a comfortable breakfast together.

For some time longer they continued to stand or drift about in groups talking. Mozart was looking for somebody, apparently for the future bride; but since she did not happen to be there at the moment, he naïvely put the question intended for her directly to Franziska, who was standing close by: "Well, and what did you think of our Don Giovanni on the whole? What good fortune can you prophesy for him?"

"I will try," she rejoined with a laugh, "to answer as well as I can in place of my cousin. My untutored opinion is this: that if Don Giovanni does not turn the heads of the whole world, then the good God may shut up his musical-box, for an indefinite period, that is, and give humanity to understand. . . ." "And give humanity," corrected her uncle, "a bagpipes to carry; and harden men's hearts so that they worship strange gods."

"Heaven preserve us!" laughed Mozart. "But there! in the course of the next sixty or seventy years, when I am long dead and gone, many a false prophet shall arise."

Eugenie came up with the Baron and Max, and imperceptibly the conversation took a fresh turn, once more becoming grave and weighty, so that before the company dispersed again, the composer had the pleasure of hearing a number of fine and pregnant observations of a kind flattering to his hopes.

It was long after midnight before they dispersed; for till then none of them had realized how greatly they needed rest.

On the following day, the weather being in no way inferior to that of the day before, by ten o'clock a smart travelling-carriage, packed with the belongings of the two guests from Vienna, was seen standing in the courtyard of the Schloss. The Count stood before it with Mozart, shortly before the horses were led out, and asked him how he liked it.

"Very much. It seems extremely comfortable."

"Good! Then will you give me the pleasure of keeping it as a remembrance of me?"

"What! Are you in earnest?"

"How could I be otherwise?"

"Holy Saints! Konstanze! Here!" he called up to the window from which she was looking out with the others. "The carriage is for me! In future you shall ride in your own carriage!"

He threw his arms round the donor, who was smiling broadly, then walked round his new property, looking at it from every point of view, opened the door, threw himself down inside, and called out to them: "I feel as grand and distinguished as the Chevalier Gluck!*

---

*Christoph Willibald von Gluck (1714–87) had been living in Vienna since 1748.

Won't they stare in Vienna!"

"I hope," said the Countess, "that on your way back from Prague we shall see your conveyance all begarlanded with wreaths."

Not long after this merry scene, the carriage which had been the subject of so many eulogies really began to move off, and, drawn by a smart pair, drove at a brisk trot down to the main road. The Count sent his own horses with them as far as Wittingau, where they were to hire post-horses.

When good, kind people have enlivened our house with their presence for a while, bringing a fresh and quickened stir of life into our existence by their invigorating mental atmosphere, and causing us to experience to the full the blessedness of hospitality, their departure always leaves us with a comfortless sense of flatness for the rest of the day, at least—supposing, that is, that we are entirely thrown back upon our own resources again.

But this last condition, at least, did not affect the party at the Schloss. Franziska's parents, it is true, and the old aunt with them, also took their departure immediately afterwards; but the young lady herself and the future bridegroom remained behind, to say nothing of Max. As for Eugenie, with whom we are here more particularly concerned, this superlatively precious experience had affected her more deeply than all the rest, so it might well be imagined that she could find nothing wanting, nothing amiss, and nothing that could damp her joy. Her perfect happiness in the man she truly loved had just received its formal sanction, and this could not fail to outweigh everything else; indeed this, the noblest and most beautiful experience that could have moved her heart, was fused inevitably with the fullness of her bliss. Or it would have been had she been able to live that day and the one before only in the present, and afterwards in nothing but the pure enjoyment of its after-effects. But already during the evening, while his wife had been telling her story, a slight dread had come over her on behalf of him whose lovable presentment was then delighting her. This premonition still agitated the lower depths of her consciousness all the while Mozart was playing, looming through all the ineffable charm and mysterious horror of the music; and finally the anecdote with the same suggestion that he had casually related about himself had surprised and shocked her profoundly. So sure, so absolutely certain did she feel that this man would rapidly and inevitably be consumed away in the flame of his own ardor, that he could not possibly be more than a fleeting apparition upon earth, if only because this world was in truth incapable of bearing the overwhelming richness of that which he would lavish upon it.

This and much more beside had ebbed and flowed in her bosom on the previous day, while the confused echoes of Don Giovanni were still reverberating in her inward ear. It was not till towards morning that she fell asleep, worn out with fatigue.

The three ladies had now settled down with their work in the garden, and the men were keeping them company; since the conversation naturally turned at first upon no other subject than Mozart, Eugenie made no secret of her fears. Nobody was in the least inclined to share them, though the Baron entered into them to the full. In hours of happiness and moods of sheer human emotion and gratitude, men are wont to brush aside with all their might any thoughts of disaster that do not directly affect themselves. The most forcible and tempting proofs to the contrary were put forward, especially by her uncle, and how gladly did Eugenie listen to them all! A little more and she would really have been convinced that she had seen things in too gloomy a light.

A few moments later, as she passed through the great saloon upstairs, which had just been cleaned and set to rights again, and whose green damask curtains, now drawn across the window, admitted only a soft twilight gloom, she paused sadly before the piano. She gazed long and thoughtfully down at the keys which he had been the last to touch, then softly closed the lid and turned the key with jealous care, so that no other hand should open it again for a long time to come. As she turned away, she chanced to put a few song-books back in their right place. An old sheet of paper fell out, a copy of a Bohemian folksong* that Franziska had often sung in earlier days, and she herself too. She picked it up, though not before she had stepped upon it. In such a mood as hers, the most natural occurrence may easily appear a portent. But however she might interpret it, the tenor of the song was such that, as she once more perused the simple verses, hot tears fell from her eyes.

---

*The "Bohemian folksong" is, of course, a poem of Mörike's. It was set to music by Robert Franz (Op. 26, No. 6) soon after publication. There are a number of other settings, including one by Hugo Wolf, *Mörike Lieder*, No. 39.

ACKNOWLEDGMENTS

Every reasonable effort has been made to locate the owners of rights to previously published translations printed here. We gratefully acknowledge permission to reprint the following material:

From *Limestone and Other Stories* by Adalbert Stifter, English translation copyright © 1968 by David Luke. Reprinted by permission of Harcourt Brace Jovanovich, Inc., and John Johnson Limited.

The Jew's Beech by Annette von Droste-Hülshoff, translated by Lionel and Doris Thomas, is reproduced by kind permission of John Calder (Publishers) Limited, London.

The Black Spider by Jeremias Gotthelf, translated by H. M. Waidson, is reproduced by kind permission of John Calder (Publishers) Limited, London, and Riverrun Press Inc., New York.

The Poor Musician by Franz Grillparzer, translated by J. F. Hargraves and J. G. Cumming, is reprinted by kind permission of Berg Publishers.

THE GERMAN LIBRARY
in 100 Volumes

Gottfried von Strassburg
Tristan and Isolde
Edited and Revised by Francis G. Gentry
Foreword by C. Stephen Jaeger

German Medieval Tales
Edited by Francis G. Gentry
Foreword by Thomas Berger

German Humanism and Reformation
Edited by Reinhard P. Becker
Foreword by Roland Bainton

Immanuel Kant
Philosophical Writings
Edited by Ernst Behler
Foreword by René Wellek

Frederich Schiller
Plays: Intrigue and Love and Don Carlos
Edited by Walter Hinderer
Foreword by Gordon Craig

German Romantic Criticism
Edited by A. Leslie Willson
Foreword by Ernst Behler

Heinrich von Kleist
Plays
Edited by Walter Hinderer
Foreword by E. L. Doctorow

E.T.A. Hoffman
Tales
Edited by Victor Lange

German Literary Fairy Tales
Edited by Frank G. Ryder and Robert M. Browning
Introduction by Gordon Birrell
Foreword by John Gardiner